Human Rights and Drug Control: Access to Controlled Essential Medicines in Resource-Constrained Countries

School of Human Rights Research Series, Volume 80.

The titles published in this series are listed at the end of this volume.

Human Rights and Drug Control: Access to Controlled Essential Medicines in Resource-Constrained Countries

Marie Elske Gispen

intersentia

Cambridge – Antwerp – Portland

Intersentia Ltd
Sheraton House | Castle Park
Cambridge | CB3 0AX | United Kingdom
Tel.: +44 1223 370 170 | Fax: +44 1223 370 169
Email: mail@intersentia.co.uk
www.intersentia.com | www.intersentia.co.uk

Distribution for the UK and Ireland:
NBN International
Airport Business Centre, 10 Thornbury Road
Plymouth, PL6 7 PP
United Kingdom
Tel.: +44 1752 202 301 | Fax: +44 1752 202 331
Email: orders@nbninternational.com

Distribution for Europe and all other countries:
Intersentia Publishing nv
Groenstraat 31
2640 Mortsel
Belgium
Tel.: +32 3 680 15 50 | Fax: +32 3 658 71 21
Email: mail@intersentia.be

Distribution for the USA and Canada:
International Specialized Book Services
920 NE 58th Ave. Suite 300
Portland, OR 97213
USA
Tel.: +1 800 944 6190 (toll free) | Fax: +1 503 280 8832
Email: info@isbs.com

Human Rights and Drug Control: Access to Controlled Essential Medicines
in Resource-Constrained Countries

Typesetting: Editing Department, School of Law, Utrecht University

ISBN 978-1-78068-454-3
D/2017/7849/3
NUR 828

British Library Cataloguing in Publication Data. A catalogue record for this book is available from the British Library.

ACKNOWLEDGEMENTS

To my grandfather David de Wied (1925-2004)

Whilst interning at the Essential Medicines and Pharmaceutical Products Department of the World Health Organization in 2010, Hans Hogerzeil and Richard Laing inspired me to work on essential medicines. Returning to the Netherlands with a strong interest in health and human rights matters, it was eventually Adriaan van Es and his team at the International Federation for Health and Human Rights Organizations who introduced me to the pressing issue of the unavailability of *controlled* medicines. I am grateful for them to – perhaps without realizing – shape my academic interest. The confrontation with the large human suffering involved in the unavailability of controlled medicines and the apparent inconsistencies in law to improve their medical availability and use inspired me to eventually carry out the present study.

I am indebted to a range of institutions that enabled me to write this dissertation and to many people, who challenged, guided, encouraged, and supported me throughout this process. I would first like to recognize the Medicines Evaluation Board of the Netherlands and Utrecht University's focus and mass area 'Conflicts and Human Rights' for their research grants. I would also like to thank the members of the reading committee: Professor Deryck Beyleveld, Professor Antoine Buyse, Professor Bert Leufkens, Professor Titia Loenen, and Professor Brigit Toebes.

A heartfelt thank you goes out to my two supervisors: Professor Jenny Goldschmidt and Professor Marcus Düwell. I could not have wished for a better collaboration and team. I thank you for your support on all fronts and your confidence in me. Jenny, I am grateful for your mentorship; your critical reflection on law and the bigger picture, trust in me as a person, and personal involvement go beyond expression. Marcus, the way in which you structured my thinking and argumentation inspires me. I am grateful for your academic encouragement and I look forward to our continued collaboration.

Whilst many claim the opposite, writing a dissertation has been far from a lonely endeavour for me. I wish to thank my colleagues and PhD peers – past and present – of the Netherlands Institute of Human Rights (SIM) in particular, and Utrecht University more generally, for their friendship, collegiality, and challenging debates. I also wish to thank my colleagues at the International Law Department of Groningen University: I am appreciative for the warm welcome you have given me, both professionally and personally. Having spent various moments abroad, I am also indebted to the colleagues at Durham Law School (UK), the team of the African Palliative Care Association (UG), the Latvian Centre for Human Rights (LV), and the staff at the Brocher Foundation (CH).

It is always tricky to include or exclude names, yet I feel like a range of individuals deserve to be thanked separately. Deryck Beyleveld, thank you for your time and patience to teach me about ethical reflection. I truly enjoyed our collaboration in Durham, Utrecht, and Geneva and hope more is to come. Brigit Toebes, thank you for the trust you had in me by appointing me as a post-doc researcher before I had even officially finished my dissertation. I am excited to have joined the team at the Global Health Law Groningen Research Centre. Fatia Kiyange, I am happy that our collaboration in Uganda developed into a dear friendship. A particular thank you also goes out for the fantastic help in editing to Shan Patel, but also to Titia Hijmans van den Bergh, Klaartje Hoeberechts, and Titia Kloos of Utrecht University's editing department, and staff of Intersentia. All errors remaining are entirely my own.

Saskia Bal, your friendship and support means a lot to me. I always enjoy our *biertje* and *bitterbal* at the Faculty Club and I miss our time at Drift 15. Brianne McGonignle-Leyh, work bestie, dear friend, and *Paranymph,* I thank you for the many years at SIM and I am very excited we managed to merge our research interests in joint projects. Furthermore, I would also like to recognize my friends outside academia. Karen Bal, Maike van den Berg, Anne-Claire Bijmolt, Jef Croonen, and Peggy Simon; thank you for being my close friends. I feel privileged to rely on our long-standing friendships. A particular thank you goes out to Maike. We have a joint academic interest that I enjoy deeply; thank you for being my *Paranymph.*

Last but certainly not least, I wish to pay my deepest gratitude to my family. My dear *Omoes*, I am proud to share this great moment with you. We both miss *Opa* terribly at this event, knowing how proud he, like you, would be to witness one of his grandchildren obtaining a PhD degree. I thank you for what you taught me and for the warm home you have always provided for me. I also wish to thank my sisters Nathalie, Eliane, Lúthien, and Charlotte for keeping me – as the youngest – with both feet on the ground.

My parents always told me that I should never have to thank them for the support they give me. However, I feel like an exception is appropriate here. *Pap* and *Mam*, who would ever have thought that I would pursue an academic career at the crossroads of our fields of interest? I could not have been more proud to share this moment with you and I value every step you walk along with me in life: thank you.

Dearest Paul, where should I start with thanking you? I thank you for your unwavering support, patience, unconditional love, and companionship: you make me smile. *Nakupenda sana mpenzi.*

Contents

List of Abbreviations

AAAQ	Availability Accessibility Acceptability Quality
ACHPR	African Charter on Human and Peoples' Rights
ACRWC	African Convention on the Rights and Welfare of the Child
AIDS	Acquired Immune Deficiency Syndrome
APCA	African Palliative Care Association
ATOME	Access To Opioid Medication in Europe project
CAT	Convention against Torture and Other Cruel, Inhuman or Degrading Treatment and Punishment
CED	Convention for the Protection of All Persons from Enforced Disappearance
CEDAW	Convention on the Elimination of All Forms of Discrimination Against Women
CERD	Convention on the Elimination of All Forms of Racial Discrimination
CESCR	Committee on Economic, Social and Cultural Rights
CFREU	Charter on the Fundamental Rights of the European Union
CIDT	Cruel, Inhuman and Degrading Treatment
CND	Commission on Narcotic Drugs
CP	Civil and Political
CRC	Convention on the Rights of the Child
CRPD	Convention on the Rights of Persons with Disabilities
ECHR	European Convention on Human Rights and Fundamental Freedoms
ECOSOC	Economic and Social Council
ECtHR	European Court of Human Rights and Fundamental Freedoms
DNA	Deoxyribonucleic Acid
EMA	European Medicine Agency
ESC	Economic, Social and Cultural
EU	European Union
GP	General Practitioner
HAU	Hospice Africa Uganda
HDI	Human Development Index
HICs	High Income Countries
HIV	Human Immunodeficiency Virus
IACtHR	Inter-American Court of Human Rights
ICCPR	International Covenant on Civil and Political Rights
ICESCR	International Covenant on Economic, Social and Cultural Rights

ICMW	International Convention on the Protection of the Rights of All Migrant Workers and Members of their Families
INCB	International Narcotics Control Board
ILC	International Law Commission
JMS	Joint Medical Store (Uganda)
LCHR	Latvian Centre on Human Rights
LMICs	Low and Middle Income Countries
MDGs	Millennium Development Goals
NDA	National Drug Authority (Uganda)
NHI	National Health Inspectorate (Latvia)
NHS	National Health Service (Latvia)
NMS	National Medical Store (Uganda)
PCAU	Palliative Care Association of Uganda
PGC	Principle of Generic Consistency
RESC	Revised European Social Charter
SAM	State Agency of Medicines (Latvia)
SDGs	Sustainable Development Goals
UDHR	Universal Declaration of Human Rights
UN	United Nations
UNAIDS	United Nations Programme on HIV/AIDS
UNGA	United Nations General Assembly
UNGASS	United Nations General Assembly Special Session
UNODC	United Nations Office on Drugs and Crime
USSR	Union of Soviet Socialist Republics
VCLT	Vienna Convention on the Law of Treaties
VDPA	Vienna Declaration and Programme of Action
WHA	World Health Assembly
WHO	World Health Organization

Table of Instruments

International

Charter of the United Nations (adopted 24 October 1945) 1 UNTS XVI.
Statute of the International Court of Justice (adopted 26 June 1945, entered into force 24 October 1945) 33 UNTS 993.
Constitution of the World Health Organization (adopted 22 July 1946, entered into force 7 April 1948) 14 UNTS 185.
Universal Declaration of Human Rights (adopted 10 December 1948) UNGA Res 217 A(III).
Single Convention on Narcotic Drugs (adopted 30 March 1961, entered into force 13 December 1964, as amended in 1972) 520 UNTS 151.
International Convention on the Elimination of All Forms of Racial Discrimination (adopted 7 March 1966, entered into force 4 January 1969) 660 UNTS 195.
International Covenant on Economic, Social and Cultural Rights (adopted 16 December 1966, entered into force 3 January 1976) 993 UNTS 3.
Optional Protocol to the International Covenant on Economic, Social and Cultural Rights (adopted 10 December 2008, entered into force 5 May 2013) UN Doc A/RES/63/118.
International Covenant on Civil and Political Rights (adopted 16 December 1966, entered into force 23 March 1976) 999 UNTS 171.
Optional Protocol to the International Covenant on Civil and Political Rights (adopted 16 December 1966, entered into force 23 March 1976) 999 UNTS 171.
Vienna Convention on the Law of Treaties (adopted 23 May 1969, entered into force 27 January 1980) 1155 UNTS 331.
Convention on Psychotropic Substances (adopted 21 February 1971, entered into force 16 August 1976) 1901 UNTS 175.
Convention on the Elimination of All Forms of Discrimination Against Women (adopted 18 December 1979, entered into force 3 September 1981) 1249 UNTS 13.
Convention against Torture and Other Cruel, Inhuman or Degrading Treatment or Punishment (adopted 10 December 1984, entered into force 26 June 1987) 1465 UNTS 85.
United Nations Convention Against the Illicit Traffic in Narcotic Drugs and Psychotropic Substances (adopted 20 December 1988, entered into force 11 November 1990) 1582 UNTS 95.
International Convention on the Protection of the Rights of All Migrant Workers and Members of their Families (adopted 18 December 1990, entered into force 1 July 2003) 2220 UNTS 3.

Convention on the Rights of the Child (adopted 20 November 1989, entered into force 2 September 1990) 1577 UNTS 3.

Optional Protocol to the Convention on the Rights of the Child on the Involvement of Children in Armed Conflict (adopted 25 May 2000, entered into force 12 February 2002) 2173 UNTS 222.

Optional Protocol to the Convention on the Rights of the Child on the Sale of Children, Child Prostitution and Child Pornography (adopted 25 May 2000, entered into force 18 January 2002) 2171 UNTS 227.

Convention on the Rights of Persons with Disabilities (adopted 13 December 2006, entered into force 3 May 2008) 2515 UNTS 3.

Optional Protocol to the Convention on the Rights of Persons with Disabilities (adopted 13 December 2006, entered into force 3 May 2008) UN Doc A/RES/61/106.

International Convention for the Protection of All Persons from Enforced Disappearance (adopted 20 December 2006, entered into force 23 December 2010) 2716 UNTS 3.

Regional

Africa

African Charter on Human and Peoples' Rights (adopted 27 June 1981, entered into force 21 October 1986) 1520 UNTS 217.

Protocol to the African Charter on Human and Peoples' Rights on the Establishment of an African Court on Human and Peoples' Rights (adopted 10 June 1998, entered into force 25 January 2004) OAU Doc OAU/LEG/EXP/AFCHPR/PROT(III).

African Charter on the Rights and Welfare of the Child (adopted 1 July 1990, entered into force 29 November 1999) OAU Doc CAB/LEG/24.9/49.

Protocol to the African Charter on Human and Peoples' Rights on the Rights of Women in Africa (adopted 7 November 2003, entered into force 25 November 2005) OAU Doc CAB/LEG/66.6.

The East African Community HIV & Aids Prevention and Management Bill of 2012.

Americas

American Declaration on the Rights and Duties of Man (adopted 2 May 1948) OAS Doc OEA/Ser.L.V/II.82 doc.6 rev.1.

American Convention on Human Rights (adopted 22 November 1969, entered into force 18 July 1978) 1144 UNTS 123.

Additional Protocol to the American Convention on Human Rights in the Area of Economic, Social, and Cultural Rights (adopted 17 November 1988, entered into force 16 November 1999) OASTS 69.

Inter-American Convention to Prevent and Punish Torture (adopted 9 December 1985, entered into force 28 February 1987) OASTS 67.

Europe

European Convention for the Protection of Human Rights and Fundamental Freedoms (adopted 4 November 1950, entered into force 3 September 1953, as amended) 213 UNTS 222.
European Convention for the Prevention of Torture and Inhuman or Degrading Treatment or Punishment (adopted 26 November 1987, entered into force 1 February 1989) ETS 126.
Revised European Social Charter (adopted 3 May 1996, entered into force 1 July 1999) ETS 163.
Additional Protocol to the European Social Charter (adopted 5 May 1988, not yet in force) ETS 128.
Convention for the protection of Human Rights and Dignity of the Human Being with regard to the Application of Biology and Medicine (adopted 4 April 1997, entered into force 1 December 1999) ETS 164.
Charter of Fundamental Rights of the European Union [2000] OJ C364/1 (as amended).
Council Directive 2001/83/EC of 6 November 2001 on the Community code relating to medicinal products for human use (Medicinal Products for Human Use Directive) [2001] OJ L311/67.

National

Latvia

Constitution of the Republic of Latvia, 1922 (as amended).
Law on International Treaties of the Republic of Latvia of 1994.
Medicines and Related Substances Act 101 of 1995.
Law on Procedures for the Legal Trade of the Narcotic and Psychotropic Substances and Medicinal Products of 1996 (as amended).
Law on Precursors of 1996 (as amended).
Constitutional Court Law of 1997.
Pharmaceutical Law of 1997 (as amended).
Criminal Law of 1998 (as amended).
Latvian Administrative Violations Code of 2007.

Spain

Constitución Española.

Uganda

National Drug Policy and Authority Act of 1993.
Constitution of the Republic of Uganda, 1995.

Medicines and Related Substances Act 101 of 1995.
Local Governments Act of 1997.
National Drug Authority (Prescription and Supply of Certain Narcotic Analgesic Drugs) Regulations, Statutory Instruments 14/2004.
Narcotic Drugs and Psychotropic Substances (Control) Act of 2015.

USA

Food and Drugs Regulation, 21 CFR 314.80 (2015).

Table of Cases

International

HR Committee

HR Committee, *Irving Phillip v Trinidad and Tobago* (Comm no 594/1992).
HR Committee, *Eustace Henry and Everald Douglas v Jamaica* (Comm no 571/1994).
HR Committee, *Dennis Lobban v Jamaica* (Comm no 797/1998).
HR Committee, *Manuel Wackenheim v France* (Comm no 854/1999).
HR Committee, *Oleg Pustovalov v Russian Federation* (Comm no 1232/2003).
HR Committee, *Saed Shams and Ors v Australia* (Comm no 1255, 1256, 1259, 1260, 1266, 1268, 1270, and 1288/2004).
HR Committee, *Prince v South Africa* (Comm no 1474/2006).
HR Committee, *Omar Faruk Bozbey v Turkmenistan* (Comm no 1530/2006).

Regional

European Court of Human Rights

D. v the United Kingdom (1997) 24 EHRR 423.
Rehbock v Slovenia ECHR 2000-XII 645.
Bensaid v the United Kingdom (2001) 33 EHRR 10.
McGlinchey and Ors v the United Kingdom (2003) 37 EHRR 41.
Holomiov v Moldova App no 30649/05 (ECtHR, 7 November 2006).
Hummatov v Azerbaijan App nos 9852/03 and 13413/04 (ECtHR, 29 November 2007).
Bragadireanu v Romania App no 22088/04 (ECtHR, 6 December 2007).
Mikhaniv v Ukraine App no 75522/01 (ECtHR, 6 November 2008).
N. v the United Kingdom (2008) 47 EHRR 39.
Okhrimenko v Ukraine App no 53896/07 (ECtHR, 15 October 2009).
Zakharkin v Russia App no 1555/04 (ECtHR, 10 June 2010).
A.B. v Russia App no 1439/06 (ECtHR, 14 October 2010).
Logvinenko v Ukraine App no 13448/07 (ECtHR, 14 October 2010).
Goginashvili v Georgia App no 47729/08 (ECtHR, 4 October 2011).

Inter-American Court of Human Rights

Cantoral Benavides v Peru (Reparations, and Costs) Inter-American Court of Human Rights Series C No 88 (3 December 2001).
Gutiérrez Soler v Colombia (Merits, Reparations, and Costs) Inter-American Court of Human Rights Series C No 132 (12 September 2005).
Indigenous Community Yakye Axa v Paraguay (Merits, Reparations, and Costs) Inter-American Court of Human Rights Series C No 125 (6 February 2006).
Sawhoyamaxa Indigenous Community of the Enxet People v Paraguay (Merits, Reparations, and Costs) Inter-American Court of Human Rights Series C No 146 (29 March 2006).
Damião Ximenes Lopes v Brazil (Merits, Reparations, and Costs) Inter-American Court of Human Rights Series C No 149 (4 July 2006).
Fernández Ortega and Ors v México (Preliminary Objection, Merits, Reparations, and Costs) Inter-American Court of Human Rights Series C No 215 (30 August 2010).

Inter-American Commission of Human Rights

Joined Cases 12.067, 12.068 and 12.086 *Michael Edwards, Omar Hall and Brian Schroeter and Jeronimo Bolweg v the Bahamas* (Merits) Inter-American Commission of Human Rights Report No 48/01 (4 April 2001).
Case 12.158 *Benedict Jacob v Granada* (Merits) Inter-American Commission of Human Rights Report No 56/02 (21 October 2002).
Case 12.275 *Denton Aitiken v Jamaica* (Merits) Inter-American Commission of Human Rights Report No 58/02 (21 October 2002).
Case 12.417 *Whitley Myrie v Jamaica* (Merits) Inter-American Commission of Human Rights Report No 41/04 (12 October 2004).
Case 12.476 *Oscar Elías Biscet et al. v Cuba* (Merits) Inter-American Commission of Human Rights Report No 67/06 (21 October 2006).
Case 12.265 *Chad Roger Goodman v the Bahamas* (Merits) Inter-American Commission of Human Rights Report No 78/07 (15 October 2007).
Case 12.296 *Dexter Lendore v Trinidad and Tobago* (Merits) Inter-American Commission of Human Rights Report No 28/09 (20 March 2009).

African Commission of Human and Peoples' Rights

Free Legal Assistance Group and Ors v Democratic Republic of Congo, ACHPR Commission, Comm no 25/89, 47/90, 56-91 and 100/93 (4 April 1996).
Media Rights Agenda and Ors v Nigeria, ACHPR Commission, Comm no 105/93, 128/94, 130/94 and 152/96 (31 October 1998).
Huri-Laws v Nigeria, ACHPR Commission, Comm no 225/98 (6 November 2000).
Democratic Republic of Congo v Burundi, Rwanda and Uganda, ACHPR Commission, Comm no 227/99 (29 May 2003).

Purohit and Moore v The Gambia, ACHPR Commission, Comm no 241/01 (29 May 2003).
Garreth Anver Prince v South Africa, ACHPR Commission, Comm no 225/02 (7 December 2004).
Egyptian Initiative for Personal Rights and INTERIGHTS v Egypt, ACHPR Commission, Comm no 323/06 (12 October 2013).

National

BVerfG, 21.06.1977 (1 BvL 14/76), NJW 1977, 1525.
Conseil d'Etat n° 136727 du 27 octobre 1995.
Glenda López and Ors v Instituto Venezolano de los Seguros Sociales (IVSS), Expediente 00-1343 [1997] Tribunal Supremo de Justicia de la República Bolivariana de Venezuela.
Cruz del Valle Bermúdez and Ors v MSAS, Expediente 15.789 [1999] Tribunal Supremo de Justicia de la República Bolivariana de Venezuela.
Prince v President of the Law Society of the Cape of Good Hope and Others (CCT36/00) [2000] ZACC 28.
People living with HIV, Expediente 3.599-2001-10-16 [2001] Corte Suprema de Chile.
Minister of Health and Others v Treatment Action Campaign and Others (No 2) (CCT8/02) [2002] ZACC 15.
Azanca Alhelí Meza García v Peru, Expediente 2945-2003-AA/TC [2004] Tribunal Constitucional del Perú.
HR (9 January 2007), ECLI:NL:HR:2007:AZ2497.
Rb Haarlem (26 March 2009), ECLI:NL:RBHAA:2009:BH9844.
Roberts Mutulis v the Republic of Latvia (Case No 2008-48-01) [2009] LVCC 6 (29 September 2009).
Hof Amsterdam (24 February 2012), ECLI:NL:GHAMS:2012:BV6888.
Center for Health Human Rights & Development (CEHURD) and 3 Ors v Attorney General (Constitutional Petition No 16/2011) [2012] UGCC 4 (5 June 2012).
Vitālijs Orlovs and 19 Ors v the Republic of Latvia (Case No 2012-14-03) [2013] LVCC 6 (9 April 2013).

List of Figures and Tables

Figures

Tables

Part 1

Concept and Problem

Chapter 1
Introduction

It is time for regulations that put lives and safety first.
Kofi Annan, 2016[1]

1.1 A bird's-eye view

The general topic of this book is access to controlled essential medicines under the interplay of human rights and drug-control norms. The exact focus and approach are elaborated in this introductory chapter. For the purpose of definition, controlled essential medicines are those medicines whose active substance is listed in one of the schedules of the international drug-control treaties, which regulate their availability and accessibility. Yet at the same time, these medicines appear on the Model List of Essential Medicines as developed by the World Health Organization (WHO), meaning that human rights law also regulates their availability and accessibility.[2] Controlled substances are all those substances scheduled under the international drug-control treaties. It is important to distinguish between controlled *medicine* and controlled *substance* because only part of all controlled substances has a clear and evidence-based medical potential.

---

1 KA Annan, 'Lift the Ban! Kofi Annan on Why It's Time to Legalize Drugs' *Der Spiegel* (22 February 2016) <www.spiegel.de/international/world/kofi-annan-on-why-drug-bans-are-ineffective-a-107840 2.html> accessed 31 August 2016.

2 The term 'controlled medicines' is not necessarily a medical classification but a legal term instead. The international drug-control treaties include different lists or schedules of medicines, which determine the level of protection and use of these medicines. Chapter 2, Section 2.4 will deal with this issue in more detail. For now, it suffices to acknowledge that controlled medicines are 'listed' or 'scheduled' under the international drug-control treaties, meaning that they more generally fall within their legal realm. See also WHO, 'Model List of Essential Medicines' (19th edn, August 2015) <www.who.int/medicines/publications/essentialmedicines/EML_2015_FINAL_amended_NOV2015.pdf?ua=1> accessed 31 August 2016 (WHO Model List of Essential Medicines). As a result of this focus, the case of medicinal cannabis use falls outside the remit of this book because medicinal cannabis, by an omission demonstrated in Chapter 2, is not listed as an essential medicine on the WHO Model List of Essential Medicines. On medicinal cannabis and international drug control, see eg DR Bewley-Taylor, *International Drug Control: Consensus Fractured* (CUP 2012).

Throughout this study, morphine and codeine, essential pain-control medicines, serve as leading examples.[3] This implies that the central topic is addressed from both a (general) controlled essential medicines perspective, as well as a specific (or applied) pain-control medicine angle. It is important to clearly mark this purposeful distinction from the start so as to avoid confusion in concept, focus, and analysis throughout the book. The reason for this differentiation is that the interplay of human rights and drug-control norms affect more medicines than just morphine and codeine, and thus warrants the inclusion of a more general focus. However, in terms of application, it will be more insightful to concentrate on part of the medicines involved in order to strengthen and deepen the analysis.

The issue of controlled essential medicines and the severity of their absence are best demonstrated by the situation of Remedios Ramirez Facio, a 73-year-old woman with pancreatic cancer. In an interview with Human Rights Watch, Remedios said: '[With the pain] I didn't have the desire to do anything. I wasn't hungry and didn't want to walk (…) nothing. It would anger me when people spoke to me (…) [With palliative care] I have come back to life.'[4]

Remedios receives palliative care[5] at Mexico's National Cancer Institute.[6] She is lucky to receive this treatment including pain-control medication such as morphine, which drastically changed her life. In many countries of all levels of development opioid analgesics – opium containing painkillers – such as morphine are almost unavailable or inaccessible.[7] Morphine is not just indispensable for adequate chronic pain treatment (and palliative care) but is also vital in treating acute trauma, and for

3 WHO Model List of Essential Medicines (n 2). See also Single Convention on Narcotic Drugs (adopted 30 March 1961, entered into force 13 December 1964, as amended in 1972) 520 UNTS 151 (Single Convention) schs I-II.
4 Human Rights Watch, *Care When There is no Cure* (HRW 2014) 20.
5 The WHO defines palliative care as 'an approach that improves the quality of life of patients and their families facing the problem associated with life-threatening illness, through the prevention and relief of suffering by means of early identification and impeccable assessment and treatment of pain and other problems, physical, psychosocial and spiritual'. See WHO, 'Definition of Palliative Care' <www.who.int/cancer/palliative/definition/en/> accessed 31 August 2016. Morphine and codeine are essential medicines for pain control, which is a vital component of palliative care. See WHO, 'Cancer Pain Ladder for Adults' <www.who.int/cancer/palliative/painladder/en/> accessed 31 August 2016 (WHO Pain Ladder).
6 Human Rights Watch (n 4) 20.
7 B Duthey and W Scholten, 'Adequacy of Opioid Analgesic Consumption at Country, Global, and Regional Levels in 2010, its Relationship with Development Level, and Changes Compared with 2006' (2014) 47 Journal of Pain and Symptom Management 283.

pre and post-surgery care.[8] In spite of their importance, Duthey and Scholten found there is virtually no consumption of opioid analgesics in 66 per cent of the global population, that it is very low in 10 per cent, low in 3 per cent, moderate in 4 per cent, and adequate in a mere 7.5 per cent.[9]

Although fair or equitable access to quality medication is also problematic in the developed world, the undersupply of medicine including opioid medicines is most acute in Low- and Middle-Income Countries.[10] Effectively, the world is facing a lopsided supply/demand chain when it comes to opioid analgesics. Data from 2009 demonstrates that 90 per cent of all consumption occurred in Australia, Canada, New Zealand, the United States of America, and several European countries, whereas 80 per cent of the global population lives in developing regions.[11] By means of example, only 0.2 per cent of the global distribution of morphine consumption was traced to the African region in that same year.[12] Duthey and Scholten similarly found that the unavailability of opioid medication was most serious in the African region.[13] As a result of skewed distribution, millions of patients across the world remain in dire need of such medicines, as access is virtually non-existent.[14]

Consequently, this public health deficit leads to numerous patients, already living in lesser-advanced circumstances, suffering daily in disabling, degrading, and sometimes even inhumane conditions.[15] The suffering caused, thus, raises serious

8 See the WHO Pain Ladder (n 5) which defines when strong opioids such as morphine should be used to treat moderate to severe pain. Morphine is not the only medicine used to treat such pain, yet it remains the most common medicine used for this purpose. On essential medicines in palliative care including pain control more generally, see J Cleary, 'Essential Medicines in Palliative Care' (2014) 28 Palliative Medicine 291.

9 Duthey and Scholten (n 7).

10 ibid 286-287. See on the problems of medicine access in the developed world eg B Obrist and others, 'Access to Health Care in Contexts of Livelihood Insecurity: A Framework for Analysis and Action' (2007) PLOS Medicine 1584, 1584; P Stephens, 'Access to Medicines: Common Problems, Common Solutions?' (DPhil thesis, Utrecht University 2016) 11.

11 INCB, *Availability of Internationally Controlled Drugs: Ensuring Adequate Access for Medical and Scientific Purposes* (INCB 2011) 2. On global patterns of consumption, see also INCB, *Availability of Internationally Controlled Drugs: Ensuring Adequate Access for Medical and Scientific Purposes. Indispensable, Adequately Available and Not Unduly Restricted* (INCB 2016) 12-27.

12 id.

13 Duthey and Scholten (n 7) 285.

14 The unavailability of controlled medicines does not only include morphine for pain treatment. Also other controlled medications such as medicines for obstetric complications and in opioid dependence treatment remain largely unavailable. On this topic, see eg WHO, 'Access to Controlled Essential Medicines Programme: Improving Access to Medications Controlled under International Drug Conventions' (April 2012) WHO Briefing Note <www.who.int/medicines/areas/quality_safety/ACMP_BrNote_Genrl_E N_Apr2012.pdf?ua=1> accessed 31 August 2016.

15 As will be discussed in Chapter 2, this suffering puts huge pressure on the individual patient, caregivers, and society at large.

concerns in light of human rights protection.[16] For instance, States have obligations under the right to health to ensure adequate treatment and care is available.[17] States must also protect people from inhuman and degrading treatment under the freedom from torture and cruel, inhuman, and degrading treatment.[18] More generally, such seriously disabling suffering could infringe upon human dignity, which human rights are set to integrally protect and promote.

There are many factors potentially contributing to the unavailability of medicines. Some of these factors are general in nature, i.e. independent of the specific context of a medicine or medicine group. Examples include infrastructure and geographic accessibility of health facilities and services. Other factors are substance-specific in nature, i.e. might come into play exactly because of the particular context of a medicine or medicine group, or aggravate general factors because of that. In the case of controlled medicines, there might be many of these general factors. It can also be questioned whether the international drug control treaties themselves might be such a medicine-specific factor obstructing access to controlled medicines such as morphine. The distinction between general and substance-specific challenges serves to demonstrate how the international drug-control treaties might fit into a larger picture of complexities in global medicine provision.[19]

---

16 F Brennan, DB Carr and M Cousins, 'Pain Management: A Fundamental Human Right' (2007) 105 Anesthesia & Analgesia 205; D Lohman, R Schleifer and JJ Amon, 'Access to Pain Treatment as a Human Right' (2010) 8 BMC Medicine 1; MEC Gispen, *Poor Access to Pain Treatment* (International Federation of Health and Human Rights Organization 2011); MEC Gispen, 'A Human Rights View on Access to Controlled Substances for Medical Purposes under the International Drug Control Framework' (2013) 719 European Journal of Pharmacology 16; L Radbruch and others, 'The Lisbon Challenge: Acknowledging Palliative Care as a Human Right' (2013) 16 Journal of Palliative Medicine 301; D Lohman, 'Pain Care as a Human Right' (2014) 14 Pain Practice 199. On human rights claims to access controlled medicines more generally, see WHO, 'Access to Analgesics and to Other Controlled Medications' <www.who.i nt/medicines/areas/quality_safety/access_Contr_Med/en/> accessed 31 August 2016. Notably, most of the work on the access to controlled medicines and human rights is still mainly focused on pain-control medicines.

17 International Covenant on Economic, Social and Cultural Rights (adopted 16 December 1966, entered into force 3 January 1976) 993 UNTS 3 (ICESCR) art 12.

18 Convention against Torture and Other Cruel, Inhuman or Degrading Treatment or Punishment (adopted 10 December 1984, entered into force 26 June 1987) 1465 UNTS 85, arts 1, 16.

19 Chapter 2 gives a more in-depth overview of general and substance-specific factors.

There could be many legislative, policy, regulatory, educational, informational, financial, and political challenges to the access to morphine for pain treatment.[20] One of the underlying reasons for these potential challenges in morphine provision are the fear and myths surrounding the safe and responsible use of morphine. Amongst many policymakers, doctors, patients, pharmacists, nurses, family members, and spiritual leaders, the fear remains that morphine use would impair legal capacity, be addictive, or would hasten death and cause social disorder as a consequence.[21] This fear ultimately reveals a fundamental dilemma: controlled substances may be saints and sinners.[22]

As saints, if used with due respect for medical guidelines, controlled substances are essential to the provision of adequate medical care. Notably, in the context of medical use, controlled substances are referred to as controlled medicines throughout the book. Up until today, controlled medicines are vital for the provision of adequate medical care. For instance, morphine is still considered the most effective medicine for the treatment of pain alongside a range of non-opioid analgesics.[23] As sinners, if used for non-medical purposes, however, controlled substances may lead to dependence and addiction disorders.[24] For instance, the recreational use of heroin (like morphine a derivate of opium) may lead to dependency and addiction disorders.

20 See Brennan, Carr and Cousins (n 16); R Harding and others, 'Provision of Pain- and Symptom-Relieving Drugs for HIV/AIDS in Sub-Saharan Africa' (2010) 40 Journal of Pain and Symptom Management 405, 412; L Thomas, D Lohman and JJ Amon, 'Access to Pain Treatment and Palliative Care: A Human Rights Analysis' (2010) 24 Temple International & Comparative Law Journal 365, 370-378; Gispen, *Poor Access to Pain Treatment* (n 16) 13-15; Global Commission on Drug Policy, *The Negative Impact of Drug Control on Public Health: The Global Crisis of Avoidable Pain* (GCDP 2015).

21 DS Bennett and DB Carr, 'Opiophobia as a Barrier to the Treatment of Pain' (2002) 16 Journal of Pain & Palliative Care Pharmacotherapy 105; A Rhodin, 'The Rise of Opiophobia: Is History a Barrier to Prescribing?' (2006) 30 Journal of Pain & Palliative Care Pharmacotherapy 31. This fear is largely considered ill-founded in light of the bulk of evidence-based research demonstrating the opposite. However, due to the socio-legal nature of this book, it falls outside its remit to make any medical value judgments.

22 The term 'saints and sinners' is inspired by the LIFE Before Death campaign in which it is questioned whether opium is to be considered 'sinner' or 'saint'. See 'Opium, Sinner or Saint? Life Before Death Film No 22' (*Pain Policy*, 15 October 2011) <https://painpolicy.wordpress.com/2011/10/15/opium-sinner-or-saint-life-before-death-film-no-22/> accessed 31 August 2016.

23 In the absence of alternative pharmacotherapies to alleviate pain, the relief of pain is still a prominent priority in present pharmacotherapy research, see KM Foley and others 'Pain Control for People with Cancer and AIDS' in DT Jamison and others (eds), *Disease Control Priorities in Developing Countries* (2nd edn, OUP 2006) 981; WHO, *Ensuring Balance in National Policies on Controlled Substances: Guidance for Availability and Accessibility of Controlled Medicines* (WHO 2011) 13-14. See also text to n 8.

24 The term addiction is sensitive due to the stigma attached to it. While acknowledging this sensitivity, the terms addiction and dependency disorder are used interchangeably throughout this study to refer to the potentially serious negative consequences of non-medical drug use.

Therefore, in the context of non-medical use, controlled substances are referred to as drugs throughout this book. Obviously, drug dependence and addiction are a threat to the protection of public health at both the level of the individual user and society as a whole. Not only does the use of illicit drugs undermine a country's socio-economic development, it also contributes significantly to crime, instability, and insecurity.[25] Globally, it is estimated that 16 million people inject drugs, of whom 3 million are Human Immunodeficiency Virus (HIV)-infected.[26] Apart from social exclusion, stigmatization, and discrimination, drug users face an additional risk of HIV, hepatitis B, and hepatitis C infections.[27]

Rationally, it is imperative to regulate the use of these substances in order to promote, as well as protect, public health. In particular because there are many controlled substances that have 'abuse potential' and do not necessarily possess evidence-based medical potential.[28] Yet, 'there seems to be no standard pharmacological classification of drugs which divides them exhaustively into mutually exclusive categories'.[29] This is demonstrated for instance by the case of derivatives from opium such as morphine and heroin, with the question being what the desired or aspired level and manner of regulating controlled substances is.[30] To regulate this dual nature of controlled substances, the international community, over a period of a hundred years, has adopted a criminal-law based system of control.[31] To date, the system receives much criticism in relation to human rights protection. In fact, Barrett and Nowak submit that '[t]he "war on drugs" is now more widespread and higher in financial and human cost than ever, and has impacted negatively across borders and across human rights protections'.[32]

---

25 UNODC, *World Drug Report 2012* (UNODC 2012) iii (UNODC Report 2012).

26 WHO, 'HIV/AIDS' <www.who.int/hiv/topics/idu/en/> accessed 31 August 2016.

27 See J Ahern, J Stuber and S Galea, 'Stigma, Discrimination and the Health of Illicit Drug Users' (2007) 88 Drug and Alcohol Dependence 188, 188-189; WHO, *Ensuring Balance in National Policies on Controlled Substances* (n 23).

28 S Luper-Foy and C Brown (eds), *Drugs, Morality, and the Law* (Garland Publishing 1994) ix.

29 ibid xi.

30 This duality is not necessarily unique to controlled substances. There have also been recent discussions on the regulation of antibiotics addressing a similar conflict in the protection of public health. Their use is vital to the provision of adequate medical care and in combating bacterial infections. Yet their overuse results in resistance, which makes it more difficult to combat bacterial infections. Hence in relation to the use of antibiotics, there are also two public-health concerns that might conflict with each other.

31 UNODC Report 2012 (n 25).

32 D Barrett and M Nowak, 'The United Nations and Drug Policy: Towards a Human Rights-Based Approach' in A Constantinides and N Zaikos (eds), *The Diversity of International Law: Essays in Honour of Professor Kalliopi K Koufa* (Martinus Nijhoff Publishers 2009) 449.

In brief, the international drug-control treaties operate on a delicate equilibrium: States have to control diversion of controlled substances whilst ensuring their medical and scientific availability. This foundational notion is often referred to as the 'principle of balance'.[33] To give effect to the aforementioned principle, a general prohibition clause has been adopted which prohibits all production, manufacturing, import/export, trade, distribution, administration, and use of controlled substances.[34] The single legitimate exception to this otherwise strict rule only allows for medical and scientific usage of the substances in question.[35] To further guide States in their efforts to comply with this general obligation, many additional provisions have been adopted that include administrative and procedural obligations to monitor the use of controlled medicines. From a wide variety of perspectives, however, this general prohibition clause, the additional provisions, and in particular administrative and procedural obligations and specific trade and distribution requirements to monitor the use of controlled medicines, are questioned.

Concerned with the unmet demand for controlled medicines such as morphine, this book specifically analyses the interface of human rights and international drug-control norms on access to controlled medicine provision in resource-constrained countries.[36] As mentioned, in doing so it takes the access to morphine for pain control, like in the case of Remedios, as an example.[37]

33 Sometimes also referred to as the 'Vienna consensus'. This, however, refers to the fact that only medical and scientific purposes are considered a legitimate exception in the international drug-control treaties for the use of controlled substances. On the term 'Vienna consensus', N Boister, 'Waltzing on the Vienna Consensus on Drug Control? Tensions in the International System for Control of Drugs' (2016) Leiden Journal of International Law 389. This balanced notion, or rather 'Vienna consensus', is frequently challenged in the context of religious, traditional, and/or recreational use. See also text to n 45.

34 Single Convention, art 4.

35 id.

36 In this book, 'resource-constrained countries' refers also to countries which are moderately resource-constrained but have seriously constrained health systems, and/or resource-rich countries with such geographically remote areas that constraints in service delivery in these regions is similar to the conditions in generally resource-constrained countries. For readability, the study refers only to resource-constrained countries yet, as illustrated, means to include all those mentioned above. See eg C Coleman and others 'The International Cancer Expert Corps (ICEC): A Unique Global Mentoring Model for Building Sustainable Expertise in Low-and Lower-Middle Income Countries and Geographically Remote Areas in Resource Rich Countries' (2015) 81 Annals of Global Health 20.

37 To use morphine as an example of a larger group of controlled medicines does not mean that the discussions, findings, and conclusions presented will only apply to the availability of morphine. Especially at the conceptual level, this study is relevant to the broader field of controlled medicines as well. Defining a normative basis of drug control in human rights norms essentially deals with the underlying public health predicament, which, in distinct ways, underlies the regulation of controlled substances in general.

1.2 Research design

1.2.1 State of the art of human rights and drug-control research

In April 2016, the United Nations General Assembly held a Special Session (UNGASS) on the world's drug problem and reform initiatives, in which human rights perspectives were included.[38] In the run-up to this session, human rights law had often been referred to as the compass in drug-control efforts. Human rights norms should guide the international community and States in balancing the dual nature of controlled substances.[39] A human rights approach is also much called for in the academic and policy-oriented discussion.[40] However, the event itself received substantial criticism of civil society organizations stating 'UNGASS is now perilously close to representing a serious systemic failure of the [United Nations (UN)] system' challenging the 'non-inclusive and non-transparent nature of the preparatory process'.[41] The criticism mainly relates to the drafting process of the special session's Outcome Document in which developing countries who lack a permanent representation in Vienna were not assisted in their taking part in the preparatory process, progressive reform initiatives were wiped off the table without careful consideration, and the use of progressive language was blocked.[42] However promising the event was, the outcome of UNGASS 2016 has been received as disappointing from a human rights perspective by many.[43] As Lohman acknowledges '[t]he increased focus on health and human rights (...) is welcome, but as long as the dominantly court-and-cops approach to fighting drugs continues, the toll [taken by] the fight will far outweigh

38 D Lohman and N Burke-Shyne, 'The Impact of International Drug Policy on Access to Controlled Medicines' (Open Society Foundations 2015).

39 This issue has for instance been widely debated at the Equitable Access to Controlled Medicines Brocher Symposium (Hermance, Switzerland, 8-9 October 2015).

40 See eg D Barrett and others, 'Recalibrating the Regime: The Need for a Human Rights-Based Approach to International Drug Policy' (The Beckley Foundation 2008) <www.hrw.org/sites/default/files/related_material/beckley0308exec.pdf> accessed 31 August 2016; Barrett and Nowak (n 32); Gispen, 'Access to Controlled Substances' (n 16); Global Commission on Drug Policy, *Taking Control: Pathways to Drug Policies that Work* (GCDP 2014); MM Sánchez-Moreno, 'The Human Rights Case for Drug Reform: How Drug Criminalization Destroys Lives, Feeds Abuses, and Subverts the Rule of Law' in Human Rights Watch (ed), *World Report* (HRW 2014); S Rolles and others, *The Alternative World Drug Report* (2nd edn, Transform Drug Policy Foundation 2016).

41 Civil Society Statement, 'The UNGASS Outcome Document: Diplomacy or Denialism?' (14 March 2016) <www.tni.org/en/article/the-ungass-outcome-document-diplomacy-or-denialism> accessed 31 August 2016.

42 ibid.

43 See 'World Drug Problem: UN Adopts New Framework for Policies to 'Put People First' (*UN News Centre*, 19 April 2016) <www.un.org/apps/news/story.asp?NewsID=53723#.VyN1U03VyUm> accessed 31 August 2016; D Lohman, 'A Missed Opportunity to End the War on Drugs' (*IDPC*, 25 April 2016) <http://idpc.net/alerts/2016/04/a-missed-opportunity-to-end-the-war-on-drugs> accessed 31 August 2016.

the damage [caused by] the drugs themselves'.[44] For this reason, the aftermath of the UNGASS 2016 has fuelled debates on the continuous need for human rights and drug-control research.

In existing research, human rights law is frequently invoked and mostly used to support the position of a certain group of individuals (e.g. patients, drug users, traditional users, religious users or women, children, HIV and Acquired Immune Deficiency Syndrome (AIDS) patients), and/or in relation to the access to medicines or to drug enforcement. Such studies are generally set up to challenge the prohibitive approach of the international drug-control treaties or any of their implications. Or, alternatively, to propose an alternative framework in which the particular situation these groups of individuals should be understood.[45] In other words, human rights law is used to challenge or support political and legal decision-making in the field of drug control.[46] From a more general public international law perspective, scholars research the interface of human rights and drug-control norms, yet do not necessarily apply this work specifically to the case of controlled medicines.[47] Moreover, the interface between human rights and public health is also studied.[48] This current body of research covers ethical, legal, and societal dilemmas.[49]

---

44 Lohman, 'A Missed Opportunity' (n 43).

45 On human rights and access to pain control and palliative care, see eg Brennan, Carr and Cousins (n 16); AL Taylor, 'Addressing the Global Tragedy of Needless Pain: Rethinking the United Nations Single Convention on Narcotic Drugs' (2007) 35 Journal of Law, Medicines and Ethics 556; Lohman, Schleifer and Amon (n 16); Gispen, *Poor Access to Pain Treatment* (n 16); Radbruch and others (n 16); Lohman, 'Pain Care' (n 16). On human rights, drug control, and access to controlled medicines eg KI Pettus, 'Rhetoric and the Road to Hell: The International Narcotics Control Regime and Access to Essential Medicines' (2012) 1 Bulletin Health Policy and Law 1; Gispen, 'Access to Controlled Substances' (n 16). See also on human rights and the rights of drug users and/or drug use as such, A Stevens, 'Drug Policy, Harm and Human Rights: A Rationalist Approach' (2011) 22 International Journal of Drug Policy 399; PHPHMC van Kempen and MI Fedorova, *Internationaal Recht en Cannabis* (Kluwer 2014); D Wolfe and others, 'Human Rights and Access to Hepatitis C Treatment for People who Inject Drugs' (2015) 26 International Journal of Drug Policy 1072; C Walsh, 'Psychedelics and Cognitive Liberty: Reimaging Drug Policy through the Prism of Human Rights' (2016) 29 International Journal of Drug Policy 80. Or on children's rights and drug control, D Barrett, *The Impacts of Drugs Policies on Children and Young People* (Open Society Foundations 2015), and on human rights and traditional and religious drug use, BC Labate and C Canvar (eds), *Prohibition, Religious Freedom and Human Rights: Regulating Traditional Drug Use* (Springer 2014).

46 On the development dimension of drug control and its human rights angle, see R Schleifer, J Sagredo and T Avafia, 'Addressing the Development Dimensions of Drug Policy' (UNDP 2015).

47 RM Lines, *Human Rights and Drug Control in International Law* (CUP *forthcoming*).

48 N Hunt, 'Public Health or Human Rights: What Comes First?' (2004) 15 International Journal of Drug Policy 231.

49 Strikingly, the large majority of work that has included human rights arguments has one or more doctors as author(s). Much less has been written on human rights and drug control strictly from the legal perspective or by those with a legal background.

This existing body of work largely focuses on the effects of the present international drug-control regime on human rights protection, but does not necessarily look at the substantive legal and moral implications of framing a human rights approach to drug control. Such studies are valuable but leave out the potentially distinct way in which human rights and drug-control norms could shape and balance the two competing public health concerns: 'access to medicines' and 'control of diversion'. Redefining this basis allows one to really understand drug-control matters from a human rights perspective and prevents a mere injection of human rights into a structure which in itself is questioned as to whether it is morally, legally or politically in conflict with human rights norms. If one really wanted to push for any change in relation to the effects of the international drug-control regime in the area of access to medicine provision, Pettus suggests, the internal structures of the international drug-control system itself have to be reviewed.[50] Indeed in order to exactly understand the particular case of controlled medicines, the theoretical consequences, as well as practical implications of injecting human rights into drug control, should be taken into account. Only then can human rights perform a compass role and guide legitimate law and policy-making in the field of drug control. Understanding what it means to talk about a human rights approach to drug control to support access to controlled medicines in resource-constrained countries, in particular by looking at the internal legal structures, is exactly what this book aims to do.

Moreover, although it seems largely accepted that control mechanisms of the international drug-control treaties monitoring the access to controlled medicines might be problematic, there has been no research into their practical implications beyond acknowledging their potential complexity.[51] These potential complexities have been studied insufficiently both from the perspective of the application of the drug-control treaties itself, as well as in relation to the access to medicine provision in accordance with human rights norms. In other words, people speak of potential difficulties of compliance, yet there is little research-based understanding as to what it really means for States to comply with said procedures.

It is therefore clear that the current body of work is relevant but has left a gap in terms of understanding the human rights basis of drug control in general, and in understanding the access to controlled medicine provision in resource-constrained countries in particular.

---

50 Pettus (n 45) 1.

51 See eg S Berterame and others, 'Use of and Barriers to Access to Opioid Analgesics: A Worldwide, Regional, and National Study' (2016) 387 The Lancet 1644, 1653. The study was supported by the INCB, the monitoring body of the international drug control treaties. Their view on this matter is also briefly presented in the text at n 58.

1.2.2 Research approach

Concerned about the unmet demand for controlled medicines such as morphine, this book analyses the interface of human rights and international drug-control norms on the access to controlled medicine provision in resource-constrained countries. In order to clarify what it means to talk about human rights as a compass in drug-control matters, the present book utilizes a design study. A design study sets out by proposing an intervention or new measure to improve a situation or to solve a problem.[52] This book aims to improve an existing situation.

This book is set up to describe the global public health deficit caused by poor access to controlled medicines and its causes. Of the many potential hampering factors, this study focusses on one of these causes: the international drug-control treaties and their monitoring mechanisms, including specific regulatory demands. The book proposes a human rights approach by developing a normative basis for drug control in human rights norms.[53] Yet from a methodological perspective, designing a new approach requires it to be applied to an existing situation or norm in order to test its impact and feasibility so as to create a desirable outcome or resolve an undesirable outcome.[54] In line with the focus of this research, such application means to understand whether international and domestic procedures to regulate the accessibility and availability of controlled medicines would be human-rights compliant. More specifically, it also requires one to know what the real implications of in particular the control mechanisms of the international drug-control system are for the local service provision. To this end, two qualitative country studies are conducted. The book thus includes a normative framework as well as a more applied component.

Normative framework

This book develops a normative framework by scrutinizing the international drug-control system's foundational 'principle of balance' in light of human rights norms. Reconsidering this balanced foundation of international drug-control norms is necessary because of the unbalanced outcome said principle has in practice. Balancing two competing interests or claims, such as the conflict inherent to the dual nature of controlled substances, presupposes a certain standard on the basis of which the

52 I Curry-Summer and others, *Research Skills* (Ars Aequi Libri 2010) 18.

53 As mentioned earlier, access to medicines and drug control are also discussed and framed as public-health and economic issues, meaning that any new interpretation of this area could also be explored from these perspectives. Any of such alternatives, however, fall outside the scope of this work and, as such, are not discussed.

54 Curry-Summer and others (n 52) 18.

balancing between these two aspects can be determined.[55] In other words, one needs a standard or criterion to determine the legitimacy of drug-control regulation. Human rights law and the moral principles on which human rights rest represent a normative framework that can be used to legitimately balance competing interests.

Human rights norms seek to protect individuals from illegitimate state interference and empower individuals with entitlement claims to demand certain goods and services.[56] As such, the present framework of human rights both invokes corresponding negative (refraining from action/interference) and positive (demanding focused/targeted action) legal and moral rights and obligations.[57] One can understand human rights as the way they are institutionalized (law) as well as in light of the moral principles on which they rest (ethics). Human rights principles are further claimed to carry normative priority because they protect the inherent dignity of each and every person on a non-discriminatory basis, setting standards as to what is acceptable and what not, i.e. which law, policy, or action is legitimate and which is not, as well as which interest should take priority over other interests in case of a rights-claims clash.[58] This book will explore the theoretical and concrete implications of understanding drug-control matters in the framework of legitimacy established by human rights.

Yet, exactly because human rights determine a framework of legitimate balancing of competing interests, one could question how the predicament of ensuring access to controlled medicines and the protection against dispersion and hazardous non-medical use of controlled substances would be framed and balanced in human rights. It is particularly important to address such concerns because the way in which the dual nature of controlled substances is regulated should not be based on arbitrary or political decision-making. Instead, attempts should be made to follow a system of law that is supported by consistent logical argumentation, thereby legitimizing any decision-making in the field of drug control and access to medicines. The form of logical argumentation does not need to derive its authority or accuracy from human rights language per se.

In light of the predicament outlined above, various questions arise when attempting to shape and understand a model of drug control in compliance with human rights

55 Balancing does not necessarily mean that both aspects should be treated in an equal or exclusively similar manner.

56 To 'protect' is used here more generally and does not directly relate to the trichotomy of the human rights obligation to 'respect, protect, and fulfil'. This is addressed in more detail in Chapter 3.

57 Negative rights/obligations often imply freedom rights and a government refraining from action or interference. Positive rights/obligations imply entitlement claims to goods and services which demand focused and targeted state action.

58 The normative priority of human rights *law* in light of other fields of public international law is disputed. See for a further discussion on this matter Chapter 2, Section 2.2.

norms. For instance, 'Are people free to use drugs or should governments prohibit their use and protect people from the potential negative consequences of drug use?', 'Should we be concerned with ensuring access to medicines?', and 'Is this concern any different in relation to controlled medicines?'. Moreover, 'What if denying the use of drugs then leads to people no longer receiving medicines, is that a problem?', 'Should we care about that at all?'. Such questions essentially deal with values of protecting and promoting human dignity. 'Should people be protected from the hazardous use of listed substances or are people free to do so as long as their actions do not harm others?'. In other words, 'Would a strict regulation of drug control be paternalistic or a legitimate protection of public health and order in light of human rights norms?'. On the other hand, 'What are the values supporting access to controlled medicines?', 'Would it be a direct infringement on human dignity if no adequate care was available?'. Yet most strikingly, what happens if any efforts in relation to drug control conflict with efforts to secure medical access? Hence 'How should one frame these values when they are in conflict with each other?'. Once it becomes clear in what way human rights would be setting standards in the regulating of the dual nature of controlled substances, the question arises what the exact normative conditions and criteria are determining state obligations to protect human rights in this particular domain.

Notably, in line with the book's central focus, the intertwined complexity at hand is the potential inherent public health conflict of ensuring access to medicines and controlling diversion. In an attempt to resolve this tension in human rights law and theory, this study thus elaborates on claims to access controlled medicines and control diversion of controlled substances to protect public health and order. In line with this focus, the scope and content of state obligations are related to these two aspects based on the right to health and the freedom from cruel, inhuman and degrading treatment primarily. Aspects of traditional, religious, cultural, and recreational use are only addressed if relevant and necessary to understand the juxtaposition described. This focus, however, does not deprive the study of its broader relevance to human rights and drug-control research.

Application and implementation

Following the normative analysis, the second issue addressed relates to the application of the human rights approach analysed within the remits of the international drug-control treaties. In light of the general context of access to medicine provision, administrative and procedural drug-control requirements, including specific trade and distribution requirements, are questioned as to potentially complicate medicine provision in resource-constrained countries.[59] Taylor submits in this respect for instance that it is widely understood that countries simply ban a medicine once it falls within the scope of the international drug-control treaties.[60] Even the International Narcotics Control Board – the monitoring body of the international drug control treaties – refers to the implications of the administrative and procedural obligations to monitor and control access to controlled medicines as the potential heart of the problem.[61]

Yet if the implications of the administrative and procedural drug-control obligations are at the heart of the problem, then would this also frustrate resource-constrained countries in the protection of human rights? More specifically the question would arise as to how this claimed technical challenge of the international drug-control treaties relates to human rights obligations to realize access to health facilities, goods, and services, including medicines. And should a human rights approach to drug control invoke alternative procedures?

Qualitative country studies in Uganda and Latvia have been conducted. These country studies go beyond a strict legal analysis and serve the purpose of understanding the real implications of the administrative and procedural mechanisms, including specific trade and distribution requirements, in the local service provision.[62] The implications for such local service provision are considered in light of the normative criteria as developed from human rights norms to ensure access to controlled medication.

1.2.3 Research questions

In order to design a human rights approach to drug control to advance the access to controlled medicines in resource-constrained countries, the central research question to be addressed is:

---

59 Taylor (n 45); Pettus (n 45); MEC Gispen, 'Reconciling International Obligations and Local Realities: Provision of Pain Control Medication in Resource-Constrained Countries – Experiences from Uganda' in M Hesselman, A de Wolff and BCA Toebes (eds), *Essential Public Service Provision* (Routledge *forthcoming*). Marks discusses in light of human rights protection that it is important to focus on the root cause of human rights violations. This analogue discussion is relevant in light of Pettus' observation to focus on the internal structure of the international drug-control treaty instead of its external effects. See S Marks, 'Human Rights and Root Causes' (2011) 74 The Modern Law Review 57.

60 Taylor (n 45).

61 R Yans, 'Statement by the President of the International Narcotics Control Board' (Fifth Session of the African Union Conference of Ministers for Drug Control, Addis-Ababa, Ethiopia, 11-12 October 2012) 3 <www.incb.org/documents/Speeches/Speeches2012/2012_October_CAMDC5_111012_eng.pdf> accessed 31 August 2016.

62 This is further elaborated on in Section 1.3.3.

Which structural, mandate-related, or behavioural changes, if any, does a human rights approach imply in the field of drug control focused on the access to controlled medicines provision in resource-constrained countries in particular?

Structural changes are understood to include any aspect of legal-technical or institutional amendments. In contrast, mandate-related changes refer to any aspects related to the mandate of the various actors involved, including both drug-control and human rights bodies. In the context of this book, behavioural changes refer to any aspect related to the interpretation and attitude of the individuals occupying a position in any of the drug-control and human rights bodies.

As will be further elaborated below, this book starts with a conceptual analysis to better understand the concept and problems of access to controlled medicines in the relevant context. From this conceptual component and in line with the central research question various positive legal, normative ethical, and implementation-related questions arise which are addressed in subsequent parts.

The sub-questions are:

1) How would human rights norms frame the regulation of controlled substances, given their dual individual and public-health implications?

The first sub-question implies a need to address previously introduced issues, such as which values support access to medicine efforts and which support controlling drug diversion. Would these values be in conflict with each other and, if so, how would human rights norms frame such conflicts?

2) What are the conditions based on human rights norms, if any, in line with which States have to ensure the provision of controlled medicines?

The second sub-question elaborates on the requirements of access to medicine provision in accordance with human rights norms, but also focuses on the way in which morphine, in particular, should be made available in accordance with human rights norms. Morphine (for pain treatment) is mentioned specifically because throughout the book it is used as the central example.

3) How, if at all, can a normative framework as developed under sub-questions 1-2 be included in the structures of the present international drug-control system?

This last sub-question essentially outlines what the implications of implementing the current drug-control regime are for human-rights compliant access to medicine provision. It deals specifically with the perceived intensity of complying with the international drug-control treaties' monitoring mechanisms in resource-constrained countries, and/or countries with seriously constrained health systems.

1.2.4 Context of general access to medicines and human rights research

Much has been written on the access to medicines from a wide range of perspectives. The general aspects of this work, i.e. not dealing with any medicine-specific issue or context, may be relevant to the present research. Studies on the access to medicines are primarily conducted from the perspective of health systems, pharmaco-epidemiology, global health, or public health. In fact, the existing body of work deals in various ways with some of the challenges presented above.[63] However, it is difficult to understand the case of controlled medicines solely in light of the general body of work on the access to medicines. Instead, exactly because controlled medicines are listed under the international drug control treaties and their availability and accessibility is thus regulated by this framework of law, the medicine-specific context should be taken into account. It could also very well be true that a group of medicines is distinct insofar that it makes general access to medicine research only partly relevant. This is the case when it comes to controlled medicines. While specific in focus the book clearly adds a valuable component to the general access to medicines debate and, in doing so, advances and supports its comprehensiveness.

Similar to general access to medicines research, access to medicines and law and human rights approaches are also only partly applied in this book. Existing research on the access to medicines, law, and human rights largely focuses on intellectual property law, patent law, and trade law, and perhaps lacks a comprehensive overarching view.[64] These studies often fail to connect human rights law to frameworks of law other than those mentioned above. Despite their value and being much needed, the present study demonstrates that such approaches are not sufficiently equipped to deal with the current controversies regarding the access to controlled medicine provision. It is for this reason that these studies are only partly relied on here. Other access to medicine and human rights research focuses on defining a human rights-

63 See eg A Cameron, 'Understanding Access to Medicines in Low-and Middle-Income Countries Through the Use of Price and Availability Indicators' (DPhil thesis, Utrecht University 2013); M Bidgeli and others, 'Access to Medicines from a Health System Perspective' (2013) 28 Health Policy and Planning 692; Stephens (n 10).

64 See eg SP Marks, 'Access to Essential Medicines as a Component of the Right to Health' in A Clapham and M Robinson (eds), *Realizing the Right to Health*, vol 3 (Rüffers & Rub 2009); J Sellin, *Access to Medicines* (Intersentia 2014); SP Zinzombe, *The Right to Health, Pharmaceutical Corporations and Intellectual Property: Access to Medicines* (Intersentia 2015).

based approach to medicines through accountability mechanisms and court cases.[65] Again, such work is valuable in the case of controlled medicines and will be taken into account throughout this book. Regardless, a more comprehensive approach is needed in the case of controlled substances due to the interface with international drug-control treaties.

1.3 Methodology

1.3.1 Law and other disciplines

The issues at stake in drug control pertain to a range of different disciplines. This book reflects a legal theoretical analysis of the structure and foundations of human rights as relevant to access to medicines and drug-control regulation. While legal at its core, the research requires additional input from disciplines including ethics, the life sciences, and the social sciences. Such additional input is necessary to answer the central research question. The study is therefore carried out at the intersection of a variety of disciplines. In practice, this means that the research methods used are not restricted to the gamut of traditional legal methods, but include ethical analysis and a selection of qualitative empirical methods as well.[66]

1.3.2 Legal and ethical analysis

An ethical and legal analysis is needed to produce an answer to the first sub-question on framing the regulation of controlled substances in human rights. The system of human rights law needs to be explained in terms of positive law to understand how the two aspects of drug control would relate to each other under human rights law. It would undermine or detract from the formal relevance of human rights law and the integrated interpretation suggested if such a new foundation were not supported by ethical reflection, because it is important to demonstrate that a human rights foundation of a drug-control system is not an arbitrary interpretation of international

65 See eg HV Hogerzeil and others, 'Is Access to Essential Medicines as Part of the Fulfilment of the Right to Health Enforceable Through the Courts?' (2006) 368 The Lancet 305; M Forzley, DM Walker and MEC Gispen, 'Essential Laws for Medicines Access: A Pilot Study on National Legislation' (WHO 2014) <http://apps.who.int/medicinedocs/documents/s21443en/s21443en.pdf> accessed 31 August 2016. Litigating health rights and enforcing access to medicines via court cases is also contested, see eg AE Yamin and S Gloppen (eds), *Litigating Health Rights: Can Courts Bring More Justice to Health?* (HUP 2011), and in particular, OL Motta Ferraz, 'Brazil: Health Inequalities, Rights, and Courts: The Social Impact of the Judicialization of Health' in AE Yamin and S Gloppen (eds), *Litigating Health Rights: Can Courts Bring More Justice to Health?* (HUP 2011).

66 After 1 January 2016 no systematic review has been carried out. Additional information published after that date has only been added if directly relevant to the central message and purpose of this book.

law but is justified by a logically consistent argument: a type of argumentation, which as mentioned in Section 1.2.2, one may expect from any legal framework. An ethical analysis is needed to further conceptualize human rights law and justify the approach presented.

Throughout the book, human rights will be interpreted internally in the first place. In other words, the validity of the system of human rights as such will not be discussed. The analysis, both legal and ethical, is based on the assumptions reflected in positive law. In theories of practical philosophy and ethics, the human rights framework as a whole is questioned in many ways.[67] However, there is also a plethora of studies which support the foundations of human rights law as adopted in positive norms, attempt to further explain the validity of these assumptions, and elaborate on their normative implications. Theories supporting the human rights regime are relied on because the aim of this book is not to discuss the philosophy of human rights in general. The nature of this book is rather to create a normative basis, as well as to outline the practical implications, of a legitimate system of drug control to advance access to controlled medicine. In the present human rights system, human dignity is often understood as the foundation of and justification for human rights.[68] In the context of bioethics,[69] human dignity in its foundational role is often understood as a claim to facilitate the ability of human beings to lead an autonomous life.[70] In line with this foundational role of human dignity, human rights will be conceptualized and justified by ethical theories supporting such a claim to foster autonomy, which

67 See eg O O'Neil, 'The Dark Side of Human Rights' (2005) 81 International Affairs 427.

68 Universal Declaration of Human Rights (adopted 10 December 1948) UNGA Res 217 A(III), art 1; International Covenant on Civil and Political Rights (adopted 16 December 1966, entered into force 23 March 1976) 999 UNTS 171, prmbl; ICESCR, prmbl. Although stated in positive law, Waldron contests and questions whether human dignity is the foundation of human rights. See for his critique J Waldron, 'Is Dignity the Foundation of Human Rights' (2013) NYU Public Law & Legal Theory Research Paper 12/73 <http://papers.ssrn.com/sol3/papers.cfm?abstract_id=2196074> accessed 31 August 2016. Moreover, McCrudden questions whether human dignity as the foundation of human rights could really further the universal nature of human rights due to its varied judicial interpretations, C McCrudden, 'Human Dignity and Judicial Interpretation of Human Rights' (2008) 19 The European Journal of International Law 655.

69 Bioethics is a branch of ethics focusing on medical and biological concerns. Given the underlying problem the present study ultimately deals with – the juxtaposition underlying the regulation of controlled substances – the ethical concerns addressed are clearly bioethical in nature.

70 D Beyleveld and R Brownsword, *Human Dignity in Bioethics and Biolaw* (OUP 2001) 12-13. See also Macklin's critique on human dignity as including nothing more than a claim to autonomy; R Macklin, 'Dignity is a Useless Concept' (2003) 327 The British Medical Journal 1419. This claim is not entirely disputed, yet the point of the study is not to test the validity of this assumption, as that would amount to challenging the human rights regime as such, but instead to understand the public-health deficit of access to medicines and control of diversion through the prism of human rights law. On human dignity, see C McCrudden (ed), *Understanding Human Dignity* (OUP 2013); M Düwell and others (eds), *The Cambridge Handbook of Human Dignity* (CUP 2014).

in itself is a concept interpreted in various ways.[71] Where relevant and necessary, opposing arguments and different viewpoints are presented. By no means should the analysis presented be considered as the only one possible. Instead, the conceptual analysis aims to produce a valid and logically consistent argument operating on the assumptions of the current (positive) human rights framework itself.

Further legal analysis is needed to define the scope and remit of the different obligations at stake, in particular to define what it means to ensure access to controlled medicines, in order to produce an answer to the second sub-question on the conditions according to which States have to ensure controlled medicines provision in accordance with human rights. What exactly do States have to do for their efforts to potentially be sufficient? The legal and ethical analysis may determine how the two values (access and control) relate to each other under human rights law, but this does not necessarily say anything about what exactly States must do. It is therefore important to disentangle the normative scope and content of relevant positive human rights norms as well as elaborate on relevant case law and highly authoritative soft-law documents such as general comments.

Interpretation of sources

The methods used in the normative analysis include: (i) the review of relevant international and national legal frameworks, including hard-law and soft-law mechanisms and jurisprudence when relevant; and (ii) literature research. In relation to the former, the material is collected on the basis of the sources of international law as defined in the Statute of the International Court of Justice.[72] These include international treaties and conventions, rules of customary international law, *jus cogens*, judicial decisions of international, regional, and national institutions, and the most highly regarded academic writings. Additionally, other sources such as official UN documentation, documents of inter-governmental organizations, and non-governmental organizations are consulted.

The normative analysis is carried out using a mix of traditional legal methods and qualitative methods. Traditional legal methods are employed in the form of plain

71 Macklin (n 70) adopts a very a narrow interpretation of autonomy, making it more of a negative freedom allowing people to choose what they want. Beauchamp and Childress, on the other hand, see autonomy as one of the four principles of bioethics (autonomy, nonmaleficience, beneficience, and justice). Any bioethical concern should be weighed within these four pillar concepts; TL Beauchamp and JF Childress, *Principles of Biomedical Ethics* (7th edn, OUP 2013). Beyleveld and Brownsword (n 70), in turn, regard human dignity as the basis of the entire system of human rights. They view autonomy as an explication of the value dignity.

72 Statute of the International Court of Justice (adopted 26 June 1945, entered into force 24 October 1945) 33 UNTS 993, art 38(1).

reading of texts, and techniques of interpretation, systematization, and argumentation, as well as a qualitative method of document analysis. Such analysis gives due weight to the context of a document. To provide further context and gain a comprehensive understanding of the deficit of unavailable controlled medicines in light of drug-control requirements and human rights, relevant newspaper articles and general news reports are also consulted and analysed.

1.3.3 Country studies

It is important to gain on-the-ground insights to produce an answer to the third research question on the implementation of the human rights approach analysed within the remits of the international drug-control treaties. One could review legislation to see whether the monitoring system of the international drug-control treaties is compliant with human rights norms on paper. Though in the context of the general complexity of access to medicine provision, as briefly hinted to in Section 1.1 and as elaborated upon in Chapter 2, local insight into constraints, if they exist at all, in complying with the aforementioned procedures is of great added value. In order to understand whether access to medicines in accordance with human rights law could be realized through the current means of the international drug-control system, one should understand what the practical burden is, if any, of the administrative and procedural obligations to monitor access to controlled medicines. To gain this insight two qualitative country studies are carried out using a case study approach.

Qualitative case study research often approaches 'how' or 'why' questions over which the researcher has little control – as the research is focused on a real-life contextual phenomenon.[73] The use of qualitative case studies, however, allows for a deepening of the understanding of a certain phenomenon through contextual research. To understand the real, on-the-ground implications of these provisions it is valuable to use qualitative techniques to understand in what way, if at all, the actors working in the procedures feel frustrated, obstructed, or challenged in their provision of services (in accordance with human rights).[74] In other words, how, if at all, can the normative basis as developed in the book's normative part be implemented using the present means of the international drug-control treaties themselves? Uganda and Latvia have been selected as case study countries and the relevant bodies have

---

73 RK Yin, *Case Study Research: Design and Methods* (4th edn, SAGE Publications 2009) 2, 9, 18, 32.
74 On the potential of qualitative research to provide insight into the perception of participants in a certain phenomenon, for instance in light of research on health workers and controlled medicine provision, see eg R Barbour, *Introducing Qualitative Research* (SAGE Publications 2008).

granted ethical approval.[75] It is important to note that although some comparisons will be made, strictly speaking the case studies are not set up to be comparative. The country selection criteria, research design, as well as country-specific application of the methodology, will be elaborated on in Chapter 5, directly preceding the two country study chapters.

1.4 Aims and ambitions

Essentially, this book aims to explore what it means to view international drug-control law and human rights law both in theory and practice as mutually reinforcing, instead of viewing them as exclusive frameworks of law in relation to controlled medicine provision. From an academic perspective, it aims to both fill a gap and inform the current body of knowledge on the interplay of human rights and drug control. It also wishes to complement and contribute to a more comprehensive assessment of general access to medicines, and access to medicines and human rights research in particular. It further aims to overcome the more traditional – and general – legal analysis by enunciating a legal theoretical analysis relying on a multidisciplinary selection of methods.

From a law and policy-making perspective, this book aims to inform current political debates on what it means to interpret drug-control regulation in the context of human rights and, in particular, inform current drug-reform initiatives. To do so, it aims to provide for human rights-based normative requirements and thresholds with which current drug-control reform initiatives can be explored. Hence, it is hoped that this research adds to the current debates on international drug-control reform, the public-health deficit, and human rights violations presently taking place as a result of drug-control efforts. Inasmuch, this study aims to directly respond to the desires expressed to foster a human rights approach to drug-control regulation. Finally, it is hoped that a normative framework as designed in this book, if used in its guiding capacity, can directly affect the approaches of national and international policymakers and legislators, so as to stimulate human rights compliant policy changes in the field of controlled medicine regulation and advance their availability on a global scale.

75 The study design of the case study in Uganda was approved by the Medical Ethics Review Committee of the University Medical Centre Utrecht (14-244/C), and the Uganda National Council for Science and Technology (SS 3477). The study design of the case study in Latvia was also approved by the Medical Ethics Review Committee of the University Medical Centre Utrecht (14-532/C).

1.5 Output and relevance

The research output is twofold: (i) the book produces an overview of what makes a normative framework for a human rights approach to drug control; and (ii) provides normative recommendations in the field of international drug control pertaining to structural, mandate-related, and behavioural changes necessary to implement the proposed approach.

The academic relevance is both specific and general in nature. The study contributes to a better understanding of human rights and drug-control debates and the contemporary implications of the international drug-control treaties on the access to medicine provision. Still specifically related to the field of drug control, the book supports theories of drug control by injecting human rights law. More broadly, the book contributes to a better understanding of access to medicine research, taking the case of controlled medicines as an example. In such capacity, it might also contribute to understanding the way in which different norms, regulations, or other norm-deriving sources such as culture and religion, relate to each other in different stages of the pharmaceutical life cycle.[76] In doing so, the book does not just contribute to a comprehensive academic understanding of fair access to medicines, but also informs policy debates on this matter. From a public international law and human rights perspective, the academic significance lies in its addition to the existing body of knowledge on the conceptualization of human rights norms and their relevance and applicability to other fields of law and particularly public international law. More specifically, the book contributes to clarifying the realization of positive obligations and the challenges therein. As such, this book offers a way to integrate different theoretical understandings of human rights and enunciates how to synthesize those with practice. Moreover, as was referred to in Sections 1.2.1 and 1.2.4, the research questions fill a knowledge gap in this multifaceted and multidisciplinary field.

The creation of a human rights approach to drug control to improve access to controlled medicines carries significant relevance for society at large as well. Policymakers and legislators can use the framework proposed in this book as a guide. If used in such a guiding capacity, the book may initiate real practical steps leading towards better access to controlled medicines. As such, any initiated policy changes based on the outcomes of this book may contribute to creating a better, dignified living standard for individuals suffering unbearable pain by allowing them access to sufficient pain

76 The 'pharmaceutical life cycle' is a modern term that refers to the artificial life cycle of medicines. The cycle is split into three separate stages: (i) development; (ii) registration; and (iii) consumer use (ie use by patients). Briefly, medicine development equals fair access to medicines. Norms and regulations apply throughout the entire process, raising serious questions of human rights protection and intersections of norm-deriving sources and legal frameworks at all different stages.

and palliative care treatment, the subsequent effect of which can have a significant positive impact on people's day-to-day lives.

1.6 Structure

The book is divided into four main parts: (i) concept and problem; (ii) normative framework; (iii) country studies; and (iv) conclusions and recommendations.

Part 1: Concept and Problem consists of Chapters 1 and 2. *Chapter 1* briefly introduces the central research problem, the research design, and the methodology employed in this book. As the first chapter can only briefly highlight the issue at hand, *Chapter 2* will provide further context and disentangle the issue of access to controlled essential medicine provision in its entirety. As such, the chapter presents a more comprehensive view of the legal context of a human rights approach to drug control. In addition, the chapter reflects the background, framing, and focus of the approach taken. The chapter will demonstrate that the research approach, in fact, takes a funnel perspective.

Part 2: Normative Framework consists of Chapters 3 and 4 and addresses sub-questions 1 and 2. *Chapter 3* presents a doctrinal analysis and situates the contradiction in drug-control regulation within human rights law. To this end, the chapter distinguishes what balancing in human rights constitutes more generally and applies these general findings to the access to controlled medicines, and the prevention of diversion and abuse to protect public health and order. Moreover, the chapter analyses the criteria relevant to monitoring implementation and enforcement of a human rights approach to drug control, which also makes it a prelude to Part 3 of the book (Country Studies). *Chapter 4* addresses whether one can normatively defend a human rights approach to drug control as constructed in Chapter 3. The chapter briefly elaborates on the relationship between morality, ethics, and human rights for the purpose of methodological clarity and to explain the analytical lens used. Operating on the assumptions of human rights law, the chapter analyses human dignity as the foundation of human rights, and its conceptualization and justification, in relation to the access to medicines and aspects of drug control.

While Chapters 3 and 4 have the same purpose, namely to situate the 'principle of balance' in human rights norms, the legal and ethical analyses are separately addressed to avoid confusion. This is also done to be sensitive to and distinguish between human rights law and human rights theory.

Part 3: Country Studies includes Chapters 5-7 and deals with sub-question 3. *Chapter 5* includes a brief introduction to the case studies including the general methodology and research approach used. The chapter serves to bridge the gap between the conceptual and the applied level. *Chapters 6* and *7* will address the country situations in Uganda and Latvia, respectively. Both chapters include a short introduction to the country-specific research approach. After a general country profile, findings are structured by addressing specific administration and trade and distribution requirements as included in Articles 17 and 30 of the Single Convention on Narcotic Drugs (Single Convention), and data collection, analysis and reporting as included in Articles 19-20 of the Single Convention separately. The chapters conclude by discussing the findings in light of the human rights approach established in Part 2.

Part 4: Conclusions and Recommendations comprises Chapter 8. In *Chapter 8* the studies' general conclusions are presented by linking up the conceptual and applied analysis (Parts 2 and 3) and by formulating recommendations. The first part of the book demonstrated how the present research focus was derived from general aspects, and the conclusion will present an outlook for the broader field as well. In doing so, it will discuss the strong example that controlled medicines may provide in the context of general access to medicines research, pharmaceutical policy analysis, and the realization of positive obligations – i.e. obligations requiring focused state action. Moreover, the chapter will consider this example in relation to the realization of positive obligations in resource-poor regions.

Chapter 2
Access to Controlled Essential Medicines: Context, Background, Framing, and Focus

2.1 Introduction

This book analyses the reciprocity of human rights and international drug-control norms regarding the access to controlled essential medicine provision in resource-constrained countries.[1] As also stated in the previous chapter, access to medicines such as morphine and codeine for pain and palliative care treatment is the leading example used throughout this study. While Chapter 1 only briefly introduced the topic, this chapter supplies further context, background, framing, and focus. In that capacity, the present chapter provides both the starting point of the normative analysis, i.e. the normative framework, elaborated in Part 2 of the book, and serves to place the relevance of the analysis and results (Chapter 8) in context.

This chapter commences by situating the approach taken in international public law, regardless of any substantive implications (Section 2.2). In doing so, the chapter addresses the current debates on the interpretation of international law and its interaction with different subfields of international law. Following this contextualization, the chapter then widens its (funnel) focus to cover human rights, drug control, controlled essential medicines, and resource-constrained countries. The chapter provides a background to medicines regulation in health systems (Section 2.3) and frames the concept of (controlled) essential medicines (Section 2.4). Subsequently, the chapter addresses the global crisis of pain control medicines as an example (Section 2.5). Ultimately, and more specifically, the chapter elaborates on the relevant aspects of the international drug-control treaties (Section 2.6).

Notably, Chapter 1 already clearly demonstrated that the unavailability or inaccessibility of controlled medication is a serious human rights concern and that States have obligations under human rights law to address the concomitant suffering. Apart from situating the human rights approach elaborated in this book within the ambit of international law, any substantive human rights issues can be found in Part 2 and are not discussed in this chapter.

---

1 For the purpose of this book, the term 'resource-constrained countries' is used as an umbrella term. It also refers to countries with large remote areas or generally seriously constrained health systems.

2.2 Context of a human rights approach to drug control in international law

Prior to elaborating the funnel focus in this book, the human rights approach analysed – notwithstanding its substantive implications – is placed into the broader discussion on the integration of different international legal regimes. The section commences with an analysis of international institutional law and its relevance to international human rights and drug-control treaties. Subsequently, it places the approach taken in the context of the 'fragmentation debate' and the general rules of treaty interpretation.

2.2.1 International institutional law

Drug-control bodies such as the International Narcotics Control Board (INCB) have long shunned human rights language.[2] For a long time the INCB claimed that human rights were not included in their mandate, thus preventing them from speaking out against any human rights issues related to drug control. In 2012, the president of the INCB refused to express an opinion on e.g. the death penalty, forced labour, and rehabilitation camps in relation to human rights protection. He dismissed a question by civil society on the matter, asserting that the absence of human rights in the INCB's mandate precluded the Board from making any statements on the topic.[3] After having received much criticism, actors like the INCB have slightly adapted their stance on this subject. Now more actively than ever, drug-control bodies include human rights language in their reporting and statements.[4] A human rights approach to drug control is, however, not a matter for political decision-making, but reflects a legitimate interpretation of public international law.

---

2 The INCB is the treaty-based monitoring body of the international drug-control treaties.

3 'INCB's Tortured Logic' (*TNI Drugs & Democracy*, 3 April 2012) <http://undrugcontrol.info/en/weblog/it em/3332-incbs-tortured-logic> accessed 31 August 2016.

4 See eg CND Res 51/12 'Strengthening Cooperation between the United Nations Office on Drugs and Crime and Other United Nations Entities for the Promotion of Human Rights in the Implementation of the International Drug Control Treaties' (2008); UNODC, 'UNODC and the Promotion and Protection of Human Rights' (2012) Position Paper <www.unodc.org/documents/justice-and-prison-reform/UNO DC_Human_rights_position_paper_2012.pdf> accessed 31 August 2016; L Naidoo, 'Statement by President of the International Narcotics Control Board' (Fifty-Eighth Session of the Commission on Narcotic Drugs, Vienna, Austria, 9-17 March 2015) <www.incb.org/documents/Speeches/Speeches2015/Statement_INCB_President_CND_2015_UNGASS_06_03_15V_1_cl_INCB_logo.pdf> accessed 31 August 2016; W Sipp, 'Statement by the President of the International Narcotics Control Board' (Reconvened Fifty-Eighth Session of the Commission on Narcotic Drugs, Vienna, Austria, 9 December 2015) <www.incb.org/documents/Speeches/Speeches2015/statement_reconvened_CND_session.pdf> accessed 31 August 2016; INCB, *Report of the International Narcotics Control Board for 2014* (INCB 2015); INCB, *Report of the International Narcotics Control Board for 2015* (INCB 2016) iv, paras 23, 36-37.

The international drug-control treaties fall under the auspices of the UN. In the preamble of the 1961 Single Convention on Narcotic Drugs (Single Convention), State Parties acknowledge the competence of the UN in the field of drug control.[5] This same recognition is found expressed in Articles 5 and 6 of the Single Convention. As set out in Article 1 of the Charter of the United Nations (UN Charter), one of the core objectives of the UN is '(...) promoting and encouraging respect for human rights and fundamental freedoms for all without distinction as to race, sex, language, or religion (...)'.[6] Any Member State to the UN Charter and any institution affiliated to the UN or falling under its auspices should observe the UN's core objectives.

The question of whether the INCB is bound to act within the scope of the UN Charter is analogous to discussions on the accountability of UN Specialized Agencies such as the World Health Organization (WHO), World Trade Organization, or International Monetary Fund under international human rights law. Both types of bodies rely on their independence when claiming human rights to fall outside the remit of their mandate. Skogli asserts, however, that UN Specialized Agencies have a 'substantial obligation to ensure that human rights are not violated through [their] policies' and possess 'procedural obligations to include a human rights check in the planning, implementation and evaluation stages of programmes and projects'.[7] Hence, together with Member States, any actor mandated to observe the treaties should adhere to the core objectives of the UN and, in other words, respect human rights in the manner suggested by Skogli.

In case of conflicting obligations or interests, Article 103 of the UN Charter states that the provisions of the Charter shall take precedence. In other words, it would constitute a violation of the Charter if the normative foundation, application, interpretation, and implementation of the international drug-control treaties were to undermine the respect of human rights. Article 30 of the Vienna Convention on the Law of Treaties (VCLT), moreover, reinforces the supremacy of the Charter and its content.[8] Paragraph 3 of this article reads:

---

5 Single Convention on Narcotic Drugs (adopted 30 March 1961, entered into force 13 December 1964) 520 UNTS 151 (Single Convention) prmbl.

6 Charter of the United Nations (adopted 24 October 1945) 1 UNTS XVI (UN Charter) art 1.

7 SI Skogly, 'The Human Rights Obligations of the World Bank and IMF' in W van Genugten, P Hunt and S Mathews (eds), *World Bank, IMF and Human Rights* (Wolf Legal Publishers 2003) 78.

8 Vienna Convention on the Law of Treaties (adopted 23 May 1969, entered into force 27 January 1980) 1155 UNTS 331 (VCLT) art 30; A Orakhelashvili, 'Article 30 Convention of 1969' in O Corten and P Kleinne (eds), *The Vienna Conventions on the Law of Treaties: A Commentary* (vol 1, OUP 2011) 770.

> When all the parties to the earlier treaty are parties also to the later treaty but the earlier treaty is not terminated or suspended in operation under article 59, the earlier treaty applies only to the extent that its provisions are compatible with those of the later treaty.[9]

The UN Charter lists the respect for human rights as one of its core pillars. However, the general human rights obligations, including those related to the access to controlled medicines and aspects of drug control, are at a minimum specified in the 1969 International Covenant on Civil and Political Rights (ICCPR) and the International Covenant on Economic, Social and Cultural Rights (ICESCR).[10] In other words, for States that have ratified both of the aforementioned covenants and the Single Convention, the latter ought to be interpreted in such a way as to be compatible with the provisions contained in the ICCPR and the ICESCR.[11] A similar line of reasoning applies to obligations relevant to the access to controlled medicines and aspects of drug control based on subsequent human rights treaties, including those with a more specific focus on non-discrimination, women, torture, children, migrant workers, and disability.[12]

2.2.2 Fragmentation of international law and the hierarchy of norms

Stating that the international drug-control treaties ought to be interpreted in a way which observes human rights norms, touches on debates about the hierarchy in international legal norms. It falls outside the ambit of this book to enter into extensive

9 VCLT, art 30(3). Some scholars consider Article 30 VCLT a 'difficult' provision dealing with complex legal principles such as, for instance, the difference in the regional scope of a treaty or successive treaty on the same subject matter. A common example in this respect is environmental law. Such discussions, however, fall outside the ambit of the present research. See for comparison, M Fitzmaurice and O Elias, *Contemporary Issues in the Law of Treaties* (Eleven International Publishing 2005) 318-319.

10 International Covenant on Civil and Political Rights (adopted 16 December 1966, entered into force 23 March 1976) 999 UNTS 171 (ICCPR); International Covenant on Economic, Social and Cultural Rights (adopted 16 December 1966, entered into force 3 January 1976) 993 UNTS 3 (ICESCR). This will be further elaborated on in Chapter 3.

11 What such integration generally implies in terms of substantive law will be further elaborated on when discussing the normative framework in Part 2 of the book.

12 Respectively the International Convention on the Elimination of All Forms of Racial Discrimination (adopted 7 March 1966, entered into force 4 January 1969) 660 UNTS 195 (CERD); Convention on the Elimination of All Forms of Discrimination Against Women (adopted 18 December 1979, entered into force 3 September 1981) 1249 UNTS 13 (CEDAW); Convention Against Torture and Other Cruel, Inhuman or Degrading Treatment or Punishment (adopted 10 December 1984, entered into force 26 June 1987) 1465 UNTS 85 (CAT); Convention on the Rights of the Child (adopted 20 November 1989, entered into force 2 September 1990) 1577 UNTS 3 (CRC); International Convention on the Protection of the Rights of All Migrant Workers and Members of their Families (adopted 18 December 1990, entered into force 1 July 2003) 2220 UNTS 3 (ICRMW); Convention on the Rights of Persons with Disabilities (adopted 13 December 2006, entered into force 3 May 2008) 2515 UNTS 3 (CRPD).

substantive discussions on this subject. Such discussions are so complex and nuanced that they warrant standalone research. That said, it would be erroneous, not to mention difficult, to fully neglect these discussions and solely rely on international institutional law as a justification for a human rights approach to drug control.

Article 38 of the Statute of the International Court of Justice sets out the sources of international law to include conventions, customary law, and general principles of law, but does not explicitly establish a hierarchy among these sources.[13] In a textual interpretation, some scholars regard all sources of international law to be horizontal, i.e. no source of international law takes precedence. Others, however, contend that even though the sources are horizontal *stricto sensu*, there is an informal hierarchy, where treaty law generally takes precedence over customary law, local custom takes precedence over general customary law, special law trumps general law, and peremptory norms (*jus cogens*) are superior to all.[14] *Jus cogens*, as the international community has accepted, refers to those norms from which no derogation is permissible.

The proliferation of international institutions and international regimes on specific issues such as trade, drug control, and the environment has led some scholars to become concerned about the fragmentation of international law. This concern arose in particular in the context of the horizontal nature of international norms. If no overarching source of internationally set standards existed in relation to potential disputes and overlap between the various institutional and regime specifications presently witnessed in international law, one would risk a 'loss of overall control'.[15]

The concern about fragmentation of international law reveals a clear difference between two normative traditions. Essentially, one either argues that there is a hegemonic overarching normative structure setting standards in an attempt to legitimize international institutional powers. In that case, an overarching normative structure may support the settling of conflicts between different sources or subfields

13 Statute of the International Court of Justice (adopted 26 June 1945, entered into force 24 October 1945) 33 UNTS 993, art 38.
14 See ILC, 'Report of the Study Group of the International Law Commission on the Fragmentation of International Law: Difficulties Arising from the Diversification and Expansion of International Law' (13 April 2006) UN Doc A/CN.4/L.682, para 85 (ILC Report); J Vidmar, 'Norm Conflicts and Hierarchy in International Law: Towards a Vertical International Legal System?' in E de Wet and J Vidmar (eds), *Hierarchy in International Law* (OUP 2012) 20.
15 M Koskenniemi and P Leino, 'Fragmentation of International Law? Postmodern Anxieties' (2002) 15 Leiden Journal of International Law 553, 553, 555; ILC Report (n 14) para 324.

of law (constitutionalism).[16] One, on the other hand, might also argue that there is no overarching normative structure. Instead, international law comprises all of the subfields of special law, which deprives human rights of any claimed normative priority. This means that conflicts between any of these subfields of law cannot be settled by reference to an overarching constitutionalist document or norm (legal pluralism).[17] This latter view is more in line with the primary concern in the fragmentation debate –asserting that eventually international law as a holistic system will no longer hold and will fall apart into 'limited systems with little or no interrelationship'.[18] Both the position of and the role ascribed to human rights norms in these different normative traditions are very different.

In a constitutionalist interpretation of international law, human rights may be the hegemonic overarching normative structure setting standards to legitimize international institutional powers. In a legal pluralist interpretation of international law, however, the human rights framework is considered to exist on equal footing with any other subfield of international law. As such, it is deprived of its so-claimed normative priority. By its very nature, a horizontal system of norms implies that no law can *prima facie* take priority or trump another law.[19]

Moving away from a tendency to push for the trumping powers of human rights, some scholars seek human rights commitment by mainstreaming human rights. Inspired by 'gender mainstreaming discussions', McCrudden defines human rights mainstreaming as the '(…) reorganization, improvement, development and evaluation of policy processes, so that a human rights perspective is incorporated in all policies at all levels and at all stages, by the actors normally involved in policy-making.'[20] Koskenniemi, however, regards such mainstreaming as 'a project for seizing institutional power that

---

16 See on this E de Wet, 'The International Constitutional Order' (2006) 55 International and Comparative Law Quarterly 51, 56; M Scheinin, 'Impact on the Law of Treaties' in M Kamminga and M Scheinin (eds), *The Impact of Human Rights Law on General International Law* (OUP 2009) 23-36, 29.

17 See eg De Wet (n 16) 56; D Kennedy, 'One, Two, Three, Many Legal Orders: Legal Pluralism and the Cosmopolitan Dream' (2006/2007) NYU Review of Law and Social Change 641, 642. In the context of this book, legal pluralism should only be understood as to reflect the idea that international law is a collection of equally important regimes of law. The plurality this collection reflects lies at the heart of the terminology of legal pluralism when attempting to understand the sources and structures of international law.

18 M Shaw, *International Law* (6th edn, CUP 2008) 65.

19 See eg Vidmar (n 14) 13.

20 C McCrudden, 'Mainstreaming Human Rights' University of Michigan (2004) Public Law & Legal Theory Research Paper Series No 47 <http://papers.ssrn.com/sol3/papers.cfm?abstract_id=568642> accessed 31 August 2016.

is profoundly ambiguous in its effects'.[21] According to Koskenniemi, mainstreaming human rights is impossible because this would still assert a normative priority. In Koskienniemi's words such normative priority would be problematic '[b]ecause there are no authoritative lists of prelegislative rights (...)' and policymakers or politicians can frame anything they want in human rights wording.[22]

One can indeed question whether or not a prelegislative set of rights exists. Yet, the fact that any right can be invoked or challenged from competing perspectives is not problematic as such. What it ultimately boils down to is how human rights norms set standards as to what is considered legitimate and what is not. From a philosophical perspective, a real dilemma is one that cannot be solved. Legally speaking, however, any conflict should be resolved and, thus, positive human rights norms have to indicate which aspect of a conflict should take legitimate priority. This reflects more of a constitutionalist interpretation of international law as also reflected in this book.[23] For, as Scheinin aptly puts it, 'human rights law should not be reduced to one of many branches of international law, and (...) human rights lawyers should not join in the chorus singing the song of fragmentation'.[24] Instead, human rights law should be guiding in the interpretation of international law. According to Scheinin, within the fragmentation approach to international law, a legal pluralist interpretation, i.e. interpreting international law as a collection of equally important branches, would paradoxically only contribute to its erosion.[25]

Scholars in favour of an international constitutional legal order plead for greater normativity. Human rights scholars in particular seek an objective binding force – i.e. a hegemonic overarching normative source granting legitimate powers to international institutions.[26] As De Wet puts it, an international regime in which the UN Charter may play an institutional and substantive role, connecting the various regional systems expressing universal values as well as international regimes clustering certain sectors (e.g. trade, drug control, environment), would support the constitutionalism of international law. In other words, such an overarching international system of universal values, as De Wet describes it, would give international institutions legitimate powers and may provide for a basis on which or a tool with which to settle any conflicts between different regimes.[27] Some scholars submit that international institutional

21 See M Koskenniemi, 'Human Rights Mainstreaming as a Strategy for Institutional Power' (2010) 1 Humanity 47, 47.
22 ibid 49.
23 Chapter 4 contains an ethical analysis in which morality and law are considered as related instead of mutually exclusive and discusses the existence, if at all, of a prelegislative set of rights.
24 Scheinin (n 16) 28.
25 ibid 28-29.
26 De Wet (n 16) 56-57; Scheinin (n 16) 28.
27 De Wet (n 16) 56.

law itself reinforces 'the special community importance of the UN Charter'.[28] These arguments are based on Article 103 of the UN Charter, as addressed above, stating that the Charter takes precedence in case of conflict. This has elevated the UN Charter to a superior position in international law.[29]

As was mentioned in Chapter 1, human rights norms are claimed to possess normative priority because they protect the inherent dignity of each and every person on a non-discriminatory basis. Human rights set standards as to what is acceptable and what is not. This means that they provide a framework to determine what law, policy, or action is legitimate and what is not, as well as which interest should take priority over other interests in case of a rights-claims clash. Considering human rights not just as a sub-regime of international law, but also partly as *erga omnes* obligations, *jus cogens*, and a set of moral universal values, therefore implies that human rights norms are dominant over other norms.[30] *Erga omnes* obligations are obligations that States have towards the entire international community, even if the obligation originated in a bilateral treaty between two parties. It is commonly asserted that *erga omnes* obligations mainly emerge from human rights and humanitarian law.[31] It is submitted here that human rights are dominant to the extent that any limitation of a human right should be justified in the human rights norms itself.

The fact that human rights norms in their modern positive legal structure were only articulated and adopted after the Second World War does not change this argument. Positive human rights norms that may apply to drug control are not a mere set of arbitrary rules.[32] Instead, these norms reflect a certain way of thinking; an idea about what makes a just society, how the individual should be protected from illegitimate state interference, and how the State should act as a guardian to enable individuals to live a dignified life. Moreover, the underlying assumptions of what makes a just society, or in what way conflicting interests such as the predicament caused by substances like opium should be dealt with, is not a random selection of norms or ideas. In contrast, these assumptions and foundational principles can be addressed in a logical manner for which the human rights framework is contingently important,

---

28 Vidmar (n 14) 18.

29 ibid. Vidmar submits, however, that the hierarchy of the UN Charter is not absolute, as it is commonly accepted that limitations or exceptions to Article 103 exist.

30 Although there increasingly is formal recognition of a hierarchy in international law in which human rights are, in part, lifted to the level of *jus cogens* or peremptory norms of international law, legal practice demonstrates that it is doubtful whether such elevated priority status effectively contributes to human rights protection. See on this eg E de Wet, 'Jus Cogens and Obligations Erga Omnes' in D Shelton (ed), *The Oxford Handbook of International Human Rights Law* (OUP 2013) 560.

31 See eg De Wet, 'International Constitutional Order' (n 16) 55; ILC Report (n 14) para 392.

32 Chapter 3 includes a largely doctrinal legal analysis of the law as *is* in relation to access to medicines and aspects of drug control in particular.

though not necessary. In essence, a moral interpretation of how to understand the juxtaposition underlying drug-control regulation would be a human rights compliant approach to said regulation. This even if one does not want to accept any normative priority of the positive human rights framework.

What it substantively means to talk about a human rights approach to drug control still remains unclear.[33] What is meant by the argument presented above is that human rights ought to be granted a certain normative priority when interpreting other legal frameworks, including the international drug-control treaties. This does not mean that one should dismiss the entire international drug-control system in the same breath. Nor does this mean that one should a priori disregard any legal structure not strictly falling within the scope of human rights law or explicitly observing human rights norms. What it means is that, at the very least, as McCrudden argued, human rights should be mainstreamed. It is submitted here that the extent to and the manner in which depends on the specific case.

Should one not be convinced by a constitutionalist interpretation of international norms, one must inevitably opt for a legal pluralist interpretation. What is important is that even such legal pluralist conception would not detract from the formal relevance of human rights to the international drug-control treaties. When perceiving human rights norms strictly as a positive legal framework operating within the broader field of public international law, one cannot establish an a priori superior human rights argument. International legal norms are, after all, viewed as horizontal in such argument.[34] Yet, even if one moves away from the trumping force of human rights or even consider mainstreaming human rights at a policy level as a reinforced claim of its normative authority, the international drug-control treaties still have to be interpreted in the context of human rights norms. Human rights in themselves are relevant to drug-control matters as being standard-setting in the field of access to (controlled) medicines and should be taken into account on the basis of the general rules of treaty interpretation.

2.2.3 General rules of treaty interpretation and the principle of systemic integration

Scheinin submits that it might be reasonably problematic to grant human rights normative priority, thus trumping power in positive law. A strict positivist reading of the VCLT would construct human rights as one out of the many special law regimes, which would deprive it of its claimed normative priority. This would decrease

33 This will be addressed in Part 2 of the book.
34 ILC Report (n 14) para 324.

its substantive normative potential.[35] Moreover, in a strict legal reading, human rights law is special simply because it does not just invoke traditional multilateral obligations between States but also corresponding rights and obligations, anchoring the individual rights-holder at its core. However, as mentioned above, even via the general rules of treaty interpretation one could establish the procedural relevance of human rights. Even if one were to view human rights norms as having no trumping authority.

Article 31 VCLT states that a treaty should be interpreted in good faith and in light of its context, object, and purpose. The context of the purpose of a treaty includes, among other aspects, '[a]ny relevant rules of international law applicable in the relations between the parties'.[36] McLachlan contends that the rules of treaty interpretation set forth by Article 31 VCLT are often referred to as the 'principle of systemic integration'.[37] In his view, said principle is of constitutional value to the international legal order.[38] In his words:

> [t]he foundation of this principle is that treaties are themselves creatures of international law. However wide their subject matter, they are all nevertheless limited in scope and are predicated for their existence and operation on being part of the international law system. As such they must be 'applied and interpreted against the background of the general principles of international law', and, as Verzijl put it in the extract above, a treaty must be deemed 'to refer to such principles for all questions which it does not itself resolve expressly and in a different way'.[39]

Context is therefore important in treaty interpretation, as law only makes sense in its context.[40] In explaining the position of special law in relation to general law, the International Law Commission (ILC) highlighted in 2006 that 'no rule, treaty or custom, however special its subject-matter or limited the number of States concerned by it, applies in a vacuum'.[41] When it comes to the international drug laws, however,

---

35 See on the substantial normative potential of human rights in a constitutionalist interpretation of international law Scheinin (n 16) 31.

36 VCLT, art 31(3c). Some scholars hold that the application of the law of treaties to human rights treaties might at times to be problematic in a strictly positivist reading of the VCLT. The main concerns are that the VCLT is written for State-to-State relations only. Moreover, scholars hold the VCLT to be written as if States bear the sole responsibility for the monitoring of compliance with their international obligations. See Scheinin (n 16) 27.

37 C McLachlan, 'The Principle of Systemic Integration and Article 31(3)(c) of the Vienna Convention' (2005) 54 International and Comparative Law Quarterly 279, 280.

38 id.

39 id (citations omitted) citing A McNair, *The Law of Treaties* (OUP 1961) 466.

40 ibid 286.

41 ILC Report (n 14) para 120.

they seem to have been developed and interpreted in a rather isolated fashion.[42] A potential conflict between the human rights framework and the drug-control framework would, when interpreting international law from a fragmented perspective and thus considering it a collection of horizontal branches, be one between two special frameworks of law. The ILC explains in its same 2006 report that settling tensions or conflicts between two different branches of international law depends on 'the relevant frame of legal interpretation' that one chooses.[43]

As was mentioned in Chapter 1 and repeated in the present chapter, as much as drug-control norms are, human rights law is also standard-setting in the field of access to medicines, including controlled medicines. Thus, human rights norms are clearly part of the relevant context in which the international drug-control treaties should be interpreted. The fact that the ICCPR, ICESCR, and the international drug-control treaties enjoy almost global ratification only strengthens this premise. Taking human rights law into account is therefore not just an arbitrary decision, but supports enhancing a consistent international legal order. Based on analogous exercises of systemic integration, McLachlan submits that the importance of the system of law to be integrated (*in casu* human rights) is not so much grounded in a claimed normative priority or an overriding nature. Instead, the importance is that such other rules '(...) may perform a systemic or constitutional function in describing the operation of the international legal order, and in establishing a common set of underlying principles which inform it'.[44]

To summarize, a human rights approach to drug control is, in either interpretation, a legitimate and warranted interpretation of international law in relation to the access to controlled medicines and certain aspects of drug control. In this context, the background and framing of the access to controlled medicines in light of drug-control regulation is elaborated. As mentioned in the introduction, doing so reflects a funnel approach. With medicine regulation in health systems in mind, this book analyses the interface of human rights and international drug-control norms on the access to controlled essential medicine provision in resource-constrained countries.

---

42 See eg D Barrett and M Nowak, 'The United Nations and Drug Policy: Towards a Human Rights-Based Approach' in A Constantinides and N Zaikos (eds), *The Diversity of International Law: Essays in Honour of Professor Kalliopi K Koufa* (Martinus Nijhoff Publishers 2009) 461-465.

43 ILC Report (n 14) para 55.

44 C McLachlan, 'Investment Treaties and General International Law' (2008) 57 International and Comparative Law Quarterly 361, 373.

2.3 Background of medicines regulation in health systems

Medicines regulation in health systems is presented as the background that supports the book's central focus on human rights, international drug control, access to controlled essential medicines, and resource-constrained countries.[45] The section begins by introducing the 'pharmaceutical life cycle' as a timeline and framework within which to place medicines regulation in the first place. Then, it addresses the multifaceted challenges in medicines access in the context of regulations based on the primary medicine regulatory review process (up until market approval of new medicines). In doing so, the section also touches on external aspects such as other relevant legal frameworks, post-market authorization distribution, and aspects related to medicine use.

2.3.1 The pharmaceutical life cycle

The development, registration, distribution, and use of medicines is a highly complex and global enterprise involving not just different nations, but also regional frameworks.[46] The pharmaceutical, medicine, or drug life cycle[47] is a common term to refer to the entire process of medicine discovery, development and registration, and eventually consumer use. The cycle includes a lengthy process, which starts with the search for active substances and the application for permission to test a new substance on humans. After the regulatory agency mandated to oversee this process approves an 'investigational new drugs'[48] application, initial testing on humans in the form

45 Generating context regarding medicines regulation in health systems not only helps frame the case of controlled essential medicines, but also demonstrates that the book operates in the outer layers of regulatory sciences and the public health monitoring mandate of regulatory agencies. Regulatory science covers evidence-based decision-making on market authorization of new medicines. See on this topic, CC Gispen-de Wied and HGM Leufkens, 'From Molecule to Market Access: Drug Regulatory Science as an Upcoming Discipline' (2013) 719 European Journal of Pharmacology 9. 'Evidence-based' means that any selection or decision-making process, policy, or any other aspect of regulation, is based on scientific data.

46 Global medicine development is often referred to as global drug development, in which 'drugs' therefore means 'medicines'. However, for the purpose of clarity and consistency, this study refers to global medicine development and the plural term 'drugs' is only used in the context of dependency disorders.

47 Similarly to the remark above, this cycle is often paradoxically referred to as the drug development cycle. Because of the dual connotation of the word 'drugs' – especially in the context of this book – the words 'medicines' or 'pharmaceuticals' are used instead.

48 I Hägglöf and Å Holmgren, 'Regulatory Affairs' in HP Rang (ed), *Drug Discovery and Development: Technology in Transition* (Elsevier 2006) 284. Paradoxically or at least rather confusingly 'drugs' refers to medicines here and not to illicit substances. It was decided *not* to change the common way of referencing this type of application in pharmaceutical regulation so as to avoid confusion.

of clinical trials[49] follows. Such testing, in its most favourable outcome, results in a pharmaceutical company's application for the authorization of a newly developed medicine on the pharmaceutical market. Only if these tests have proven to be of high quality, to be safe, and to be effective, will the regulatory agency review the entire dossier and, ultimately, grant market authorization.[50] Notably, the regulatory agency bases its judgment concerning market approval on the outcome of conducted clinical trials and is, in principle, not responsible for any ethical reviews necessary for the granting of permission to execute these trials.

On average, the process up until market approval is estimated to take at least ten years and cost 1.8 billion US dollars from the initial discovery to market authorization.[51] In this regard, see Figure 2.1 below for a visualization of the key aspects in the pharmaceutical life cycle.[52]

Figure 2.1 Pharmaceutical life cycle (1)

Discovery	**Development**		**Access**
Identification by pharmaceutical company of an active substance with potential beneficial health impact and initial approved testing on humans	Approved efficacy, clinical and comparative studies carried out by pharmaceutical company to submit the application dossier for regulatory review and market authorization by regulatory agencies (domestic or regional)	*Market authorizations*	Post-marketing surveillance and *patient use*

Rang considers the interests of pharmaceutical companies in developing products that address societal health needs to be financial as well as altruistic.[53] More often than not, however, pharmaceutical companies are said to be driven solely by the profits needed to recover their research and development costs. In fact, as also acknowledged by Rang, the balance between altruism and profits is often questioned. Many sceptics claim that profits, instead of the protection of public health, dominate

49 The WHO states '(...) for the purposes of registration, a clinical trial is any research study that prospectively assigns human participants or groups of humans to one or more health-related interventions to evaluate the effects on health outcomes.' WHO, 'Clinical Trials' <www.who.int/topics/clinical_tri als/en/> accessed 31 August 2016.

50 Hägglöf and Holmgren (n 48) 285.

51 SM Paul and others, 'How to Improve R&D Productivity: The Pharmaceutical Industry's Grand Challenge' (2010) 9 Nature Review Drug Discovery 203.

52 The figure is inspired by Fig 20.2 in Hägglöf and Holmgren (n 48) 284. 'Patient use' is italicized because this points to which stage of the pharmaceutical life cycle this book focuses on.

53 HP Rang (ed), *Drug Discovery and Development: Technology in Transition* (Elsevier 2006) vii.

the pharmaceutical industry.[54] Paul and colleagues, in that regard, assert that the current business model underlying the pharmaceutical industry needs to be revisited because 'without a dramatic increase in R&D [i.e. research and development] productivity, today's pharmaceutical industry cannot sustain sufficient innovation to replace the loss of revenues'.[55] The loss of revenues may hamper the production of innovative medicines which, according to the authors, is mainly due to the expiration of important patents and the decreasing number of innovative medicines being approved by regulatory agencies.[56]

Apart from assessing marketing approval on the basis of scientific research, national and regional medicine regulatory agencies should also perform post-marketing surveillance despite the absence of an active mandate to support the realization of access to medicines on the ground. Pharmaceutical companies, in addition, have the legal obligation to monitor their product, update regulatory agencies when adverse reactions occur, and provide safety information and 'post-trial access', i.e. access to medicines necessary to carry out tests in real-life conditions.[57] The agencies, in turn, have the responsibility to deposit such information in registries.[58] Apart from post-marketing surveillance, no absolute data on the real-life availability and use of medicines is taken into account during this primary regulatory review process (see e.g. Figure 2.2).

54 id.

55 Paul and others (n 51) 203.

56 ibid.

57 In a European context, these obligations are laid down in Council Directive 2001/83/EC of 6 November 2001 on the Community code relating to medicinal products for human use (Medicinal Products for Human Use Directive) [2001] OJ L311/67, arts 104-107. In the American context, these obligations are laid down in the FDA Food and Drugs Regulation, 21 CFR 314.80 (2015). In context of the South African Medicine Control Council (MCC), relevant obligations are enshrined in the Medicines and Related Substances Act 101 of 1995, s 10(2b). Obligations in the Japanese system can be found at the Pharmaceuticals and Medical Devices Agency, 'About PMDA' <www.pmda.go.jp/english/about-pmda/0004.html> accessed 31 August 2016.

58 Questions of enforcement arise in light of recent research, which has demonstrated the very low rate of post-market authorization studies submitted to regulatory agencies. However, this issue falls outside the scope of this book and will not be discussed further. C Jonker presented her work on the submission of post-market authorization studies at the Netherlands Medicine Evaluation Board Science Day 2016 (Utrecht, the Netherlands, 5 February 2016). See also EMA, 'Reflection Paper on Ethical and GCP Aspects of Clinical Trials of Medicinal Products for Human use Conducted Outside of the EU/EEA and Submitted in Marketing Authorisation Applications to the EU Regulatory Authorities' (16 April 2012) EMA/121340/2011, 28.

Figure 2.2 Pharmaceutical life cycle (2)

Discovery	**Development**		**Access**
Identification by pharmaceutical company of an active substance with potential beneficial health impact and initial approved testing on humans	Approved efficacy, clinical and comparative studies carried out by pharmaceutical company to submit the application dossier for regulatory review and market authorization by regulatory agencies (domestic or regional)	*Market authorization*	Post-marketing surveillance and patient use

Application dossier (Discovery → Development)

Medicine lifeline dossier (Discovery → Access)

As opposed to the 'application dossier', which includes information up until the moment of market authorization, the 'medicine lifeline dossier' also includes data on post-market authorization surveillance in order to secure the safe use of medicines. Data on patient use is not included in the application dossier.

2.3.2 Access to medicines and pharmaceutical regulation

The ultimate objective in the pharmaceutical life cycle, or its overarching purpose, is at least implicitly the assurance of the medicine's availability. For instance, in the European context, Council Directive 2001/83 states that '[t]he essential aim of any rules governing the production, distribution and use of medicinal products must be to safeguard public health.'[59] When describing the European Union's (EU) regulatory system for medicines, the European Medicines Agency (EMA) lists the purpose of regulation to be '[t]o guarantee the protection of public health and to ensure the availability of high quality, safe, and efficacious medicines for European citizens.' The EMA stresses that 'all medicines must be authorized before they can be placed on the [pharmaceutical] market in the EU', i.e. the regulatory chain described above must be completed, before ensuring availability of these medicines.[60] Similarly, the Food and Drugs Administration – the US medicine regulatory authority – is responsible for 'protecting the public health by assuring the safety, effectiveness, quality and security of human (…) [medicines]'.[61] The Japanese authorities, a standard-setter in Asia, also

59 Medicinal Products for Human Use Directive, prmbl.
60 EMA, 'The European Regulatory System for Medicines and the European Medicines Agency: A Consistent Approach to Medicines Regulation across the European Union' (2014) EMA/437313/2014, 2.
61 FDA, 'FDA Fundamentals' (12 March 2015) <www.fda.gov/AboutFDA/Transparency/Basics/ucm192695.htm> accessed 31 August 2016.

explicitly stress their public-health mandate.[62] The South African authorities do so more implicitly.[63]

Regional and domestic regulatory agencies, but also other bodies such as the European Commission, thus support public health, instead of financial return, as the ultimate *raison d'être* for the development of new medicines. In fact, the growth of the pharmaceutical industry is generally seen as a response to disease, which 'has been recognized as an enemy of humankind since civilization began'.[64] In other words, one could argue that the ultimate objective of pharmaceutical regulation is the fair availability of safe and efficacious medicines. Notably, as will be discussed in the subsequent chapters, fair access can be viewed as human rights compliant access. However, for the purpose of this book, medicine availability is interpreted as actual consumer use of medication by patients in regions where these medicines are most needed.[65] As such, availability does not only refer to new and expensive patented medicines, but also to those unpatented medicines which have been approved and allowed onto the pharmaceutical market for a long time. One must note, however, that a clear financial incentive for pharmaceutical companies to establish a market for the latter may be lacking. Morphine for pain control is such an example.[66]

2.3.3 Multifaceted challenges of medicine access in the broader health system

Although public health, and implicitly medicine access, can be viewed as the equitable objective of pharmaceutical regulation, successful medicine provision largely depends on the interplay of formal and informal rules in the context of local realities governing the pharmaceutical life cycle at large. As set out above, many laws, regulations, and norms apply throughout the primary medicine regulatory review process. Such *internal* laws and regulations mostly include quality and ethical review standards related to testing new substances, and intellectual property law designed to facilitate the recovery of investments and the protection of the product in question.

62 See PMDA (n 57).

63 See MCC, 'About' <www.mccza.com/About> accessed 31 August 2016.

64 HP Rang, 'The Development of the Pharmaceutical Industry' in HP Rang (ed), *Drug Discovery and Development: Technology in Transition* (Elsevier 2006) 3.

65 Cameron submits that what is most important for an individual visiting a health clinic is that the right medicine is physically available at the right time at the same clinic as where the individual is, referring to such a conception of medicine availability and accessibility as 'true access'. See A Cameron, 'Understanding Access to Medicines in Low-and Middle-Income Countries through the Use of Price and Availability Indicators' (DPhil thesis, Utrecht University 2013) 220, 228.

66 This issue was discussed at the Equitable Access to Controlled Medicines Brocher Symposium (Hermance, Switzerland, 8-9 October 2015).

In addition to these internal regulations, there is a large number of *external* laws, regulations, norms, and values that might have a certain impact on the different stages of the pharmaceutical life cycle and therefore also on current trends of innovative medicines, personalized medicines, and access to medicines as the cycle's equitable objective. The interplay between these internal and external regulations is of vital importance when investigating whether any of these norms, intentionally or unintentionally, have an impact on medicine availability and accessibility.

Implications of and challenges in access to medicine provision

The question about whether or not internal and external norms, intentionally or unintentionally, could complicate or obstruct medicine provision largely depends on the medicine-specific and/or institutional context of implementation and compliance. Implementation of or compliance with any of such norms or regulations and medicine provision in accordance with relevant regulations, presupposes an impressive series of steps and actions having been taken.

For example, from a health systems perspective, access to health facilities, goods, and services, including medicines, essentially presupposes a well-functioning and appropriately designed health system, which requires a smooth and high-quality infrastructure, adequate preservation requirements, and affordable pricing mechanisms, all of which should be free from health-sector corruption. Moreover, access to medicine provision also implies a need for sufficient information services and education on the rationale use of medicines.[67] From a law, governance, and policy perspective, service delivery (including access to medicine provision) presupposes legitimate institutional and bureaucratic functioning at both the organization and at state level.[68] Appropriate priority-setting in line with international standards allows one to address the key urgencies in a country with due respect for vulnerable and marginalized sections of society, equitable distribution of human resources, while taking health and other social expenditure into account.[69] The incidental or structural lack of such preconditions could make it more complicated to provide for services.

---

67 See eg M Bideli and others, 'Access to Medicines from a Health Systems Perspective' (2013) 28 Health Policy and Planning 692.

68 cf MM Lee, G Walter-Drop and J Wiesel, 'Taking the State (Back) Out? Statehood and the Delivery of Collective Goods' (2014) 27 Governance 635, 635. Lee, Walter-Drop, and Wiesel submit more generally that the provision of goods and services, as argued here to include medicines, requires a State to function. Moreover, see on legal aspects and securing access to medicines M Forzley, DM Walker and MEC Gispen, 'Essential Laws for Medicines Access: A Pilot Study on National Legislation' (WHO 2014) <http://apps.w ho.int/medicinedocs/documents/s21443en/s21443en.pdf> accessed 31 August 2016.

69 See eg WHO, *How to Develop and Implement a National Drug Policy* (2nd edn, WHO 2001).

Resource-constrained countries, States with large remote areas, and Low- and Middle-Income Countries (LMICs) in general, often do not possess the general preconditions mentioned above. This could be caused by financial and economic crisis, result from austerity measures affecting the health system,[70] or be due to insufficient insight into the State's needs. If service delivery is complex in such countries, then presumably evidence-based needs assessments may also be difficult to carry out in countries with large remote areas, regardless of its socio-economic or development status. This may be further complicated by the general suboptimal conditions under which a resource-constrained country has to provide for services.[71] For this reason, such general factors, e.g. poor infrastructure, unfit health systems, health-system failure, health-sector corruption, insufficient resources, and inefficient allocation of resources, may complicate compliance with regulation. More specifically, these are factors that could obfuscate access to medicine provision in accordance with international standards.

General and substance-specific challenges

The aforementioned conditions or lack thereof could be labelled as general challenges to medicine provision. They might complicate medicine provision in accordance with international regulations regardless of a medicine's therapeutic or legal classification, i.e. the medicine-specific context. One must note that these factors do not always complicate the provision of medicines, and that regulations do not always apply to all medicines regardless of the country. It is merely submitted that these factors *could* play a role in the provision of medicines regardless of their therapeutic or legal classification. The way in which or the extent to which such factors might manifest themselves depends on other aspects, such as the level of corruption in a country or the country's general socio-economic status.[72] Moreover, Hogerzeil and colleagues submit that general challenges in access to medicine provision do not always demand highly innovative or difficult interventions. These authors contend that even within existing budgets and structures much can be achieved in advancing the access to medicines for non-communicable diseases, for instance.[73]

70 G Dussault, T Correia and C Pontes, 'Impact of the Economic Crisis on Human Resources for Health Policies in Southern EU Countries' (2015) 25 European Journal of Public Health 32.

71 See eg R Harding and others, 'Availability of Essential Drugs for Managing HIV-related Pain and Symptoms within 120 PEPFAR- Funded Health Facilities in East Africa: A Cross-Sectional Survey with Onsite Verification' (2014) 28 Palliative Medicine 293, 294.

72 On the detrimental effect of health-sector corruption on health-service delivery in a human rights context, see BCA Toebes, 'Human Rights, Health Sector Abuse and Corruption' (2011) HRHW Working Paper No 64 <www.du.edu/korbel/hrhw/workingpapers/2011/64-toebes-2011.pdf> accessed 31 August 2016.

73 HV Hogerzeil and others, 'Promotion of Access to Essential Medicines for Non-Communicable Diseases: Practical Implications of the UN Political Declaration' (2013) 381 The Lancet 680.

As opposed to general challenges, substance-specific challenges could come into play in the context of a certain group of medicines. Substance-specific challenges could therefore be quintessential to some medicine groups whilst being relatively insignificant to others. Taking a substance-specific approach, in other words, requires one to focus on various normative frameworks as relevant to the different medicine groups. Despite its seeming a mere technicality, distinguishing between more general and substance-specific challenges helps us understand why it is important to primarily focus on a particular aspect for a certain group of medicines and why that same focus ought to be merely implicit for other medicines. Relating it to this book more concretely: the availability of controlled medicines might not only be complicated by general factors – which could also be aggravated by specific concerns – but potentially also by more substance-specific challenges in particular. As will be demonstrated below, a key substance-specific challenge in the provision of controlled medicines may be the international drug-control framework itself. Other examples, which lie beyond the scope of this book, relate to observing intellectual-property laws, to trade-law regimes, and to the access to affordable antiretroviral treatment.

Taking into account multifaceted aspects of medicines access is of vital importance to address medicines regulation in health systems. For instance, one has to take into account externalities such as other regulatory frameworks, as well as post-marketing distribution, provision, and use-related aspects in order to truly bring about medicine development that addresses society's most pressing needs.[74] This is not assumed to be part of the mandate of regulatory agencies as such.[75] It is argued, however, that one simply cannot understand the access to medicines and medicine regulatory issues without taking the legal and post-market authorization context of medicine distribution, provision, and use into account. This relevance certainly does not only apply to controlled medicine, but controlled medicines definitely represent a strong case study. The interplay of internal and external regulations, and general and specific

74 Most medicine regulatory agencies have medicine shortages databases to record and show which medicines are either short in stock or out of stock entirely. Other than these databases, which merely reflect hick-ups in the supply/demand chain, there is no recording of real-life access or gaps between the absolute need and registered demand.

75 Redefining mandates and responsibilities within the pharmaceutical life cycle at large is a separate issue that falls outside the scope of this book.

challenges, could vary per medicine group or classification, which means that access to medicines research should be sensitive to this intersectionality.[76]

2.4 Framing the concept of essential medicines

For the purpose of definition and scope, it is important to frame the concept of essential medicines and determine which medicines would classify as *controlled* essential medicines. In this section, the development and framing of the concept of essential medicines is introduced first. Subsequently the section turns to the criteria for developing a national medicines list. Finally, the section maps an overview of the so-called controlled essential medicines.[77]

2.4.1 Development of the WHO Model List of Essential Medicines

The WHO defines essential medicines as those medicines that satisfy a population's priority health needs.[78] In 1975, the World Health Assembly (WHA) – the WHO's decision-making body – asked the WHO to guide and assist Member States in developing and implementing national medicine policies. The question was in particular to assist States in selecting a list of affordable quality essential medicines corresponding to national health needs.[79] In response to this request, the WHO published its first Model List of Essential Medicines in 1977.[80] A year later, with the adoption of the Declaration of Alma-Ata, the concept of essential medicines officially became one of the eight key components in primary healthcare.[81]

---

76 Intersectionality is a term borrowed from equality and non-discrimination studies. It reflects the sensitivity warranted when different aspects of, in this case medicine provision and the obstructions thereto, should be understood as intersectional, revealing a multidimensional complexity often found in medicine provision. In the context of this book, controlled medicine provision may neither be complex due to human resources per se nor merely due to additional regulatory requirements. However, viewing these two aspects as intersecting reveals such complexity. See also Section 2.5.3. On intersectionality more generally, see eg K Crenshaw, 'Mapping the Margins: Intersectionality, Identify Politics, and Violence against Women of Color' (1991) 43 Stanford Law Review 1241.

77 Controlled essential medicines are those medicines of which the active substance is listed under the international drug-control treaties and at the same time appears on the WHO Model List of Essential Medicines. See also Chapter 1 in comparison.

78 WHO, 'Essential Medicines' <www.who.int/topics/essential_medicines/en/> accessed 31 August 2016.

79 WHA Res 28.66 'Prophylactic and Therapeutic Substances' (29 May 1975) 2.

80 WHO, *The Selection of Essential Drugs* (Technical Report Series 615, WHO 1977) 21 (WHO Technical Report).

81 Declaration of Alma-Ata (International Conference on Primary Health Care, Alma-Ata, USSR, 6-12 September 1978) s VII(3) <www.who.int/publications/almaata_declaration_en.pdf> accessed 31 August 2016. See also J Sellin, *Access to Medicines* (Intersentia 2014) 24-25.

The WHO Expert Committee on the Selection and Use of Essential Medicines updates the list every two years.[82] The committee is appointed by the WHO Director General and decides which medicines are deleted from or added to the list.[83] Since 1977, 38 lists have been published. In 2007, the WHO made a significant contribution to the concept of essential medicines in relation to children. The WHA, in that same year, had called for 'better medicines for children'[84] to which the WHO reacted by adopting the first specialized List of Essential Medicines for Children.[85]

Over time, the selection and adoption procedure of the lists has changed significantly. In the early days, essential medicines were defined as '(...) of utmost importance, basic, indispensable and necessary for the health and needs of the population'.[86] Selection of medicines was often based on expert decisions and selection criteria mainly focused on low-priced medication.[87] Laing and colleagues assert in this respect that '[b]efore 1991, inclusion of medicines in the list was mainly a result of applications from WHO programme staff and the pharmaceutical industry.'[88] As of 2002, the WHO refined the definition of essential to include '[t]hose that satisfy the priority health care needs of the population.'[89] In addition to this adjustment, the selection process gradually changed to become evidence-based.[90] Since its first publication, the total number of medicines included in the list has increased significantly.[91] Morphine, one of the most important medicines to treat moderate to severe pain, has been on the list from the start.[92]

2.4.2 Developing a national essential medicines list

Generally, developing countries have been more active in adopting national essential medicines lists modelled on the WHO Model List of Essential Medicines than more developed nations.[93] The process of developing a national essential medicines list always begins with identifying a country's key disease burden and the most common

82 R van den Ham, L Bero and R Laing, 'Selection of Essential Medicines' in L Bero and others (revs), *World Medicines Situation Report 2011* (3rd edn, WHO 2011) 2.
83 R Laing and others, '25 Years of the WHO Essential Medicines Lists: Progress and Challenges' (2003) 361 The Lancet 1723, 1724.
84 WHA Res 60.20 'Better Medicines for Children' (23 May 2007). See also Laing and others (n 83).
85 For a milestone overview of the development of the concept of essential medicines, see Laing and others (n 83).
86 Laing and others (n 83) 1724.
87 Van den Ham, Bero and Laing (n 82) 4.
88 Laing and others (n 83) 1724 (citations omitted) citing Mary Couper, personal communication.
89 WHO, 'Essential Medicines' (n 78).
90 Van den Ham, Bero and Laing (n 82) 3. See also Laing and others (n 83) 1723. See text at n 45.
91 Van den Ham, Bero and Laing (n 82) 5.
92 WHO Technical Report (n 80).
93 Van den Ham, Bero and Laing (n 82) 7.

health needs and problems. Standard treatment guidelines should then be established to assist prescribers in their clinical decision-making. It is a common strategy to include medicines on the national list that appear in evidence-based standard treatment guidelines.[94]

The WHO recognizes tensions between developing such standard treatment guidelines and the adoption of national essential medicines list. If developed successfully, however, a national essential medicines list can be a helpful tool. It can assist States in allocating their limited resources to address primary and the most common health concerns in a rational and affordable manner.[95] Key factors determining the successful implementation of essential medicines lists include: a transparent process of revisiting and updating; establishing a link between essential medicines lists and clinical guidelines; active consultation of key stakeholders such as clinicians and the public; ensuring the list is widely available and accessible; and, finally, ensuring regular updates to make sure the list is up-to-date with the latest therapeutic advances.[96]

As opposed to how it was in the past, low costs are no longer a leading selection criterion when selecting essential medicines. Currently, selection depends on the medicine's public health relevance, evidence-based efficacy and safety, and comparative cost-effectiveness.[97] The selection criteria have been further refined because the WHO considers that:

> [e]ssential medicines are intended to be available within the context of functioning health systems at all times in adequate amounts, in the appropriate dosage forms, with assured quality and adequate information, and at a price the individual and the community can afford.[98]

In its Medium-Term Strategic Plan for 2008-2013, the WHO adopted progress indicators to measure access to medicines implementation and realization. As was described in the WHO Essential Laws for Medicine Access report, the indicators include: government commitment; rational selection; affordable prices; sustainable

---

94 The bottom-up approach reflected in the consultation and development of treatment guidelines reflects the real needs of and common health problems in a country, which a top-down approach to the development of a national essential medicine list would not. See on this for instance WHO, 'Selection of Essential Medicines' (2002) Policy Perspectives on Medicines Series No 4 <http://apps.who.int/medicinedocs/pdf/s2 296e/s2296e.pdf> accessed 31 August 2016.

95 Van den Ham, Bero and Laing (n 82) 5.

96 WHO, 'Selection of Essential Medicines' (n 94).

97 WHO, 'Essential Medicines' (n 78).

98 id.

financing; and reliable systems.[99] As indicated above, the number of medicines included in the WHO Model List of Essential Medicines has increased over the years. A number of these medicines classify as *controlled* medicines and are therefore of particular relevance to this book.

2.4.3 List of controlled essential medicines and treatments

As was introduced in Chapter 1, controlled medicines are those medicines of which the active substance is listed under the international drug control treaties. Controlled *essential* medicines are also listed under drug control treaties, but also appear on the WHO Model List of Essential Medicines. Said list consists of a core and a complementary part. The medicines that appear on the core list are the most efficacious, safe, and cost-effective in addressing priority health conditions. These medicines are needed in a basic healthcare system. Medicines appearing on the complementary part, on the other hand, are essential priority medicines that, despite being cost-effective and safe, are either unaffordable or demand specialized healthcare facilities, services, or know-how.[100] See Table 2.1 below for a breakdown of all controlled essential medicines.

Table 2.1 Overview of controlled essential medicines

<table>
<tr><th rowspan="2">Medicine</th><th colspan="2">WHO Model List of Essential Medicines (2015)</th><th rowspan="2">International drug control treaty</th></tr>
<tr><th>Therapeutic category</th><th>Core/complementary list</th></tr>
<tr><td>Codeine</td><td>Opioid analgesic; Antidiarrheal</td><td>Core</td><td>Single Convention (Schedule II)</td></tr>
<tr><td>Morphine</td><td>Opioid analgesic; Preoperative sedative</td><td>Core</td><td>Single Convention (Schedule I)</td></tr>
<tr><td>Methadone</td><td rowspan="2">Opioid dependence agonist for the treatment of opioid dependence disorders</td><td>Complementary</td><td>Single Convention (Schedule I)</td></tr>
<tr><td>Buprenorphine</td><td>Complementary</td><td>1971 Convention (Schedule III)</td></tr>
<tr><td>Diazepam</td><td>Anxiolytic; Antiepileptic; anticonvulsant; Preoperative sedative; to treat common symptoms in palliative care</td><td>Core</td><td>1971 Convention (Schedule IV)</td></tr>
</table>

99 See Forzley, Walker and Gispen (n 68) 6. See also WHO, 'Equitable Access to Essential Medicines: A Framework for Collective Action' (2004) Policy Perspectives on Medicines Series No 8 <http://apps.who.i nt/iris/bitstream/10665/68571/1/WHO_EDM_2004.4_eng.pdf> accessed 31 August 2016.

100 Laing and others (n 83) 1724; van den Ham, Bero and Laing (n 82) 2.

Medicine	WHO Model List of Essential Medicines (2015)		International drug control treaty
	Therapeutic category	*Core/complementary list*	
Phenobarbital	Anticonvulsant; antiepileptic	Core	1971 Convention (Schedule IV)
Ergometrine	Oxytocics; obstetric emergency	Core	1988 Convention (Table I)
Ephedrine	Obstetric emergency, local anaesthetic. Used to prevent hypotension in spinal anaesthesia during delivery	Complementary	
Potassium permanganate	Anti-infective	Core	1988 Convention (Table II)

Opioid analgesics such as codeine and morphine (see Table 2.1), painkillers of which the active substance is derived of the active component of opium, are controlled medicines included in the core WHO Model List of Essential Medicines and, as such, should be available in each basic healthcare system.[101] Nevertheless, as already briefly touched on in Chapter 1, the public health crisis central to this book is their global unavailability.

2.5 The example of the global crisis of unavailable pain-control medication

This section provides a more detailed overview of which patient groups, at what scale, suffer from the inaccessibility of exactly which controlled medicines otherwise important for treatments. This information allows one to obtain a clearer image of the key groups of rights-holders this book is ultimately set up to deal with. Such an overview not only allows the book to operate on the correct scientific assumptions, but also serves to define the normative analysis conducted in Part 2 (Normative Framework). This section commences with tracing patterns in the global burden of pain and distinguishes various pain syndromes. The section then turns to standard treatment guidelines and the result of unavailability of medicine. Subsequently, it briefly highlights the political action taken to counter such unavailability. Finally, in the context of the multifaceted challenges of access to medicine in health systems, the section presents an overview of the challenges that might obstruct the access to pain-control medication.

101 Indicated in italics in Table 2.1, diazepam is partly relevant as being an essential medicine to treat common side effects in palliative care. If relevant, explicit links are traced to diazepam when discussing pain-control and palliative care issues.

2.5.1 Patterns in the global burden of pain

Providing access to affordable medicine in developing countries was a target included by the international community in the 2015 Millennium Development Goals (MDGs). The taskforce report of the MDGs highlights, as do the aforementioned sections of this book, the serious deficit that remains in terms of access to medicine provision and, in particular, stresses the problematic situation that prevails in the developing world.[102] To address this ongoing deficit, the international community has set itself a new target in the Sustainable Development Goals. By 2030, universal coverage in the access to essential safe, quality, affordable, and efficacious medicines should be achieved.[103] Such efforts toward greater achievement in ensuring access to medicines evidently also include access to pain-control medication.

As was mentioned in Chapter 1, Duthey and Scholten concluded that there are serious constraints in the global consumption of opioid analgesics.[104] In modelling (the adequacy of) opioid consumption, Duthey and Scholten calculated that 66 per cent of the global population shows virtually no consumption of opioid analgesics, 10 per cent has a very low intake, for 3 per cent consumption is low, for 4 per cent it is moderate, and for 7.5 per cent it is adequate.[105] When comparing these results to earlier research, it becomes evident that the use of opioid analgesics has increased slightly since 2006.[106]

Examining morphine consumption data over a period of 30 years, Hastie and colleagues found serious global inequities in supply/demand of opioid analgesics to continue to exist, despite a general regional increase of consumption.[107] Chapter 1 indicated that, in 2009, 90 per cent of all opioid consumption was traced to Australia,

---

102 MDG Gap Task Force, *Millennium Development Goal 8: Taking Stock of the Global Partnership for Development* (UN 2015) iii.

103 See UNGA Res 70/1 'Transforming our World: The 2030 Agenda for Sustainable Development' (21 October 2015) UN Doc A/RES/70/1, Goal 3, Target 3.8.

104 B Duthey and WK Scholten, 'Adequacy of Opioid Analgesics Consumption at Country, Global, and Regional Levels in 2010, its Relationship with Development Level, and Changes Compared with 2006' (2014) 47 Journal of Pain and Symptom Management 283.

105 id. Although the need for opioid analgesics differs per country, as does the indication for which pain control is considered the appropriate treatment strategy, Section 2.5.2. will indicate that pain-control medicines are not just needed in chronic, but also in acute care, and are therefore integrally relevant to any health system.

106 MJ Seya and others, 'A First Comparison between the Consumption of and the Need for Opioid Analgesics at Country, Regional, and Global Levels' (2011) 25 Journal of Pain & Palliative Care Pharmacotherapy 6. Based on 2006 figures, Seya and others found that 83% of the global population had low to non-existent access to opioid analgesics and only 7% had adequate access.

107 See B Hastie and others, 'An Examination of Global and Regional Opioid Consumption Trends 1980-2011' (2014) 28 Journal of Pain & Palliative Care Pharmacotherapy 259, 259.

Canada, New Zealand, the United States of America, and a range of European countries.[108] Hastie and colleagues similarly demonstrate that in 2011, a mere 8 per cent of global opioid consumption was traced back to LMICs while 92 per cent was found in High-Income Countries (HICs). Such a continued discrepancy sustains these inequities and the serious social injustice that follows. The impact of this disparity becomes more visible when one is reminded that, at that same time, only 17 per cent of the global population lived in HICs as opposed to 83 per cent living in LMICs.[109]

Such stark disparities and inequities reinforce the general global North and global South divide. In terms of geographical dispersal, Duthey and Scholten also demonstrate that the unavailability of opioid analgesics is not just traced to the developing world but that it hits the Sub-Sahara African region the hardest.[110] A recent study by Berterame and colleagues used longitudinal data to complement previous descriptive work. Their results indicate that worldwide the use of opioid analgesics doubled between 2001-03 and 2011-13.[111] However, the authors found this global increase to be the result of a significantly higher consumption level in HICs (North America, Oceania, and Western and Central Europe) rather than a substantial increase in the developing world.[112] This finding supports earlier data and, once more, reflects the stark disparities in global consumption patterns.[113] Moreover, in its recent 2015 report, the INCB maps global patterns of opioid analgesics use in particular.[114] In support of the data referenced above, the INCB observes in relation to the regional context that:

> [m]easuring the levels of consumption of opioid analgesics against cancer rates reveals insufficient consumption in parts of Africa, Asia, Central America, and the Caribbean, Eastern and South-Eastern Europe and some small island States in Oceania. Inadequate opioid availability to treat pain related to AIDS seems to be pronounced in sub-Saharan

108 INCB, *Availability of Internationally Controlled Drugs: Ensuring Adequate Access for Medical and Scientific Purposes* (INCB 2011) 2 (INCB Availability Report 2011). On global patterns of consumption, see also INCB, *Availability of Internationally Controlled Drugs: Ensuring Adequate Access for Medical and Scientific Purposes. Indispensable, Adequately Available and Not Unduly Restricted* (INCB 2016) 12-27 (INCB Availability Report 2016).

109 B Hastie and others (n 107) 261.

110 Duthey and Scholten (n 104) 285.

111 S Berterame and others, 'Use of and Barriers to Access to Opioid Analgesics: A Worldwide, Regional, and National Study' (2016) 387 The Lancet 1644, 1653. The study was supported by the INCB. See also J Cleary, A Husain and M Maurer, 'Increasing Worldwide Access to Medical Opioids' (2016) 387 The Lancet 1597, 1597.

112 Berterame and others (n 111).

113 id.

114 The INCB's position and mandate in overseeing the annual estimation and quarterly statistical return procedures are further elaborated on in Sections 2.6.3-2.6.5 of this Chapter. The INCB has an invaluable global data set because of the annual country-specific consumption data it receives.

African and Asian countries. In addition, even in the presence of high levels of national consumption, access for some sectors of the population (rural and poor communities) may be limited provision of palliative care services.[115]

Clearly, the data shows that the need and unmet demand for opioid analgesics, in particular to treat pain syndromes, is most acute in the developing world. Apart from the global pattern of use, the pattern of demand is mainly traced to cancer and HIV/AIDS patients.[116] On a global scale, 14 million new cancer cases were detected in 2012. In that same year, 8.2 million cancer-related deaths occurred.[117] Most of these patients were located in developing countries. With the global shift of the burden of diseases in mind and with an increase of non-communicable diseases in the developing world, the need for pain-control treatment is further increasing in those regions.[118] Global cancer statistics demonstrate that in 2012, 57 per cent of all new cancer incidences, 65 per cent of all cancer mortalities, and 48 per cent of the five-year prevalent cancer incidents were traced to the developing world.[119] López-Gómez and colleagues even estimate that by 2020, almost 70 per cent of all cancer incidences will be traced to the developing regions.[120]

Although the HIV/AIDS epidemic has stagnated and is starting to decrease, 36.9 million people remained HIV-positive in 2014. This number is increasing since more and more people have access to antiretroviral treatment and, thus, prolong their life. In 2015, 15.8 million HIV-infected patients were on antiretroviral therapy, which globally amounts to a treatment coverage of 40 per cent based on 2014 numbers.[121] The United Nations Programme on HIV/AIDS (UNAIDS) emphasizes that such a vast increase in access to treatment was deemed almost impossible in 2000. In

115 INCB, *Report for 2015* (n 4) ix.

116 See eg KM Foley and others, 'Pain Control for People with Cancer and AIDS' in DT Jamison and others (eds), *Disease Control Priorities in Developing Countries* (2nd edn, OUP 2006).

117 WHO, 'Cancer' (February 2015) Factsheet No 297 <www.who.int/mediacentre/factsheets/fs297/en/> accessed 31 August 2016.

118 See A Merriman, *Audacity to Love* (The Irish Hospice Foundation 2010) 36-41; W Kaplan and C Mathers, 'Global Health Trends: Global Burden of Disease and Pharmaceutical Needs' in L Bero and others (revs), *World Medicines Situation Report 2011* (3rd edn, WHO 2011) 2; Hogerzeil and others (n 73) 681.

119 International Agency for Research on Cancer, 'GLOBOCAN 2012: Estimated Cancer Incidence, Mortality and Prevalence Worldwide' <http://globocan.iarc.fr/Pages/fact_sheets_cancer.aspx> accessed 31 August 2016.

120 M López-Gómez and others, 'Cancer in Developing Countries: The Next Most Preventable Pandemic. The Global Problem of Cancer' (2013) 88 Critical Reviews in Oncology/Hematology 117, 120.

121 Such a vast increase in access to treatment was believed nearly impossible in 2000 as in that year only 1% of patients had access to treatment, see UNAIDS, 'AIDS by the Numbers 2015' (UNAIDS 2015) 3 <www.unaids.org/sites/default/files/media_asset/AIDS_by_the_numbers_2015_en.pdf> accessed 31 August 2016.

that year, only 1 per cent of patients had access to treatment. Although the HIV/AIDS pandemic has been successfully stagnated, UNAIDS stresses that joint efforts are still required to prevent 28 million HIV infections and 21 million AIDS-related mortalities.[122] Moreover, the current crisis still hits the developing region hardest. In fact, the increase in patients' access to antiretroviral treatment might bring about a new challenge, as opioid analgesics are needed to address HIV-related pain.[123]

The patient group to which this book relates can therefore largely be divided into cancer patients on the one hand, and HIV/AIDS patients on the other. As will become apparent in the course of the book, in these patient groups special attention should be given to society's most vulnerable and marginalized individuals. This should at least include the elderly, women, children, and people living in remote communities.

2.5.2 Standard treatment guidelines and results of inadequate treatment

As can be seen in Table 2.1 in Section 2.4.3, codeine and morphine are both essential medicines for the treatment of pain conditions.[124] This means that both medicines should be included in each basic healthcare system and that their therapeutic classification indicates them to be needed in both acute and chronic medical interventions.

In terms of acute medical interventions, morphine and codeine are essential to trauma care and to the treatment of acute pain syndromes. Morphine, in particular, is also used in pre- and post-surgery care. In reference to the WHO Model List of Essential Medicines the WHO states that pain-control medicines are essential to trauma care so as to provide acute pain control to injured patients. Morphine and codeine, or equivalents, are listed as an essential medicine for pain, fever, and inflammation in the WHO's Guidelines for Essential Trauma Care and should, according to these guidelines, also be available at the most basic healthcare level.[125] The minimization of pain is one of the three key aspects fundamental to trauma care.[126] In terms of operative care, morphine and codeine are both considered crucial for post-operative

122 id.

123 On chronic pain in HIV-infected patients, see eg D Krashin, J Merrill and A Trescot, 'Opioids in the Management of HIV-Related Pain' (2012) 15 Pain Physician 157; L Uebelacker and others, 'Chronic Pain in HIV-Infected Patients: Relationship to Depression, Substance Use, and Mental Health and Pain Treatment' (2015) 16 Pain Medicine 1870.

124 Codeine is also important for antidiarrheal treatment and morphine, in addition to being a pain-control medicine, is also a pre-surgery sedative. These therapeutic classifications are, however, not addressed further in this study.

125 C Mock and others, *Guidelines for Essential Trauma Care* (WHO 2004) 51.

126 ibid 11.

pain control.[127] In relation to chronic medical interventions, morphine is vital to palliative care in general and for the treatment of chronic pain conditions in particular.

The WHO has developed a standard guideline for pain control, which is commonly referred to as the WHO Pain Relief Ladder.[128] The ladder was introduced to assist with the determination of pain relief interventions for adult cancer patients. Since then, the ladder has turned into a common standard applicable also to HIV-related pain-relief efforts. The three-step approach gradually increases opioid medication alongside the persistence or increase of pain from mild to moderate or severe. Codeine is generally preferred to treat mild to moderate pain, whereas morphine is used to treat moderate to severe pain. The ladder also sets forth the need for adjuvants – additional medication – to treat common side effects such as obstipation. This is an important observation that implies not just the need for the availability of or accessibility to pain-control medication, but also signifies that their pre-eminent position in treatment plans is connected to the accessibility of such adjuvants. Moreover, patients preferably take pain-control medication orally, following a strict time schedule with due respect for the personal conditions of the patient in question as well as the treatment's responsiveness.[129]

Pain control is not the only, though clearly a central component of palliative care. According to the WHO:

> [p]alliative care is an approach that improves the quality of life of patients and their families facing the problem associated with life-threatening illness, through the prevention and relief of suffering by means of early identification and impeccable assessment and treatment of pain and other problems, physical, psychosocial and spiritual.[130]

Generally speaking, one needs palliative care when suffering an incurable medical condition that leads to such discomfort that it cannot be left unattended. Notably, palliative care is not strictly bound to end-of-life situations, yet it is often needed in the final phase of one's life. Palliative care differs from euthanasia or physician-assisted suicide in that, for instance, morphine should have no role in the euthanasia procedure.

---

127 See eg M Dobson and others, *Surgical Care at the District Hospital* (WHO 2003) 5, 9.

128 WHO, 'Cancer Pain Ladder for Adults' <www.who.int/cancer/palliative/painladder/en/> accessed 31 August 2016 (WHO Pain Ladder). In its original form, the ladder is disputed by scholarly work by eg G Vargas-Schaffer, 'Is the WHO Analgesic Ladder Still Valid?' (2010) 56 Canadian Family Physician 514; JC Ballantyne, E Kalso and C Stannard, 'WHO Analgesic Ladder: A Good Concept Gone Astray' (2016) 352 The British Medical Journal 1 <http://dx.doi.org/10.1136/bmj.i20> accessed 31 August 2016.

129 WHO, *Cancer Pain Relief* (2nd edn, WHO 1996) 14-15.

130 WHO, 'Definition of Palliative Care' <www.who.int/cancer/palliative/definition/en/> accessed 31 August 2016.

For euthanasia, as advised by pharmacologists, a coma inducer and a neuromuscular blocker should be used.[131] However, patients opting for euthanasia, if allowed in the respective domestic legal system, often do receive pain-control medication including morphine as part of their palliative care or pain-control treatment. A mistake often made in this respect is to view morphine as part of the euthanasia procedure, which strictly speaking it is not. Such an erroneous assumption complicates discussions concerning autonomy and wellbeing, particularly in relation to 'opiophobia' and with respect to the complexity of establishing the right patient-specific treatment dose.[132]

The strain on governments to improve access to palliative care and access to pain-control medication in particular is significant and severe. Especially countries that suffer from resource constraints or where large parts of the population live in remote areas without sufficient access to health facilities, goods, and services (regardless of the available resources) experience much pressure.[133] In such cases, healthcare often remains at the palliate level, which means that when curative treatment is not available or comes too late, palliative care and pain control are, if available, the only alternatives. This is particularly problematic when one bears in mind the immense

131 KNMG/KNMP, 'Guidelines for the Practice of Euthanasia and Physician-Assisted Suicide' (5th edn, KNMG 2012) <www.knmp.nl/downloads/guidelines-for-the-practice-of-euthanasia.pdf> accessed 31 August 2016.

132 This is often referred to as 'opiophobia', which is 'the irrational and undocumented fear that appropriate opioid use will lead patients to become addicts'. D Bennett and D Carr, 'Opiophobia as a Barrier to the Treatment of Pain' (2002) Journal of Pain & Palliative Care Pharmacotherapy 105, 106. General practice often demonstrates that it is not so easy to establish the patient-specific treatment dose and schedule recommended, even though palliative medicine advises that titration of opioids usually suffices to achieve the optimal effect. Titration of opioids means to find the right dose by either increasing or decreasing it in very small steps and observing the differences. Errors in establishing the right dose and schedule often cause side effects such as a drowsy feeling or hallucination, both of which can be addressed effectively in their distinct ways. For instance, a drowsy feeling is often the result of an overly high dose. Lowering or altering the dose might decrease this feeling. Hallucination usually only occurs in the first 48 hours and can be treated effectively with adjuvant medication. Adequate (at least daily) clinical observation and evaluation, and if necessary adaptation of the daily dosage, usually establishes a situation of optimal palliative wellbeing. Ill-treatment such as inadequate dosage or absent clinical observation and evaluation might underlie the difficulties in establishing the right treatment dose and schedule. If not improved, the idea that morphine diminishes legal capacity and as such may be a dangerous medicine to be used only in end-of-life situations may find traction, which has already happened to a large extent. As a point of demarcation, any questions concerning euthanasia and autonomy go beyond the scope of this study and are therefore left unaddressed. Email from A van Es, General practitioner, 'SCEN-Arts' (consultant end-of-life decisions), and Director of the International Federation of Health and Human Rights Organization to author (21 March 2016).

133 See eg C Coleman and others, 'The International Cancer Expert Corps (ICEC): A Unique Global Mentoring Model for Building Sustainable Expertise in Low-and Lower-Middle Income Countries and Geographically Remote Areas in Resource Rich Countries' (2015) 81 Annals of Global Health 20.

increase in the prevalence of non-communicable diseases in developing countries. In 2011, the UN General Assembly adopted a political declaration stating, among other aspects, that the international community should '[c]ontribute to efforts to improve access to and affordability of medicines and technologies in the prevention and control of non-communicable diseases.'[134] Such a statement furthermore supports the call to ensure access to palliative care and pain-control medication.

According to Foley and colleagues, pain is the most important symptom or discomfort for which patients seek medical care.[135] There is no single or fixed definition of pain.[136] The International Association of the Study of Pain defines pain as 'an unpleasant sensory and emotional experience associated with actual or potential tissue damage, or described in terms of such damage.'[137] Pain is not only a common side effect of disease patterns or treatments, but can also be regarded as a disease entity as such.[138] From a patient perspective, pain is often divided into disease-related or treatment-related pain. Foley and colleagues submit that disease-related pain is most common in developing countries, as patients in these regions often visit health clinics at a late(r) stage when the disease in question has already led to significant discomfort.[139]

As the story of Remedios in Chapter 1 demonstrates, the difference between access and no access can be enormous. Over time, studies have consistently shown that suffering from chronic pain conditions leads to a higher risk of anxiety or depression disorders among patients and, furthermore, has the potential to even increase pain perceptions.[140] Moreover, untreated pain disables patients and prevents them from taking care of family, sustaining their own income, enjoying free time, and taking part in social activities. This does not only put immense pressure on individual patients, but also affects caregivers and society as a whole. Studies even demonstrate that caregivers sometimes have to leave their job to care for a terminally ill relative.[141] As a result, inadequate or no access to pain-control medication or palliative care could

---

134 UNGA Res 66/2 'Political Declaration of the High-level Meeting of the General Assembly on the Prevention and Control of Non-communicable Diseases' (24 January 2012) UN Doc A/Res/66/2, para 44(e).

135 Foley and others (n 116) 981.

136 JMA Stitsen and others (eds), *Farmalogie* (2nd edn, Elsevier 2001) 101-105; MEC Gispen, *Poor Access to Pain Treatment* (International Federation of Health and Human Rights Organization 2011) 12.

137 International Association for the Study of Pain, 'IASP Taxonomy' (22 May 2012) <www.iasp-pain.org/Taxonomy#Pain> accessed 31 August 2016.

138 F Brennan, DB Carr and M Cousins, 'Pain Management: A Fundamental Human Right' (2007) 105 Anesthesia & Analgesia 205; Gispen (n 136) 34.

139 Foley and others (n 116) 982.

140 id; K Wiech and I Tracey, 'The Influence of Negative Emotions on Pain: Behavioural Effects and Neural Mechanisms' (2009) 47 NeuroImage 987.

141 Foley and others (n 116) 981.

seriously harm human dignity.[142] As was also set out in Chapter 1, both on moral and legal grounds, States have human rights obligations to redress the suffering caused by the unavailability of these medicines and to ensure the medicines are available at all. On which norms the obligations are based exactly and what their precise scope and content are, will be further elaborated in Part 2 of the book (Normative Framework).

2.5.3 Overview of challenges to access pain-control medication

As described in Section 2.3.3, both general and substance-specific challenges could also occur in the provision of controlled medicines. Chapter 1, furthermore, has shown that there could be many legislative, policy, regulatory, educational, informational, financial, and political challenges regarding the access to morphine for pain treatment. These challenges could be both general and specific in nature.[143] Many studies, both dated and more recent, describe and analyse the various barriers or challenges to the access to pain-control medication in particular. In different wordings or phrasing, these studies largely describe a similar set of factors contributing to their unavailability.[144] Table 2.2 provides a non-exhaustive overview.

142 On discussion about human dignity and pain experiences, see eg D Pullman, 'Human Dignity and the Ethics and Aesthetics of Pain and Suffering' (2002) 23 Theoretical Medicine 75. It is not submitted that this book necessarily ties in with the moral arguments presented; a link is merely established between discussions on human dignity and unmitigated pain.

143 Gispen (n 136) 13-15.

144 For scholarly work on the barriers/challenges to access opioid analgesics, see Brennan, Carr and Cousins (n 138); D Lohman, R Schleifer and JJ Amon, 'Access to Pain Treatment as a Human Right' (2010) 8 BMC Medicine 1; Gispen (n 136). For strictly legal aspects, see eg M Vranken and others, 'Legal Barriers in Accessing Opioid Medicines: Results of the ATOME Quick Scan of National Legislation of Eastern European Countries' (2014) 48 Journal of Pain and Symptom Management 1135. For a variety of regional perspectives, see eg J Cleary and others, 'Formulary Availability and Regulatory Barriers to Accessibility of Opioids for Cancer Pain in Africa: A Report from the Global Opioid Policy Initiative (GOPI)' (2013) 24 Annals of Oncology xi14; J Cleary and others, 'Formulary Availability and Regulatory Barriers to Accessibility of Opioids for Cancer Pain in Asia: A Report from the Global Opioid Policy Initiative (GOPI)' (2013) 24 Annals of Oncology xi24; J Cleary and others, 'Formulary Availability and Regulatory Barriers to Accessibility of Opioids for Cancer Pain in Latin America and the Caribbean: A Report from the Global Opioid Policy Initiative (GOPI)' (2013) Annals of Oncology xi41; J Cleary and others, 'Formulary Availability and Regulatory Barriers to Accessibility of Opioids for Cancer Pain in the Middle East: A Report from the Global Opioid Policy Initiative (GOPI)' (2013) 24 Annals of Oncology xi51.

Table 2.2 General and specific challenges to the access to pain-control medication

General challenges	Specific challenges
Intellectual property law	**International drug-control regulations**
Restricted financial resources	• *International and domestic trade and distribution control measures*
Restricted human resources	• *(Additional domestic) regulatory procedures*
Infrastructure and sourcing	Perception and fear of addiction and diversion
Human resources	Education on rational use
Quality-control standards	Fear of criminal sanctions
Cultural and religious attitudes	Lack of legal framework embedding access to types of treatment for which pain-control medication is relevant

Examples are manifold. On a general level, one of the underlying causes of a variety of potential challenges in morphine provision are the fears and myths surrounding the safe and responsible use of the medicine. As mentioned above, this is often referred to as 'opiophobia'.[145] The fear that the use of morphine would impair legal capacity, be addictive, or would hasten death is closely related to the dilemma described in Chapter 1. Education on its rationale use, as well as the perception of pain-control medication, therefore remains problematic as the palliative care aspect of pain control is neither specifically addressed in medical curricula, nor in pharmacy education.

From the wide range of potential factors, the book singles out the international drug-control treaties as a potential substance-specific challenge to medicine provision.[146] It is important to understand the interface between human rights and drug-control norms, as both frameworks set standards in the context of the production, manufacturing, distribution, trade in, and distribution and use of controlled medicines. Apart from the normative relevance addressed in subsequent sections, this focus is particularly relevant from a more practical perspective in the context of pharmaceutical regulation.

As was stressed in Chapter 1, some countries prohibit the registration of a medicine due to the administrative and regulatory burden that the international drug-control treaties would impose on the State. This despite the fact that, as will be discussed below, international drug-control treaties themselves neither effectuate standards as to the quality of medicines per se, nor set any standards regarding the clinical use of medicines. As a result, cheap medicine (e.g. morphine) could remain excluded

145 Bennett and Carr (n 132) 106.

146 This does not mean that none of the other challenges are mentioned. The entire exclusion thereof would be impossible as medicine provision generally depends on a multifaceted pallet of factors, which renders it unfeasible to discuss the potential challenge posed by international drug-control treaties in a strict vacuum.

from the pharmaceutical market due to post-market regulatory frameworks that have nothing to do with the primary medicine registration process. Not licensing morphine, despite the public health impact that will result from the decision, significantly complicates patients' access to this medicine. In other words, external post-marketing regulations, such as the international drug-control treaties, might seriously thwart successful access to medicine provision.

2.6 A specific focus on the international drug-control system as a central regulatory framework and potential challenge

This section elaborates on the international drug-control system as a central regulatory framework of controlled medicine provision and illustrates how it can be a challenge to the consumer of said medicines. Addressing the international drug-control treaties in particular is the last piece of the puzzle required to understand the funnel focus in this book. This section first elaborates on the framework's normative foundation, after which it turns to distinguish the obligations that are relevant to the provision of pain-control medication. Subsequently, the section outlines the actors involved and their various monitoring mandates, as well as the manner in which they interpret the aforementioned treaties. Finally, the nature, scope, and implications of the administrative and procedural obligations, which regulate the access to medicine provision under the international drug-control system, are elaborated on.

Such an overview, in addition, doubles as background information for the normative framework to be discussed in Part 2 of the book. Moreover, it helps one understand whether a human rights approach to drug control can be realized within the ambit of the administrative and procedural requirements in international drug-control treaties. This is dealt with in detail in the country studies included in the book (see Part 3).

2.6.1 Towards a system of international drug control

A brief history of regulation

As was mentioned in Chapter 1, the current international regime developed from a public-health oriented system to a criminal-law based system of control. In response to what is known as the Chinese opium epidemic, global action was taken to adopt international standards on drug control.[147] Until the mid-19th century, the use of

147 See H Ghodse (ed), *International Drug Control into the 21st Century* (Ashgate 2008) 89-90, 92-93; UNODC, *World Drug Report* (UNODC 2008) 117 (UNODC Report 2008); MEC Gispen, 'A Human Rights View on Access to Controlled Substances for Medical Purposes under the International Drug Control Framework' (2013) 719 European Journal of Pharmacology 16, 18.

controlled substances, in particular opioid analgesics, remained fairly unrestricted.[148] If regulated at all, drug-control regulations were mainly national or bilateral in nature.[149] It was not until the Chinese Opium Wars that calls for international regulation emerged. The Opium Wars had rapidly increased opium production in China, which in turn had led to a surge in consumption too. As a result, China counted 13.5 million opium addicts in the early 20th century, 'account[ing] for 27 per cent of the adult male population' and putting immense strain on the Chinese society.[150] The Chinese government, in a bid to acquire assistance in handling such a high number of drug users and in the hope of rehabilitating their society, reached out to the international community. As a response to this call, the United States initiated the establishment of the Shanghai International Opium Commission in 1909.[151] This pivotal moment marks the start of over 100 years of international drug control.

Towards the current system of control

When drafting the first international drug-control conventions, States took the duality of using hazardous substances into account. Wright asserts that States unequivocally denounced the use of hazardous substances and viewed medicinal use as the only licit form of substance use.[152] States further recognized that illicit use should be diminished. Yet, efforts primarily focused on control measures.[153] In the course of four decades, a long list of international opium conventions was adopted and repealed. Drug control, in the international context, first became a matter of concern to the League of Nations and later the UN. Some of the cornerstones of the current enforcement regime, including predecessors of the system's monitoring mechanisms, were developed and adopted at this early stage.[154] None of the conventions, however, captured the level of control desired by States.[155] Eventually, after drug

148 Gispen, 'Access to Controlled Substances' (n 147) 18.

149 RM Lines, 'The 'Fifth Stage' of Drug Control: International Law, Dynamic Interpretation and Human Rights' (DPhil thesis, Middlesex University 2014) 29-30.

150 L Lu, Y Fang and X Wang, 'Drug Abuse in China: Past, Present and Future' (2008) 28 Cellular and Molecular Neurobiology 479, 481. See also UNODC Report 2008 (n 147) 18, 179; Gispen, 'Access to Controlled Substances' (n 147) 18; Lines (n 149) 29-30.

151 UNODC Report 2008 (n 147) 18; Gispen, 'Access to Controlled Substances' (n 147) 18; Lines (n 149) 29-30.

152 H Wright, 'International Opium Commission' (1909) 3 American Journal of International Law 828, 859.

153 See eg IG Waddell, 'International Narcotics Control' (1970) 64 American Journal of International Law 310, 310-315; D Bewley-Taylor and M Jelsma, 'Regime Change: Re-Visiting the 1961 Single Convention on Narcotic Drugs' (2011) 23 International Journal of Drug Policy 72, 73; Gispen, 'Access to Controlled Substances' (n 147) 18.

154 For an in-depth overview of drug-control regulation under the League of Nations and later under the United Nations, see Ghodse (n 147) 82-84; Lines (n 149) 29-51.

155 See eg UNODC Report 2008 (n 147) 177-198.

control became an issue of concern to the UN, the intention was expressed within the UN framework to adopt one comprehensive convention that would render all previous conventions moot.[156] That all-encompassing instrument became a reality when States adopted the Single Convention in 1961, which was amended in 1972. Notwithstanding its comprehensive nature, the scope of international drug control was expanded further with the adoption of the 1971 Convention on Psychotropic Substances[157] and the 1988 United Nations Convention Against the Illicit Traffic in Narcotic Drugs and Psychotropic Substances.[158] These three treaties together form the current international drug-control system.

2.6.2 Normative foundation and the 'principle of balance'

In a textual interpretation, the treaties regulate the dual nature of controlled substances in a balanced manner: State Parties have to ban the illicit use of controlled substances whilst maximizing their medical availability. Such duality, and the accompanying concern, is explicitly mentioned in the preambles of both the Single Convention and the 1971 Convention. In relation to ensuring the access to medicines, State Parties recognize that '[t]he medical use of narcotic drugs continues to be indispensable for the relief of pain and suffering (...) and adequate provisions must be adopted to ensure the availability of narcotic drugs for such purposes.'[159]

Whereas the Single Convention only refers to pain control and pain medication in particular, the preamble of the 1971 Convention stresses that State Parties recognize the need to ensure that adequate treatment, relying on the range of psychotropic substances listed under the international drug-control treaties, is available. The 1971 Convention stipulates that '[t]he use of psychotropic substances for medical and scientific purposes is indispensable and that their availability for such purposes should not be unduly restricted'.[160]

These same preambles express the need to prevent and reduce drug-associated harm, both in a public health and a social welfare context. The preamble of the Single Convention echoes that 'addiction to narcotic drugs constitutes a serious evil for

---

156 See A Lande, 'The Single Convention on Narcotic Drugs, 1961' (1962) 16 International Organization 776, 776-777.

157 Convention on Psychotropic Substances (adopted 21 February 1971, entered into force 16 August 1976) 1901 UNTS 175 (1971 Convention).

158 United Nations Convention Against the Illicit Traffic in Narcotic Drugs and Psychotropic Substances (adopted 20 December 1988, entered into force 11 November 1990) 1582 UNTS 95 (1988 Convention).

159 Single Convention, prmbl.

160 1971 Convention, prmbl.

the individual and is fraught with social and economic danger to mankind'.[161] The 1971 Convention implicitly reaffirms, but also extends, this notion by stressing that ratifying States are 'determined to prevent and combat abuse of [psychotropic] substances and the illicit traffic to which it gives rise.'[162] The WHO has framed this outset as the central 'principle of balance'.

> The central 'principle of balance' represents a dual obligation of governments to establish a system of control that ensures the adequate availability of controlled substances for medical and scientific purposes, while simultaneously preventing abuse, diversion and trafficking.[163]

This balancing act may differ depending on the substance it relates to. A system of scheduling determines which substances fall under what exact scope and level of control, and thus affects the manner in which States should regulate. Considering this book's specific focus on pain-control medication, i.e. morphine and codeine, only the relevant legal structure of the Single Convention will be discussed. After all, morphine and codeine appear in the first schedule (list) of the Single Convention.[164]

2.6.3 Obligations relevant to the provision of pain-control medication

State Parties to the Single Convention have to observe a general obligation, which includes a strict prohibition that gives effect to this 'principle of balance'. Article 4, in that regard, mandates State Parties to take all '(...) legislative and administrative measures as may be necessary (...) to limit exclusively to medical and scientific purposes the production, manufacture, export, import, distribution of, trade in, use and possession of drugs.'[165] The Single Convention, furthermore, sets several additional standards relating to the level and scope of control of the non-medical use of controlled substances to be maintained in domestic law. For instance, State Parties are not to allow the possession of controlled substances (except under legal authority).[166] Any breach of the strict prohibition clause should, within the limits of country-specific constitutional safeguards, be considered a punishable offence under

161 Single Convention, prmbl.
162 1971 Convention, prmbl.
163 WHO, *Ensuring Balance in National Policies on Controlled Substances: Guidance for Availability and Accessibility of Controlled Medicines* (WHO 2011) 11.
164 Where deemed necessary and relevant, links to the other drug-control treaties are provided.
165 Single Convention, art 4. On the basis of Article 2(1) of the Single Convention, substances listed on Schedule I (including morphine and codeine) are subject to all measures of control of said Convention, including in particular Articles 4(c) and 19-21 (referring to the monitoring mechanisms as addressed below).
166 ibid art 33.

domestic law.[167] The Single Convention is not a self-executive instrument, meaning that State Parties have to adopt domestic legislation to give effect to the conditions and obligations contained in it. In addition to the general obligation, State Parties also have an explicit obligation to take measures to combat the abuse of listed substances.[168] Such additional provisions, when viewed jointly, reflect an extended framework of law that guides States in their control efforts.

In the context of ensuring the medicinal use of controlled substances, however, the Single Convention does not set out such detailed supplementary obligations. In other words, the Convention only enshrines a general obligation to ensure the access to listed substances for medical and scientific purposes. Yet no subsequent provisions include any reference to the desired level of access, for instance. On the other hand, the convention does provide an extensive regulatory system with respect to the global import/export of controlled medicines and their domestic manufacturing, distribution, trade, and usage. The Single Convention, moreover, contains a comprehensive monitoring mechanism consisting of three distinct obligations. As briefly introduced in Chapter 1, these obligations require State Parties to:

i) maintain a *special administration* for the purpose of complying with the provisions as included in the Single Convention (Article 17 Single Convention);
ii) to submit to the INCB an *annual estimate* specifying, amongst other figures, the quantities of drugs to be consumed next calendar year for medical and scientific purposes, and quantities necessary in addition to special stocks[169] (Article 19 Single Convention);
iii) to furnish the INCB annually with *statistical returns* on official forms specifying, amongst other elements, the consumption of drugs, the production of drugs and the imports and exports of drugs and poppy straw (raw material) (Article 20 Single Convention).

In conjunction with these administrative and procedural obligations, States have to comply with specific trade and distribution requirements. Controlled essential medicines should be available on prescription, if deemed necessary written on official forms, dispensed by authorized staff and control facilities that operate in the trade or distribution of controlled medicines.[170] Adequate compliance with these monitoring procedures and specific obligations is important because these administrative and procedural obligations, in essence, reflect a global regulatory structure of import

167 ibid art 36.
168 ibid art 38.
169 Drugs to be consumed for medical and scientific purposes should be understood as controlled medicines.
170 Single Convention, art 30.

and export licences. This, it would seem, becomes irrelevant to any self-sufficient State that does not rely on either import or export for the assurance of access to pain-control medication. However, as was already described, the pharmaceutical life cycle and, more generally, medicine development is a highly complex and truly global enterprise. Consequently, any State not complying with the control procedures mentioned above would essentially be side-lined.[171]

2.6.4 Actors, functions, and monitoring mandates relevant to ensuring the access to pain-control medication

Commission on Narcotic Drugs

The Commission on Narcotic Drugs (CND) is the political body of the international drug-control treaties.[172] The CND is a committee of the UN's Economic and Social Council (ECOSOC) and is mandated to monitor the world's drug problem, develop strategies on the topic, and issue recommendations.[173] The Commission meets annually in Vienna, where it holds open sessions to review the progress made in reaching international and domestic drug-control objectives.[174] The CND is also mandated to determine if changes in the scope of control are required and, if so, to make the necessary adjustments.[175] Following advice by the WHO (see below), the CND may decide to include or delete a substance from any schedule or decide to move a substance from one schedule to another. This clearly means that the CND is at the heart of the international drug-control system; scheduling is the key determinant defining the exact level of control applicable to a certain substance.[176] Furthermore, the Commission may raise any issue with the INCB relevant to its functioning and may issue recommendations on the implementation of the aims and provisions of the Single Convention.[177] Moreover, the CND may, among other tasks, bring any recommendations it adopts under these Conventions to the attention of non-parties.[178]

---

171 MEC Gispen, 'Reconciling International Obligations and Local Realities: Provision of Pain Control Medication in Resource-Constrained Countries – Experiences from Uganda' in M Hesselman, A de Wolff and BCA Toebes (eds), *Essential Public Service Provision* (Routledge *forthcoming*).

172 ECOSOC Res 1946 'Commission on Narcotic Drugs' (16 February 1946) UN Doc E/RES/1946/9(I); Ghodse (n 147) 22; Lines (n 149) 62.

173 ECOSOC Res 1946; Lines (n 149) 62.

174 Ghodse (n 147) 22; Lines (n 149) 62.

175 Single Convention, art 3.

176 See also C Hallam, D Bewley-Taylor and M Jelsma, 'Scheduling in the International Drug Control System' (2014) TNI Series on Legislative Reform of Drug Policies No 25 <www.tni.org/files/download/dlr25_0.pdf> accessed 31 August 2016.

177 Single Convention, art 8.

178 id.

International Narcotics Control Board

The INCB is the monitoring body of the international drug-control treaties, including the Single Convention.[179] As defined in Article 9 of the Single Convention, the INCB's mandate includes monitoring compliance with the administrative and procedural obligations listed above (in particular Articles 19 and 20). As enumerated in Article 12 of the Single Convention, its particular tasks in this regard include: (i) to fix the date by and manner in which estimates need to be submitted; (ii) to establish estimates – insofar as possible – on behalf of governments failing to submit an estimate; and (iii) to complete estimates if it deems it necessary after examining a submitted estimate. The INCB's mandate in terms of the statistical return requirements is similar and codified in Article 13 of the Single Convention. More generally, Article 14 of the Single Convention sets out the measures available to the Board to ensure the Single Convention's execution.

Under explicit conditions, the INCB could also request open consultations, ask for explanations from States on certain provisions, call on governments to take remedial measures, propose the execution of a study within the territory of a State, or call for the attention of other State Parties, the ECOSOC, and the CND when it deems collective action to be necessary.[180] Moreover, the Board can recommend import and export embargos, and is free to publish a report on any issue relevant to measures set out in Article 14 itself. Despite seemingly representing an extensive list of options, the aforementioned measures reflect a relatively weak enforcement mechanism with soft-law characteristics. Yet, it is this type of political, rather than strictly legal, enforcement mechanism to which the drafters of the convention committed themselves. The nature of these measures is similar to those contained in the mandates of other international legal treaty bodies. However, in addition or as an alternative to these measures, the INCB may recommend to relevant UN Specialized Agencies and competent bodies that a State, upon consent, should receive technical or financial assistance to carry out obligations set forth in the Single Convention.[181]

---

179 See also Ghodse (n 147) 22-23.

180 Single Convention, art 14.

181 ibid art 14*bis*. In the last three annual reports of the INCB, technical assistance was only requested by a specific government or discussed by the INCB itself in relation to the control of diversion and harm reduction. While access to medicines is part of the dual nature of the international drug-control system, technical support has neither been discussed nor suggested in relation to the provision of controlled medicines or for the purpose of compliance with the administrative and procedural obligations set out in Section 2.6.3. It is, in addition, unclear whether the INCB executes its mandate of art 14*bis* when technical assistance is discussed at all. See, by omission, INCB, *Report of the International Narcotics Control Board for 2013* (INCB 2014); INCB, *Report for 2014* (n 4); INCB, *Report for 2015* (n 4).

United Nations Office on Drugs and Crime

The United Nations Office on Drugs and Crime (UNODC) houses with the INCB Secretariat in Vienna and is the key programmatic actor in the international drug-control system. It was established to facilitate a 'programme of technical assistance in narcotics control within the regular budget of the United Nations.'[182] As such, it is tasked to provide assistance to governments in overcoming their fight against illicit drugs, crime, and terrorism.[183] In particular the UNODC's role in the provision of technical assistance is noteworthy.[184] Its work, in terms of technical assistance, is based on three pillars: (i) to conduct field-based technical cooperation projects; (ii) to increase the body of knowledge on drug issues through research and analytical work; and (iii) to fulfil a normative role in assisting States in the ratification and implementation of the international drug-control conventions.[185]

World Health Organization

The WHO maintains a key programmatic and norm-setting position in the field of global health issues. As a UN Specialized Agency it is mandated with an advisory role in the international drug-control system. The WHO leads the Access to Controlled Medications Programme, flagging the public health deficit of the poor access to medicines under the present system. It also helps States overcome their struggles in providing access by, for instance, publishing guidelines. In relation to the drug-control conventions, the WHO has an advisory function regarding the scheduling of substances and the scope of control. If it believes that any substances should be added to or removed from one of the Schedules, it may inform the UN Secretary-General and provide evidence-based information on the medical and non-medical effects of the substance in question.[186] The WHO may also nominate five candidates with a medical or pharmacological background from which the ECOSOC elects three experts to serve on the INCB (the remaining ten are selected from a list provided by parties and non-parties to the UN alike).[187]

182 UNGA Res 1395 (XIV) (20 November 1959) para 1; Lines (n 149) 70.
183 See UNODC, 'Commission on Narcotic Drugs' <www.unodc.org/unodc/en/commissions/CND/> accessed 31 August 2016.
184 Ghodse (n 147) 24.
185 UNODC, 'Commission on Narcotic Drugs' (n 183).
186 Single Convention, art 3(1).
187 ibid art 9(1b).

2.6.5 Treaty interpretation, normative guidance and technical support to comply with the relevant administrative and procedural obligations

Managing a control system based on estimates presupposes that these estimates articulate the real on-the-ground need for medicines in an accurate manner. In the context of the multifaceted challenges to provide access to medicines, articulating realistic and sufficient estimates might be difficult. In fact, the INCB itself held that adequate capacity, both in terms of financial expenditure and human resources, is a *conditio sine qua non* for the production of accurate estimates. This, in turn, means that a range of procedures has the potential to affect vital aspects of the deficit in controlled medicine provision.[188] Still, it is crucial to articulate estimates sufficiently covering country-specific needs as the 'estimate system' essentially regulates the import/export of all controlled medicines.

The WHO and INCB have jointly published technical support and training manuals to assist countries in drawing up estimates and in complying with their estimating and reporting obligations. Previously, the INCB has published training manuals targeted at national administrators, guiding them in how to submit the correct documents so as to accurately reflect the true needs of patients.[189] In its communications, the INCB calls upon States to ensure that the challenges to service provision are identified in order to take appropriate measures to increase access, on the one hand, and implement sufficient monitoring and control systems, on the other.[190] Yet, these manuals only refer to the more methodological aspects of implementation and compliance, and lack any normative criteria defining access to or availability of controlled medicines.[191]

---

188 R Yans, 'Statement by the President of the International Narcotics Control Board' (Fifth Session of the African Union Conference of Ministers for Drug Control, Addis-Ababa, Ethiopia, 11-12 October 2012) 3 <www.incb.org/documents/Speeches/Speeches2012/2012_October_CAMDC5_111012_eng.pdf> accessed 31 August 2016. Part 3 will elaborate on this link in the context of realizing human rights standards of access to medicines provision through the mechanisms of the international drug-control treaties.

189 See INCB, 'Training Manual: 1961 Single Convention on Narcotic Drugs. Part 1: The International Control System for Narcotic Drugs' (INCB 2005) <www.incb.org/documents/Narcotic-Drugs/Training-Materials/English/PART_I_English.pdf> accessed 31 August 2016; INCB and WHO, *Guide on Estimating Requirements for Substances under International Control* (INCB 2012).

190 See eg INCB, *Report of the International Narcotics Control Board for 2010* (INCB 2011) v.

191 The INCB does refer to the fact that availability does not only include physical availability and practical access, but also includes financial aspects such as affordability. However, it does not refer to this in a comprehensive or structural way so as to guide States at the normative level. W Sipp, 'Statement by the President of the International Narcotics Control Board' (Fifty-Ninth Session of the Commission on Narcotic Drugs, Vienna, Austria, 17 March 2016) 3 <www.incb.org/documents/Speeches/Speeche s2016/Speech_CND_item_6_d.pdf> accessed 31 August 2016.

Together with the WHO, the INCB recommends State Parties to use three methods which may prove helpful in producing estimates reflecting the real country-specific needs: (i) consumption-based methods; (ii) service-based methods; and (iii) morbidity-based methods.[192] Without entering into a complex methodological discussion, which would go beyond the scope of this book, it is important to explain that both consumption-based and service-based methods use the registered need, i.e. consumption within a country as the main unit of analysis. The data collected is either representative of the entire country or is a mere sample of health facilities. In both cases, the estimates made essentially reflect the number of people presenting themselves to a doctor to obtain treatment. As Sections 2.3.3 and 2.5 have indicated, a structural and serious problem presents itself here because the actual need for pain-control medication is, in resource-constrained countries, often far greater than the actual medical consumption of medicines.

As opposed to the first two methods, the third method relies on epidemiological data – data on the incidence and prevalence of diseases or the conditions in a region or country.[193] As such, this method may be useful to analyse the absolute need in a country, regardless of the number of patients presenting their conditions to medical professionals. The method presupposes up-to-date and comprehensive insight into local, regional, and national disease patterns, whose existence may not be taken as a given in resource-constrained countries and in countries with large remote areas.[194] Apart from estimate-related and statistical return procedures, the WHO and INCB do not provide any specific guidance in their joint reporting on how States should handle the storage and distribution for monitoring and control purposes. Notwithstanding this lack of guidance, both bodies acknowledge storage and distribution to be an integral component of good pharmaceutical procurement and stress its value for monitoring and control purposes. Regardless, they do not refer to the specific trade and distribution requirements stipulated in Article 30 of the Single Convention.[195]

In case of insufficient estimates or increased demands, States may submit supplementary estimates to the INCB.[196] Given its monitoring mandate, the INCB acts as a gatekeeper and plays a pivotal role in ensuring the access to medicines under the international drug-control system. In the contrast to the two other administrative and procedural obligations (managing a separate administration and submitting quarterly statistical returns), no additional normative guidance is provided. More generally, the INCB in

192 INCB and WHO (n 189) 46-52. See also Gispen, 'Reconciling International Obligations' (n 171).
193 id.
194 Especially in the context of this third method, there could be little difference between resource-constrained countries and countries with large remote areas. See eg Coleman and others (n 133).
195 INCB and WHO (n 189) 5.
196 Single Convention, arts 12(4) and 19(3).

particular has been criticized for following a one-sided treaty interpretation despite the inherent duality underlying the international drug-control system.[197] Scholars and the international community assert that the majority of recommendations, guidance, and reporting of the INCB is focused on the control of diversion and is unbalanced when compared to the access to controlled medicines. This despite the increased awareness of and focus on the access to controlled medicines.[198]

2.6.6 Overview of administrative and procedural obligations to ensure access to medicines

Table 2.3 provides an overview of the normative basis as well as an outline of the purpose of the three main administrative and procedural obligations relating to the provision of controlled medicines. Additionally, the table provides an obligation-specific visualization of the normative guidance and technical support provided to State Parties, or the lack thereof, in order to improve effective implementation of said procedures.

197 See eg AL Taylor, 'Addressing the Global Tragedy of Needless Pain: Rethinking the United Nations Single Convention on Narcotic Drugs' (2007) 35 Journal of Law, Medicines and Ethics 556; KI Pettus, 'Rhetoric and the Road to Hell: The International Narcotics Control Regime and Access to Essential Medicines' (2012) 1 Bulletin Health Policy and Law 1; Gispen, 'Access to Controlled Substances' (n 147) 19; Global Commission on Drug Policy, *The Negative Impact of Drug Control on Public Health: The Global Crisis of Avoidable Pain* (GCDP 2015) 11-12.

198 The INCB has focused various technical reports on access to medicine provision. See eg INCB Availability Report 2011 (n 108); INCB Availability Report 2016 (n 108).

Table 2.3 Overview of administrative and procedural obligations

Obligation and legal basis	Implication and purpose	Normative guidance (on domestic interpretation)	Technical support (for domestic implementation)
Art. 17 Single Convention (separate administration)	Managing a separate administration to track the licit medical/scientific supply/demand chain.	–	–
Art. 19 Single Convention (annual estimate)	Submit annual estimates to the INCB reflecting the estimated need of controlled substances for medical (and scientific) purposes for the next calendar year, i.e. estimates submitted in 2016 reflect the calculated need for 2017. The purpose is to track and monitor the licit medical and scientific supply/demand chain.	The WHO and INCB jointly recommend States to rely on combined consumption-based and morbidity-based methods to draft their estimates. Such combined methods are claimed to produce the most comprehensive and accurate overview.	
Art. 20 Single Convention (quarterly statistical return)	Submit quarterly statistical returns reflecting the amounts of controlled substances used for medical (and scientific) purposes including an overview of (medical) consumption. The purpose is to track and monitor the licit medical/scientific supply/demand chain.	–	–
Art. 30 Single Convention (trade and distribution requirements)	Ensure controlled medicines are only available on prescription, if deemed necessary on official forms dispensed by authorized staff. Facilities which engage in trade or distribution of controlled medicines should be monitored.	The WHO and INCB only describe the importance of storage and distribution for the purpose of monitoring and control.	The WHO and INCB do not give any specific guidance in their joint reporting on how this should be done in light of the specific trade and distribution requirements

2.7 Conclusion

Much has been discussed in this chapter. The important 'take home messages' or rather 'take along for further reading messages' are manifold. First, human rights are integrally relevant to the interpretation of the international drug-control treaties, whether one grants human rights normative priority or not. This book, in line with a constitutionalist interpretation of international law, grants human rights such priority. Such an approach survives the criticism of international public lawyers claiming the opposite because human rights have to be integrated also on the basis of the general rules of treaty interpretation. It is submitted here that a human rights approach to drug control is not based on arbitrary political decisions, but seen as a legitimate interpretation of international law on all accounts. Yet, the question remains what this implies *in concreto* (see Part 2 for further analysis).

Second, medicine regulation is a complex and global enterprise of which ensuring access to medicines is implicitly the overarching aim. To this end, medicine regulation and market approval of new medicines should be steered towards and focused on reaching those most in need. Yet, viewing the access to medicines in the context of health systems more broadly demonstrates many challenges that may hamper the provision of medicines. These challenges may originate from or exist in the context of regulations that are internal and external to the primary medicine regulatory process. This chapter established that these challenges could either be considered general or substance-specific. In other words, there is a range of challenges that may hamper medicine provision at any stage of the pharmaceutical life cycle, regardless of the legal or therapeutic classification of a medicine.

On the other hand, there are also substance-specific challenges, which come into play exactly because of this legal or therapeutic classification of a medicine and, thus, the medicine-specific context. For various reasons, the implications of medicine provision in accordance with international standards may make it even more complex for resource-constrained countries to provide access to medicines. It is therefore important to focus on these countries in particular. In light of the various challenges, moreover, the chapter has used a funnel perspective to demonstrate why it is important to focus on the international drug-control treaties in particular when viewing the access to controlled medication in accordance with human rights norms.

Third, from the wider selection of essential medicines, i.e. those medicines that aim to satisfy the priority health needs of a country, one can select controlled essential medicines. Pain-control medication, such as morphine and codeine, is both part of the core list of the WHO Model List of Essential Medicines and listed under the Single Convention. This chapter has clearly demonstrated in detail the serious social injustice embedded in the global crisis of unavailable pain-control medication. Those living in LMICs suffer most. The patient groups on which this book focuses are cancer and HIV/AIDS patients, with special attention to those living in remote areas, the elderly, children, women, and otherwise vulnerable and marginalized members of society.

Finally, this chapter has discussed the balanced manner in which the international drug-control treaties aim to regulate the dual nature of controlled substances. It is commonly asserted that *de jure* horizontal balancing has led to *de facto* control efforts dominating the access to medicine efforts. It is not the right place here to go into overly great detail regarding this issue. What is important to take along into the discussion of the normative framework (in Part 2) is the balanced yet prohibitive approach that the international drug-control treaties take regarding drug control in order to regulate the dual nature of substances. The issue central to Part 2 is whether human rights law and theory provide for any arguments to support such an approach. Indeed, the issue is how human rights norms would situate the juxtaposition of drug control and inform governments on how to create a system of control that is set up to balance obligations to ensure access whilst preventing diversion and abuse.

It is this idea of balancing that needs further analysis from a human rights perspective in order to reconsider the international drug-control system as such. Apart from these doctrinal and normative aspects, the relevant message to take along into the country studies (in Part 3) is not so much the balanced outset, but rather the technical implications of the administrative and procedural obligations, as well as the specific trade and distribution requirements applicable to the access to controlled medicine provision under the international drug-control system. The potential constraints in service provision, both structural and incidental, both substance-specific and general in nature, are of crucial importance to determine whether any human rights approach to balance drug-control regulation can be secured through the mechanisms of the international drug-control system as it stands.

Part 2

Normative Framework

Chapter 3
Access to Controlled Essential Medicines and Aspects of Drug Control in Human Rights Law

3.1 Introduction

In search of a human rights approach to drug control to address the issue of access to controlled essential medicines, one has to situate the international drug-control treaties' foundational 'principle of balance' in human rights *law*.[1] This chapter offers a largely doctrinal legal analysis focusing on the role of the State.[2] Although the legal framework is addressed from a general perspective, applicability mainly hinges on whether States have signed and ratified the different treaties and conventions analysed.

As stressed in Chapter 2, the 'principle of balance' captures the idea that States have to maximize the access to controlled medicines whilst minimizing their diversion.[3] This is the World Health Organization's (WHO) interpretation of the strict prohibition clause adopted in Article 4 of the 1961 Single Convention on Narcotic Drugs (Single Convention).[4] However, in light of the structures of human rights law, the question is whether human rights law would support the 'principle of balance' as interpreted and

---

1 Law is emphasized here to avoid confusion. Part 2 of the book includes a legal and an ethical analysis, which each in their distinct way address a similar issue: situating the 'principle of balance' in human rights norms. While the present chapter deals with doctrinal issues, Chapter 4 discusses normative questions about the law (*lex ferenda*).

2 Human rights law is state-centric. It is traditionally distinct from other fields of international law due to the rights and obligations it enumerates at the state-individual level as opposed to state-to-state obligations. Nonetheless, human rights law includes inter-state obligations as well as obligations between private parties. See M Scheinin, 'Characteristics of Human Rights Norms' in C Krause and M Scheinin (eds), *International Protection of Human Rights: A Textbook* (Institute for Human Rights Åbo Akademi University 2009) 19. The scope of the traditional relationship is increasingly discussed in light of non-state actors, acknowledging their importance in human rights protection. Examples of such non-state actors include Non-Governmental Organizations, armed groups, and pharmaceutical companies. D Weissbrodt, 'Roles and Responsibilities of Non-State Actors' in D Shelton (ed), *The Oxford Handbook of International Human Rights Law* (OUP 2013) 719. See for examples respectively, KMA Fortin, *The Accountability of Armed Groups under Human Rights Law* (DPhil thesis, Utrecht University 2015); SP Zinzombe, *The Right to Health, Pharmaceutical Corporations and Intellectual Property: Access to Medicines* (Intersentia 2015).

3 In the context of this study, the prevention aspect includes protection against the use of hazardous substances to safeguard public health and the public order.

4 WHO, *Ensuring Balance in National Policies on Controlled Substances: Guidance for Availability and Accessibility of Controlled Medicines* (WHO 2011) 11. See also Single Convention on Narcotic

constructed in the international drug-control system. Or, if not, would human rights law frame the balancing of the access to controlled medicines and the protection against hazardous use in a different way?[5] And, if so, what would the difference be? More generally, these questions reflect on the meaning of such balancing in the context of human rights law.

Balancing is a particularly interesting exercise in human rights law: human rights law provides a framework of legitimate interferences with rights and interests, balancing *between* different rights and interests and/or interferences, as well as balancing in terms of priority-setting for the realization of a *specific* right.[6] According to Porat, the act of balancing – or weighing interests – usually includes three steps: (i) the identification of the various considerations or interests involved; (ii) the attribution of a normative value to each of these considerations based on their importance; and (iii) the scaling of all considerations and their normative value.[7] In order to balance the access to controlled medicines with aspects of drug control in human rights law, one needs to understand how human rights law would frame either of these aforementioned aspects. Moreover, one must cognize what determines the importance of a certain norm and how norms relate to one another.

Against the backdrop of Porat's three-step structure of balancing, this chapter commences with an elaboration on the nature and legal status of human rights (Section 3.2) as well as the mechanisms for their implementation and enforcement (Section 3.3). These sections provide a general understanding of the fundament on which medicine-access claims are based and illustrate how States should discharge their obligations based on such a claim. Yet, perhaps most significantly, this general overview also provides a lens, a legal structure, through which to see how such a claim relates to the

---

Drugs (adopted 30 March 1961, entered into force 13 December 1964) 520 UNTS 151 (Single Convention) art 4. The article enunciates the dual obligation of governments to manage a system of drug control that prevents dispersion and abuse while supportive to the medical use of controlled substances. See Chapter 2, Section 2.6.

5 The issue is not just how and on what basis human rights law conceptualizes a claim to access controlled medicines. Such a narrow approach would fail to address the juxtaposition underlying the regulation of controlled substances in a holistic manner. Instead, one has to understand a claim to access medicines in relation to the way in which States have to discharge their obligations to prevent dispersion of controlled substances, protect public health, and safeguard the public order.

6 Rights and interests are intentionally mentioned separately here because individual rights protection may be different from obligations to protect societal interests such as public health, the public order, safety, and security. Section 3.3 deals with the criteria within human rights law that organize this legitimacy of balancing between, and priority-setting within, specific rights protection measures, including those securing societal interests.

7 I Porat, 'The Dual Model of Balancing: A Model for the Proper Scope of Balancing in Constitutional Law' 27 (2005-2006) Cardozo Law Review 1393, 1399. While used in the context of constitutional law, Porat's structure of balancing may be applicable to any field of law, including human rights law.

protection against the hazardous use of controlled substances in human rights law.[8] In other words, these general aspects are relevant when exploring if and how human rights law balances different rights and interests, or aspects of rights, in the implementation and enforcement of rights. Subsequently, the chapter applies the general parameters relevant to balancing in human rights law, as described in Sections 3.2 and 3.3. It does so by analysing a substantive claim to access to controlled medicines on the basis of, primarily, the right to health (Section 3.4) and, complementarily, the prohibition of torture, cruel, inhuman, and degrading treatment (CIDT) (Section 3.5).[9] Throughout these sections, the chapter necessarily also explores arguments in relation to the protection against hazardous use and addresses how States should appreciate their dual obligations in accordance with human rights law.

The arguments presented rely on legal and case-law analysis, and on literature review. In line with what has been expressed in Chapter 1, the interpretation of legal sources is based on Article 38 of the Statute of the International Court of Justice.[10] The selection of legal norms, in turn, is based on their direct relevance or clear complementary potential.[11] Supporting literature has been gathered from law-specific and general databases. An extensive case-law analysis is carried out.[12] Case law has been systematically gathered and inspected at the international, regional, and domestic level, using databases such as those of the Netherlands Institute of Human

8 In line with this book's central focus on access to controlled medicines and drug control, other aspects such as religious, cultural, traditional, and/or recreational use are only addressed if relevant to understand any question of proportionality in relation to the protection against hazardous use. This focus does not deprive the study of its broader relevance, as it demonstrates and provides for legal norms, criteria, and principles instructive to the interpretation of drug-control matters in the first place. See also text at n 3.

9 As will be briefly touched on in Section 3.4, the access to medicines is litigated on the basis of a range of rights, including the right to health, the right to life, the prohibition of torture and CIDT, the principle of non-discrimination, and the right to family life. The chapter does not outline all these rights. Rather, it limits itself to a discussion of the right to health and the prohibition of torture and CIDT. Access to medicines naturally fits within the ambit of the right to health. The second example is introduced to complement this analysis. The reason for this is mainly that the prohibition of torture and CIDT is a much stronger right in terms of enforceability and justiciability, although less explicit in terms of scope and application. Access to medicines could, in addition, also be understood in light of disability law or with specific foci on women and children. While especially disability law as a field of human rights protection is considered to be of much added value to the understanding of access to medicines and, in particular, pain-control medicines for chronic conditions, the chapter will not present an in-depth analysis for reasons similar to those explained above. If relevant, the chapter will make reference to relevant discussions or analogous interpretations supporting or undermining the general arguments presented in this part of the book.

10 Statute of the International Court of Justice (adopted 26 June 1945, entered into force 24 October 1945) 33 UNTS 993 (ICJ Statute).

11 Compare text at n 9.

12 The case-law analysis was carried out in August 2013 and no additional cases have been included since then.

Rights (currently hosted by the UN), HUDOC (the case-law finder of Council of Europe), the African Human Rights Case Law Identifier, and the case-law finder of the Centre for Justice and International Law. In total, 476 cases were identified of which 148 were considered relevant.[13] Claims in these cases were, for example, based on the denial or inadequate access to medicines (in- and out-prison) and on the denial or inadequacy of medical care in terms of not receiving medication (when needed). The criteria used are blind to a medicine's controlled status.[14] Cases in which access to medicines is referred to in the outline of the facts but in which this is not mentioned or referred to in the actual claim are considered irrelevant.

3.2 The human rights framework in brief

This section briefly describes the structure of the human rights framework. Since the interpretation and reconstruction of the normative basis of drug-control regulation finds its roots in this legal framework, the latter is addressed in more detail than the international drug-control framework was in Chapter 2. Nonetheless, it would be unnecessarily lengthy to address each and every aspect of it. As such, this section provides an overview of the key human rights instruments and analyses the categories of human rights, their nature, and the typology of obligations. Such an outline allows one to distinguish the parameters which determine balancing in human rights law and to situate the juxtaposition of drug-control regulation therein.

3.2.1 Human rights instruments

The modern interpretation of human rights law is chiefly based on the international human rights documents adopted after the atrocities of World Word II.[15] In fact,

---

13 The relevance was assessed by using the Ctrl-F function for: **medicines** and **medication**. If there were no hits, the function was also used to search for **medical** because some search engines broaden the search scope to *medi**.

14 The decision was made not to search for controlled medicines specifically because human rights law does not distinguish between controlled or uncontrolled medicines. The only distinction human rights law manages to make is essential medicines. See also Chapter 2.

15 The idea of human rights is much older and has been captured in many different ways prior to adoption of the international legal system of human rights currently in force. On the history of the human rights framework, see eg C Tomuschat, *Human Rights: Between Idealism and Realism* (2nd edn, OUP 2008) 5-24; I Bantekas and L Oette, *International Human Rights: Law and Practice* (CUP 2013) 11-19; PG Lauren, 'The Foundations of Justice and Human Rights in Early Legal Texts and Thought' in D Shelton (ed), *The Oxford Handbook of International Human Rights Law* (OUP 2013) 164. The modern understanding of human rights reflects the mainstream traditional interpretation. Both the idea of human rights as well as its legal framework are also much contested. Critics mainly argue that human rights law, and international law in general, is Eurocentric and lacks a third-world perspective, both in theory and in practice. Arguing human rights operates in a neo-colonialist fashion, and human rights theory and practice need to be revisited and decolonized. On

human rights became part of international law through the adoption of the Charter of the United Nations (UN Charter). One of the purposes of the UN, which was established in 1945 by the adoption of the Charter, is to promote and encourage 'respect for human rights and for fundamental freedoms'.[16] With the Holocaust in mind, the international community subsequently adopted the Universal Declaration of Human Rights (UDHR) in 1948.[17] The UDHR is often understood as elaborating the explicit human rights obligations of States, as derived from the UN Charter.[18]

The UDHR voices a clear universal message against any violations of people's rights and indicates which rights should be secured and realized in order to protect human dignity, the foundational principle upon which human rights rest.[19] The UDHR includes both civil and political rights (CP rights) and economic, social, and cultural rights (ESC rights). Traditionally, in law, CP rights are freedom rights, such as the prohibition of torture and CIDT, the freedom of speech, and the right to vote.[20] By contrast, ESC rights are rights to socioeconomic goods and services, such as the right to health and to education. It is often said that due to the international community's inability to unanimously agree on the content and status of the various rights and duties included in the UDHR, the list of rights was adopted as a declaration. The lack of unanimity on the status of CP and ESC rights was, and still is, largely political and ideological in nature.[21]

---

criticism of human rights, see eg B Rajagopal, 'Counter-Hegemonic International Law: Rethinking Human Rights and Development as a Third World Strategy' (2006) 27 Third World Quarterly 767; JM Barreto (ed), *Human Rights from a Third World Perspective: Critique, History and International Law* (CUP 2013). This criticism is acknowledged and referred to if necessary and relevant throughout the analysis.

16 Charter of the United Nations (adopted 24 October 1945) 1 UNTS XVI, art 1(3).

17 A Samnøy, 'The Origins of the Universal Declaration of Human Rights' in G Alfredsson and A Eide (eds), *The Universal Declaration of Human Rights: A Common Standard of Achievement* (Martinus Nijhoff Publishers 1999) 3; M Sepúlveda and others, *Human Rights Reference Handbook* (4th edn, Icelandic Human Rights Centre 2009) 5; J Donnelly, *International Human Rights* (3rd edn, Westview Press 2013) 25. See also Universal Declaration of Human Rights (adopted 10 December 1948 UNGA Res 217 A(III) (UDHR).

18 A Eide and others, *The Universal Declaration of Human Right: A Commentary* (SUP 1992); H Hannum, 'The Status of the Universal Declaration of Human Rights in National and International Law' (1995-1996) 25 Georgia Journal of International and Comparative Law 287, 353; BG Ramcharan, 'The Law-Making Process: From Declaration to Treaty to Custom to Prevention' in D Shelton (ed), *The Oxford Handbook of International Human Rights Law* (OUP 2013) 508.

19 Notably, human dignity may play a significant role in the discussion on how to reconsider the 'principle of balance' in human rights norms. The substantive analysis of these issues is left to Chapter 4 in order to avoid any confusion about what the law as is regulates and how one should reflect on such an outcome from a philosophical perspective.

20 Section 3.2.2 addresses what this categorization of rights implies both formally and substantively.

21 Excerpts of substantive negotiations at the time of adoption of the UDHR demonstrate the divergent ideological and political positions of States on the different rights included in the UDHR. The United Kingdom, for instance, was in favour of adopting the UDHR as a binding treaty instead

In this context, adopting a declaration was deemed a step towards codified universal basic principles, which were to be elaborated in a treaty or covenant at a later time.[22] Consequently, in 1966, the International Covenant on Economic Social and Cultural Rights (ICESCR) and the International Covenant on Civil and Political Rights (ICCPR) were adopted to grant legal effect to the rights and freedoms secured in the Declaration.[23] The mere fact that two covenants – instead of one – were concluded, demonstrates that in the mid-sixties the international community was still unable to reach a unanimous decision regarding the status of the different categories of rights enunciated in the UDHR.[24] Providing the UDHR with legal limbs, the two 1966 covenants are, together with the UDHR, often referred to as the international bill of rights.

In addition to the international bill of rights, the international community adopted a variety of other (core) human rights instruments, focusing on obligations in relation to specific areas of human rights protection, including on racial discrimination, discrimination against women, torture and other degrading treatment, children, migrant workers, enforced disappearance, and disability.[25] Human rights protection

---

of declaration (as it is now). It, however, only wished to do so if ESC rights were not included. Moreover, the USSR was much involved in discussing the inclusion of ESC rights as opposed to the US which, like the British delegation, preferred to exclude ESC rights from a universally binding text. These different positions still influence and colour debates about human rights and their enforcement and justiciability. This is further discussed in Sections 3.2.2-3.2.3. Samnøy explains that, for the sake of adopting one document to which all parties could consent, controversial ideas were excluded from the text, provisions and formulations were drafted rather vaguely, limitation clauses were included to temper the absolute nature of human rights, and explicit references to the source or foundation of human rights was excluded. See Samnøy (n 17) 10-11, 14-18. This latter aspect will also be moderated in Chapter 4.

22 Bantekas and Oette (n 15) 20.

23 International Covenant on Economic Social and Cultural Rights (adopted 16 December 1966, entered into force 3 January 1976) 993 UNTS 3 (ICESCR); International Covenant on Civil and Political Rights (adopted 16 December 1966, entered into force 23 March 1976) 999 UNTS 171 (ICCPR).

24 B Saul, D Kinley and J Mobray (eds), *The International Covenant on Economic, Social, and Cultural Rights: Commentary, Cases, and Materials* (OUP 2014) 134-135; AEM Leijten, *Core Rights and the Protection of Socio-Economic Interests by the European Court of Human Rights* (DPhil thesis, Leiden University 2015) 186.

25 Respectively, International Convention on the Elimination of All Forms of Racial Discrimination (adopted 7 March 1966, entered into force 4 January 1969) 660 UNTS 195 (CERD); Convention on the Elimination of All Forms of Discrimination Against Women (adopted 18 December 1979, entered into force 3 September 1981) 1249 UNTS 13 (CEDAW); Convention against Torture and Other Cruel, Inhuman or Degrading Treatment or Punishment (adopted 10 December 1984, entered into force 26 June 1987) 1465 UNTS 85 (CAT); Convention on the Rights of the Child (adopted 20 November 1989, entered into force 2 September 1990) 1577 UNTS 3 (CRC); International Convention on the Protection of the Rights of All Migrant Workers and Members of their Families (adopted 18 December 1990, entered into force 1 July 2003) 2220 UNTS 3 (ICRMW); International

has, moreover, also been advanced regionally. At the European, African, and Inter-American level, instruments have been adopted which significantly contribute to the realization and protection of human rights in the aforementioned contexts.[26] To different degrees, these instruments may be relevant in order to understand the access to controlled medicines and other aspects of drug control in human rights law. Human rights are, furthermore, also protected in domestic legal systems in their own distinct ways. Domestic clauses are, however, not analysed in this chapter.

Although human rights instruments, including treaties and covenants, are the primary source of human rights law, they are not its only source.[27] It is commonly asserted that at least some of the rights the UDHR sets out have obtained the status of customary international law.[28] The lack of an exclusive and authoritative view regarding which rights would, or would not, be lifted to this status of international law, however, makes the argument subject to dispute.[29] Of some, certainly not all, human rights it is also argued that these are peremptory norms of international law – *jus cogens*.[30]

Convention for the Protection of All Persons from Enforced Disappearance (adopted 20 December 2006, entered into force 23 December 2010) 2716 UNTS 3; Convention on the Rights of Persons with Disabilities (adopted 13 December 2006, entered into force 3 May 2008) 2515 UNTS 3 (CRPD).

26 European Convention for the Protection of Human Rights and Fundamental Freedoms (adopted 4 November 1950, entered into force 3 September 1953, as amended) 213 UNTS 222 (ECHR); Charter of Fundamental Rights of the European Union [2000] OJ C364/1 (as amended); Revised European Social Charter (adopted 3 May 1996, entered into force 1 July 1999) ETS 163 (RESC); African Charter on Human and Peoples' Rights (adopted 27 June 1981, entered into force 21 October 1986) 1520 UNTS 217 (ACHPR); American Convention on Human Rights (adopted 22 November 1969, entered into force 18 July 1978) 1144 UNTS 123 (ACHR); Sepúlveda and others (n 17) 6. The Asian and Arab region have not adopted a similar human rights instrument at the regional level, only a declaration proclaiming human rights. On human rights protection in Asia and the Arab world, see respectively Y Ghai, 'Understanding Human Rights in Asia' in C Krause and M Scheinin (eds), *International Protection of Human Rights: A Textbook* (Institute for Human Rights Åbo Akademi University 2009) 547; M Rishmawi, 'The Revised Arab Charter on Human Rights' in C Krause and M Scheinin (eds), *International Protection of Human Rights: A Textbook* (Institute for Human Rights Åbo Akademi University 2009) 529.

27 The sources of international law and human rights law alike are listed in Article 38 of the ICJ Statute. On the source of international human rights law, see also C Chinkin, 'Sources' in D Moeckli, S Shah and S Sivakumaran (eds), *International Human Rights Law* (2nd edn, OUP 2014) 81.

28 See O de Schutter, 'The Status of Human Rights in International Law' in C Krause and M Scheinin (eds), *International Protection of Human Rights: A Textbook* (Institute for Human Rights Åbo Akademi University 2009) 41; Sepúlveda and others (n 17) 22.

29 See Hannum (n 18) 340; Sepúlveda and others (n 17) 22. Customary international law is comprised of evidenced state practices that are believed to be required by law. Two issues usually emerge: proving a 'virtually uniform and consistent State practice' and demonstrating that this practice constitutes *opinio juris* – the belief that such practice is 'required by law (...) rather than (...) some other reason such as diplomatic nicety or etiquette'. See Chinkin (n 27) 81-82.

30 As mentioned in Chapter 2, peremptory norms of international law are those norms regarding which the international community has accepted no derogation to be permissible. See eg de Schutter (n 28) 47-50; Chinkin (n 27) 84-85.

Although this is an interesting debate, the details of the status of rights are only subjected to a cursory discussion when relevant (in Sections 3.4 and 3.5).

3.2.2 Categories of rights

As indicated above and evident in most human rights instruments, human rights are traditionally divided into two categories: CP rights and ESC rights. To understand the manner in which human rights relate to one another, it is important to provide some insight into the current discussions on the categorization of rights. Although rather general in nature, such insight is valuable when attempting to understand the manner in which access to medicines and protection against hazardous use are related in human rights law.

Apart from a CP/ESC distinction, some scholars distinguish between classic and social rights, in which the former correspond to negative obligations and the latter require state action.[31] Others, in turn, differentiate between fundamental and basic rights. Appealing to a certain core or essence, and as such fundamental rights, is often a response to the concern that the proliferation of human rights protection would be detrimental to their significance.[32] There are, moreover, also scholars and legal traditions in which human rights are understood as freedoms, civil liberties, or generations of rights.[33] The latter interpretation builds on the traditional distinction between CP and ESC rights.

The generational distinction of rights (i.e. first, second, and third) implies viewing CP rights (first generation) as claims to necessary freedoms and ESC rights (second generation) as relating to equality. Third-generation rights, transcending the traditional dichotomy of CP and ESC rights, represent collective claims or group rights that have only been marginally accepted or received formal recognition. However, thus far only the right to development has received formal recognition as a so-called third-generation or collective right at the international level.[34] Regardless of how one frames the different categories of rights, dividing human rights into the ICESCR and the ICCPR 'has left its mark on the human rights discourse and sometimes overshadowed the fact that human rights cannot be neatly divided into two (or three) categories'.[35] Either way, any classification of rights 'correspond[s] more to conceptual premises

31 Sepúlveda and others (n 17) 7.

32 ibid 11. For an introduction on core rights as a classification of human rights, see also T van Boven, 'Categories of Rights' in D Moeckli, S Shah and S Sivakumaran (eds), *International Human Rights Law* (2nd edn, OUP 2014) 150-152.

33 Sepúlveda and others (n 17) 12-13.

34 ibid 13. See also Van Boven (n 32) 147.

35 Scheinin (n 2) 23.

than to realities'.[36] Any of these fairly strict classifications is therefore increasingly out of place,[37] especially in light of the modern common understanding that both positive and negative obligations are relevant to any human right and not limited to either CP or ESC rights.

3.2.3 Typology of obligations

The classic distinction between CP/ESC rights and negative/positive obligations is fuelled by divergent political and ideological stances on the role of the State in providing socio-economic goods and services.[38] Moving away from this rather strict distinction, state obligations are increasingly referred to and understood in a tripartite structure: to respect, protect, and fulfil *all* human rights and, thus, transcend the traditional dichotomy of CP and ESC rights. Similar to getting a grasp of the categorization of rights, understanding the typology of obligations helps frame the manner in which access to medicines and the prevention of dispersion should eventually be balanced, if at all, in human rights law.

The three types of obligations – to respect, protect, and fulfil – essentially operate on a scale with, on the one end, refraining from interference and, on the other, positive action.[39] The obligation to respect is the most negative in nature, demanding States to refrain from action in order to ensure the effective enjoyment of a right.[40] The obligation to protect is situated in the middle of the spectrum and includes both positive and negative elements. Concretely, protecting a right means that States have

36 Van Boven (n 32) 143.

37 Scheinin recognizes that it is difficult to classify some human rights in such fixed interpretation. Moreover, other than the ICESCR and the ICCPR, many other core human rights instruments – both international and regional – do not distinguish between CP or ESC rights claims but include references to human rights that contain both aspects. Scheinin (n 2) 23.

38 In human rights *law*, negative obligations are generally understood as requiring States to refrain from taking action – ie an obligation of non-interference. As opposed to negative obligations, positive obligations are understood as obligations that require States to take active steps to achieve the full realization and enjoyment of a specific right. On positive and negative obligations, see also Bantekas and Oette (n 15) 76-77. Human rights *law* is emphasized in the context of positive and negative obligations because the scope and definition provided here is strictly legal in nature. With Chapter 4 in mind, it is important to observe that positive and negative obligations may be understood differently in philosophical literature. Compare with text at n 21 on the political and ideological background of the framing of CP and ESC rights.

39 IE Koch, 'Dichotomies, Trichotomies, or Waves of Duties?' (2005) 5 Human Rights Law Review 81, 82.

40 id. For instance, a negative obligation flowing from the civil right to life implies that a State simply refrains from arbitrarily taking someone's life. It is not submitted here, however, that the right to life only includes negative elements. In fact, the opposite is argued: that the realization of all rights includes both positive and negative obligations. The example used here only helps illustrate the spectrum of respect, protect, and fulfil.

to ensure individuals are protected from interference with their right by, for instance, third parties.[41] The obligation to fulfil resides on the far positive side of the spectrum and requires the adoption of legislation and effective judicial systems, as well as the allocation of adequate resources and state planning for the full realization of a right.[42]

Different UN treaty bodies rely on the tripartite classification to interpret the scope and content of obligations relating to a certain right. When doing so, these treaty bodies often also rely on a mix of concepts, including the dichotomies of positive/negative obligations, and obligations of conduct and result.[43] The tripartite categorization of obligations does not entail any order of priority. In reality, however, respecting, protecting, and fulfilling human rights can be understood as a concept with fluid boundaries, applicable to all rights. One simply cannot theoretically link a specific right to a specific type of obligation. As Koch submits, 'some [situations] are so complex that they require efforts that fall within all three levels: respect, protection and fulfilment'.[44] In other words, despite its status as a CP or ESC right, the realization of any right demands a State to both take focused action as well as to refrain from interference. Yet, regardless of any classification or genealogy of rights and subsequent typology of obligations, human rights are generally understood as being equal in nature.

3.2.4 Universal and interdependent nature

Human rights are universal, making them applicable to all human beings under all circumstances.[45] They are interdependent which means a specific human right, or its

41 id. Taking the right to life as an example again, the obligation to protect moves towards a more positive-oriented obligation in relation to this right. In addition to the obligation on States not to arbitrarily kill a person, States also have to protect individuals against others who (might) violate their right to life. Protecting against third-party interference presupposes a more active and plan-oriented State, as well as the allocation of substantial resources to organize and pay for such protection (eg by having a police force).

42 id. For instance, the right to freedom of speech includes a right to protest. However, if you want to exercise your right to free speech and protest a controversial topic, the State may not just have an obligation not to interfere and ensure others do not either, but also has an obligation to implement a certain organizational structure, which is positive in nature, to enable you to exercise your right.

43 See CESCR, 'General Comment No 3: The Nature of States' Parties Obligations (Art. 2, Para. 1 of the Covenant)' adopted at the Fifth Session (14 December 1990) UN Doc E/1991/23; Scheinin (n 2) 26.

44 Koch (n 39) 92.

45 Universalism is often challenged from the perspective of cultural relativism. Cultural relativism entails the idea that 'some or all beliefs, values, norms and practices are not universally valid, but valid only for some cultures', see M Freeman, 'Universalism of Human Rights and Cultural Relativism' in S Sheeran and N Rodley (eds), *Routledge Handbook of International Human Rights Law* (Routledge 2013) 51. Traditionally, the discussion mainly focuses on whether a universalist approach to human rights is sensitive or open to cultural aspects that are by their very nature contextual. A more modern interpretation of this old discussion holds that it is commonly accepted,

exercise or enjoyment, may be invalid in absence of another human right. Moreover, human rights are equal by nature, meaning that Signatory or State Parties to a treaty have obligations to respect, protect, and fulfil all human rights equally.[46]

The universality of and equality in and amongst human rights is firmly embedded in the preamble of the UN Charter. Moreover, Article 1 of the UDHR dictates that '[a]ll human beings are born free and equal in dignity and rights'.[47] Being born in equal dignity and with identical rights clearly refers to the equality people share in being the rights holders of human rights. Such rights-holder equality, moreover, says something about the way in which human rights relate to one another and the obligations of States to respect these rights. As mentioned earlier, this interdependence of human rights and their non-hierarchical nature essentially implies that States have obligations to protect all human rights equally. At the 1993 World Conference on Human Rights held in Vienna, the universal, interdependent nature of human rights was once more unequivocally affirmed. Delegates, including representatives of 171 States, adopted the Vienna Declaration and Programme of Action which holds that '[a]ll human rights are universal, indivisible and interdependent and interrelated'.[48]

---

and to some extent necessary, that with due respect for the norms set out in the legal frameworks, the exact implementation is contextual. See also E Brems, 'Reconciling Universality and Diversity in International Human Rights: A Theoretical and Methodological Framework and Its Application in the Context of Islam' (2004) 3 Human Rights Review 5; SE Merry, 'Legal Transplants and Cultural Translation: Making Human Rights in the Vernacular' in M Goodale (ed), *Human Rights: An Anthropological Reader* (Blackwell 2009). This study is sympathetic to the idea that inclusion and diversity is a necessary part of universalism. Given the global nature of medicine development and curtailing drug abuse, there is a need for a global regulatory framework; law could be an adequate instrument to meet this need. Therein, the book partly distinguishes itself from the newly emerged 'Receptor Approach', which predominantly advocates using social institutions rather than laws to implement international (human rights) standards. See on the receptor approach, T Zwart, 'Using Local Culture to Further the Implementation of International Human Rights: The Receptor Approach' (2012) 34 Human Rights Quarterly 546; Y Donders and V Vleugel, 'The Receptor Approach: A New Human Rights Kid on the Block or Old Wine in New Bags?' (2014) 36 Human Rights Quarterly 654. Chapter 4 also touches on the universality of human rights norms.

46 Vienna Convention on the Law of Treaties (adopted 22 May 1969, entered into force 27 January 1980) 1155 UNTS 331 (VCLT) art 18 holds that States cannot act contrary to the object and purpose of a treaty when it has, amongst other conditions, signed the treaty. When a State signs a treaty the State consents to the object and purpose of that treaty. Signing itself does not yet demand implementation of all specific provisions the treaty sets forth, but the State may no longer breach or act contrary to its object and purpose. In its future planning, a State already has to take into account the scope and application of the treaty it signed. JE Goldschmidt and MEC Gispen, '*Aanvullend Rapport Ratficatie... En dan?*' (SIM 2012) 12. In addition, following VCLT art 19, unless the treaty under review prohibits reservations, States may adopt reservations upon ratification of a treaty, including human rights treaties, if these are not contrary to the object and purpose of the treaty. The permissibility of reservations is not discussed further.

47 UDHR, art 1.

48 'Vienna Declaration and Programme of Action' UN World Conference on Human Rights (Vienna,

Human rights belong to everyone, without any discrimination, at every time, regardless of any formal recognition, and all human rights are equally important.[49]

The idea that human rights are interdependent and non-hierarchical in nature transcends the dichotomy or trichotomy of rights, or any of their classifications. For what would be the point of having a right to vote – thinking in classifications of rights: a CP or first-generation right – if you are ill and bedridden due to a lack of access to health services? Your right to vote could help you claim access to health services by voting for the political party that supports strengthening the health system. However, the current lack thereof is keeping you from physically going to the polling station to cast your vote and claim your right to access health services – an ESC or second-generation right.

Given the fact that human rights protection is theoretically equal in nature, regardless of the question under which right access to medicines and aspects of drug-control regulation falls, one can conclude that, in principle, States have obligations towards the protection of all human rights and thus towards any aspect of drug-control regulation equally. Notably, these obligations can be positive and negative in relation to any right at stake. States, in other words, have obligations to address all aspects of drug control, if falling within the substantive scope of a specific human right, equally.

Despite this theoretically equal nature, human rights might require priority-setting or balancing given that States are often faced with limited budgets and are constrained in their abilities when discharging their obligations. Moreover, different rights claims might compete with each other in their effective enjoyment. Such claims include clashes that may be horizontal (individual-individual/non-State actor) and vertical (individual-State, concerning the protection of societal concerns such as public order, safety, and health). It is impossible to foresee all manifest or non-manifest conflicts in the enjoyment of specific human rights or in the enjoyment of a specific human right and the interest of society. In fact, it happens regularly that practice demonstrates that different individual-individual and individual-societal interests are in competition. Human rights law provides a framework to determine in which cases

---

14-25 June 1993) (25 June 1993) UN Doc A/CONF.157/23 (VDPA) para 5. According to Jensen, the 1994 World Conference was held due to the significant political changes that occurred prior to the conference. Its purpose was 'to lay new foundations for international human rights protection in the post-Cold War'. SLB Jensen, *The Making of International Human Rights: The 1960s, Decolonization, and the Reconstruction of Global Values* (CUP 2016) 1. Although international human rights law is often much contested from a third-world perspective, it is important to signal that the universal and interrelated nature of human rights was reaffirmed at a truly global event organized to reconsider and shape international human rights.

49 See also OHCHR, 'World Conference on Human Rights' <www.ohchr.org/EN/ABOUTUS/ Pages/ ViennaWC.aspx> accessed 31 August 2016.

a State is allowed to or obliged to prioritize aspects of its obligations over others, the legitimacy of any interference with human rights, and the balancing between these interferences and rights in general. As mentioned in the introduction to this chapter, the question is whether one may legitimately prioritize in operationalizing *specific* human rights, and/or legitimately limit and thus balance between *different* human rights and legitimate interferences. Ultimately, as also submitted in Chapter 2, any limitation of a human right is only legitimate if justified in human rights norms itself.

3.3 Implementation and enforcement of human rights

This section deals with the implementation and enforcement of human rights to ensure their effective enjoyment. The section starts with an analysis of priority-setting within the realization of *a specific right*. In doing so, it introduces the concepts 'immediate and progressive realization' and 'minimum core rights protection'. Then, an exploration relating to the legitimacy of limitations of rights to balance the protection of *different rights or interests* will follow. In terms of limitations of rights, this section turns to the status of rights and their obligations, referring to absolute and relative rights, and to the use of limitation clauses. Finally, aspects of monitoring and accountability are addressed.

Although no substantive question about access to medicines and aspects of drug control has been tackled yet, this section delves into the criteria that exist in human rights law to legitimately prioritize a right, or element thereof, over another. In other words, it explores important indicators for the way in which human rights law recognizes balancing and weighing of different rights and their aspects. Notably, human dignity may be a yardstick in rights enforcement. As the fundamental principle of human rights law, it cannot be equated with others and thus acts as a source, informing the interpretation of human rights norms in its widest sense. As mentioned in the introduction, the discussion of human dignity in relation to access to medicines and drug control specifically is left until Chapter 4.

3.3.1 Immediate and progressive realization

Although theoretically understood as equal in nature and listed in the UDHR with similar importance, practice demonstrates that the realization of, in particular, ESC rights is complex.[50] However, one must note, that the adoption of the ICESCR Optional Protocol can be seen as an important indicator for the recognition of ESC

50 Leijten (n 24) 186. The philosopher Charles Beitz notes that 'it is not even clear how we should conceive of "enforcement" in relation to some of the requirements of human rights doctrine', see CR Beitz, *The Idea of Human Rights* (OUP 2009) 3.

rights as 'important international norms with significant practical application'.[51] Yet, many governments still allocate more attention to the adjudication, realization, and enforcement of CP rights. The latter, in part, due to their political opinion(s) on the status of ESC rights and due to the disparate *urgency of realization* that the obligations of both CP and ESC rights are assigned.[52] Urgency of realization, although an uncommon term in human rights scholarship and practice, refers to the grading approach human rights law maintains in guiding States in their efforts to implement and enforce specific human rights.[53]

The state obligations grounded in CP rights are all conceptualized in absolute terminology. States, moreover, have to discharge these obligations immediately. Many of the individual rights clauses of the ICCPR, in one way or another, include phrases such as 'no one shall be' or 'everyone has the right to' and 'all persons shall be or have'. ESC rights included in the ICESCR, on the other hand, are phrased more ambiguously and instead start with 'the State Parties to the Covenant recognize'. Indeed, whereas the ICCPR frames rights as individual rights, the ICESCR elaborates on the responsibilities of States towards the recognition of certain rights.[54] Article 2 ICCPR sets out that States have to 'adopt laws or other measures as may be necessary to give effect to the rights recognized in the present Covenant'.[55] In General Comment 31, the Human Rights Committee (HR Committee), the monitoring body of the ICCPR, interprets this general obligation to imply that States have to discharge their obligations immediately.[56] In other words, at the moment of ratification of the ICCPR, States have to realize all the rights recognized by the covenant. In line with the typology of obligations set out in Section 3.2.3, realizing CP rights includes both negative and positive elements and obligations to respect, protect, and fulfil human

---

51 Saul, Kinley and Mobray (n 24) 3.

52 ibid 3, 134; B Klein Goldewijk and B de Gaay Fortman, *Where Needs Meet Rights* (WCC Publications 1999) ix-x. Saul, Kinley and Mobray (n 24) elaborate that 'the different trajectory of each category of rights [ie CP and ESC rights] was set by the splintering of human rights into the two separate covenants of 1966'. CP rights 'were largely seen as immediately applicable and typically justiciable, whereas [ESC rights] were viewed as subject only to progressive realization through measures of State policy'. See also text at n 21.

53 From a philosophical perspective, Beitz (n 50) 142 similarly refers to the 'different degrees of urgency' of rights protection and acknowledges that claims may be weighed differently. This is discussed in Chapter 4.

54 See eg ICCPR, art 6 which states that '[e]very human being has the inherent right to life'; ICESCR, art 12 reads: '[t]he States Parties to the present Covenant recognize the right of everyone to the enjoyment of the highest attainable standard of physical and mental health.' See also Leijten (n 24) 186-187.

55 ICCPR, art 2.

56 HR Committee, 'General Comment No 31: The Nature of the General Legal Obligation Imposed on States Parties to the Covenant' adopted at the Eightieth Session (29 March 2004) UN Doc CCPR/C/21/Rev.1/Add.13, para 5-6. See also Scheinin (n 2) 28.

rights regardless of their traditional classification. Even though Scheinin observes that the realization of CP rights in practice mainly relates to their promotion and protection, it is submitted here that indeed *all* human rights are subject to the tripartite obligations and the realization of any right always includes both positive and negative elements.[57]

In contrast, Article 2 ICESCR enshrines that State Parties should take steps with the maximum of resources available 'to achiev[e] progressively the full realization of the rights recognized in the present Covenant'. In other words, States have obligations towards the realization of ESC rights, which are progressive instead of immediate in nature. Moreover, this vastly different requirement means that the extent to which ESC rights are realized may differ significantly per country, as it is dependent entirely on the amount of resources available and allocable.[58]

Furthermore, States to some extent are free to choose their preferred means of rights implementation.[59] Yet, in the context of socioeconomic rights, the Committee on Economic, Social and Cultural Rights (CESCR), the monitoring body of the ICESCR, requires any step towards full realization to be targeted and time-bound.[60] This means that progressive realization should not be understood as an open-ended obligation.[61] The provision of socio-economic goods, especially those that go hand-in-hand with serious resource demands, is complex. In the context of day-to-day realities, and looking at the aspired level of full realization of any ESC right, it seems only rational to allow for certain priority-setting to discharge obligations of progressive realization. As a result, although ESC rights do not have to be realized overnight, a (pre)defined time plan in which they clearly differ from CP rights is required.[62] Although in itself an acknowledgment of the fact that for many countries full realization of ESC rights would simply be impossible, any retrogressive measures are prohibited within this requirement.[63] Essentially, the CESCR submits that the concept of progressive realization is:

57 id.

58 Leijten (n 24) 187. For a comment on the duality of progressive realization, see CESCR, 'GC No 3' (n 43) para 9.

59 N Ando, 'National Implementation and Interpretation' in D Shelton (ed), *The Oxford Handbook of International Human Rights Law* (OUP 2013) 709.

60 CESCR, 'GC No 3' (n 43) para 2.

61 E Riedel, 'Economic, Social, and Cultural Rights' in C Krause and M Scheinin (eds), *International Protection of Human Rights: A Textbook* (Institute for Human Rights Åbo Akademi University 2009) 137.

62 CESCR, 'GC No 3' (n 43) para 9.

63 id; Leijten (n 24) 188.

> (…) on the one hand a necessary flexibility device, reflecting the realities of the real world and the difficulties involved for any country in ensuring full realization of economic, social and cultural rights. On the other hand, the phrase must be read in the light of the overall objective, indeed the *raison d'être*, of the Covenant which is to establish clear obligations for States parties in respect of the full realization of the rights in question.[64]

It therefore lies at the very heart of the concept of progressive realization that States also have to protect a certain minimum core.

3.3.2 Minimum core rights protection

The notion of minimum core rights protection or 'minimum cores' reflects an attempt to establish a legal content for, in particular, economic and social rights.[65] The minimum core approach helps to structure issues in terms of priority-setting for the realization of ESC rights, which is necessary in light of resource constraints.[66] Drawing on its experience in examining state compliance with the ICESCR, the CESCR 'is of the view that a minimum core obligation to ensure the satisfaction of, at the very least, minimum essential levels of each of the rights [recognized by the ICESCR] is incumbent upon every State party'.[67] Such minimum core rights protection safeguards the *raison d'être* (very essence) of the ICESCR. These core obligations are implicitly considered obligations of immediate effect and should at least be prioritized when discharging ESC rights obligations.[68] One could say that each State not observing its core obligations *prima facie* fails to effectively discharge its obligations based on the ICESCR.

In circumstances in which a State fails to realize core obligations effectively and attributes such failing to a lack of available resources, a State has to demonstrate that it made every effort to prioritize the minimum core obligations and has indeed allocated all available resources to attempt to satisfy these obligations.[69] Nevertheless, even if the insufficiency of resources is successfully demonstrated, any State Party to the ICESCR still has the obligation to ensure the 'widest possible enjoyment of the relevant rights under the prevailing circumstances'.[70]

---

64 CESCR, 'GC No 3' (n 43) para 9.

65 Young understands the minimum core concept as an attempt to address 'notoriously indeterminate claims' which are socio-economic in nature. KG Young, 'The Minimum Core of Economic and Social Rights: A Concept in Search of Content' (2008) 33 The Yale Journal of International Law 113, 113.

66 D Bilchitz, 'Socio-Economic Rights, Economic Crisis, and Legal Doctrine' (2014) 12 International Journal of Constitutional Law 710, 712.

67 CESCR, 'GC No 3' (n 43) para 10.

68 ibid para 1.

69 ibid para 10.

70 ibid para 11.

The Maastricht Guidelines on Violations of Economic, Social, and Cultural Rights underpin the immediate status of core obligations. In line with these guidelines, a violation of an ESC right through an act of omission includes 'the failure to implement without delay a right which it is required by the Covenant to provide immediately'.[71] Only core rights are discussed in light of having certain priority over other elements of rights. This means that the CESCR states that the ICESCR invokes some instant obligations as opposed to the more general concept of progressive realization. One could therefore hold that, in content, core obligations are of priority and, thus, of immediate effect as opposed to subject to progressive realization.[72]

The most contentious question in the protection of minimum core rights concerns who decides what exactly constitutes the core of a right and what does not.[73] Such concern is particularly relevant when minimum core rights protection is used as a criterion to determine the permissibility of infringements upon rights.[74] In this context, core rights protection is therefore also an important aspect to understand the legitimacy of balancing *between different rights*.

An analysis of the different ways in which minimum cores have emerged in the CESCR's General Comments demonstrates a certain overlap. The CESCR might consider one aspect to be part of the core of the right to health, whilst also explicitly mentioning it as a core obligation under another ESC right. For instance, access to food and mitigation of hunger are both aspects of the right to health, on the one hand, and the right to food, on the other.[75] One can trace such overlap back to the underlying determinants of health. However, as Leijten importantly observes, such overlap is also present in the core rights of the ICESCR more generally.[76] Leijten distinguishes five subcategories in the minimum cores concept:

1) Non-discrimination;
2) Disadvantaged and marginalized individuals and groups;
3) Strategic;
4) Procedural;
5) Subsistence minimum.[77]

---

71 Maastricht Guidelines on Violations of Economic, Social and Cultural Rights (26 January 1977) guideline 15(h).
72 See also Leijten (n 24) 190-192.
73 Young (n 65) 115. It goes beyond the scope of this research to enter into an extensive discussion on this matter.
74 ibid 116.
75 Leijten (n 24) 210.
76 id.
77 ibid 210-212.

Regardless of the aspect of ESC rights protection, both non-discrimination and the protection of vulnerable and marginalized groups are of central importance. Leijten distinguishes strategic cores as being requirements to implement, embed, and monitor the full realization of a right – e.g. through the adoption of strategy or action plans. Procedural cores are requirements of essential importance in relation to, for example, forced evictions. Much like the strategic requirements, procedural requirements provide for the means, the structure, or the framework needed to result in the equitable realization of ESC rights.[78] Finally, subsistence minimum obligations are material in nature and, in one way or another, essentially a basic need.[79] Leijten also rightly states that either obligations of conduct and result, positive and negative obligations, or the tripartite obligation – to respect, protect, and fulfil human rights – could apply to any aspect of priority (and therefore core) and progressive realization (and therefore a more peripheral aspect of an ESC right).[80]

The status of the obligations, as based on a particular right, informs the standing of such obligation in States' efforts to ensure the effective realization of the right in general. This in itself can be understood as the normative value a consideration or value should be assigned corresponding to the status it generates in legal doctrine.[81] This status, whether progressive or priority, guides and determines the legitimacy, if any, of prioritizing one element of a right over another during the realization of a *specific* right. Here, it is irrelevant whether core aspects are general, strategic, procedural, or basic in light of Leijten's categorization. As Leijten demonstrated, one should understand the core elements in these subcategories to gain a better understanding of their meaning and scope. However, the CESCR adopted a different approach. It includes various well-reasoned lists of core obligations based on which it assigns priority status to rights (and their elements), guiding States in the implementation and realization of ESC rights in particular. The question, then, is what this framework of priority-setting, as developed in the context of the right to health specifically, adds to the debate when situating and reconsidering the 'principle of balance' in human rights law (see Section 3.4).

3.3.3 Limitations of rights

Alongside any priority-related aspect in discharging human rights obligations, human rights law also elaborates the limitations of rights. Despite *a priori* being equal in nature, some rights may be legitimately limited and others may not.

---

78 ibid 212.
79 id.
80 ibid 210.
81 This resembles the second step in the act of balancing, as mentioned in the introductory section of this chapter. See Porat (n 7) 1399.

Such permissibility of limitations becomes particularly important when balancing competing rights claims.[82] Whether or not to allow or prohibit any limitation of a right is mainly determined by the status of the rights involved.

According to Scheinin, law can be divided into rules and principles. Any legal norm is, moreover, either a rule or a principle. Rules should be – and are – applied 'in an all-or-nothing fashion', meaning that when a situation 'falls within the scope of application of a rule, the rule determines the outcome of the case' without any further consideration.[83] Principles, in contrast, 'are characterized by a dimension of weight and are applied through a process of weighing and balancing that takes into account also competing principles and optimizes the realization of all of them'.[84] In other words, settling any conflict between rules demands one to scrutinize the scope of the application of the rules involved. Settling conflicts between competing principles, on the other hand, demands one to balance and weigh the different interests the principles present. This distinction in the nature of a legal norm can also be applied to human rights norms.[85]

In human rights law, one would commonly consider rules to be absolute rights and principles to equate with relative rights. Generally speaking, one could classify rights as relative, with only a very limited group labelled as absolute.[86] Gerards asserts that the permissibility of limitations and therefore also the balancing of these rights has gradually been determined based on this status:

I. Absolute rights, no interference is justified;
II. Absolute, not *notstandfeste* (non-derogable) rights, rights that may be legitimately restricted in times of war;
III. Relative rights with a specific limitation clause;

---

82 While Dworkin's work on balancing individual rights with the interests of society is also very relevant to the discussion on balancing in human rights, this falls outside the scope of this study. As mentioned, Chapter 3 is largely doctrinal in nature. The normative analysis of Chapter 4 is framed on the foundations of human rights law and not necessarily only related to balancing between different interests as such.

83 Scheinin (n 2) 32.

84 id. Notably, operating on the assumptions of modern human rights law, human dignity as a central human rights principle can never act as a mediating principle, but is instead a foundational principle; a normative source of the principles as set out here. Chapter 4 will expand on human dignity in its foundational role and will also demonstrate why human dignity is a different type of principle in the context of the logic of modern human rights law.

85 Bearing in mind the way in which human rights *law* regulates the juxtaposition of drug control, it is important to observe that rules and principles are explained differently in philosophical terms. In philosophy, principles are usually understood as being much more fundamental than rules. See also Chapter 4.

86 Scheinin (n 2) 31.

IV. Relative rights with a general limitation clause;
V. Relative rights with an implicit limitation clause;
VI. Other rights.[87]

Absolute rights without any permissible limitation include non-derogable rights such as the freedom from torture and CIDT, and the freedom from slavery. The application of these rights does not leave room for balancing but rather 'call[s] the interpreter to concentrate on defining' its scope of application instead.[88] In contrast, any limitations to rights in any of the other aforementioned categories should be balanced by means of a proportionality test. In State-individual relationships, such a proportionality test implies weighing a pressing social need (the interest of society to limit the right) against the individual interest of executing and thus safeguarding a right. This means that central to this balancing exercise is the cost-benefit analysis of pursuing the goal in light of the individual interest. Concretely, this question generally relates to reconciling societal interests with individual rights protection.[89] The proportionality test is, for that purpose, a valuable tool with which to substantiate and guide public policy decision-making.

Gerards distinguishes several key and subsidiary standards relevant to the determination of the legitimacy of interference, including the legality, necessity, subsidiarity, and proportionality of any limitation of a right.[90] The status of a right thus informs the standing of a *specific* right in relation to other rights and/or a pressing social need reflecting the interest of society. Such a status, and the legal codification thereof, also impacts the legitimacy, if any, of interfering with a *specific* right and *ipso facto* the balancing *between* different rights. The latter is, in particular, determined by the presence – or absence – of a limitation clause and the specific basis this clause creates on which to interfere with or limit the right in question. The absolutism and relativism of rights shapes the notion of balancing in human rights law. Although a valuable and much-needed exercise, drawing on comparative discussions in constitutional law, balancing is also questioned. Bomhoff, for instance, states that balancing 'can be both an admission of the limitations of formal legal analysis and an attempt to stretch formal legal reasoning as far as it might go'.[91] Acknowledging

87 Gerards elaborates on these rights on the basis of the work of the ECtHR in particular. Nevertheless, the overview is still also instructive to the understanding of a framework of the permissibility of limitations of rights in general. JH Gerards, *EVRM-Algemene Beginselen* (SDU Uitgevers 2011) 103 (translated by author).
88 Scheinin (n 2) 32.
89 In relation to the right to health and potential inner-health protection conflicts that exist, see Saul, Kinley and Mobray (n 24) 981-984.
90 Gerards (n 87) 97.
91 J Bomhoff, *Balancing Constitutional Rights: The Origins and Meanings of Postwar Legal Discourse* (CUP 2013) 8.

this criticism, the dominant approach in human rights law is applied, including the various differentiations of balancing addressed in this section.

However, before doing so, it is important to briefly move away from the discussion on balancing and address the more general aspects of monitoring and accountability, which are crucial for the translation from theory into practice – and bring human rights 'home'.[92]

3.3.4 Monitoring and accountability

In order for human rights to be effective in demanding state action or non-interference, rights should be enforceable (i.e. anchored in legislation which can be executed) and justiciable (i.e. litigable in Court). The rights holder should, moreover, be able to hold a duty bearer accountable in order to safeguard this effectiveness.[93] There is little point in having a right if there is no manner in which to claim it. In fact, as Potts indicates, 'concrete cases of individuals and groups seeking government accountability show that the real challenge is to convert this legal commitment into specific measures of implementation'.[94]

Accountability mechanisms can be manifold, traditionally including courts and tribunals, and currently being increasingly extended to include mandates of Special Rapporteurs and UN treaty bodies.[95] Varying per right, at the heart of the accountability process, the range of mechanisms available continues to expand to encompass not only naming and shaming, but also transparency alongside legal sanctions (so too for the right to health).[96] In the context of ESC-rights protection more generally, common

---

92 'Bringing human rights home' is a term often used in human rights scholarship. The term refers to bridging theory and practice, and implies that it is important to focus on the actual realization and monitoring of human rights in order to ensure that those who are deprived of them are given a position to enjoy their rights.

93 As Fortin sets out, the concept of accountability is to be understood as distinct from responsibility. If responsible under human rights law, a duty bearer has the obligation to provide for reparation. Accountability is generally held to be a wider notion in which not just responsibility, and thus the obligation to provide for reparation, is found, but the accountability framework also includes a State (in the traditional sense) that 'has a duty to provide an explanation for an act which is apparently contrary to international law', see Fortin (n 2) 16. Although Fortin later applies the notion of accountability to the particular position of armed groups in international law, the analysis presented provides a clear general overview of accountability as a central concept of human rights law. Any discussion on the notion of accountability necessarily also touches on discussions on the traditional dichotomous interpretation of the State and individual as respectively duty bearer and rights holder. Compare with text at n 2.

94 H Potts, *Accountability and the Right to the Highest Attainable Standard of Health* (Human Rights Centre 2008) 7.

95 See Fortin (n 2) 19.

96 Potts (n 94) 7.

mechanisms to ensure the implementation of obligations of progressive and priority realization are state reporting and international monitoring.[97] Court cases, individual complaints, and state reporting are addressed in this section.

Court cases

Court cases can be a suitable mechanism to hold governments accountable for, in particular, their commitment to core obligations of priority with immediate effect. The enforceability and justiciability of ESC rights – or lack thereof – is central to much debate. In fact, many governments do not codify ESC rights as legal *rights* at the domestic level, but as principles or political aspirations instead. Nevertheless, so-called indirect justiciability (i.e. litigating for socio-economic goods on the basis of CP rights) allows for aspects usually falling within the scope of ESC rights to be claimed through courts in legal systems in which ESC rights itself are neither considered legally enforceable nor justiciable.[98] Case law of the European Court of Human Rights (ECtHR) and the Inter-American Court of Human Rights (IACtHR) on socioeconomic matters exemplifies such a trend. Yet, even when viewing CP and ESC rights on a more equal footing in this sense, the issue is no longer whether socio-economic entitlements can be adjudicated via courts, as case law has evidenced it can – either via ESC rights or through CP rights (indirect justiciability). Rather, the issue is 'where to draw the line between judicial and legislative powers when the disputed measures are resource-demanding and their legal basis vaguely worded'.[99] Indeed, in relation to the access to medicines in particular, the Inter-American human rights system has produced insightful case law, imposing clear-cut positive obligations on States to ensure the access to healthcare (and medicines) within a reasonable distance. Vulnerable and marginalized groups of society must, in particular, be protected. These cases have, however, mainly been based on the right to life and are therefore not scrutinized further in Section 3.4.[100]

Although in line with the international bill of rights, ESC rights should (ideally) be understood as enforceable and justiciable, the question remains whether courtrooms are the best venue through which to implement ESC-rights entitlements effectively into domestic law. The impact and effectiveness of ESC-rights litigation or their

97 The impact and effectiveness of state reporting under the UN treaty bodies is also questioned. See J Krommendijk, *The Domestic Impact and Effectiveness of the Process of State Reporting under UN Human Rights Treaties in the Netherlands, New Zealand and Finland* (Intersentia 2014).

98 On the indirect protection of ESC rights, see Van Boven (n 32) 147-150.

99 Koch (n 39) 102.

100 See eg *Indigenous Community Yakye Axa v Paraguay* (Merits, Reparations, and Costs) Inter-American Court of Human Rights Series C No 125 (6 February 2006); *Sawhoyamaxa Indigenous Community of the Enxet People v Paraguay* (Merits, Reparations, and Costs) Inter-American Court of Human Rights Series C No 146 (29 March 2006); *Damião Ximenes Lopes v Brazil* (Merits, Reparations, and Costs) Inter-American Court of Human Rights Series C No 149 (4 July 2006).

judicialization have been increasingly questioned in terms of the real benefit it brings to its rights holders, especially in relation to the right to health. Would court-ordered access to socio-economic goods and services really improve their practical availability? A striking example can be found in parts of Brazil, where an overloaded health system is unable to deal with the high amount of court-ordered prescriptions of medicines.[101] Despite the fact that such strenuous court-mandated medicine provision and its practical implications bring important human rights questions to light, it falls beyond the scope of the present study to go into these matters extensively.

Individual complaints procedures and state reporting

Individual complaints procedures may be open to rights holders via the different Optional Protocols supplementing the core human rights instruments. One must note to this end the critically different ways in which CP and ESC rights are granted legal effect, if any, through these individual complaints procedures. Moreover, the Optional Protocol that includes the ICESCR-based complaints procedure has only recently entered into force, whereas that of the ICCPR's Optional Protocol has been available to individuals much longer.[102]

In addition to the individual complaints procedures, UN human rights treaty bodies are mandated to oversee the implementation of human rights treaties by means of state reporting, through which the State and the respective UN treaty body enter into a constructive dialogue.[103] In the context of the ICESCR, the CESCR is mandated to supervise and monitor whether States effectively discharge their progressive and immediate/priority obligations. In doing so, States traditionally have to submit an initial report within two years following ratification (of the ICESCR) and periodic reports every five years thereafter.[104] Yet, in light of divergent rules regarding state reporting, former UN Secretary-General Kofi Annan called for a harmonization

---

101 See OL Motta Ferraz, 'Brazil: Health Inequalities, Rights and Courts: The Social Impact of the Judicialization of Health' in AE Yamin and S Gloppen (eds), *Litigating Health Rights: Can Courts Bring More Justice to Health?* (HUP 2011) 97.

102 Optional Protocol to the International Covenant on Civil and Political Rights (adopted 16 December 1966, entered into force 23 March 1976) 999 UNTS 171; Optional Protocol to the International Covenant on Economic, Social and Cultural Rights (adopted 10 December 2008, entered into force 5 May 2013) UN Doc A/RES/63/118.

103 No country-specific reporting is addressed because the implementation of rights largely depends on a country's context, which makes such reporting unlikely to yield the information sought.

104 CESCR, 'General Comment No 1: Reporting by States Parties' adopted at the Thirteenth Session (27 July 1981) UN Doc E/1989/22, 2. The initial report should reflect the situation relating to socio-economic rights (as included in the ICESCR) starting at the date of ratification. Progress reports should reflect the level of and manner in which States work towards achieving full realization of the rights enunciated in the ICESCR. See also ESCR-Net, 'Background Information on the ICESCR' <www.escr-net.org/resources/section-5-background-information-icescr> accessed 31 August 2016.

of the state reporting procedures in 2002. Revision of these procedures led to the requirement to submit a common core document – relevant to all human rights treaty monitoring procedures – and a treaty-specific document relevant to the particular treaty under review.[105] The CESCR requires States to refer specifically to its General Comments and explicitly notes that reports may not be general in nature.[106] In other words, States have to explicitly demonstrate whether they are really devoting all available resources in a timely and constructive manner to realizing the fullest potential of a right laid down in the ICESCR.

3.3.5 Overview of findings

To summarize, human rights law provides for a clear legal framework with which competing interests or clashes may be balanced. Human rights law further demonstrates that balancing does not necessarily mean that each interest involved is lifted to a strictly or formally equal level, and attributed similar weight. In fact, balancing denotes that a balanced approach in human rights law may be one in which one interest dominates because of its 'assigned (…) value or (…) weight according to its respective importance'.[107] Moreover, having elaborated upon the most relevant legal thresholds, the key aspects to be applied integrally throughout the following sections are as follows:

1. All human rights are equal in nature. A hierarchy in discharging human rights obligations and balancing in human rights protection may be legitimate, if justifiable in human rights law itself.
2. Any priority-setting or legitimate balancing is determined by:
   a. The status of rights and obligations as being absolute or relative and the applicability, if any, of limitation clauses and the proportionality test applied;
   b. The urgency of realization (priority/immediate or progressive) of a specific human rights obligation and core rights protection.
3. Accountability mechanisms are of vital importance to ensure the effectiveness of any rights claim. Yet these are in themselves not undisputed.

---

105 OHCHR, 'Enhancing the Human Rights Treaty Body System' <www2.ohchr.org/english/bo dies/treaty/CCD.htm> accessed 31 August 2016. See also IHRI 'Report of the Inter-Committee Technical Working Group on Harmonized Guidelines on Reporting under the International Human Rights Treaties, Including Guidelines on a Common Core Document and Treaty-Specific Documents' (10 May 2006) UN Doc HRI/MC/2006/3. For a more recent overview of the working methods and reporting requirements of all UN treaty bodies, see IHRI 'Report on the Working Methods of the Human Rights Treaty Bodies Relating to the State Party Reporting Process' in 'Note by the Secretariat' (23 May 2011) UN Doc HRI/ICM/2011/4.

106 CESCR 'Guidelines on Treaty-Specific Documents to be Submitted by States Parties under Articles 16 and 17 of the International Covenant on Economic, Social, and Cultural Rights' in 'Note by the Secretary-General' (24 March 2009) UN Doc E/C.12/2008/2, para 3, annex part A.

107 Porat (n 7) 1399.

Having dealt with key characteristics of human rights norms and the framework human rights law provides to legitimately operationalize and balance human rights, it is important to move on to a more topic-specific discussion relating to the substantive claim of access to medicines (in relation to drug-control matters).

3.4 The right to health

The following section analyses the right to health in general as well as specifically applied to the access to medicines and aspects of drug control. In doing so, it deals with the concept and legal codification of the right to health, its scope and content, and their application to controlled medicines and drug control in particular. Moreover, the section deals with relevant obligations based on the right to health, criteria for their realization, priority-setting and related limitations, and to the right to health more generally.[108]

3.4.1 Concept and legal codification

Good health is crucial to an individual's well-being and is, as such, a precondition to live a dignified life.[109] In fact, 'health is a fundamental human right indispensable for the exercise of other human rights'.[110] As a normative concept, the right to health was first expressed in the 1946 WHO Constitution and has ever since been reinforced in many international and regional documents.[111] According to the WHO, 'health is a state of complete physical, mental and social well-being and not merely the absence of disease or infirmity'.[112] Taking into account biological and genetic factors, socio-

108 The section refers to hard and soft law documents, case law, and literature.

109 E Riedel, 'The Human Right to Health: Conceptual Foundations' in A Clapham and M Robinson (eds), *Realizing the Right to Health* (Rüffers & Rub 2009) 21. On the conceptual foundations of the right to health more widely, see J Tobin, *The Right to Health in International Law* (OUP 2012).

110 CESCR, 'General Comment No 14: The Right to the Highest Attainable Standard of Health (Art. 12)' adopted at the Twenty-Second Session (11 August 2000) UN Doc E/c.12/2000/4, para 1. On global health law more generally, see L Gostin, *Global Health Law* (HUP 2014).

111 BCA Toebes, *The Right to Health as a Human Right in International Law* (Intersentia 1999) 23; Riedel, 'The Human Right to Health' (n 109) 21.

112 Constitution of the World Health Organization (adopted 22 July 1946, entered into force 7 April 1948) 14 UNTS 185. The WHO's definition of health is embraced by some, yet much contested by others. Those who embrace the term find it important that the definition recognizes mental and social aspects of well-being alongside the more traditional physical aspects of health. See eg BCA Toebes, 'Schets van het Internationaal Gezondheidsrecht' Tijdschrift voor Gezondheidsrecht (*forthcoming*). Yet, others hold the term to be too wide and deem it to allow the medicalization of all aspects of well-being, which is considered harmful for current health trends. See eg B Mason Meier and AM Fox, 'Development as Health: Employing the Collective Right to Development to Achieve the Goals of the Individual Right to Health' (2008) 30 Human Rights Quarterly 259, 298; M Huber and others, 'How Should We Define Health?' (2011) The British Medical Journal 343. Tobin (n 109) also deals with this discussion.

economic preconditions, and available state resources, the right to health should not be understood as the right to be healthy but instead as a right to the highest attainable standard of health.[113]

The right to health is, moreover, an inclusive right, which signifies that its scope is extended by including the underlying determinants of health too. The CESCR sets out that the right to health does not just include fundamental aspects such as basic health services, maternal care, healthcare facilities, and adequate information, but also includes clean and safe drinking water, and adequate housing as underlying determinants. The notion of underlying determinants can be traced back to the interdependence of human rights and the preconditions needed to enjoy a right in the first place. More generally, the CESCR explicitly states that the right to health should be considered as interrelated with other human rights.[114] For what is the point of having access to basic health services if one lacks adequate housing? The lack of protection against the weather would, after all, increase one's risk of falling ill in the first place.[115]

The right to health classifies as an ESC right in human rights law and is, as inspired by the WHO Constitution, enshrined in many international, regional, and domestic treaties and laws. At the international level, the general legal codifications of the right include Articles 25 UDHR and 12 ICESCR. Other human rights instruments, although focused on their particular areas of human rights protection, also refer to the right to health.[116]

At the regional level, the most general references to the right to health are found in Article 16 of the African Convention on Human and Peoples Rights (ACHPR), Article 11 of the American Declaration on the Rights and Duties of Man, Article 10 of the Additional Protocol to the American Convention on Human Rights in the Area of Economic, Social, and Cultural Rights, Articles 11, 19, and 23 of the Revised

113 CESCR, 'GC 14' (n 110) para 9; OHCHR/WHO, *The Right to Health* (OHCHR 2008) 5; Toebes, *The Right to Health* (n 111) 16-17; Riedel, 'The Human Right to Health' (n 109) 28; Tobin (n 109) 121.

114 CESCR, 'GC 14' (n 110) para 3.

115 ibid para 4; OHCHR/WHO, *The Right to Health* (n 113) 3; Toebes, *The Right to Health* (n 111) 254-258; Sepúlveda and others (n 17) 311; M Ssenyonjo, *Economic, Social and Cultural Rights in International Law* (Hart Publishing 2009) 327-330. Tobin discusses the potential danger of viewing the right to health as an inclusive right that includes underlying determinants of health. He questions whether such approach 'inflates' the right to health, see Tobin (n 109) 130.

116 CRPD, arts 16, 24-26; CRC, arts 23-24; CEDAW, arts 12, 14; VDPA, arts 18, 31, 41; ICRMW, arts 28, 45; CERD, art 5; UNGA Res 70/175 'United Nations Standard Minimum Rules for the Treatment of Prisoners' (8 January 2016) UN Doc A/RES/70/175 (Nelson Mandela Rules) rules 24-35.

European Social Charter, and Article 35 of the Charter on the Fundamental Rights of the European Union.[117]

The right to health or access to healthcare facilities, goods, and services is also codified in many legislative acts and constitutions at the domestic level.[118] Of this extensive list of legal provisions, Article 12 ICESCR is considered one of the most important provisions enshrining the right to health.[119]

3.4.2 The scope and content of Article 12 ICESCR

Article 12 ICESCR provides that States should 'recognize the right of everyone to the enjoyment of the highest attainable standard of physical and mental health' (right to health).[120] This article provides detailed guidance concerning the steps that States have to take towards the realization of the right to health:

a. To reduce the stillbirth-rate and infant mortality and provide for the healthy development of the child;
b. To improve all aspects of environmental and industrial hygiene;
c. To prevent, treat, and control epidemics, endemics, occupational, and other diseases;
d. To create conditions in which one can assure all medical service and medical attention in the event of sickness.[121]

---

117 RESC, prmbl; Additional Protocol to the European Social Charter (adopted 5 May 1988, not yet in force) ETS 128, art 4; African Charter on the Rights and Welfare of the Child (adopted 1 July 1990, entered into force 29 November 1999) OAU Doc CAB/LEG/24.9/49, prmbl, art 14; Protocol to the African Charter on Human and Peoples' Rights on the Rights of Women in Africa (adopted 7 November 2003, entered into force 25 November 2005) OAU Doc CAB/LEG/66.6, art 14; American Declaration on the Rights and Duties of Man (adopted 2 May 1948) OAS Doc OEA/Ser.L.V/II.82 doc.6 rev.1; Additional Protocol to the American Convention on Human Rights in the Area of Economic, Social, and Cultural Rights (adopted 17 November 1988, entered into force 16 November 1999) OASTS 69.

118 See SK Perehudoff, RO Laing and HV Hogerzeil, 'Access to Essential Medicines in National Constitutions' (2010) 88 Bulletin of the World Health Organization 800. SK Perehudoff, B Toebes and HV Hogerzeil, 'Access to Essential Medicines in National Constitutions: Progress Since 2008' (2016) 18 Health and Human Rights 1.

119 Toebes, *The Right to Health* (n 111) 27. It is chosen to use Article 12 ICESCR and not Article 25 UDHR as a starting point because the first is a treaty and the latter a declaration. Other references of the right to health are stipulated in more specific human rights treaties or regional treaties and are therefore not suitable as a starting point for the argumentation.

120 The right to health is challenged as an individual right. Scholars like Mason Meier and Fox, for instance, submit that health matters transcend the level of individual rights protection and should rather be understood as a collective right. More specifically, they explore the potential of the right to development as a tool 'to ameliorate underlying determinants of ill-health through development processes that bolster public health systems'. See Mason Meier and Fox (n 112) 262.

121 ICESCR, art 12.2.

The scope and content of Article 12 and the obligations it invokes are further elaborated by the CESCR in General Comment 14.[122] In short, the CESCR interprets the direction in which States have to take the steps outlined above as to imply: (i) 'the right to maternal, child and reproductive health'; (ii) 'the right to healthy natural and workplace environments'; (iii) 'the right to prevention, treatment, and control of diseases'; and (iv) 'the right to healthcare facilities, goods, and services'.[123] It also specifically elaborates on what it considers the obligation to respect, protect, and fulfil the right to health to mean. Apart from the CESCR, the Committee on the Rights of the Child (CRC Committee), the monitoring body for the Convention of the Rights of the Child (CRC), and the African Commission on Human and Peoples' Rights (ACHPR Commission) also interpret the right to health to include the right to access healthcare facilities, goods, and services.[124]

Bearing in mind the list of controlled essential medicines and treatments (Chapter 2), any of these specifications of the right to health may be relevant in the case of controlled medicines. With due respect for the key focus of this study, arguments on the scope of access to pain-control medication and other controlled medicines are dealt with separately.

3.4.3 Access to pain-control medicines

According to the CESCR, 'the right to treatment includes the creation of a system of urgent medical care in cases of accidents, epidemics and similar health hazards, and the provision of disaster relief and humanitarian assistance in emergency situations,' including in particular HIV/AIDS.[125] Health systems in Low- and Middle-Income Countries (LMICs) are often designed to respond to acute epidemic outbreaks or other health emergencies such as HIV/AIDS. In view of the patterns of the global

122 Although not legally binding, General Comments are often regarded as highly authoritative soft-law documents, pivotal to the constructive and coherent interpretation, application, and implementation of rights, including the right to health. In fact, especially General Comment 14 is criticized for 'going far beyond what the treaty itself provides and what the States Parties believe to be the obligation they have accepted'. K Gorove, 'Shifting Norms in International Health Law' (2004) 98 American Society of International Law Proceedings 18-20, as cited in Mason Meier and Fox (n 112) 313.

123 CESCR, 'GC 14' (n 110) paras 14-17. In light of the proliferation of human rights norms, such specification should clearly not be considered as a 'new right' but rather as one of an 'existing right' applicable to a particular situation, emphasizing the gravity of the situation or instead calling for targeted and focused state action in this area.

124 CRC Committee, 'General Comment No 4: Adolescent Health and the Development in the Context of the Convention on the Rights of the Child' adopted at the Thirty-Third Session (1 July 2003) UN Doc CRC/GC/2003/4, para 39-c; ACHPR Commission, 'Pretoria Declaration on Economic, Social, and Cultural Rights in Africa' (2004) <www.achpr.org/files/instruments/pretoria-declaration/achpr_instr_decla_pretoria_esc_rights_2004_eng.pdf> accessed 31 August 2016 (Pretoria Declaration).

125 CESCR, 'GC 14' (n 110) para 16.

burden of pain, as set out in Chapter 2, palliative care and therefore also pain control are of vital importance to address the HIV/AIDS epidemic in a holistic manner.

More specifically, the ACHPR Commission stresses that States should prevent and treat HIV/AIDS and other major diseases with high mortality rates, and should adopt national mechanisms with which they can respond to both epidemic and endemic diseases.[126] The East African Community, a regional intergovernmental organization, highlighted in their HIV & Aids Prevention and Management Bill of 2012 that palliative care is intrinsic to home-based care; healthcare services should therefore include access to medicines and States should ensure equitable access to HIV/AIDS treatment in particular. These home-based programmes should be supported by a regulatory framework that ensures the respect for human rights and the availability of quality care.[127]

Increasingly, the health systems of LMICs are confronted with endemic chronic illnesses and non-communicable diseases, and are to respond to these.[128] Yet, the (potential) lack or inadequate standard of curative care in these regions in itself calls for effective palliative care, which relies heavily on the availability of pain-control medicines such as morphine and codeine.[129] Notably, following this line of reasoning, one could also claim access to diazepam to treat common symptoms in palliative care.

Moreover, the CESCR explicitly interprets access to essential medicines to be part of ensuring access to healthcare facilities, goods, and services.[130] As was also demonstrated in Chapter 2, morphine and codeine are the most common pain-control medicines (appearing on the WHO Model List of Essential Medicines). Any claim to access pain-control medicines therefore falls within the scope of Article 12.2(d) ICESCR. Pain patients, but also those in need of acute, surgical, and palliative care, classify as rights holders in such a claim.

---

126 See Pretoria Declaration, para 7; ACHPR Commission, 'Draft Principles and Guidelines on Economic, Social and Cultural Rights in the African Charter on Human and Peoples' Rights' (2011) para xix <www.achpr.org/files/instruments/economic-social-cultural/achpr_instr_guide_draft_esc_rights_eng.pdf> accessed 31 August 2016 (Draft Principles and Guidelines).

127 The East African Community HIV & Aids Prevention and Management Bill of 2012, cls 2, 5, 44. The EAC includes the Republics of Burundi, Kenya, Rwanda, Tanzania, and Uganda.

128 See WHO, *The Global Burden of Disease: 2004 Update* (WHO 2008) 50; A Cameron, *Access to Medicines in Low- and Middle- Income Countries Through the Use of Price and Availability Indicators* (DPhil thesis, Utrecht University 2013) 47.

129 See Chapter 2.

130 CESCR, 'GC 14' (n 110) para 17.

3.4.4 Access to other controlled essential medicines

Apart from pain-control medication, access to controlled medicines more generally may also fall within the scope of the right to health. First, one must note that human rights law does not distinguish between controlled or uncontrolled medicines.[131] Any claim to access *controlled* medicines, therefore, falls squarely within the ambit of access to medicines as a human right. Implicitly, one may argue that controlled medicines, as much as any other medicine, fall within the remit of the obligation to ensure access to healthcare facilities, goods, and services. Second, along the same line of reasoning, controlled medicines which are also controlled *essential* medicines also fall within the obligation of States to ensure access.[132]

Additional arguments can, moreover, be presented in relation to specific controlled essential medicines. For example, the CESCR understands the right to maternal, child, and reproductive health to include emergency obstetric care.[133] In line with the WHO Model List of Essential Medicines, ergometrine and ephedrine are necessary for an obstetric emergency.[134] Any claim to access these particular controlled medicines therefore falls within the scope of Article 12.2(a) ICESCR. In such a scenario, mothers in childbirth would classify as rights holders in the claim.

Moreover, as also outlined by the CESCR, the obligation to ensure access to healthcare facilities, goods, and services also includes the availability of rehabilitative services.[135] Rehabilitative services may include harm reduction programmes, including opioid dependence therapy.[136] Methadone and buprenorphine both appear on the WHO Model List of Essential Medicines as agonists for opioid dependence therapies. Any claim to access these particular controlled medicines would therefore fall within the scope of Article 12.2(c) ICESCR. Problematic drug users, for whom opioid dependence therapy could be a medically relevant intervention, would classify as rights holders in such claim.

Finally, diazepam and phenobarbital necessary for epilepsy treatment fall within the general claim to access healthcare facilities, goods, and services. Any claim to access

---

131 Compare with text at n 14.

132 For an overview of all controlled medicines, see Chapter 2, Section 2.4.3 (Table 2.1).

133 CESCR, 'GC 14' (n 110) para 14.

134 See Chapter 2, Section 2.4.3 (Table 2.1). See also WHO, 'Model List of Essential Medicines' (19th edn, August 2015) <www.who.int/selection_medicines/committees/expert/20/EML_2 015_ FINAL_amended_AUG2015.pdf?ua=1> accessed 31 August 2016.

135 CESCR, 'GC 14' (n 110) para 17.

136 On harm reduction and human rights, see also S Takahashi, 'Drug Control, Human Rights, and the Right to the Highest Attainable Standard of Health: By No Means Straightforward Issues' (2009) Human Rights Quarterly 748.

these particular medicines should be based on Article 12.2(d) ICESCR. In this case, epilepsy patients would be those to classify as rights holders in the claim.

3.4.5 Protection against the hazardous use of substances

As much as access to controlled medicines and in particular pain-control medicines falls within the ambit of the right to health, so does the protection against the hazardous use of substances. The juxtaposition of drug control as a tension within the protection of public health is at its minimum also a tension in view of different elements of the right to health.[137]

Similar to submitting that access to opioid-dependence therapies can be based on Article 12.2(c) ICESCR, one can also hold access to methadone and buprenorphine to fall within the scope of the obligation to ensure natural environments. The CESCR interprets Article 12.2(b) to include discouraging 'the abuse of alcohol, and the use of tobacco, drugs and other harmful substances'.[138] The question that one can raise, although empirical in nature, relates to what the most humane and effective way of discouraging or countering drug use would be, both for the sake of the drug users as well as society as a whole?[139]

Although this is not the place to make extensive value judgments about empirical studies, evidence implies that complete abstention programmes leave drug users dealing with withdrawal symptoms without any form of treatment. Such approaches, the same studies show, are generally ineffective and lead to preventable casualties and inhumane suffering.[140] Moreover, longitudinally, drug use has not decreased.[141] Harm reduction programmes, on the other hand, are designed to reduce the harm of drug use to the individual user, and to society in general, by focusing on behavioural modification.[142] In these programmes, drug users are perceived as patients rather

137 The juxtaposition of drug control as an inner-health conflict is discussed in Chapter 1.

138 CESCR, 'GC 14' (n 110) para 15.

139 Takahashi argues that 'harm reduction does nothing to address the abuse of the drugs itself; that is not its objective'. However the point is not necessarily only what the purpose of harm reduction is beyond the individual, but also what its effect in terms of public health and order are, including in relation to discouragement. Takahashi (n 136) 767.

140 D Barrett and others, 'Recalibrating the Regime: The Need for a Human Rights-Based Approach to International Drug Policy' 5 (The Beckley Foundation 2008) <www.hrw.org/legacy/pub /2008/hivaids/beckley0308.pdf> accessed 31 August 2016.

141 See P Reuter and F Trautmann (eds), *A Report on Global Illicit Drug Markets 1998-2007* (European Communities 2009) 53; Global Commission on Drug Policy, *War on Drugs* (GCDP 2011) 4.

142 See N Ezard, 'Public Health, Human Rights and the Harm Reduction Paradigm: From Risk Reduction to Vulnerability Reduction' (2001) 12 International Journal of Drug Policy 207, 207; International Harm Reduction Association, 'What is Harm Reduction?' (2009) <www.ihra.net/files/2010/05/31/IHRA_HRStatement.pdf> accessed 31 August 2016.

than criminals and are offered substitute treatment to avoid the cruelties of complete abstention. Such programmes are held to enable drug users to take part in society. Moreover, these interventions remove users' incentive to steal or display violent behaviour to obtain their daily high. This is not only beneficial to the individual but has proven effective in terms of costs and safety for society.[143] Contrary to the empirical studies demonstrating the ineffectiveness of prohibitive rehabilitative services, harm-reduction programmes, such as methadone-substitute treatment, have demonstrated to be effective in reducing drug-associated harms in both the public health and the social welfare context. As such, these measures, and therefore the accessibility of methadone and buprenorphine, could contribute to ensuring a natural (societal) environment in which drug use is, from a public health and human rights perspective, countered in a humane and effective way. Any claim to access these particular controlled medicines could accordingly fall within the scope of Article 12.2(b) ICESCR. Problematic drug users, here too, would classify as rights holders in such a claim.

In addition to reduction of harm, discouraging drug use also includes more general prevention campaigning. Moreover, in relation to recreational drug use, Van Kempen and Fedorova argue that States have a positive obligation under the ICESCR to fight the illegal drugs trade.[144]

3.4.6 Relevant obligations to respect, protect, and fulfil

States have, as indicated before, both negative and positive obligations under the right to health. In fact, the CESCR outlines what falls specifically within the scope of respecting, protecting, and fulfilling this right. The obligation to *respect* the right to health includes 'refraining from denying or limiting equal access for all persons, including prisoners or detainees, minorities, asylum seekers and illegal immigrants, to preventive, curative and palliative health services'.[145] Inasmuch, the obligation to respect also implies ensuring equal access to pain-control medicines. In relation to ensuring access to medicines in particular, the CESCR asserts that the obligation to respect implies States must abstain 'from marketing unsafe drugs [i.e. medicines in the context of this book]'.[146]

143 See DP Wilson and others, 'The Cost-Effectiveness of Harm Reduction' (2015) 26 International Journal of Drug Policy s5.

144 PHPHMC van Kempen and MI Fedorova, *Internationaal Recht en Cannabis II: Regulering van Cannabisteelt en -Handel voor Recreatief Gebruik: Positieve Mensenrechtenverplichtingen versus VN-Drugsverdragen* (Wolters Kluwer 2016) 80.

145 CESCR, 'GC 14' (n 110) para 34.

146 id.

The CESCR recognizes the obligation to *protect* to imply that States have 'to control the marketing of medical equipment and medicines by third parties'.[147] More generally, States have a duty to adopt legislation to ensure equal access to healthcare, ensure that the privatization of health services does not impede 'the availability, accessibility, acceptability and quality of health facilities, goods and services', and to make sure that health personnel is adequately skilled and trained.[148] Although not discussed in terms of the substantive elements of the right to health, especially adequate training is relevant in relation to the assumed practical controversies of pain-control medication and the myths surrounding its use (as described in Chapter 2).

Finally, the CESCR understands the obligation to *fulfil* to denote that States must 'give sufficient recognition to the right to health (...) [in] national political and legal systems'.[149] Moreover, States should ensure that a public-health infrastructure is put into place, which focuses in particular on rural areas. This means that States should also ensure adequate training for and sufficient availability of healthcare facilities and medical personnel.[150] The obligation to fulfil is generally viewed as a positive obligation to facilitate: 'enable and assist individuals and communities to enjoy the right to health'.[151] Moreover, the CESCR explicitly states that the obligation to fulfil the right to health implies implementing information campaigns on the abuse of drugs and other harmful substances.[152] While it becomes evident that States have to take active measures, the question remains, nonetheless: What determines whether States have discharged their obligations satisfactorily or, rather, what guides States in discharging their obligations in the first place? This aspect of implementation and enforcement is not necessarily relevant to the exercise of balancing, but is vital to Part 3 of the research.

3.4.7 The AAAQ standard of healthcare

The CESCR has interpreted the right to health to include four interrelated elements: all aspects of the right to health should be available, accessible, acceptable, and of quality. According to the CESCR, the 'precise application [of these elements depends] on the conditions prevailing in a particular State'.[153] Jointly these four criteria are

147 ibid para 35.
148 id.
149 id.
150 ibid para 36.
151 ibid para 37.
152 ibid para 36. Such a statement does not yet say anything about the level or type of control envisioned, see Van Kempen and Fedorova (n 144) 46.
153 CESCR, 'GC 14' (n 110) para 12.

often referred to as the Availability, Accessibility, Acceptability, and Quality (AAAQ) standard of healthcare. Table 3.1 provides an enumeration of the content per criterion.

Table 3.1 The AAAQ standard of healthcare[154]

Criterion	Summary of content
Availability	Functioning public health and healthcare facilities, goods and services, and programmes should be available. Such services should be available in sufficient quantity and address the underlying determinants of health as well. Essential medicines, as defined in the WHO Action Programme on Essential Drugs (medicines in context of the present study), are explicitly understood as part of the availability criterion.[155]
Accessibility	Healthcare facilities, goods, and services should be both physically available and economically accessible (affordable) to all segments of society on a non-discriminatory basis. Accessibility also includes information accessibility, i.e. the potential of seeking and receiving impartial and adequate information about health issues. Moreover, healthcare facilities, goods, and services should be within safe physical reach of people, in particular to those living in rural areas.[156]
Acceptability	Any medical care or health facility, good, or service, should be culturally appropriate, and respecting and observing medical ethics. Cultural sensitivity implies that there is no 'one size fits all approach' to health services and specific measures could be warranted to protect, in particular, the position of vulnerable and marginalized groups of society.[157]
Quality	Any health facility, good, or service should be of sufficient scientific quality, i.e. scientifically approved, medicines should not be past their expiration date, and medical staff has to be adequately skilled.[158]

States have to realize access to controlled medicines and to the treatments for which they are relevant in general, and access to pain-control medication and palliative care in particular with due respect for these four elements. More generally, it is clear that, both implicitly and explicitly, States equally have obligations in terms of public-health aspects of drug control and these obligations too should be realized in accordance with the AAAQ standard of healthcare. Nevertheless, as illustrated in Section 3.3, some form of prioritization may be allowed or perhaps even required during the realization of a specific right, including the right to health.

154 An adjusted version of this table was published before in MEC Gispen, 'Reconciling International Obligations and Local Realities: Provision of Pain Control Medication in Resource-Constrained Countries – Experiences from Uganda' in M Hesselman, A de Wolff and BCA Toebes (eds), *Essential Public Service Provision* (Routledge *forthcoming*).

155 CESCR, 'GC 14' (n 110) para 12(a).

156 ibid para 12(b).

157 ibid para 12(c).

158 ibid para 12(d).

3.4.8 The principle of non-discrimination

The principle of non-discrimination and the protection of vulnerable groups is in itself a core obligation, in line with Leijten's analysis.[159] Article 2.2 ICESCR mandates State Parties to the ICESCR to guarantee all rights set out in the ICESCR on a non-discriminatory basis.[160] Article 3 of the ICESCR, moreover, addresses the equality of people in the enjoyment of socio-economic rights, including the right to health.[161] Drawing on the principle of non-discrimination, effective realization of the right to health is viewed as requiring special attention to be given to the needs of some members of society, including women, children, the elderly, persons with disabilities, persons infected with HIV/AIDS, and members of ethnic minorities or otherwise marginalized groups, such as injection drug users.[162] Drug users, however, are not explicitly referred to as a vulnerable group by the CESCR.[163] In light of the empirical evidence, one could consider injection drug users as part of a vulnerable group and, therefore, advocate for enhanced protection of their rights.[164]

The CRC Committee, in addition, interprets the right to health of children in relation to HIV/AIDS treatment to embody the right to equal access to comprehensive HIV/AIDS treatment, including HIV-related medicines (and therefore implicitly also pain-control medication).[165] The Committee on the Elimination of Discrimination Against Women (CEDAW Committee) interprets the right to health in light of the ICCPR, ICESCR, the Convention on the Elimination of Racial Discrimination, and the CRC. According to the CEDAW Committee, States should, in particular in relation to HIV/AIDS, take specific measures to combat diseases among women and implement a national health plan to that end.[166] The focus on women in healthcare is reaffirmed once more by the Committee on the Protection of the Rights of All Migrant Workers and Members of their Families, the monitoring body of the convention of the same name.[167] The ACHPR Commission stresses, moreover, that access to maternal

---

159 See Section 3.3.2.

160 ICESCR, art 2.2.

161 ibid art 3.

162 CESCR, 'GC 14' (n 110) paras 18-27. On the stigmatization and marginalization of drug-users, see also J Ahern, J Stuber and S Galea, 'Stigma, Discrimination and the Health of Illicit Drug Users' (2007) 88 Drug and Alcohol Dependence 188.

163 See by omission CESCR, 'GC 3' (n 43).

164 The WHO explicitly refers to the vulnerability of injection drug users and their particular vulnerability to contract an HIV infection, see WHO, 'Health and Human Rights' (December 2015) Factsheet No 323 <www.who.int/mediacentre/factsheets/fs323/en/> accessed 31 August 2016.

165 CRC Committee, 'General Comment No 3: HIV/AIDS and the Rights of the Child' adopted at the Thirty-Second Session (17 March 2003) UN Doc CRC/GC/2003/1, para 25.

166 CEDAW Committee, 'General Comment No 24: Women and Health (Art. 12)' adopted at the Twentieth Session (1999) UN Doc A/41/45, paras 4, 5, 17, 29.

167 ICRMW Committee, 'General Comment No 1: Migrant Domestic Workers' (23 February 2011)

healthcare services should be based on the life-cycle approach to health. Likewise, the ACHPR Commission points out that humane and dignified care should be available for the elderly, and for people suffering from mental and physical disabilities.[168]

Any cluster of individuals involved in any drug-control matter, whether it is access to controlled medicines or protection against hazardous use, may belong to a vulnerable or marginalized group. Non-discrimination is therefore pivotal in the interpretation, application, implementation, and enforcement of any specific right, including the right to health. That said, at this stage it is still little more than informative for the reconstruction of the 'principle of balance' as such.

3.4.9 Priority realization

Priority realization of the access to medicines

Article 12 ICESCR shows the progressive nature of the right to health. As opposed to the immediate terminology often included in CP-rights provisions, the wording 'highest attainable standard of physical and mental health', as well as the wording 'steps to be taken by the States Parties (…) to achieve full realization', indicates that the implementation of the right to health is a gradual process.[169] By no means does this progressive nature imply that obligations based on the right to health are elastic or open-ended – which can hardly be measured or monitored. As explained in Section 3.3.1, progressive realization rather implies that time-bound and targeted steps towards full realization of a given right must be taken.

In light of minimum core rights protection, the CESCR presents an explicit list of core obligations that should be prioritized over other aspects during the realization of the right to health. The CESCR specifically interprets the right to health also to invoke obligations of international assistance:

> For the avoidance of any doubt, the [CESCR] Committee [emphasizes] that it is particularly incumbent on States parties and other actors in a position to assist, to provide 'international assistance and cooperation, especially economic and technical' which enable developing countries to fulfil their core and other obligations.[170]

UN Doc CMW/C/GC/1, para 43 states that 'any medical care urgently required to avoid irreparable harm' should be available, and States should give special attention to pregnant women migrant workers with irregular status.

168 Pretoria Declaration, para 7.

169 ICESCR, art 12(1).

170 CESCR, 'GC 14' (n 110) para 45. On minimum core rights protection and the role of international assistance therein, see Section 3.3.2.

The manner in which the prioritized realization of core obligations is extended to include obligations of international assistance is particularly relevant in light of Article 14*bis* Single Convention.[171] Article 14*bis* provides the legal basis for the technical or financial assistance a State, upon consent, may receive from specialized UN agencies and competent bodies. Whereas the Single Convention only refers to other bodies, not specifically States, the obligation to provide international assistance under human rights law clearly does apply to States, in particular when it comes to core rights. The question remains, however, whether one can extend this line of reasoning to include States to have the obligation to assist other States in fulfilling these obligations that stem from the international drug-control system. These obligations, as has been suggested before, also relate to human rights obligations or, at the very least, demonstrate that there is an overlap between the two systems of law. The issue emerging here is particularly important to keep in mind because:

> [f]or those many States which have difficulties in marshalling sufficient resources to build and maintain even a basic system of healthcare, international assistance and cooperation is often a vital source of funding, training, advise and expertise upon which they draw.[172]

Despite its potential, core rights protection also receives criticism. One of the main concerns is that the obligations listed as core obligations implicitly presuppose (and require) a well-organized and developed healthcare system, something many resource-constrained countries simply do not possess.[173] This criticism is very similar to the criticism on the potential burdensome nature of specific drug-control requirements discussed in Chapter 2. Even though Part 3 of this study focuses specifically on the implementation of specific drug-control requirements, criticism on the feasibility of the implementation of core obligations should be kept in mind. This is especially true because at no stage of the study is it submitted that human rights law takes local realities of services provision into account adequately. Yet, regardless of these critical views, the lists (of core rights) as developed by the CESCR still provide a yardstick to determine priority-setting when discharging obligations relating to the right to health.

In various ways, access to controlled medicines and in particular pain-control medication can be understood as part of those substantive elements or sub-rights of the right to health which are granted such priority status. Drawing on the substantive

171 See Chapter 2, Section 2.6.4 on the technical assistance clause captured in Article 14*bis* Single Convention.

172 Saul, Kinley and Mobray (n 24) 1034.

173 Leijten (n 24) 203. For criticism on the minimum core approach in light of local governance, see also O Fuo and A Du Plessis, 'In the Face of Judicial Deference: Taking the "Minimum Core" of Socio-Economic Rights to the Local Government Sphere' (2015) 19 Law, Democracy & Development 1.

application, as set out in Sections 3.4.3-3.4.4, access to controlled medicines should be realized with priority on the basis of the core obligation to:

a. [e]nsure the right of access to healthcare facilities, goods, and services on a non-discriminatory basis, especially for vulnerable or marginalized groups;
b. [p]rovide essential drugs [i.e. medicines in the context of the present study] as from time to time defined under the WHO Action Programme on Essential Drugs.[174]

In General Comment 15, the CRC Committee reaffirms that the provision of essential medicines is a core obligation under the right to health and recommends States to use the WHO Model List of Essential Medicines – and when available the WHO Model List of Essential Medicines for Children.[175] In the Pretoria Declaration on ESC rights, the ACHPR Commission considers the right to health to include the obligation to ensure the provision of affordable medicines.[176] In its Principles and Guidelines, the ACHPR Commission also lists access to essential medicines as defined in the WHO Model List of Essential Medicines, as a core obligation.[177]

Access to controlled medicines should, similarly, be realized with priority on the basis of obligations of comparable priority to:

a. [e]nsure reproductive, maternal (pre-natal as well as post-natal), and child healthcare;
b. [t]ake measures to prevent, treat, and control epidemic and endemic diseases.[178]

It is therefore clear that, at least within the framework of the right to health, States are held to prioritize access to medicines in their efforts to implement the right to health.

Progressive realization and the protection against hazardous use

In search of the margins of appreciation of claims regarding the access to controlled medicines, one might wonder whether States also have such priority obligations when it comes to controlling the non-medical use of controlled substances. As stressed above, Article 12.2(b) implies that the provision of a healthy natural environment is a state obligation.[179] The CESCR considers this obligation to specifically include the

174 CESCR, 'GC 14' (n 110) para 43.
175 CRC Committee, 'General Comment No 15: The Right of the Child to the Enjoyment of the Highest Attainable Standard of Health (Art. 24)' adopted at the Sixty-Second Session (17 April 2013) UN Doc CRC/G/GC/15, paras 67, 73-b.
176 Pretoria Declaration, para 4.
177 Draft Principles and Guidelines, para 67.
178 CESCR, 'GC 14' (n 110) para 44.
179 ibid para 15.

discouragement of drug use and of the use of other harmful substances.[180] In spite of this, as opposed to the priority status of the access to medicines, the obligation to protect against hazardous drug use is not listed as a priority obligation. In lieu of such a designation, it should be realized progressively. In fact, the obligation to discourage the use of drugs, tobacco, alcohol, or other harmful substances is phrased in general as requiring progressive realization.

In addition, the CRC Committee stresses that States should facilitate harm-reduction programmes, and that States should ratify both the international drug-control treaties and the WHO Framework Convention on Tobacco Control.[181] This explicit reference to the international drug-control framework is, on the normative level, one of the first signs of interaction between the two systems. Although not linked specifically to harm-reduction measures, the ACHPR Commission stated in its 2011 draft declaration on ESC rights that States should take measures to combat the use of contaminated needles and syringes, and to ensure the protection of a healthy environment.[182] The ACHPR Commission also noted that States should review their national legislation, criminal laws, and penal system to adequately address public health issues.[183]

One must underline, however, that it is not submitted here that any aspect of drug-control regulation other than securing access to controlled medicines is in itself less legitimate. Instead, human rights law merely proposes that States prioritize their efforts to secure access to medicines so as to secure the very essence of the right to health. As indicated in Section 3.3.2, progressive realization may never give rise to the adoption of retrogressive measures and core rights protection also plays a role in the determination of the permissibility of limitations of rights. That being said, the question is whether there are aspects of drug control, and in particular, aspects of access to medicine provision that can legitimately limit the right to health.

3.4.10 Limitations of the right to health

In light of the aforementioned, the answer to the question of whether drug control could limit the right to health and efforts to secure access to medicines would be in the negative. However, this would be too simplistic an answer since the right to health is a relative right that includes a general limitation clause. To this end, Article 4 ICESCR sets out that any right contained in the ICESCR, including the right to health, 'may [be] subject (...) to such limitations as are determined by law only in so far as this may be compatible with the nature of these rights and solely for the purpose

180 id.
181 CRC Committee, 'GC 15' (n 175) para 66.
182 Draft Principles and Guidelines, paras xxxvi, vlv.
183 ibid para xlvi.

of promoting the general welfare in a democratic society.'[184] This limitation clause should be interpreted as to protect the rights of individuals rather than facilitating States to adopt limitations on ESC rights.[185]

In relation to recreational drug use, Van Kempen and Fedorova argue that States have a positive obligation to fight illegal drug trade and to discharge this obligation in a manner that does not impair the protection of other ESC rights. Bearing the previous section in mind, this includes access to medicine provision.[186] While one can discern the obligation not to impair the protection on other ESC rights in Article 4 ICESCR, Van Kempen and Fedorova base the obligation to fight illegal drug trade on country-specific Concluding Observations. These observations are neither binding nor do they have the same general authoritative status as General Comments. Hence, the issue remains as to where to draw the line when reconciling public health interests and aspects of individual health rights.[187]

The CESCR does not elaborate much on the legitimacy of limitations of the right to health beyond emphasising that Article 4 ICESCR should be understood as to protect the interests of individuals. It is not a tool with which a State can limit their efforts in securing the maximum realization of the rights set out in the ICESCR.

Proportionality

There is no case law that deals with the legitimacy of a limitation to the access to medicine on the basis of drug-control efforts. If such a case were to present itself, it would have to be resolved with the proportionality test in mind (see Section 3.3.3). Case law on the freedom of religion, the use of controlled substances for religious purposes, and the protection of public order, can provide insight into how such a test may be substantiated.

Different religious groups hold that the use of psychotropic substances, such as cannabis and ayahuasca, is an intrinsic element of their religious practice. Rastafaris, for example, consider cannabis consumption as central to their religion. Similarly, in the Santo Daime church, drinking ayahuasca tea is considered part of their religious practice.[188]

---

184 ICESCR, art 5.
185 CESCR, 'GC 14' (n 110) para 28.
186 Van Kempen and Fedorova (n 144) 80.
187 Where to draw this line was already subject to debate during the drafting of the ICESCR, see Saul, Kinley and Mobray (n 24) 981.
188 Rastafari is an Africa-oriented religion which originated in the 1930s in Jamaica. In the Rastafari religion the use of marijuana is considered sacred. See BBC, 'Worship and Customs' <www.bbc.

A landmark case in which drug-control efforts were challenged from a religious perspective is *Garreth Prince*, over which the South African Constitutional Court, the ACHPR Commission, and the HR Committee each presided.[189] The case concerned a South African lawyer who was denied admittance to the Law Society of the Cape of Good Hope due to two convictions for cannabis possession and his express intention to keep using the substance because his Rastafari religion required it. Despite the appellant fulfilling all academic requirements, the Law Society found him 'not a fit and proper person to be admitted as an attorney'.[190] In first instance, the appellant claimed that the Law Society's decision violated his freedom of religion. Later he submitted that the 1992 South African Drugs and Drug Trafficking Act and the 1965 Medicines and Related Substances Control Act violated his freedom of religion and requested an exception to the ban of cannabis use to be made for religious purposes.[191] All bodies deciding on the matter acknowledged that cannabis use is part of the Rastafari religion and, as such, should be protected under the right to freedom of religion. In spite of this acknowledgment, the various bodies upheld the ban.

The South African Constitutional Court held that granting an exception would undermine the object of the Acts involved and that it would be 'impossible to police the exemption'.[192] Upon review of the South African Acts, their purpose was considered as 'to prevent drug abuse and to protect society as a whole'.[193] The ACHPR Commission held 'that the restrictions in the two South African legislations on the use and possession of cannabis are (...) reasonable as they serve a general purpose and [since] the Charter's protection of freedom of religion is not absolute'.[194] In addition, the HR Committee deemed that accepting an exception would create 'a system of importation, transportation and distribution to Rastafarians [which] may constitute a threat to the public at large, were any of the cannabis [to] enter into general circulation'.[195] In this context the HR Committee found it proportionate to

---

co.uk/religion/religions/rastafari/customs/customs_1.shtml> accessed 31 August 2016. Santo Daime is an early 20th century religion with roots in Brazil. For more information, see <www.santodaime.nl/> accessed 31 August 2016.

189 See respectively *Prince v President of the Law Society of the Cape of Good Hope and Others* (CCT36/00) [2000] ZACC 28; *Garreth Anver Prince v South Africa*, ACHPR Commission, Comm no 225/02 (7 December 2004); HR Committee, *Prince v South Africa* (Comm no 1474/2006).

190 *Prince v President of the Law Society* (n 189) para 2.

191 ibid paras 3, 4. In his proceedings before the ACHPR Commission and HR Committee, the appellant based his claim on Article 8 ACHPR and 18 ICCPR respectively. In the domestic, regional, and international procedures, the appellant also based his claim on other rights, including non-discrimination, the right to work, the prohibition of torture and CIDT, and the right to enjoy cultural life.

192 ibid para 8.

193 id.

194 *Garreth Anver Prince* (n 189) para 43.

195 *Prince v South Africa* (n 189) para 7.3.

uphold the general ban and forego an exemption to ensure that drugs do not end up available through illicit channels.[196]

While the different bodies ruled in favour of protection of public health in the *Prince cases*, the judicial bodies in the Netherlands have not unequivocally favoured the protection of public health and/or public order. In 2007, a case occurred in which the accused was charged with violating the Dutch Opium Act because she possessed ayahuasca (which is listed under the Opium Act). The object of the Opium Act is to protect, among other aspects, public health. The clauses stipulated in this Act, moreover, reflect obligations originating in the international drug-control treaties. The Dutch Supreme Court, however, accepted that the general prohibition clause of the Opium Act violates the freedom of religion. Nevertheless, exceptions to this rule should not be upheld because the complainant herself had raised that religious practices in the Santo Daime Church did not solely depend on ayahuasca-tea drinking and, as such, the interference did not affect the 'very essence' of the freedom of religion.[197] This also applied even though the detrimental effects of ayahuasca use were, in this particular case, considered minimal in terms of public health protection.[198]

More recently, and contrastingly, the Amsterdam Court of Appeal ruled that the Dutch Opium Act was not applicable to a case in which the appellant was caught at Schiphol Amsterdam Airport carrying a small amount of ayahuasca tea. Basing itself on the expert report which lay at the heart of the 2007 decision, the Court of Appeal ruled that the Dutch Opium Act was not to be applied, because drinking ayahuasca tea constituted a limited threat to public health (considering the limited scale on which and the controlled conditions under which consumption took place).[199]

In general, these cases demonstrate that courts at different levels rather easily accept and acknowledge the importance of the use of certain controlled substances for religious purposes. In fact, the issue is not whether or not the use of controlled substances falls within the ambit of religious freedom. Rather, the question is whether enforcing a ban on controlled substances is a legitimate interference with this right. Each in their distinct way, these cases indicate that the feasibility of managing and enforcing exceptions, the very essence of a right, and the necessity of interferences, are fundamental in shaping the outcome of the proportionality test.

---

196 id.

197 HR (9 January 2007), ECLI:NL:HR:2007:AZ2497.

198 ibid paras 3.4.2, 3.5.

199 Hof Amsterdam (24 February 2012), ECLI:NL:GHAMS:2012:BV6888. See also Rb Haarlem (26 March 2009), ECLI:NL:RBHAA:2009:BH9844.

One recognizes that the arguments presented in religious-use cases cannot be applied to the issue of the access to controlled-medicine at face value. After all, these cases merely reflect regional and domestic examples which in itself are not applicable to any country as a whole. Still, analysing the legal reasoning used in such cases helps one to think about proportionality in relation to the access to medicines and drug control in a structured manner – especially since the law is otherwise silent on this issue.[200] Yet, reflecting on these analogous cases, one could argue that drug-control regulations that would impair the availability and accessibility of medicines (either in law or in fact) are disproportionate. To this end, Chapter 2 has demonstrated the importance of pain-control medicines for specific medical interventions and treatments. Sections 3.4.3-3.4.5 subsequently demonstrated that their availability is part of the very essence of the right to health.

3.4.11 Access to medicines as a justiciable element of the right to health

Especially because the previous section has dealt with case law on the protection of public health and public order, it is worthwhile to look at the access to medicines as a justiciable element of the right to health.[201] Relevant proceedings at the international, regional, and domestic levels will be analysed for that purpose. The European human rights system, however, is not scrutinized here due to the absence of the right to health in the European Convention for the Protection of Human Rights and Fundamental Freedoms (ECHR).

At the international level, since the entry into force of its first Optional Protocol the CESCR is authorized to receive individual complaints. Nonetheless, to date, it has not (yet) received any complaints relating to the right to health.[202]

Regional and domestic cases in the African region

As will also be discussed in Section 3.5.2, States have an increased responsibility in cases of imprisonment. The ACHPR Commission held, for example, that 'to deny a

200 The law does not say anything about the proportionality of either the *de jure* or *de facto* limitation of access to medicines with the aim of protecting people against the hazardous use of controlled substances. Such a limitation is not necessarily a strict prohibition, but can also include additional requirements or higher thresholds that need to be reached when providing access to these medicines. Chapter 4 provides an ethical analysis hereon.

201 The case-law analysis is non-exhaustive and merely provides an overview of cases in which access to medicines is dealt with. Other cases, which do not deal with access to medicines specifically, are referred to for general information and contextual purposes. The overview is not intended to present an extensive analysis of the right-to-health case law.

202 For an overview of the individual complaints the CESCR has received to date, see <http://juris.ohchr.org/en/search/results?Bodies=9&sortOrder=Date> accessed 31 August 2016.

detainee access to doctors while his health is deteriorating is a violation' of the right to health.[203] Moreover, the ACHPR Commission had already stated in 1996 that 'the failure of the Government to provide basic services (...) the shortage of medicine (...) constitutes a violation [of the right to health]'.[204] Yet similarly, it also held that the right to health includes the right to healthcare facilities, goods, and services on a non-discriminatory basis.[205]

Furthermore, the ACHPR Commission considered in relation to extraterritorial obligations of socio-economic rights that access to medicines must be maintained. In this regard, for example, it considered Burundi, Rwanda, and Uganda to have violated the right to health by halting their essential medical services during their occupation of the eastern part of the Democratic Republic of the Congo.[206] Although based on a limited number of cases, the ACHPR Commission has generally produced a solid body of case law on the matter and has been explicit in defining state obligations – frequently referring to work of the UN-treaty bodies and case law of other judicial human rights bodies, such as the ECtHR.[207]

A landmark case for the African region is that of the South African *Minister of Health v Treatment Action Campaign*, which dealt with the justiciability of the right to health and access to medicines in the context of an HIV-prevention programme.[208] Here, the Constitutional Court held that the South African government had not taken adequate steps to achieve the full realization of the right to health.[209] Moreover, relying on a reasonableness approach, it required the State to remove any restrictions on the distribution and accessibility of medicines relevant to the prevention of mother-to-child HIV transmission.[210]

---

203 *Media Rights Agenda and Ors v Nigeria*, ACHPR Commission, Comm no 105/93, 128/94, 130/94 and 152/96 (31 October 1998) para 91.

204 *Free Legal Assistance Group and Ors v Democratic Republic of Congo*, ACHPR Commission, Comm no 25/89, 47/90, 56-91 and 100/93 (4 April 1996) para 47.

205 *Purohit and Moore v The Gambia,* ACHPR Commission, Comm no 241/01 (29 May 2003) para 80; *Egyptian Initiative for Personal Rights and INTERIGHTS v Egypt,* ACHPR Commission, Comm no 323/06 (12 October 2013) para 261. In the latter case, the ACHPR Commission did not accept a breach of Article 16 ACHPR because the appellant had received medical attention and the government had therefore discharged its obligations under the right to health. In the case, a woman was sexually assaulted at a protest and admitted to hospital after the event.

206 *Democratic Republic of Congo v Burundi, Rwanda and Uganda*, ACHPR Commission, Comm no 227/99 (29 May 2003) para 88.

207 See *Huri-Laws v Nigeria*, ACHPR Commission, Comm no 225/98 (6 November 2000) as an example in which the Commission refers to the case law of the ECtHR.

208 *Minister of Health and Others v Treatment Action Campaign and Others* (No 2) (CCT8/02) [2002] ZACC 15.

209 ibid para 135.

210 id. On the reasonableness approach of the South African Court in general and in relation to the *Treatment Action Campaign* case, see in particular Leijten (n 24) 228-234. See also F Coomans,

Regional and domestic cases in the Inter-American region

The IACtHR has produced a wealth of cases in which access to medicines or medical services is allocated as reparation. These cases, however, are not analysed here as they are not useful to clarify the interpretation of the access to medicines as a justiciable element of the right to health.[211] There are, moreover, many relevant examples at the domestic level throughout the region.[212] In Peru, for example, a person with AIDS submitted a constitutional petition with Peru's Ministry of Health requesting full medical care, including the permanent supply of medicines. The appellant was unable to secure treatment and medicines due to a lack of financial means. Peru's Constitutional Court accepted the petition and noted that social rights are not just programmatic goals but enforceable in court, reaffirming both the immediate and progressive nature of the right, and ordered the government of Peru to make the requested treatment available to the petitioner.[213]

In Venezuela, a group of HIV-positive citizens claimed access to medicines because they neither had the financial means nor the social security to pay for the medicines themselves. The Venezuelan Constitutional Court accepted the constitutional petition (amparo action) and ordered the Ministry of Health to make the medication available to applicants. However, it did not extend this reasoning to automatically apply to other citizens as well.[214] Subsequent to this ruling, the Court was confronted with a similar claim, again claiming access to therapy due to not being able to secure the treatment by personal efforts. In this case the Venezuelan Constitutional Court reaffirmed its earlier statement and legislation was, in turn, altered to make the treatment available to everyone.[215]

'Reviewing Implementation of Social and Economic Rights: An Assessment of the "Reasonableness" Test as Developed by the South African Constitutional Court' (2005) 65 Heidelberg Journal of International Law 167.

211 A selection of these cases include eg *Cantoral Benavides v Peru* (Reparations, and Costs) Inter-American Court of Human Rights Series C No 88 (3 December 2001); *Gutiérrez Soler v Colombia* (Merits, Reparations, and Costs) Inter-American Court of Human Rights Series C No 132 (12 September 2005); *Fernández Ortega and Ors v México* (Preliminary Objection, Merits, Reparations, and Costs) Inter-American Court of Human Rights Series C No 215 (30 August 2010).

212 HV Hogerzeil and others, 'Is Access to Essential Medicines as Part of the Fulfilment of the Right to Health Enforceable through the Courts?' (2006) 368 The Lancet 305.

213 *Azanca Alhelí Meza García v Peru*, Expediente 2945-2003-AA/TC [2004] Tribunal Constitucional del Perú.

214 *Cruz del Valle Bermúdez and Ors v MSAS*, Expediente 15.789 [1999] Tribunal Supremo de Justicia de la República Bolivariana de Venezuela.

215 *Glenda López and Ors v Instituto Venezolano de los Seguros Sociales (IVSS)*, Expediente 00-1343 [1997] Tribunal Supremo de Justicia de la República Bolivariana de Venezuela.

In Chile, the Constitutional Court stated that the government is obliged to protect the right to life and may not use a lack of financial resources to justify the failure to comply with this obligation. According to the Court, the right to life was, and is, an absolute obligation that goes beyond any financial consideration (and justification). The Chilean Ministry of Health had filed a decree ordering free medical testing and treatment for AIDS. It, however, did not do so for HIV, which according to the Constitutional Court was a breach of its obligation under the right to life. The distinction, moreover, constituted unjustified differential treatment.[216]

To conclude, even though in many legal systems the right to health in itself is not an enforceable and justiciable right, there is a variety of case law supporting the access to medicines specifically as a justiciable element of the right to health. However, as was mentioned in Section 3.3.4, this trend in itself is contested.[217] Furthermore, these cases do not address the particular juxtaposition of drug-control regulation as a public health concern.[218]

3.5 The prohibition of torture and CIDT

The following section relates the prohibition of torture and CIDT to the access-led analysis of the right to health. It does so generally and specifically in relation to the access to medicines and specific drug-control considerations. While doing so, the section deals with the concept and legal codification of the prohibition of torture and CIDT, its scope and content, and its application to the subjects studied in this book. Moreover, the section deals with interferences with the prohibition and includes an extensive case-law analysis featuring relevant obligations in this field.[219]

3.5.1 Concept and legal codification

To be free from ill-treatment, and therefore free from torture and CIDT is, similar to a state of good health and the right to health, a precondition to live a dignified life. As will also be addressed in Chapter 4, living a life in dignity is neither a value judgment nor a benchmark for what is right or wrong. It merely reflects the ability to live

216 *People living with HIV*, Expediente 3.599-2001-10-16 [2001] Corte Suprema de Chile.

217 See Motta Ferraz (n 101) 97.

218 This has no impact on understanding a claim to access controlled medicines since human rights law is blind to this term. However, it does entail that at least on the basis of the right to health, case law does not take any position on the balancing of access to controlled essential medicines and aspects of drug control.

219 The section refers to hard and soft law documents, case law, and literature. Country-specific reports have been excluded since these do not provide the generalized information one requires.

autonomously with human rights being claims to goods and services that facilitate such autonomy.[220]

There is broad consensus that acts of torture or CIDT are not only a direct violation of a person's dignity but one of the gravest violations of human rights.[221] Although not an airtight division, torture and acts of CIDT, also commonly referred to as acts of ill-treatment, occur more often in developing countries than in developed countries and are found more frequently under authoritarian regimes as opposed to liberal ones.[222] As Alston and Goodman point out, these acts may be classified into acts of ill-treatment of State Officials, on the one hand, and acts of aberrational conduct based on sheer venality, on the other.[223] Ill-treatment by State Officials often serves the purpose of extracting evidence or terrorizing a population, and frequently results in capital punishment.[224]

The prohibition of torture and CIDT is included in many international and regional legal instruments and constitutional provisions.[225] At the international level, the most general prohibition thereof is included in Article 5 UDHR, Article 7 ICCPR, and Articles 1 and 16.2 of the Convention against Torture and Other Cruel, Inhuman and Degrading Treatment or Punishment (CAT).[226] At the regional level, Article 5 ACHPR, Article 5 of the American Convention on Human Rights, Article 3 ECHR, Article 2 of the Inter-American Convention to Prevent and Punish Torture, and Article 16 of the African Convention on the Rights and Welfare of the Child prohibit such treatment.[227]

---

220 This statement should be understood in a much more nuanced context (see Chapter 4).

221 M Nowak, 'Torture and Enforced Disappearance' in C Krause and M Scheinin (eds), *International Protection of Human Rights: A Textbook* (Institute for Human Rights Åbo Akademi University 2009) 151, 182.

222 P Alston and R Goodman, *International Human Rights* (OUP 2013) 238.

223 ibid 238-239.

224 ibid 239. See also M Nowak and E McArthur, *The United Nations Convention against Torture: A Commentary* (OUP 2008) 2.

225 See eg UDHR, art 5; ICCPR, art 7; ICRMW, art 10; CRPD, art 15; ACHR, art 5; ECHR, art 3; ACHPR, art 5; Constitution of the Republic of South Africa, Act 108 of 1996, art 12; Constitución Española, art 15.

226 See also CRC, art 37; ICRMW, art 10; CRPD, art 15; and UNGA 'Body of Principles for the Protection of All Persons under Any Form of Detention or Imprisonment' (9 December 1988) UN Doc A/RES/43/173, art 6.

227 Inter-American Convention to Prevent and Punish Torture (adopted 9 December 1985, entered into force 28 February 1987) OASTS 67.

3.5.2 Distinction between torture and CIDT

Torture is most comprehensively defined in Article 1 CAT as '[a]ny act by which severe pain or suffering, whether physical or mental, is intentionally inflicted on a person in order to get a confession or any other piece of information'.[228] By omission, the CAT lacks a similar explicit reference to what defines an act of CIDT. In view of Article 16 CAT, acts of CIDT include:

> [O]ther acts of cruel, inhuman or degrading treatment or punishment which do not amount to torture as defined in article 1, when such acts are committed by or at the instigation or with the consent or acquiescence of a public official or other persons acting in an official capacity.[229]

Torture and CIDT are often referred to in one breath. There is no comprehensive definition of what constitutes an act of CIDT. Despite lacking a clear definition, differences between the two exist and are, according to the HR Committee, based on 'the nature, purpose, and severity' of an act.[230] The work of both the ECtHR and the European Commission on Human Rights (which no longer exists) has been crucial in the conceptualization of what constitutes an act of CIDT.[231]

Traditionally, CIDT was considered to be more general in nature than torture, resulting in a threshold of: (i) intent; (ii) severe suffering; (iii) and lack of justification.[232] Theoretically, the assessment of whether or not certain treatment passes this CIDT threshold depends on factors that include the treatment's duration, physical and mental effects, as well as the individual's age, sex, and health status.[233] Especially the element of intent has been a stumbling block for the interpretation of an act as an act of CIDT in many cases. Cassese holds, in this respect, that intent 'ought not to be regarded as one of the factors the absence of which warrants the conclusion that no inhuman treatment or punishment is meted out'.[234] According to Nowak and McArthur, however, intent is a crucial factor in distinguishing between CIDT and

---

228 CAT, art 1.

229 ibid art 16.

230 HR Committee, 'General Comment No 20: Article 7 (Prohibition of Torture, or Other Cruel, Inhuman or Degrading Treatment or Punishment)' adopted at the Forty-Forth Session (10 March 1992) UN Doc HRI/GEN/1/Rev.1 para 4; Sepúlveda and others (n 17) 241; MEC Gispen, *Poor Access to Pain Treatment: Advancing a Human Right to Pain Relief* (International Federation of Health and Human Rights Organizations 2011) 40.

231 A Cassese, *The Human Dimension of International Law* (OUP 2008) 229, 316; Gispen, *Poor Access to Pain Treatment* (n 230) 40.

232 id; British Medical Association, *The Medical Profession & Human Rights* (Zed Books Ltd 2001) 60.

233 Sepúlveda and others (n 17) 241.

234 Cassese (n 231) 316; Gispen, *Poor Access to Pain Treatment* (n 230) 41.

torture.[235] The difference between the two also has significant impact on the status of the right involved. Nowak and McArthur argue that 'whereas torture might be considered as absolutely prohibited, CIDT by definition is a relative concept'.[236] The relativeness of the prohibition of CIDT, as set out by Nowak and McArther, touches on potential interferences with the right at hand. They argue that in non-prison settings, i.e. in a situation in which the State does not exercise direct control over the victim, a proportionality test is the threshold to establish whether an action is to be classified as in breach of the prohibition of torture and CIDT or not.[237]

Yet in practice, the question of whether or not an act is an act of torture or CIDT is ill-defined: acts of ill-treatment often facilitate acts of torture. It is for this reason that the Committee against Torture (CAT Committee) stressed the obligations explicitly imposed on States to protect individuals against acts of torture to apply to ill-treatment by the same token.[238] In relation to the distinction between torture and CIDT, Nowak clarifies this difference by using excessive police force as an example. According to Nowak, humiliating and excessive use of force by the police outside detention, although in a situation of direct control over the victim, may lead to degrading treatment. Incrementally, the infliction of severe pain or suffering may amount to cruel or inhuman treatment. But, in line with earlier reference to Nowak and McArthur, if such treatment is considered proportional, the acts do not reach the threshold of CIDT.[239]

3.5.3 Obligations to ensure access to pain-control medicines

Apart from investigating the links between access to pain-control medicines and the prohibition of torture and CIDT in case law, it is also worthwhile to look into soft-law instruments. The normative content of the prohibition of torture and CIDT is refined in a range of General Comments and explanatory documents, both at the international and the regional level. For instance, the HR Committee has stressed explicitly in its General Comment 20 that the scope and substantive elements of the prohibition of torture, as included in the ICCPR, include the protection of patients in medical institutions as well.[240] The 'Robben Island Guidelines', adopted by the ACHPR Commission, show that prisoners should have access to medical services and medical

235 Nowak and McArther (n 224).
236 ibid 149.
237 ibid 147.
238 CAT Committee, 'General Comment No 2: Implementation of Article 2 by State Parties' (24 January 2008) UN Doc CAT/C/GC/2, para 3.
239 Nowak (n 221) 157.
240 UN Doc HRI/GEN/1/Rev.1 (n 230) para 5. For a comprehensive overview of the freedom from torture and CIDT in healthcare settings, see British Medical Association (n 232).

personnel, and that victims of ill-treatment should have access to appropriate care and medical rehabilitation.[241] These documents, however, include little reference to indicate their applicability to access to controlled essential medicines specifically or aspects of drug control more generally.

In addition, in its 2009 report, UN Special Rapporteur Manfred Nowak applied a human-rights based approach to drug policies and highlighted the hampering role of these policies in the provision of access to palliative care and pain-relief services.[242] Together with the UN Special Rapporteur on the right to the highest attainable standard of health, Anand Grover, Nowak wrote a letter to the Commission on Narcotic Drugs emphasizing States' failure to allow access to adequate pain treatment, including the use of (oral) morphine, to be in breach of the prohibition of torture and CIDT.[243]

In 2013, the Special Rapporteur on torture and CIDT, Juan Méndez, specifically listed the denial of pain treatment as an emerging form of abuse in healthcare settings.[244] Méndez outlined that '[d]enial of pain treatment involves acts of omission rather than commission, and results from neglect and poor Government policies, rather than from an intention to inflict suffering'.[245] In other words, States failing to ensure that adequate pain treatment is available by means of access to (oral) morphine are in breach of their obligations to protect individuals against ill-treatment. Nevertheless, similar to establishing an act of CIDT in other situations, assessing a violation of the prohibition of torture and CIDT in relation to the denial of pain treatment is subjected to a threshold analysis. After all, concluding that the denial of pain treatment may result in a breach of the prohibition of torture and CIDT does not mean that every case in which a person suffers pain constitutes an act of CIDT. Méndez outlined that the denial of pain treatment is only an act of CIDT:

---

241 ACHPR Commission, *Resolution on Guidelines and Measures for the Prohibition and Prevention of Torture, Cruel, Inhuman or Degrading Treatment or Punishment in Africa* (2nd edn, ACHPR 2008) paras 31, 46, 50.

242 UNHRC 'Report of the Special Rapporteur on Torture and Other Cruel, Inhuman or Degrading Treatment or Punishment' (14 January 2009) UN Doc A/HRC/10/44, paras 68-70.

243 'Joint Letter from Mr. M Nowak and Mr. A Grover to her Excellency Ms. Selma Ashipala-Musavyi, Permanent Representative of Namibia to the United Nations at Vienna, Chairperson of the 52nd Session of the Commission on Narcotic Drugs' (10 December 2008); Gispen, *Poor Access to Pain Treatment* (n 230). As also shown by the case of Remedios in Chapter 1, Human Rights Watch gave pain patients a voice to express their wish to be relieved of their pain and to die rather than to continue living in excruciating and unbearable pain. According to these reports, their experiences resembled stories of torture survivors. Human Rights Watch, *"Please do not make us suffer anymore..." Access to Pain Treatment as a Human Right* (HRW 2009) 7; Human Rights Watch, *Unbearable Pain: India's Obligation to Ensure Palliative Care* (HRW 2009) 19.

244 UNHRC 'Report of the Special Rapporteur on Torture and Other Cruel, Inhuman or Degrading Treatment or Punishment' (1 February 2013) UN Doc A/HRC/22/53, paras 51-53.

245 ibid para 54.

> [w]hen the suffering is severe and meets the minimum threshold under the prohibition against torture and ill-treatment; when the State is, or should be, aware of the suffering, including when no appropriate treatment was offered; and when the Government failed to take all reasonable steps to protect individuals' physical and mental integrity.[246]

One could therefore implicitly argue that when passing such a threshold, any claim regarding the access to these pain-control medicines could be based on Article 16 CAT. As under the right to health, all patients in need of pain-control medicines in these situations are identified as rights holder.

3.5.4 Obligations to ensure access to opioid-dependency medicines

Similarly to the way the denial of pain treatment could fall within the scope of the prohibition against torture and CIDT, one can extend this argument to harm-reduction measures and opioid-substitute medicines. One can consider such an argument as a reinforced claim to gain access to medicines, which, in the context of opioid-substitute treatment is a reinforced claim to protect public health and the public order (see Sections 3.4.4-3.4.5). Méndez emphasizes that the denial of opioid-substitute treatment is '[a] particular form of ill-treatment and possibly torture of drug users.'[247] What is more, the denial of methadone treatment is, in particular, considered a breach of the prohibition of torture and CIDT.[248] Méndez, moreover, extends this reasoning to apply to non-custodial settings as well.

Sections 3.4.4-3.4.5 situated harm-reduction measures and, in particular, opioid-dependency therapies in light of the right to health, taking into account empirical research. Data demonstrates those measures to allow drug users to participate in society in a meaningful way, to decrease drug-associated crime and instability, and to increase the protection of public health through, for example, clean needle distribution programmes.[249]

Keeping this all in mind, and in line with the reasoning presented by Mendéz, Nowak and Grover note that States maintaining a complete ban on harm-reduction programmes, including opioid-substitute treatments, are in breach of their obligations to protect under the prohibition of torture and CIDT.[250] In this light, one could also base a claim to gain access to other controlled medicines, such as opioid-dependency

246 id.
247 ibid para 73.
248 id.
249 See R Elliot and others, 'Harm Reduction, HIV/AIDS, and the Human Rights Challenge to Global Drug Control Policy' (2005) 8 Health and Human Rights 104, 110-111.
250 UN Doc A/HRC/22/53 (n 244) para 73.

medication, on the basis of Article 16 CAT. Drug users who are denied access to harm-reduction programmes, including opioid-substitute treatment, are identified as the rights holders in such a scenario.

3.5.5 Non-interference with an absolute right

The law does not clarify the permissibility of any constraints or limitations regarding the access to medicines for the purposes of protecting the public's health or the public order by regulating the use of controlled substances. Yet, if based on the prohibition of CIDT, it does. If the treatment inflicted, i.e. the denial of pain treatment, is disproportionate, any violation of this right is unlawful.[251] This argument is aggravated in cases of direct state control, in which it is more likely to find a violation of the prohibition of torture as such. Leijten affirms this idea by stressing that if any aspect of a socio-economic right falls within the scope of an absolute norm, this would result in absolute protection.[252] Yet, in line with the CAT Committee, because any obligation in relation to torture applies similarly to ill-treatment and the exact difference between the two remains hazy at best, access to pain-control medicines and, in particular, harm reduction should be considered as part of an absolute norm.

Moreover, although not unequivocally accepted, many scholars contend that the prohibition of torture and CIDT is attributed the status of *jus cogens* and, as such, has attained the status of international customary law.[253] Both elements also have non-derogable status, meaning that no situation, not even war, terrorism, natural disaster (or *force majeure*), or any other emergency situation can justify States' non-compliance with their obligations under the prohibition of torture and CIDT.[254] As supported by Alston and Goodman, this absolute and non-derogable nature of the prohibition of torture and CIDT leaves no room for balancing. This means that if access to controlled essential medicines falls within the scope of the freedom of CIDT, its protection and enforcement may not be balanced with other aspects of drug control.[255] Yet, both in relation to pain-control medicines as well as opioid-dependency medicines, the question remains what exactly States have to do to ensure access to medicines and care, as developed in case law.[256]

---

251 See CAT, arts 1, 16; Nowak (n 221) 153.

252 Leijten (n 24) 285.

253 See MN Shaw, *International Law* (6th edn, CUP 2008) 326; Sepúlveda and others (n 17) 240; Alston and Goodman (n 222) 8.

254 See HR Committee, 'GC 20' (n 240) para 3; Nowak (n 221) 157.

255 Alston and Goodman (n 222) 249.

256 While there is a bulk of human rights scholarship, and potentially also case law, on the prohibition of torture and CIDT in the context of drug-control aspects, this is not addressed further. As mentioned in the introduction, this chapter situates the 'principle of balance' in human rights law and looks into the aspects of medicine provision and the protection of society against hazardous use. An analysis of

3.5.6 Judicial review of access to medicines as part of the prohibition against torture and CIDT

Especially in legal systems in which the right to health is not acknowledged as an enforceable and justiciable right, attorneys find other ways to litigate in the interest of their client. The prohibition of torture and CIDT – as well as the right to life and right to privacy/family life – is therefore often used as a vehicle to litigate on access to medicines and healthcare issues. These cases and their analysis, being primary sources of law, are relevant to determine the scope of access to medicines, including controlled medicines, under the prohibition against torture and CIDT. Such cases, moreover, show not only the basis of an access to medicines claim under this right but also the responsibility of States in practice.

This section analyses proceedings under the international and European human rights system. The African and Inter-American human rights systems have, however, not been analysed. While of course distinct in many ways, the judicial review in these systems, relating to the access to medicines/healthcare and the prohibition of torture and CIDT, are similar to and in line with the work of the ECtHR. The IACHR Commission, for instance, maintains a strong position on these issues, stating that the denial of access to medical care constitutes a violation of the prohibition of torture and CIDT. In doing so it relies heavily on communications of the HR Committee,[257] the ECtHR,[258] and the IACtHR,[259] referring also to the UN Standard Minimum Rules for the Treatment of Prisoners (Nelson Mandela Rules).[260]

---

the individual rights potentially impaired in any other aspects of drug-control regulation is therefore not included.

257 Joined Cases 12.067, 12.068 and 12.086 *Michael Edwards, Omar Hall and Brian Schroeter and Jeronimo Bolweg v the Bahamas* (Merits) Inter-American Commission of Human Rights Report No 48/01 (4 April 2001); Case 12.158 *Benedict Jacob v Granada* (Merits) Inter-American Commission of Human Rights Report No 56/02 (21 October 2002).

258 See *Jacob* (n 257).

259 Case 12.417 *Whitley Myrie v Jamaica* (Merits) Inter-American Commission of Human Rights Report No 41/04 (12 October 2004); Case 12.265 *Chad Roger Goodman v the Bahamas* (Merits) Inter-American Commission of Human Rights Report No 78/07 (15 October 2007); Case 12.296 *Dexter Lendore v Trinidad and Tobago* (Merits) Inter-American Commission of Human rights Report No 28/09 (20 March 2009).

260 *Benedict Jacob* (n 257); Case 12.275 *Denton Aitiken v Jamaica* (Merits) Inter-American Commission of Human Rights Report No 58/02 (21 October 2002); Case 12.476 *Oscar Elías Biscet et al. v Cuba* (Merits) Inter-American Commission of Human Rights Report No 67/06 (21 October 2006). See n 113 for the Nelson Mandela Rules.

UN-treaty bodies

Looking at the work of the UN-treaty bodies, only the HR Committee has produced relevant communications on individual complaints relating to access to medicines and healthcare issues.[261] These communications are all based on Article 10.1 ICCPR – prohibition of torture and CIDT – and refer to situations in which the applicant was detained. The HR Committee accepted a violation of the prohibition of torture and CIDT to be present in cases in which the applicant claimed to have no access to medical services, including specific medical treatment and/or medicines, and in which the State did not rebut this unavailability or did only do so partially.[262] For instance, in *Lobban v Jamaica*, the appellant held that he lacked access to necessary medical, dental, and psychiatric care.[263] The Jamaican government rebutted the claim and stated that relevant medical services had been available. The Committee observed that, even if medical services were available at a given time, this did not transpire from the State Party's submission and therefore the allegations of the appellant remained undisputed.[264] In contrast, in *Pustavolov v Russian Federation* the appellant submitted that the imprisonment conditions, including the lack of access to medical assistance, violated the prohibition of torture and CIDT. In this case, the HR Committee found that the State had submitted compelling counter-arguments and therefore found no violation.[265]

European human rights system

The ECtHR has dealt with the matter of access to medicines and healthcare services on the basis of Article 3 ECHR (prohibition of torture and CIDT).[266] The difference in its reasoning in terms of custodial and non-custodial settings becomes quite clear in

---

261 As mentioned in Section 3.3.3, the UN treaty bodies may receive individual complaints. In that capacity, the UN treaty bodies act as a quasi-judicial body. No relevant cases were identified in the communications of the CAT Committee, the CERD Committee, and the CEDAW Committee. HR Committee, *Saed Shams and Ors v Australia* (Comm no 1255, 1256, 1259, 1260, 1266, 1268, 1270, and 1288/2004) was dismissed on procedural grounds.

262 See eg HR Committee, *Irving Phillip v Trinidad and Tobago* (Comm no 594/1992) para 7.4; HR Committee, *Eustace Henry and Everald Douglas v Jamaica* (Comm no 571/1994) para 9.5; HR Committee, *Dennis Lobban v Jamaica* (Comm no 797/1998) para 8.2; HR Committee, *Omar Faruk Bozbey v Turkmenistan* (Comm no 1530/2006) para 7.2.

263 *Lobban* (n 262) para 3.3.

264 ibid para 8.2.

265 HR Committee, *Oleg Pustovalov v Russian Federation* (Comm no 1232/2003) para 8.3.

266 The ECtHR deals with socio-economic aspects in general and with right to health issues more specifically, also on the basis of other rights. Analysing particular obligations in relation to the prohibition of torture and CIDT, however, this section only deals with cases based on Article 3 ECHR. On the justiciability of socio-economic rights on the basis of the ECHR, see Leijten (n 24).

the case law.[267] In custodial settings, the ECtHR maintains a test in which the quality and frequency of the care provided, if at all, and effect on the applicant's general state of health and well-being are considered.

In *Logvinenko v Ukraine*, for instance, the ECtHR held that even though the applicant had received some medical attention, the care provided was still generally insufficient in light of the applicant's rapidly deteriorating health.[268] In this case, 'the applicant asserted that the physical conditions of his detention and medical assistance for HIV and tuberculosis were incompatible with his state of health' as he had not received, amongst other things, HIV treatment.[269] The Court accepted a breach of Article 3 ECHR to have occurred and concluded that the State had 'not done what could be reasonably expected' considering 'the lack of a comprehensive approach to the applicant's medical supervision and treatment (…) and fail[ed] to ensure physical conditions reasonably adapted for his recovery process'.[270] Moreover, in *A.B. v Russia*, the ECtHR found it 'deeply disturbing' that the Russian authorities deemed it unnecessary to provide the applicant with antiretroviral treatment. The ECtHR ruled that 'the applicant was not provided with the minimum scope of medical supervision for the timely treatment of his HIV infection while in detention and thus did not receive adequate medical assistance for his condition'.[271] The Court was, furthermore, also deeply concerned that the government had been of the opinion that clinical data had not revealed the need for antiretroviral treatment.[272] In contrast, exactly because medical staff had diagnosed the applicant and supplied the necessary medication, the ECtHR found no violation of Article 3 ECHR in *Goginashvili v Georgia*.[273]

In relation to the frequency of care or medicines provided, the ECtHR held in *Bragadireanu v Romania* that having to rely on family members to access medicines whilst in prison was no violation of Article 3.[274] The applicant claimed that because the authorities did not provide him with the medicines needed, his family members

267 The vast majority of relevant ECtHR judgments pertain to in-prison and in-state facility settings. Only a handful of cases pertain to non-custodial settings.
268 *Logvinenko v Ukraine* App no 13448/07 (ECtHR, 14 October 2010).
269 ibid para 66.
270 ibid para 77.
271 *A.B. v Russia* App no 1439/06 (ECtHR, 14 October 2010) para 134.
272 ibid paras 117, 133.
273 *Goginashvili v Georgia* App no 47729/08 (ECtHR, 4 October 2011) para 81.
274 *Bragadireanu v Romania* App no 22088/04 (ECtHR, 6 December 2007). The ECtHR also found violations in a case where the applicant had to rely on family members, see *Holomiov v Moldova* App no 30649/05 (ECtHR, 7 November 2006); *Hummatov v Azerbaijan*, App nos 9852/03 and 13413/04 (ECtHR, 29 November 2007). Presumably this would need to be structural reliance, as the ECtHR also found that relying on family members for an isolated, one-off, incident is not enough to constitute a breach of Article 3 ECHR.

had to bring it to him.[275] The ECtHR held that since this had only occurred once and had not led to a deterioration of the applicant's medical condition, no violation was present.[276] In *McGlinchey and others v United Kingdom*, the Court acknowledged that the authorities had failed to provide the applicant with medicines on one occasion. In this case, however, the establishment of a violation of Article 3 ECHR was based on insufficient monitoring of her medical condition, rather than on the absence of medicines in that one instance.[277]

Though case law is plentiful, it remains unclear which standard the ECtHR uses exactly to determine the adequacy of care in general and the gravity of the absence of care and medicines in particular in relation to its minimum level of severity test. Both *Zkharakin v Russia* and *Rehbock v Slovenia* are insightful in this respect. Most notably in relation to pain control, the ECtHR accepted in *Zkharkin* that not receiving pain-control treatment, even though a doctor had prescribed this treatment, 'caused the applicant suffering attaining the minimum level of severity required to fall within the scope of Article 3'.[278] The ECtHR has also considered the actual medical condition in its reasoning. In *Rehbock*, the applicant claimed to suffer severe pain on different occasions and indicated that prison staff did not provide him with pain-control medicines. The Court held, however, that his suffering by a lack of access to these medicines was not substantiated in such a way as 'to attain a degree of severity warranting the conclusion that his right under Article 3 was thereby infringed'.[279] There are, in addition, also instances in which the ECtHR explicitly refrained from addressing the necessity, effect, or impact of pain-control medicines. In *Okhrimenko v Ukraine*, for instance, the Court explicitly held that it did not want to interfere with the doctor's expertise and, as such, did not accept a violation of Article 3 ECHR.[280]

In relation to being able to access treatment or medicines in the first place, the ECtHR accepted a violation of Article 3 ECHR in *Mikhaniv v Ukraine.* Here, the prison pharmacy ran out of stock and medicines were no longer available. The Court conceded that 'leaving a detained person without essential medical treatment as required by medical experts for his health condition over a substantial period of time and without satisfactory explanations amounts to' a violation of Article 3 ECHR.[281]

275 *Bragadireanu* (n 274) para 49.
276 ibid para 87.
277 *McGlinchey and Ors v the United Kingdom* (2003) 37 EHRR 41, paras 48, 49, 53, 57.
278 *Zakharkin v Russia* App no 1555/04 (ECtHR, 10 June 2010) para 140.
279 *Rehbock v Slovenia* ECHR 2000-XII 645, para 80.
280 *Okhrimenko v Ukraine* App no 53896/07 (ECtHR, 15 October 2009) para 71. This case is particularly interesting as the applicant claimed a violation of Article 3 ECHR because the morphine injections the applicant received for cancer treatment resulted in him relapsing into his previous drug addiction.
281 *Mikhaniv v Ukraine* App no 75522/01 (ECtHR, 6 November 2008) para 74.

In relation to non-custodial settings, relevant case law of the ECtHR supporting, or at least tracing, a link between access to healthcare and medicines and Article 3 ECHR is based on the principle of *non-refoulement*. The principle of *non-refoulement* includes the prohibition to expel people if these people run a reasonable risk to experience a violation of Article 3 ECHR at their destination and no adequate protection against such a violation would be available.[282] In relation to health matters, application of the principle of *non-refoulement* raises the question of whether expulsion would add to the victim's suffering because the standard of care is claimed to be considerably lower in the particular country to which the person is supposed to be expelled.

For instance, in *Bensaid v United Kingdom*, the ECtHR did not accept a violation of Article 3 ECHR. In this case, the applicant claimed he would not be able to have adequate access to olanzapine if sent back to Algeria. According to the ECtHR, this claim was based on hypothetical factors and it did not show whether the applicant would actually suffer ill-treatment as alternative treatment was still available.[283] It referred specifically to its ruling in *D. v United Kingdom* and stated that no such exceptional situation was applicable.[284] In *D.*, the applicant would not be able to access HIV/AIDS treatment and, given his already deteriorated state of health, the Court accepted a violation of Article 3 ECHR.[285] It remains unclear however what exactly constitute so-called hypothetical factors in the ECtHR's view.[286] Similarly to *Bensaid*, the ECtHR held in *N. v United Kingdom* that no violation of Article 3 ECHR was found because the case – not being able to access antiretroviral treatment in Uganda – was not very exceptional.[287] Apart from following the line of reasoning established in its earlier judgments, it is highly disturbing that the ECtHR recognized that once back in Uganda the applicant's quality of life and life expectancy would deteriorate rapidly, although at the time of the decision the applicant was not (yet)

282 S Joseph and A Fletcher, 'Scope of Application' in D Moeckli, S Shah and S Sivakumaran (eds), *International Human Rights Law* (2nd edn, OUP 2014) 127-128.

283 *Bensaid v the United Kingdom* (2001) 33 EHRR 10, para 38.

284 ibid para 35.

285 *D. v the United Kingdom* (1997) 24 EHRR 423, paras 53-54. In this case the ECtHR adopted the standard that: (…) aliens who have served their prison sentences and are subject to expulsion cannot in principle claim any entitlement to remain in the territory of a Contracting State in order to continue to benefit from medical, social or other forms of assistance provided by the expelling State during their stay in prison. However, in the very exceptional circumstances of this case and given the compelling humanitarian considerations at stake, it must be concluded that the implementation of the decision to remove the applicant would be a violation of Article 3 [ECHR].

286 It is common practice for any court to take into account empirical findings when rendering its judgment. In this regard it is questionable how impossible it would have been for the ECtHR to assess any empirical findings underpinning any hypothetical claim. The latter especially considering the case law it developed in relation to custodial settings in which the actual accessibility of care is a strict threshold.

287 *N. v the United Kingdom* (2008) 47 EHRR 39, para 51.

critically ill and that, as such, deciding on the rapidity of any deterioration would be pure speculation.[288]

In general, the ECtHR has delivered a strong body of case law. It seems that the foreseeability of a violation in relation to the access to medicines and the deterioration of an individual's health status due to a lack of treatment are pivotal in the outcome of the ECtHR's judicial review.[289] Lastly, in context of the study's focus on LMICs, it is noteworthy that most custodial cases claiming access to medicines or adequate care involved LMICs. In contrast, the prohibition of *non-refoulement* cases dealing with the level of care in the host country and the country to which the applicant was to be expelled included High Income Countries.

3.6 Conclusion

As was observed in the introduction, in law, balancing usually concerns three aspects: (i) the identification of the various considerations or interests involved; (ii) the assignment of a normative value to each of these considerations based on their importance; and (iii) scaling these considerations and their normative value.[290] This is exactly what this chapter has addressed in an integrated manner. It has done so in order to situate the 'principle of balance' of the international drug-control treaties within human rights law. In light of these steps, the chapter first outlined the way in which human rights law accords normative value and, subsequently, deals with framing the two aspects of the 'principle of balance' within the scope of *specific* human rights – whilst, at the same time, according these aspects their normative value and balancing them.

In terms of the normative value, the chapter demonstrated that although all rights are theoretically equal in nature, human rights law itself provides for a legal structure to implement and enforce human rights in an effective, prioritized manner. As opposed to the international drug-control regime, and in particular the Single Convention, human rights law recognizes priority-setting and balancing, if any of such priority or balancing has a basis in law itself and can be justified by human rights law. In other words, balancing or priority-setting in human rights law can never be a matter of political decision-making only but should always find a legitimate basis in any of its legal principles and concepts.

---

288 ibid para 50. In addition, it should be noted that the general rule in *D v United Kingdom* (n 285) was established with a view to prisoners receiving medical treatment whilst in prison. In *N. v the United Kingdom*, however, the applicant was an asylum seeker.

289 See eg *McGlinchey and Ors* (n 277); *Bragadireanu* (n 274); *N.* (n 287).

290 Porat (n 7) 1399. While elaborated upon in the context of constitutional law, Porat's structure of balancing may be applicable to balancing in human rights law.

In terms of framing and substantive application, any claim to access medicines, necessarily also including controlled medicines, is based on different rights. These include both CP and ESC rights and unequivocally find a basis in human rights law. Basing the argument primarily on the right to health demands one to acknowledge that the right to health might be 'weaker' from a litigation perspective, yet stronger in terms of normative scope. While it is fairly straightforward to establish the argument that access to healthcare, including medicines, is part of the prohibition of torture and CIDT, it is more complex to distinguish what States have to do exactly to ensure access to medicines on the basis of this right. Presenting the prohibition of torture and CIDT as a legally strong though complementary norm, reconstructing human rights obligations in relation to the juxtaposition of drug-control regulation has led to the following:

A human rights approach to drug control essentially means an 'access-led approach'. Access to medicines is not necessarily a more important norm from a normative perspective, but rather a weightier one under human rights law than the obligations to control the non-medical use of controlled substances. At least in the context of the right to health, the status of both elements – simply put: access and control – might be the same. The implementation and enforcement of the right to health recognizes a certain priority-setting. Access to medicines, as part of the core of the right to health, is therefore subject to priority realization. The protection against hazardous use as a more general aspect of the right to health, on the other hand, is subject to progressive realization. Although less explicit, one could say that this slight hierarchy in implementation is supported by the prohibition against torture and CIDT. Then again, the right to health may be limited to the extent that any of these limitations contribute to progressive realization of the rights set forth in the ICESCR. This study has not, and will not, however, enter into substantive arguments as to what the exact leeway ought to be, because none of these measures may limit the enjoyment of ESC rights or any claim to access controlled medicines and, in particular, pain-control and harm-reduction medicines. The prohibition against torture and CIDT complements the latter as, by its very status, it cannot be limited in any circumstance. In sum, exactly because both aspects are assigned a different normative value, any balancing of these two conflicting interests involves this difference from the outset. In other words, a balanced approach in human rights law may be a prioritized one.

In conclusion, in terms of the nature of norms, human rights law and the international drug-control treaties' *de jure* notion of balance seem rather similar.[291] The picture

291 Emphasis is added because it is often claimed that, although on paper equal in priority, the international drug-control treaties have never been established to really support and secure the access to medicines. This was extensively addressed at the Equitable Access to Controlled Medicines Brocher Symposium (Hermance, Switzerland, 8-9 October 2015).

drastically changes, however, when attempting to view drug-control matters in light of implementation and enforcement of human rights law, because the strict prohibition clause, as adopted in Article 4 Single Convention, cannot give rise to any implementation of enforcement in which access to medicines is compromised. In fact, when discharging drug-control obligations, access to medicines should be prioritized if managing a human rights approach to drug control. Inasmuch, one could argue that if indeed the access to medicines should be prioritized, one should wonder whether the strict prohibition clause of Article 4 of the Single Convention should not be reframed instead. A proportionality test may be a tool that can substantiate and guide public policy decision-making in this field.

A legal codification of the manner in which the access to medicines is prioritized in the enforcement and implementation of human rights would look like a clause in which access to medicines is the starting point and the protection against drug use the exception. In whichever form, in order to holistically argue in favour of such reconsideration, one should also conduct similar research into traditional, religious, and recreational medicinal use so as to fine-tune and reset the exact legal wording. This argument is by no means a blunt call for liberalization. It is rather the conclusion of a legal-technical argument that may result in liberalization if liberalization is the only route by means to materialise the access approach. Moreover, the question of whether such an 'access-led' approach may be justified is grounded in theories of law for which human rights are contingently important but not logically necessary. This is discussed in Chapter 4.

Finally, specifically in relation to sub-question 2, this chapter has demonstrated that if analysed in context of the right to health itself, access to controlled medicines, including pain-control medicines, is subject to the AAAQ standard of healthcare. This means that if considered holistically, any aspect of drug control, including access to medicines, should be realized in accordance with the AAAQ standard of healthcare – specifically if attempting to achieve a public health based approach to drug control in conjunction with a human rights approach. Ultimately, this begs the question whether it is feasible for States, in particular resource-constrained countries, to implement and realize access to medicines in accordance with the AAAQ standard of healthcare within the ambit of the specific administrative and procedural obligations set out in the Single Convention, including trade and distribution requirements. This is discussed in Chapters 5-7 by means of two country-specific case studies.[292]

292 Notably, if the administrative and procedural obligations of the Single Convention, including specific trade and distribution requirements, hamper States in ensuring the access to medicines, one may possibly also speak of a *de jure* limitation on any human rights claim to have access to medicines. This is further addressed and reflected on in Part 3 (Country Studies) and 4 (Conclusions and Recommendations) of this book.

Chapter 4
In Search of a Normative Justification

4.1 Introduction

In human rights law, balancing the access to (controlled essential) medicines on the one hand, with the protection of public health and public order against the hazardous use of substances on the other, differs from the balancing as framed in the international drug-control system.[1] In various ways, the obligation to ensure access to medicines is a strict obligation under human rights law and is part of the core of the right to health. Moreover, depending on the situation, access to medicines falls within the scope of the prohibition of torture and cruel, inhuman, and degrading treatment. Consequently, providing access to medicines, including controlled medicines, is a matter of priority for States.[2]

Awareness of this starting point requires a fundamentally different approach in current and future drug-control laws, policies, and regulation. Yet, questions arise about the normative justification of this interpretation – especially because human rights law itself is not explicit about how States should manage and discharge their dual obligations in the field of drug control.[3] Is it normatively defendable to argue that States must prioritize efforts to secure access to medicines over the protection against the hazardous use of controlled substances? This question touches on the justification of the priority or absoluteness of some elements of the human rights system, and the balancing between rights beyond that which is regulated by law. Addressing the issue of justification is particularly pressing because some scholars hold that (human) rights are based on incommensurable values.[4] More generally, the issue requires one to reflect on what human rights are about: to protect some basic moral standards beyond that which is written down in the law – which makes it necessary to reflect

---

1 'Controlled essential' is placed between brackets because human rights law in principle does not distinguish between controlled or uncontrolled medicines.
2 Harm-reduction measures, such as the availability of opioid-substitute medicines, should be considered as falling within the scope of this claim.
3 Chapter 3 presented a range of arguments for the reconstruction of the notion of balancing in relation to the access to medicines and the protection against hazardous drug use. However, it also demonstrated that the law as is does not explicitly deal with the juxtaposition central to this book.
4 C McCrudden, 'Human Dignity and Judicial Interpretation of Human Rights' (2008) 19 European Journal of International Law 655, 714.

on the logic behind human rights and distinguishing their underlying concepts and purposes.

One can distinguish between a principle of rights and rights as enshrined in a legal instruments programme.[5] The moral principles underlying the human rights framework are not necessarily the same as the legal rights enshrined in international human rights law.[6] In order to understand the possibility of defending an 'access-led' approach of drug-control regulation within the general structure of the human rights framework, one is required to discuss the principles that are elemental to human rights law.

With this in mind, this chapter explores whether the 'access-led' approach found in law can be morally justified. In contrast to Chapter 3, the aim of this chapter is to situate the 'principle of balance', as formulated in the international drug-control treaties, in human rights theory. The search for a more fundamental justification makes this chapter normative in nature.[7]

In terms of theory selection, the type of justification (of human rights) one defends determines the conceptualization of human rights that one presents. In other words, the content of and the role which human rights are expected to perform depend on the type of justification submitted.[8] Any balancing or priority-setting between human rights is therefore also largely influenced by said justification. As mentioned in Chapter 1, operating on the assumptions of human rights law leads one to accept human dignity as the overriding principle of the human rights system. Human dignity, in this context, should be understood as a claim to support and protect people in their ability to live their own life. This means that it is linked to the autonomy of human beings and an idea that living the life one wants to lead equates flourishing. Such a claim to autonomy, as well as the idea of 'human flourishing' and the enabling conditions necessary to protect human well-being, needs further analysis. To this end, this chapter describes two accounts of human rights that aim to justify the human rights framework instead of contesting it.[9] Both theories also view human dignity

5 S Benhabib, 'Another Universalism: On the Unity and Diversity of Human Rights' (2007) 81 Proceedings and Addresses of the American Philosophical Association 7, 10.

6 ibid; M Düwell, 'Human Dignity: Concepts, Discussions, Philosophical Perspectives' in M Düwell and others (eds), *The Cambridge Handbook of Human Dignity: Interdisciplinary Perspectives* (CUP 2014) 32. It is not argued here that there is always a gap between moral rules and legal rights. However, exactly because human rights law does not explicitly reconstruct the inner public health deficit, it is important to generate a more fundamental understanding of this matter.

7 In contrast, Chapter 3 was largely doctrinal.

8 Benhabib (n 5) 9.

9 As will be referred to throughout the chapter, there are many relevant theories of human rights that focus on agency and/or capability theory in the widest sense: theories in which human rights are

as a claim to autonomy, giving it a central overriding place in human rights.[10] This chapter analyses the capability theory, in particular as it is formulated by Martha Nussbaum, and looks into Alan Gewirth's Principle of Generic Consistency, as further substantiated by Deryck Beyleveld. Both approaches provide a philosophical account of justifying human rights and refer to ideas of autonomy and 'human flourishing' in doing so.

The chapter begins by developing an interpretation of morality and ethics, and their relation to the human rights framework, in order to substantiate the normative lens through which the analysis will take place (Section 4.2).[11] Next, the normative foundations of human rights law are analysed (Section 4.3).[12] This chapter then continues to reflect on the normative content of human dignity by analysing and applying the theories mentioned (Section 4.4). Finally, it deals with the conceptual criticism of various aspects of the argument presented (Section 4.5).

4.2 Morality, ethics and human rights

In order to fully comprehend this chapter's scope and methodology, it is important to outline how one should see the various fields of analysis in this particular chapter. For this purpose, this section briefly deals with morality and ethics, defining their meaning and purpose in light of the ambitions of this book. Subsequently, this section draws on the relevance of the relationship between law and morality for human rights law. At this stage, it is important to acknowledge that each of these topics is itself subject to extensive research. The information provided, and its application, is therefore far from exhaustive. Instead, it reflects a tailored message relevant to the central purpose of this book.

---

seen as claims to goods and services necessary for one's functioning and reaching of a certain level of well-being. However, these theories do not all operate on the premise found in human rights law. In fact, some of these theories do not aim to present a moral justification of the international human rights system at all and are therefore considered less relevant for this part of the book. See eg CR Beitz, *The Idea of Human Rights* (OUP 2009).

10 Throughout the chapter references are included, where relevant and necessary, to other theories of rights which, in their distinct ways, may be sympathetic to or critical of parts of the arguments presented.

11 Human rights are only partly relevant to the field of ethics and because theories of human rights are far from monolithic, the approach taken in this book is non-exhaustive.

12 The validity of human rights is not put to the test. The purpose of this chapter is not to discuss the philosophy of human rights in general, but rather to discuss a normative basis for a legitimate system of drug control with which to advance the access to controlled medicines based on the underlying assumptions of the international human rights framework.

4.2.1 Morality and ethics

Morality is the subject matter of ethics and reflects on how human beings should lead a 'good' life. In doing so, it asks whether certain actions are categorically either morally good (moral) or morally bad (immoral).[13] Such a categorization leads to a collection of rules of conduct that are seen to trump 'other modes of guiding action'.[14] This moral code of conduct is, moreover, categorically binding regardless of any explication – or absence thereof – in written law.[15]

Ethics is a mode of reflection on morality. It is not merely a method with which to distinguish between moral and immoral actions, but it also seeks to justify categorical moral claims, including moral obligations.[16] Some of ethics' theories deduce corresponding rights from these moral obligations. Doing so, however, immediately raises questions about why one option would be better than the other.[17] Bearing the findings of Chapter 3 in mind, one can wonder, from an ethical perspective, why access to medicines *should* be prioritized over the protection against the hazardous use of controlled substances.

Normative ethics, in turn, is the branch of moral philosophy which deals with action-guiding and with prescriptive questions regarding what we ought to do and why.[18] Analysing the role of the State here is the task of normative political philosophy. Discussing access to medicines and aspects of drug control from a normative ethical perspective not only raises the question of why one should but rather why one *ought* to prioritize access to medicines over the protection against the hazardous use of controlled substances.

Lastly, bioethics is a subfield of normative ethics that deals with the ethical aspects of medicine and biomedical research.[19] Given the subject matter of this book, the main question in this chapter will be analysed from a bioethical perspective. Nonetheless, more general philosophical and/or ethical theories concerning the human rights framework may be relevant; in particular normative political philosophy is relevant in the analysis of the role of the State.

---

13 M Düwell, *Bioethics* (Routledge 2013) 35-37. See also GE Moore, 'The Subject Matter of Ethics' in R Shafer-Landau (ed), *Ethical Theory* (2nd edn, Wiley-Blackwell 2013) 48-53.

14 A Gewirth, *Reason and Morality* (The University of Chicago Press 1978) 1.

15 id.

16 Düwell, *Bioethics* (n 13) 37. In his conceptualization of the PGC, Gewirth does the opposite. He deduces corresponding obligations using rights as a starting point. This will be further elaborated in Section 4.4.2.

17 id.

18 ibid 35, 39-40.

19 JD Arras, E Fenton and R Kukla (eds), *The Routledge Companion to Bioethics* (Routledge 2015) xxiii.

4.2.2 Morality and the law in relation to human rights

According to some scholars, applying a normative ethical approach presupposes natural law.[20] Natural law is a set of moral rules that generate their legitimacy through a transcendental norm, principle, given, or value, regardless of any explication or institutionalization in positive legal regimes or structures.[21] In such an interpretation, the legitimacy of any law – including human rights law – is grounded in categorically binding moral rules.[22] In relation to human rights, a natural-law scholar would argue 'that no political or legal order can be considered legitimate which does not subscribe to, respect, or enshrine in its constitution certain rights which human beings are entitled to qua human beings and which are thus unalterable and unrescindable'.[23]

Legal positivists, on the other hand, argue that the legitimacy of law does not depend on any moral justification. This, however, does not mean that these scholars would necessarily reject moral rules or the relevance of reflecting on the law in light of morality.[24] Rather, a legal positivist believes that the legitimacy of law is embedded in the 'legal system, insofar as it is a coherent articulation of norms, carries within it its own standards of judgment, evaluation, subordination, and subsumption'.[25] Moreover, the reluctance of some to view law and morality as mutually reinforcing is motivated by the idea that a legal order should be 'morally neutral and open to various moral convictions and worldviews'.[26]

Although the interpretation of the morality of law by natural-law scholars and legal positivists alike, and their distinction and overlap, is certainly interesting, a detailed discussion will not be entered into here. It may be noted, however, that neither field prescribes a fixed and exclusive interpretation. Rather, their interpretations rest on a dynamic continuum: especially in relation to the question 'What are human rights?', traditions in scholarship are utterly diffuse and no categorization is fixed.[27] Hoffman,

---

20 As Section 4.3.1 will elaborate, the human rights framework is traditionally often interpreted from a more natural legal perspective. Modern human rights law refers to inalienable rights grounded in human dignity. If one cannot lose human rights, then political recognition of human rights is contingently important, although not necessary. Operating on such an internal perspective, ie accepting this claim as the starting point of further analysis, means one has to acknowledge the importance of natural law and rights for the understanding of the foundations of the human rights framework.

21 See eg J Finnis, *Natural Law and Natural Rights* (2nd edn, OUP 2011) 23-24.

22 ibid.

23 Benhabib (n 5) 18.

24 R Wacks, *Understanding Jurisprudence: An Introduction to Legal Theory* (OUP 2005) 43-44.

25 Benhabib (n 5) 19.

26 Düwell, 'Human Dignity' (n 6) 32.

27 FF Hoffmann, 'Human Rights, the Self and the Other' in A Orford (ed), *International Law and Its Others* (CUP 2006); MB Dembour, 'What Are Human Rights? Four Schools of Thought' (2010) 32 Human Rights Quarterly 1.

for instance, questions whether human rights are only legal or moral rights, or whether the concept of a human right is also a discourse, idea, or practice.[28] For the purpose of this book, it suffices to acknowledge that human rights are traditionally interpreted from a more natural legal perspective.[29]

When considering human rights from a perspective according to which law and morality are related, the human rights question concerns whether human beings possess *a single right* (because they are human or because of some shared characteristic of humanity) or rights as granted by a *system of rights*? The second option would be most convincing due to its allowance for people to have more than one right.[30] Yet, it means that the human rights system is organized according to one overriding principle.[31] The next section will therefore explore whether such an overriding principle exists in human rights law, seeking to disentangle its normative foundations.

Nonetheless, at this stage it is important to observe that as a consequence, even if human rights are organized according to one superseding principle, one can still contextualize the interpretation of specific human rights. Any ethical evaluation of human rights or international law more generally allows for criticism or for one to challenge its operational, institutionalized framework – i.e. human rights law or international law as such.

Indeed, the human rights framework in general is often challenged and criticized from a Neo-Colonialist, or critical legal perspective. Critics claim that the human rights framework falls victim to the hegemony of international law, 'reinforcing pre-existing imperial tendencies in world politics'.[32] Such discussions act as the prelude

28 Hoffmann (n 27) 227.
29 J Tasioulas, 'Human Dignity and the Foundations of Human Rights' in C McCrudden (ed), *Understanding Human Dignity* (OUP 2013) 293. Section 4.3 will also demonstrate that if one scrutinizes the main human rights instruments, one finds that the references to inalienable rights as grounded in human dignity require viewing human rights as categorically binding moral rules. This does not mean that these moral claims are the same, or have to be the same, as the legal propositions set out in law. The word 'traditionally' in this sense does not refer to an old or out of date interpretation, but instead to an interpretation based on the normative foundation/assumption of the human rights framework itself.
30 Single rights theories include Hannah Arendt's argument that there is one natural right, namely the right to have rights, and Hart's conditional argument that there is one natural right – ie the right to hold rights equally. See H Arendt, *The Origins of Totalitarianism* (Harcourt 1951); HLA Hart, 'Are There Any Natural Rights?' (1955) 64 The Philosophical Review 175; CR Beitz and RE Goodin (eds), *Global Basic Rights* (2009 OUP) 5.
31 Benhabib holds that a principle of rights is not the same as a schedule of rights, cf n 5.
32 B Rajagopal, 'Counter-hegemonic International Law: Rethinking Human Rights and Development as a Third World Strategy' 27 (2006) Third World Quarterly 767, 768.

to Part 3 of this book (Country Studies) and will, as such, be discussed in Chapter 5. Nonetheless, one must note that at no stage in this book is it *a priori* contended that human rights law could not be hegemonic or that the human rights system is perfect in its current form. On the contrary, it is important to draw a clear line between the law as is and the law as ought to be, which reflects the main purpose of this chapter, and to acknowledge that it could well be that human rights law is organized incorrectly (or paradoxically) to bring about its own moral ambitions. Ultimately, the power of an ethical analysis lies precisely in its ability to bridge any potential gap between the law as it is and as it ought to be. The latter is equally the case in terms of access to controlled medicines and aspects of drug control.

4.3 Understanding the normative foundation of human rights law

This section explores the normative foundations of human rights law. In view of the approach taken in this chapter, it goes beyond *lex scripta* and distinguishes the moral principles on which the human rights framework rests. First, the section introduces human dignity as the foundation of human rights within the human rights framework. Second, it clarifies the role of human dignity and situates the matter as either a neutral, ancillary, or central principle in said framework. Especially if understood as the basis of the human rights framework, any insight into the way in which human dignity informs human rights law is significant. Reflecting on human dignity in its foundational role more substantively, the section goes on to explain the conservative and liberal view of human dignity. Finally, the section briefly addresses different philosophical approaches to autonomy, as in its traditional fashion human dignity is often considered as a claim to autonomy.

4.3.1 Human dignity as the foundation of human rights

Both at the international and regional level, there are ample examples to demonstrate that human rights documents frame human rights as being inherent to mankind, seeking to justify and legitimize them by reference to their foundation in human dignity.[33]

33 J Donnelly, *International Human Rights* (3rd edn, Westview Press 2013) 22-28; C Dupré, 'Constructing the Meaning of Human Dignity' in C McCrudden (ed), *Understanding Human Dignity* (OUP 2013) 113-116; R Brownsword, 'Human Dignity from a Legal Perspective' in M Düwell and others (eds), *The Cambridge Handbook of Human Dignity: Interdisciplinary Perspectives* (CUP 2014). Although reflecting the orthodox interpretation, the idea that human dignity is the foundation of human rights is also heavily contested. Den Hartogh, for instance, wonders whether human dignity is really the foundation of human rights or whether it rather points to the idea that human rights have a foundation, whatever this foundation substantively may be. Arguing that dignity is an empty concept, Macklin asserts that one would not even 'miss' human dignity if it were not there. R Macklin, 'Dignity is a Useless Concept' (2003) 327 The British Medical Journal 1419; G den Hartogh, 'Is Human Dignity the Ground of Human Rights?' in M Düwell and others (eds), *The Cambridge Handbook of Human*

Donnelly refers to this foundational notion of dignity found in the international bill of rights as the 'Universal Declaration Model'.[34] For instance, Article 1 of the Universal Declaration of Human Rights (UDHR) reads: '[a]ll human beings are born free and equal in dignity and rights. They are endowed with reason and conscience and should act towards one another in the spirit of brotherhood'.[35] The preambles of both the International Covenant on Civil and Political Rights and the International Covenant on Economic, Social and Cultural Rights also make reference to human rights deriving from human dignity.[36] In addition, States recognize in these preambles that the 'inherent dignity and (...) the equal and inalienable rights of all members of the human family [are] the foundation of freedom, justice and peace in the world'.[37]

In addition to those contained in the 'international bill of rights', references to dignity as the basis of human rights are also found in the nine core human rights instruments.[38]

Dignity: Interdisciplinary Perspectives (CUP 2014). Moreover, in contrast to Donnelly, Westerman questions the relationship between human rights and human dignity. According to the author, one can disagree or at least wonder whether people hold inalienable rights as stipulated in the international bill of rights and are thereby bestowed with human dignity. Or, alternatively, do people hold inalienable rights because they have human dignity? See PC Westerman, 'Natural Rights versus Human Dignity: Two Conflicting Traditions' in M Düwell and others (eds), *The Cambridge Handbook of Human Dignity: Interdisciplinary Perspectives* (CUP 2014) 108.

34 Donnelly (n 33) 28.

35 Art. 1 Universal Declaration of Human Rights (adopted 10 December 1948) UNGA Res 217 A (III) (UDHR).

36 International Covenant on Civil and Political Rights (adopted 16 December 1966, entered into force 23 March 1976) 999 UNTS 171 (ICCPR) prmbl; International Covenant on Economic, Social and Cultural Rights (adopted 16 December 1966, entered into force 3 January 1976) 993 UNTS 3 (ICESCR) prmbl.

37 id; Donnelly (n 33) 28. On the other hand, Waldron contends that in a strict textual interpretation, the preambles of the ICCPR and the ICESCR refer to 'rights and dignity as coordinate ideas, rather than deriving one from the other'. This would mean that only the UDHR would reflect a true foundational claim to dignity. J Waldron, 'Is Dignity the Foundation of Human Rights?' (2013) NYU Public Law & Legal Theory Research Paper Series Working Paper No 12-73 <http://papers.ssrn.com/sol3/papers.cfm?abstract_id=2196074> accessed 31 August 2016.

38 The International Convention on the Elimination of All Forms of Racial Discrimination (adopted 7 March 1966, entered into force 4 January 1969) 660 UNTS 195, Convention on the Elimination of All Forms of Discrimination Against Women (adopted 18 December 1979, entered into force 3 September 1981) 1249 UNTS 13, Convention on the Rights of the Child (adopted 20 November 1989, entered into force 2 September 1990) 1577 UNTS 3, and Convention on the Rights of Persons with Disabilities (adopted 13 December 2006, entered into force 3 May 2008) 2515 UNTS 3 second the foundational dignity references of the UN Charter (which also includes a fundamental reference to equal dignity) and the UDHR. The International Convention for the Protection of All Persons from Enforced Disappearance (adopted 20 December 2006, entered into force 23 December 2010) 2716 UNTS 3 only implicitly seconds the UDHR's foundational reference to human dignity. Both the Convention Against Torture and Other Cruel, Inhuman or Degrading Treatment or Punishment (adopted 10 December 1984, entered into force 26 June 1987) 1465 UNTS 85 and the International Convention on the Protection of the Rights of All Migrant Workers and Members of their Families

In addition, the 1993 Vienna Declaration and Programme of Action, which was adopted at the UN World Conference held in Vienna that same year, reinforces the claim that human beings are endowed with human rights simply in virtue of their being human. According to all representatives present at the conference '[h]uman rights and fundamental freedoms are the birthright of all human beings'.[39] Moyn coined this foundational role ascribed to dignity as 'dignitarian constitutionalism'.[40]

The constitutionalist, foundational role of human dignity is also found at the level of regional human rights protection.[41] While human dignity is well embedded in preambular texts, the concept is only marginally referred to substantively in separate provisions.[42] The lack of substantive references may raise the question whether dignity is deprived of its central role or foundational status – an issue that arises regardless of which status or role is substantively implied.

Brownsword submits that it was simply not necessary to refer to dignity repeatedly. Placing human dignity at the core of post-World War II human rights law already reflected a cosmopolitan notion thereof: 'humans have a dignity – a dignity that governments should always respect'.[43] Beyleveld and Brownsword contend more specifically that it is precisely because human dignity as the basis of human rights attracts the attention of philosophers rather than the adjudication of the legal system, that 'it is perfectly clear why human dignity, having done its work in grounding human rights, then slips into the background'.[44] Although dignity may have slipped into the background, the issue is whether it is (now) a redundant concept or rather remains a central principle for the understanding of the human rights framework.

(adopted 18 December 1990, entered into force 1 July 2003) 2220 UNTS 3 stress explicitly in their preambles that the human rights expressed in the respective treaties are based on human dignity.

39 'Vienna Declaration and Programme of Action' UN World Conference on Human Rights (Vienna, 14-25 June 1993) (25 June 1993) UN Doc A/CONF.157/23, para 1.

40 S Moyn, 'The Secret History of Constitutional Dignity' in C McCrudden (ed), *Understanding Human Dignity* (OUP 2013) 95. The relationship between human dignity and human rights is conceptualized in many ways, of which its foundational role is only one. Tasioulas (n 29) distinguishes: (i) the mere reference of human dignity in relation to 'genuine human rights'; (ii) human dignity as the distinctive feature of human rights in contrast to general ideas about moral and legal rights, which are not necessarily human rights; (iii) the foundational role of dignity, understanding human rights as grounded in human dignity.

41 Human dignity is referred to in the European Convention for the Protection of Human Rights and Fundamental Freedoms (adopted 4 November 1950, entered into force 3 September 1953, as amended) 213 UNTS 222, prmbl; and the African Charter on Human and Peoples' Rights (adopted 27 June 1981, entered into force 21 October 1986) 1520 UNTS 217, prmbl. Human dignity is referred to more substantively in relation to specific rights in the American Convention on Human Rights (adopted 22 November 1969, entered into force 18 July 1978) 1144 UNTS 123, arts 5, 6, 11.

42 D Beyleveld and R Brownsword, *Human Dignity in Bioethics and Biolaw* (OUP 2001) 12-13.

43 Brownsword (n 33) 3.

44 Beyleveld and Brownsword (n 42) 13.

4.3.2 Ancillary or central principle

Increasingly, scholars have questioned the normative content and scope of human dignity from a philosophical as well as a legal perspective.[45] Contextualizing human dignity is important precisely because of the central role human dignity occupies in the human rights discourse.[46] As Düwell observes, 'it is clear that the way [in which] we understand human dignity influences our understanding of the human rights framework as such'.[47] This is demonstrated, for example, by the central normative weight attributed to human dignity in international, regional, and domestic legal instruments.

It is often assumed that human dignity results in a categorical obligation, meaning that respect for human dignity is an obligation that overrides all other possible considerations of action. If one views human rights as being derived from human dignity, this implies that human rights also formulate categorically binding rules of action. Yet, is human dignity, or can it be, a categorical imperative? This question is addressed further below. However, even if human dignity is an articulation of a categorical imperative and human rights are categorically binding rules, this does not mean that the rights outlined in the UDHR and subsequent human rights documents are necessarily moral rights. According to Düwell, one should understand human rights as legal propositions:

> To see human rights as based on or derived from respect for human dignity would here be the recognition that it is morally required to respect human dignity, to ensure the legal provisions of the human rights would be an institutionalized answer to this moral requirement.[48]

In other words, human rights law is an institutionalization of the moral requirement to respect human dignity. This does not mean, however, that the law itself is necessarily moral because, as is addressed above, legal rights and the moral principles upon which they are based are not unequivocally the same. One can therefore very well criticize the law whilst accepting its normative foundation.

---

45 McCrudden (n 4); Dupré (n 33); Tasioulas (n 29) 293; Düwell, 'Human Dignity' (n 6).The emergence of human dignity as a subject of multidisciplinary inquiry is generally demonstrated by the wealth of recent literature written on this topic including, but not limited to, C McCrudden (ed), *Understanding Human Dignity* (OUP 2013) and M Düwell and Others (eds), *The Cambridge Handbook of Human Dignity: Interdisciplinary Perspectives* (CUP 2014).

46 Düwell, 'Human Dignity' (n 6) 27.

47 id.

48 ibid 32.

Along the same line of reasoning, Tasioulas holds that all human beings have equal human dignity. However, the set of human rights they hold 'depends also on their interests and the threshold considerations whereby those interests generate duties'.[49] It is worthwhile to acknowledge here that possessing human dignity is therefore not necessarily the same as having all human rights as enumerated in the human rights framework in a *de facto* equal manner. Rights protection, based on such reasoning, depends on the interests or needs involved. As a result, human dignity is not a redundant concept but rather the cornerstone of human rights. One can explain the central position human dignity occupies in the human rights framework by considering it as the overriding principle.

In addition, Moyn submits that human dignity became a 'crucial watchword (...) offering judicial guidance for the protection of basic values' because of the ample references to it in the international human rights framework in general and in the international bill of rights in particular.[50] Some scholars question whether human dignity is capable of fulfilling this judicial role or whether law is able to translate and adjudicate according to the moral requirements protecting human dignity.[51] Aside from addressing this criticism (see Section 4.5), at this stage of the argument it is contended that if human dignity can be such an overriding principle, then it is 'guiding for the interpretation of the entire set of human rights, and would see human rights as "derived" from human dignity'.[52] This presupposes, however, that human dignity can be a categorically binding moral principle. The question of whether or not this holds true, as well as its potential in relation to the access to medicines and drug control, is further elaborated in the following sections.

4.3.3 Different approaches to human dignity

References to the interpretation of dignity as the moral foundation of human rights are manifold.[53] Düwell maps out that dignity can be understood as a right, a norm, and as a principle.[54] Human dignity as a right could imply that an individual would hold a right with a certain special status.[55] One could argue that this means that

49 Tasioulas (n 29) 312.
50 Moyn (n 40) 95.
51 For instance, McCrudden (n 4) wrote a compelling analysis on the misguiding potential of human dignity in human rights adjudication. McCrudden's criticism is, in part, addressed in Section 4.5, translating agency accounts of human rights back into the positive human rights framework.
52 Düwell, 'Human Dignity' (n 6) 29-30.
53 To provide context; Tasioulas (n 29) indicates that viewing dignity as the foundation of the human rights framework is only one out of three ways to interpret the link between human dignity and human rights. See text at n 40.
54 Düwell, 'Human Dignity' (n 6) 28.
55 id.

human dignity is a 'container right', protecting aspects which fall outside the scope of other rights, and as such would repair the flaws of the human rights framework more generally.[56] Human dignity as a right could, in addition, also mean that people have a right to be protected against gross and structural human rights violations, which transcend the level of specific rights protection and violate any respect for the human person in general.[57] However, if one holds that human rights are derived from dignity, then dignity must have a fundamentally different meaning from human rights. Viewing it as a sort of 'super crosscutting right' is not enough.[58]

One could also see human dignity as the right to have rights.[59] A right to have rights may, at least in line with Arendt's thinking, imply that human dignity is a claim that entitles people to be or become a member of a political system, granting this person the rights of citizenship.[60] However, if human dignity is the right to have rights, and the rights one possesses are the results of political decision-making, then human dignity does not influence the scope and content of these rights.[61] This in itself would be contrary to the foundational role ascribed to dignity and as implied in the human rights framework. The human rights framework explicates that human rights are based in human dignity, which presupposes that dignity had influence and should continue to have influence over the interpretation of specific human rights. Moreover, as is mentioned in Section 4.2.2, such a single rights conception reduces human rights to one single right and cannot accommodate a set of different rights.

In addition, one could understand human dignity as a norm, which reflects the idea that one should respect humanity. In such an interpretation, human dignity could be the basis on which to 'condemn some actions as objective violations of "humanity"'.[62] As the next section will demonstrate, viewing human dignity as a norm would seriously endanger the entire human rights system. Ultimately, one can also understand human dignity as a principle. In ethics, a principle is a categorically binding imperative of action that overrides other practical – e.g. prudential – considerations.[63] Understanding human dignity as a principle, whatever this may yet imply substantively, therefore allows one to understand human rights as based on human dignity, or at least as derived from it.[64] It does so in a manner in which human

56 id.
57 id.
58 id.
59 cf text at n 30.
60 Arendt (n 30); Düwell, 'Human Dignity' (n 6) 29.
61 Düwell, 'Human Dignity' (n 6) 29.
62 id.
63 ibid 30.
64 id.

rights law is important, although not necessary.[65] In bioethics, the content of human dignity can be expounded in a conservative and a liberal manner, respectively. These two interpretations are addressed in order to demonstrate the power and necessity of viewing human dignity as formulating a categorically binding moral principle as opposed to a concrete moral norm.

4.3.4 A conservative and liberal interpretation of human dignity

The field of bioethics is imbued with dignity-related matters.[66] Addressing the various appeals to dignity, Beyleveld and Brownsword have reconstructed two different perspectives: human dignity constraint and human dignity as empowerment.[67] Human dignity as constraint is a community-based, conservative conceptualization of dignity, reflecting the protection of the dignity of a society or community rather than that of the individual as such.[68] Human dignity as empowerment, on the other hand, is an individual-based, liberal concept focused on autonomy.

Both types are claims to the constitutionalist notion that human rights are grounded in human dignity. In this sense, both concepts do not only grant human dignity a central position in the human rights framework, but also consider it as a categorically binding moral rule. While the conceptualization of Beyleveld and Brownsword is focused on the content of human dignity, instead of the role it plays in the human rights framework, one must note that, as will be elaborated upon below, human dignity as constraint often results in concrete moral norms (which may be incompatible with understanding human dignity as a principle). On the contrary, human dignity as empowerment may be the content of human dignity as a principle.

Human dignity as constraint

According to the view that considers human dignity a constraint, the protection of dignity lies in the overruling ability of a State to interfere with an individual's life in order to protect the dignity of a community or society as a whole.[69] Human dignity, in

---

65 id.

66 Think of questions such as whether it is morally acceptable or wrong to amputate a limb from a clinically healthy person upon their own request. Or, in light of this study, is it morally acceptable or wrong to treat someone's drug addiction without actively preventing dispersion and abuse in the first place? Or, is it morally acceptable or wrong to treat someone's drug addiction even though the person involved does not harm anyone and voluntarily decides to continue using? Moreover, is it morally acceptable or wrong to equate issues regarding the access to medicines to other health expenditure?

67 See Beyleveld and Brownsword (n 42).

68 ibid 1-2, 11.

69 ibid 29; SD Pattinson, *Medical law and Ethics* (3rd edn, Sweet & Maxwell 2011) 15.

such a scenario, is therefore a norm on the basis of which certain actions can be held to violate the dignity of society. Such violations would then justify States in restricting certain individual rights.[70] Along this line of thought, prostitution and dwarf-throwing would be violations of humanity or the dignity of society.[71] The French dwarf-tossing case is insightful to understand how human dignity as constraint 'works'.[72]

In the French dwarf-tossing case, it was held that the practice of dwarf-tossing – regardless of the consent of the individuals involved – would breach the *ordre public* of which human dignity is considered a key component.[73] The Conseil d'État held that a dwarf compromises his own dignity by allowing himself or herself to be used as a mere object. For this reason, local police were ordered to prohibit any platform for such entertainment.[74] In other words, state interference was deemed justifiable on the grounds of protecting human dignity, the underlying idea being that it is one thing for a person to decide to compromise his/her own dignity, but another altogether when in doing so they compromise the dignity of the community as a whole. It follows from such a conservative interpretation of dignity that one, in order to respect the dignity of the community, has a duty to refuse any compromise of one's own dignity if such an action violates the dignity of the community. Individual autonomy may therefore be subjected to or overruled by this interpretation of dignity as a constraint/dignity as a concrete moral norm.[75]

One could also frame drug control and the protection against the hazardous use and dispersion as a conservative view of dignity protection. The argument would look as follows: regardless of the individual will, consent, or interest of the person to use hazardous substances, States should protect them against such use since the mere act of using the substance compromises the dignity of society as a whole. It seems nonsensical to hold that access to medicines would be a violation of humans' dignity. The lack of access to medicines, on the other hand, would be. As a result, in the dignity as a constraint framing, one can still consider access to medicines as a vital demand. Yet, one can also use the conservative appeal to human dignity to argue in favour of a strict prohibition regarding any purpose other than the medical use of

---

70 Düwell, 'Human Dignity' (n 6) 29.

71 On human dignity and prostitution, see eg N Campagna, 'Human Dignity and Prostitution' in M Düwell and others (eds), *The Cambridge Handbook of Human Dignity: Interdisciplinary Perspectives* (CUP 2014).

72 Conseil d'Etat n° 136727 du 27 octobre 1995. See also HR Committee, *Manuel Wackenheim v France* (Comm no 854/1999) in which the Committee considered that the ban '(...) was necessary in order to protect public order, which brings into play considerations of human dignity that are compatible with the objectives of the Covenant' (para 7.4).

73 Beyleveld and Brownsword (n 42) 33-34.

74 ibid 26.

75 ibid 34. See also Düwell, 'Human Dignity' (n 6) 29.

controlled substances. Just as in the case of dwarf-tossing, the protection of human dignity would trump individual freedom and its protection.[76] Human dignity then entails the *norm* that dwarf-tossing or drug use constitutes a violation of humans' dignity.

While some might welcome this argument grounded in a foundational human dignity claim, in this capacity, human dignity represents a particular risk to the human rights framework as such. Human dignity as a norm or constraint carries the potential to support anti-law or even to undermine itself, as human dignity as a norm may favour the interest of certain social groups over others. If dignity as a norm, instead of as a principle, were still to have an overriding status in the human rights framework, human rights themselves could become a violation of human dignity. If the norm of human dignity were to function in that way, the human rights framework would compromise human dignity and human dignity as a norm could override human rights in general.[77] Although the exact definition of supporting control has yet to be examined, if it denotes strict and prohibitive approaches, then the argument demonstrates some potential. Yet, precisely because the objectivity sought is external to the human rights framework, this line of reasoning is unconvincing.

Human dignity as empowerment

By contrast, human dignity as empowerment is a more plausible interpretation. Regardless of the substantive outcome, this conceptualization of dignity reflects what Düwell would call *human dignity as a principle*, which is 'safe' for the human rights framework in general – i.e. it cannot be used as a means to undermine the idea of human rights.[78] This means that human dignity as empowerment conceptualizes human dignity as a moral rule categorically binding on all actions, trumping all practical considerations. In this context, human rights are truly derived from or based on human dignity.[79] As is postulated in the introduction, dignity as empowerment would then lead to exactly the type of conceptualization one would need in order to consider a moral justification of a human rights approach to drug control.

---

76 Protection, in this context, refers to human rights protection at large, including the tripartite obligation to respect, protect, and fulfil (See Chapter 3).

77 Düwell, 'Human Dignity' (n 6) 29. It is not contended here that arguing in favour of human dignity as constraint or human dignity as a norm necessarily means that one overthrows the human rights framework in its entirety. Instead, it is submitted that it *could* imply overthrowing the human rights framework.

78 'Safe' does not mean human rights law may not be criticized. As was also explained at the outset of this chapter, any ethical evaluation of human rights still allows for criticism or challenging of its operational framework (in this case human rights law). cf text at n 32.

79 Düwell, 'Human Dignity' (n 6) 30.

In short, human dignity as empowerment reflects a liberal approach in which dignity is the distinctive feature of humanity that justifies rights and duties.[80] According to this interpretation, humans have a certain capacity in which their specific dignity status is grounded. On the basis of this status they have rights to the protection of the conditions (of their life) that are required for the exercise of this relevant capacity.[81] More generally, one could say that human dignity grounds the right to access the conditions of human flourishing.[82] Brownsword and Beyleveld describe the concept of dignity as empowerment as giving rise to a formal scheme of three rights:

i) A right to be respected in possessing the distinct capacities of being human;
ii) A negative right against any interventions against your will which would damage the conditions essential to prospering as a human;
iii) A positive right to support and assistance in obtaining the conditions essential to your 'human flourishing'.[83]

Yet, a central issue is what this distinct capacity is, as well as how this capacity can ground and justify both negative and positive rights and obligations, which shape and revise the institutions of a social system.

---

80 Beyleveld and Brownsword (n 42) 13.

81 ibid 15.

82 There are many theories of rights that construct a theory of justice relying on a similar idea of 'human flourishing'. Examples include the basic rights theories of Pogge, Shue, and Beitz, the Capability Approach, as developed by Nussbaum, or the generic rights conceptions, as put forth by Gewirth and Beyleveld in particular. Although these theories might show similarities in the manner in which they give normative content to the goal and purpose of moral rights protection, they are distinct in their justifications. It is for that reason that they are also not necessarily directly in line with the dignity as empowerment reading, which presupposes understanding human rights via the idea that they are grounded in human dignity. D Beyleveld, *The Dialectical Necessity of Morality* (The University of Chicago Press 1991); A Gewirth, *The Community of Rights* (The University of Chicago Press 1996); H Shue, *Basic Rights: Subsistence, Affluence, and U.S. Foreign Policy* (2nd edn, Princeton University Press 1996); TW Pogge, *World Poverty and Human Rights* (2nd edn, Polity Press 2008); Beitz (n 9); Beitz and Goodin (n 30); MC Nussbaum, *Creating Capabilities: The Human Development Approach* (HUP 2011).

83 Beyleveld and Brownsword (n 42) 15. Pogge also elaborates on the notion of 'human flourishing' as to constitute a certain minimum level of well-being, see Pogge (n 82) 54. Moreover, while Tomuschat acknowledges that positive human rights duties are supported by many theories of rights, scholars like O'Neill hold that natural law, or rather human rights as moral principles, cannot give rise to positive duties. According to O'Neill, liberty rights or freedoms are the only natural rights, and any positive rights and duties such as the right to health, food, and shelter are only justified by reference to a positive legal framework enshrining these rights. Apart from seeking any objective truth, it suffices to indicate at this stage of the argument that as much as positive rights and duties are under discussion in human rights law, they are also subject to discussion in human rights theory. O O'Neill, 'The Dark Side of Human Rights' (2005) 81 International Affairs 427, 432; C Tomuschat, *Human Rights between Idealism and Realism* (2nd edn, OUP 2008) 23-24.

One can question whether this distinct capacity is the ability to value, to think, to act autonomously. It is commonly supported that the dignity-related capacity is the ability to act autonomously.[84] Beyleveld and Brownsword hold that 'if the capacity to control one's actions by reference to the choices one has made is the distinctive source of human worth, then to deny a human the opportunity to choose and control (…) is to offend against his or her dignity'.[85]

It follows that if the foundational principle of human rights is that each human being has a right to respect for his or her dignity, then both non-interference as well as assistance in obtaining conditions essential to flourishing as a human being are required.[86] In other words, protection of human dignity invokes both negative and positive rights and corresponding duties. Ultimately, the issue is how to distinguish the different conditions relevant to this idea of 'human flourishing'. We must ask ourselves which goods and services are necessary in order to live an autonomous life, i.e. a life in dignity – regardless of whether such claims are civil-political or socio-economic in nature.[87] In relation to health matters specifically, Venkatapuram holds that health justice requires such a 'supportive environment'.[88]

Consequently, if understood in line with dignity as empowerment, the human rights framework, from its very outset, ought to give rise to positive and negative rights and obligations in relation to all claims at the normative level.[89] In other words, if human dignity is the ability to act autonomously or to live an autonomous life, then human rights are positive and negative claims to goods and services are necessary to act autonomously and live an autonomous life, whatever this autonomous life or autonomous action may imply *in concreto*. To this end, as the word 'empowerment' implies, human dignity encompasses the freedom to make your own choices and restricts interference with individual lives, regardless of any presupposed good or harm. In this role, human dignity can be a 'core criterion of basic justice' and occupy a fundamental normative position in the human rights framework, as informing

84 BVerfG, 21.06.1977 (1 BvL 14/76), NJW 1977, 1525. Beyleveld and Brownsword (n 42) 15. In an autonomy-based account of human dignity, difficulties may arise in relation to the rights of comatose patients and foetuses since they do not show signs of the ability for autonomous action. In addition, difficulties may also arise in relation to the communitarianism of many non-Western societies. These concerns are addressed in Sections 4.4.2 and 4.5 respectively.

85 Beyleveld and Brownsword (n 42) 16.

86 ibid 15. For a contemporary critique on presuppositional duties, see T Hayward, 'On Prepositional Duties' (2013) 123 Ethics 264.

87 See for a debate on claim rights, L. Weimar, 'The Nature of Claim-Rights' (2013) 123 Ethics 202. In light of Chapter 3, this notion supports trumping the traditional classification between CP and ESC rights.

88 S Venkatapuram, *Health Justice* (Polity Press 2011) 1.

89 Naturally, the picture might change when it comes to the enforcement and realization of rights, as this largely depends on the context and the available resources.

the clarification of specific moral rights rather than invoking a set list of justiciable human rights.[90] This premise is the starting point for further analysis.

4.3.5 Different notions of autonomy and human dignity in bioethics

Even if one is to assume that human dignity, as the overriding principle, should be understood as a claim to autonomy to live a life in dignity, constructing such an account remains complicated. As there is no single definition of or approach to human dignity, there is no single conception of autonomy.

Autonomy is a central concept in bioethics and yet is subject to multiple interpretations within this domain. Macklin, for instance, labels dignity as a useless concept exactly because the meaning of dignity can only vaguely be determined. Macklin argues that dignity 'means no more than respect for persons or their autonomy'.[91] Beyleveld and Brownsword also trace a clear link between human dignity and autonomy in their empowerment view of human rights. However, their approaches are distinct due to their interpretation of autonomy.

While Macklin considers a very narrow interpretation of dignity, Beyleveld and Brownsword, but also scholars like Gewirth, adopt a much broader notion of autonomy and of dignity. In Macklin's argument, dignity only reflects the negative freedom to make free choices. This narrow interpretation merely invokes negative rights and duties. In contrast, the broader notion of autonomy developed by Beyleveld, Brownsword, and Gewirth, reflects both the ability to make choices and the need for positive assistance in generating the goods necessary to make that choice in the first place. In their view, autonomy is not simply the negative freedom to make choices, which merely presupposes negative rights; it also facilitates the ability to act autonomously, including the necessary preconditions for such ability, and therefore positive rights and duties.[92] According to Beyleveld and Brownsword, a foundational claim to human dignity essentially means seeing human dignity as the basis of the entire human rights system, where autonomy is the explication of dignity.

---

90 On the 'core criterion of basic justice', see Pogge (n 82) 54; Düwell, 'Human Dignity' (n 6).

91 Macklin (n 33).

92 According to Gewirth, for instance, human beings are both rights holders and duty bearers, and hold mutual obligations to rights of freedom and well-being. This correlation implies both mutual respect, as well as assistance, in obtaining goods and services necessary to enjoy rights of freedom and well-being. In fact, Gewirth considers positive rights the link to a community of rights. See Gewirth, *Community of Rights* (n 82) 6, 31; Beyleveld and Brownsword (n 42) 15; D Beyleveld, 'Human Dignity and Human Rights in Alan Gewirth's Moral Philosophy' in M Düwell and others (eds), *The Cambridge Handbook of Human Dignity: Interdisciplinary Perspectives* (CUP 2014) 232.

This interpretation generally falls within the Kantian view of dignity in which dignity is not considered as *equivalent* to autonomy but rather as a *claim* to autonomy.[93]

Beauchamp and Childress, on the other hand, regard autonomy as a mediating principle. In their view, autonomy is one of the four principles of bioethics (autonomy, non-maleficience, beneficience, and justice).[94] Any bioethical issue should be considered according to these four factors. As such, understanding dignity as an overriding principle and as the central organizing principle of the human rights framework would imply that one cannot understand autonomy in the manner that Beauchamp and Childress suggest since their understanding of autonomy implies that human dignity is a mediating norm instead of the overriding principle. The categorical claim of human dignity as the foundation of human rights does not allow one to balance human dignity with other principles. Rather, it entails that human dignity informs the explication of specific claims and the necessary balancing between these claims. Following this line of reasoning, Macklin's version would also fail to endure because of its narrow interpretation of autonomy, which limits itself only to negative freedoms.

These different interpretations reflect precisely what is argued to be one of the weaknesses of the foundational role of human dignity.[95] In fact, it leads one to question whether it can even be the foundation of human rights.[96] Notwithstanding their importance, it is helpful to set aside these criticisms for a moment and first try to understand what exactly human dignity has to bring to the table in terms of access to controlled medicines and aspects of drug-control regulation.[97]

4.4 On the normative content of human dignity as empowerment

In order to understand the way in which dignity as empowerment relates to situating the 'principle of balance' in human rights theory, one has to conceptualize and justify human rights according to theories which are supportive of enabling conditions. These accept the human rights framework and tie in with a concept of autonomy that allows dignity to act as a categorically binding moral rule. In other words, one has to explore the normative content of human dignity as advanced by these theories. Once one has some understanding of these theories and their conceptualizations, one can apply them to the access to medicines and aspects of drug control.

93 On the differences between Macklin's understanding of autonomy and dignity, and a more Kantian-based argument, see M Rosen, 'Dignity: The Case Against' in C McCrudden (ed), *Understanding Human Dignity* (OUP 2013) 150.

94 TL Beauchamp and JF Childress, *Principles of Biomedical Ethics* (7th edn, OUP 2013).

95 Macklin (n 33); Rosen (n 93) 150.

96 See Waldron (n 37).

97 This criticism is addressed in Section 4.5.

First, this section elaborates the capability approach, its general features, and its application to the access to medicines and aspects of drug control. Second, it sets out the idea of generic rights and explains the manner in which access to medicines and aspects of drug control would relate to one another on the basis of such a reading.

4.4.1 Capability theory

The capability approach is a broad normative theory focussing on people's capabilities to function. This functioning refers to a state of being of human beings in general and, in particular, to each human being's potential for well-being.[98] Functioning is value-driven and could therefore include any functioning as long as the person involved values it.[99] The approach that Nussbaum has more recently developed into a theory of human rights attempts to bring about greater social justice.[100] The focus on free choice, self-definition, and self-determination makes the theory liberal in nature. It is, however, not entirely free from paternalism.

In some situations, the theory might in fact support the idea that a State must advance individual functioning beyond individual consent or choice.[101] This is especially the case when people make choices by which they 'humiliate or debase themselves'.[102] Would this be the case for non-recreational drug use? If so, could one entertain a similar argument as applied to dwarf-tossing and prostitution, put forth by the dignity as a constraint line of reasoning (see Section 4.3.3)?[103] As will be demonstrated below, this in itself is confusing and rather controversial due to the theory's seeming reliance on different fundamental yardsticks.[104] Yet, in essence, the theory generally falls in line with the dignity as empowerment idea, while it is perhaps also sympathetic to some aspects of the framing of dignity as a constraint.

---

98 R Claassen, 'Human Dignity in the Capability Approach' in M Düwell and others (eds), *The Cambridge Handbook of Human Dignity: Interdisciplinary Perspectives* (CUP 2014) 240.

99 id.

100 The Capabilities Approach has various conceptualizations, including Amartya Sen's development approach and Martha Nussbaum's political philosophy approach, as well as a specification into health matters. See eg A Sen, 'Capability and Well-Being' in MC Nussbaum and A Sen (eds), *The Quality of Life* (OUP 1993); A Sen, 'Human Rights and Capabilities' (2005) 6 Journal of Human Development 151; JP Ruger, *Health and Social Justice* (OUP 2010); Nussbaum (n 82); Venkatapuram (n 88); Claassen (n 98) 241.

101 Claassen (n 98) 241.

102 ibid 243.

103 It is not argued here that one should uphold such an argument nor is the argument in itself supported. Rather, it is questioned whether one could argue along a similar line of reasoning on the basis of the capability approach.

104 Claassen (n 98) 243.

Capabilities

Capabilities are the conditions necessary to function, regardless of the actual functioning and the value attached to it. Functioning is the successful employment of these capabilities and therefore the actual autonomous functioning of individuals.[105] Health capability in particular 'integrates health outcome and health agency'.[106] As such, it implies the ability of a person to be healthy, which lays a correlative claim on others to assure those conditions relevant to the capability of being healthy, including the underlying determinants of health.[107] This, in turn, indicates that certain aspects of health are more important than others.[108]

More specifically, capabilities are spaces of freedom to act, or rather capabilities are not fixed opportunities presented to one another but reflect the continuous opportunity to choose and select.[109] The promotion of capabilities therefore implies the promotion of freedom and the free space to obtain freely chosen objectives, which have intrinsic value due to being freely chosen.[110] This in itself is very similar to the manner in which Pogge understands the notion of 'human flourishing': as the idea that 'human persons are flourishing [if] their lives are good, or worthwhile in the broadest sense'.[111] Yet, the challenge is, according to Pogge, to develop a theory of justice in the political discourse that reflects on and guides the way in which the institutions of any social system treat the people they affect morally and equally.[112] Nussbaum seeks this justification in a Rawlsian hypothetical social contract. This is discussed in the following section.

In order to understand the implications of the capability approach for the access to medicines and aspects of drug control, it is important to know which entitlements the theory sets forth as basic entitlements, or rather as capabilities that States should guarantee. According to Nussbaum's formulation of the theory, one can speak of basic and combined capabilities.[113] According to Nussbaum, basic capabilities are those capabilities each human person needs in order to function as a person in a

105 ibid. See also Sen, 'Capability and Well-Being' (n 110) 30-31.
106 JP Ruger, 'Health Capability: Conceptualization and Operationalization' (2010) 100 American Journal of Public Health 41, 42.
107 Venkatapuram (n 88) 1.
108 Ruger, *Health and Social Justice* (n 100) 3.
109 Nussbaum (n 82) 25.
110 id. See also MC Nussbaum, *Frontiers of Justice* (HUP 2006).
111 Pogge (n 82) 31.
112 ibid 37.
113 Combined capabilities are also referred to as substantial freedoms, whereas basic capabilities are also referred to as internal capabilities. For readability this chapter only refers to combined and basic capabilities.

fundamental sense. In fact, Nussbaum holds that personal traits are important regardless of the different socio-economic contexts in which people exercise their human rights.[114] Basic capabilities reflect the idea of basic needs.[115] As examples of these basic capacities, Nussbaum names political awareness and craft skills. The former enables individuals to place themselves in the context of the society in which they live. The latter enables individuals to earn an income, and to sustain both themselves and their family members. Because of the value attached to these basic capabilities in bringing about social justice, society has the obligation to support individual development of basic capabilities.

Combined capabilities are 'a set of interrelated opportunities [available to an individual] to choose and to act [on]'.[116] Such opportunities are interrelated in that they, on the one hand, reside inside a person, in their personal characteristics such as intellectual and emotional capacities, bodily fitness, and state of health, but, on the other, also in the socio-economic opportunities available to them.[117] As capacities differ amongst individual persons, people need different environments, including different levels of support and protection, to be enabled to flourish with the specific capacities an individual person has.[118] Combined capabilities are 'the freedoms or opportunities created by a combination of personal abilities and the political, social and economic environment'.[119]

This customizable concept allows each individual to achieve different levels of functioning in a society, which are feasible according to his or her substantial freedoms, taking into account both the capacities of the particular human being and the context of his surroundings.[120] As a result, societies hold both positive and negative obligations to create enabling conditions. The obligations society has include those to ensure access to education, health goods, facilities, services, and other social security schemes.[121] It is important to note that capabilities are not reconstructed in terms of an empirical description of human nature. Rather, they reflect the individual's 'innate faculty', which enables and contributes to development and thus to combined capabilities.[122]

114 Nussbaum, *Creating Capabilities* (n 82) 21.
115 Ruger, *Health and Social Justice* (n 100) 57.
116 Nussbaum, *Creating Capabilities* (n 82) 20.
117 ibid 21.
118 Nussbaum, *Frontiers of Justice* (n 110) 30.
119 Nussbaum, *Creating Capabilities* (n 82) 20.
120 ibid 20-21; Nussbaum, *Frontiers of Justice* (n 110).
121 Nussbaum, *Creating Capabilities* (n 82) 21.
122 ibid 21, 23-24.

Distinguishing between basic capabilities and combined capabilities is important for two reasons. First, a discrepancy may exist in that a State can support the development of basic capabilities but fail to provide a socio-political/economic context in which these basic capabilities can flourish and develop into combined capabilities. Second, there may also be disparity in that a State may develop appropriate socio-political/economic contexts, i.e. those relevant for the development of combined capabilities, but fails to support the development of basic capacities.[123] Hence, a State not providing the necessary institutional support to develop basic capabilities, but successfully securing a socio-political/economic context in which those basic capabilities, if developed, could be exercised and enjoyed, reveals the continuous interaction between basic and combined capabilities.[124]

A gradual approach

Focusing on equal dignity on the basis of innate potential means protecting and supporting agency by creating spaces of freedom rather than 'infantilis[ing] people and treat[ing] them as passive recipients of benefits'.[125] To this end, the idea of capabilities entails some kind of graded scale based on equality.

> All [individuals] should get above a certain threshold level of combined capability, in the sense not of coerced functioning but of substantial freedom to choose and act. That is what it means to treat all people with equal respect. So the attitude toward people's basic capabilities is not a meritocratic one- more innately skilled people get better treatment– but, if anything, the opposite: those who need more help to get above the threshold get more help.[126]

Clearly, this should not be understood as to imply that States have an obligation to ensure that people actively use these spaces of freedom or use these capabilities. Instead, the government merely has an obligation to ensure that the conditions necessary for autonomous functioning are accessible, but the actual use or fulfilment of these conditions is left to the people themselves.[127] In relation to health matters, health capability can never be understood as a claim to be healthy. Instead, governments hold the obligation to create a healthcare system adequately equipped to deal at least with a country's particular burden of disease. This obligation to provide care would then necessarily include harm-reduction measures. The question is, especially because according to Nussbaum the capability approach can limit individual choice

123 ibid 22.
124 On the perceptions and stereotypes in society influencing people's perspective on what they can achieve, see also Nussbaum, *Frontiers of Justice* (n 110) 73.
125 Nussbaum, *Creating Capabilities* (n 82) 30; Nussbaum, *Frontiers of Justice* (n 110) 15, 98.
126 Nussbaum, *Creating Capabilities* (n 82) 24. See also Nussbaum, *Frontiers of Justice* (n 110) 71.
127 Claassen (n 98) 241.

in exceptional circumstances, what kind of obligations States have in relation to the protection against hazardous use more generally.

In search for balance: dignity and central capabilities

According to Ruger, the selection and 'valuing' of capabilities allows one to analyse public policy.[128] This in itself seems to have much potential for the issue of access to medicines and drug control. Capabilities which demand core protection are areas of freedom of which infringements would result in lives not worthy of dignity – i.e. lives deprived of the ability to act autonomously. Aspects which are left to the political process, or rather more peripheral non-central capabilities, are areas in which infringements on freedom do not directly deprive people of the possibility of living a life of dignity.[129] The central issue is then: What constitutes a life worthy of dignity beyond attaining freely chosen purposes? Or rather, what would allow one to reconstruct a list of central capabilities guiding the interpretation of public policy?

Nussbaum proposes ten central capabilities:

1. Life
2. Bodily health
3. Bodily integrity
4. Senses, imagination, and thought
5. Emotions
6. Practical reason
7. Affiliation
8. Other species
9. Play
10. Control over one's environment
    - Political
    - Material[130]

Nussbaum, however, also places several conditions on the list she developed. First, the list has some contingent aspects. Depending on the type of justice that is aspired to, ranging from social to distributive justice, certain areas of freedom should be left to the political process.[131] The scope of these central capabilities and which rights they give rise to is a matter of democratic deliberation. Second, as fundamental political

128 Ruger, *Health and Social Justice* (n 100) 55.
129 Nussbaum, *Creating Capabilities* (n 82) 29, 31-32; Nussbaum, *Frontiers of Justice* (n 110) 78.
130 Nussbaum, *Creating Capabilities* (n 82) 33-34; Nussbaum, *Frontiers of Justice* (n 110) 76-78. Practical reason is the ability to reflect on what is good and plan one's life goals.
131 Nussbaum, *Creating Capabilities* (n 82) 36; Nussbaum, *Frontiers of Justice* (n 110) 78-79.

entitlements, capabilities should be implemented procedurally via constitutional law, in which civil rights should be granted special protection.[132]

In its application, access to medicines may fall within the scope of the capabilities of life and bodily health. One could argue that the denial of adequate access to pain-control medicines demonstrates the lack of institutional support from a State in developing basic capabilities into combined capabilities. Chronic-pain patients are limited in their functioning because the State fails to provide them with adequate access to pain-control medicines. As has been demonstrated in Chapter 2, chronic pain syndromes are disabling in nature. Patients are often bedridden and no longer able to fulfil their familial and caregiving roles, take on or sustain a job, or participate in socio-economic life more generally.

By contrast, it is not so clear-cut how aspects of drug control should be framed in terms of the list of central capabilities. One could argue that the material control over one's environment comes into play as the central capability of non-drug-users. Along this line of reasoning, one could submit that material control over one's environment includes the claim to protection from the negative consequences of drug use, such as the increased spread of infectious diseases, and general social disorder that might be caused by drug use when left unmitigated. The interests of drug users themselves, however, may also be understood in light of the capability of life and of bodily health.

In general, Nussbaum's capabilities are non-hierarchical in nature. This in itself supports the idea found in both international drug-control treaties and in human rights law that none of the aspects of drug control are *ipso facto* more important than others. Yet, would resolving matters of drug control in light of the capability approach come down to a tragic choice?

According to Nussbaum, one can settle conflicts by reference to two architectonic capabilities: affiliation and practical reason. They are architectonic in resolving clashes of interest because they are interwoven with human dignity, whereas the other capabilities are coincidental norms.[133] In other words, when 'the other' capabilities are realized complementarily to respecting human dignity, such realization or policy adopted with the aim of such realization must be rational (practical reason) and regard individuals as social beings (affiliations).[134] In addition, clashes may be resolved by using equality as a qualifying criterion, and each capability as a value by which to weigh 'by asking what respect for equal human dignity requires'.[135] Yet, similarly

132 Nussbaum, *Creating Capabilities* (n 82) 40.
133 ibid 39.
134 id.
135 ibid 40-41.

to Chapter 3, in one way or another, one is once again confronted with a tension in health protection. The real issue now becomes how either practical reason, affiliation, or equality may settle this tension. This depends on the type of justification that one embraces, because apart from the political and constitutional limitations that Nussbaum raises, the issue is rather how Nussbaum selects these central capabilities. Is she merely cherry-picking or is there a normative order behind her choice?

Reflective equilibrium

Nussbaum invokes 'the notion of dignity and of a life worthy of it' in the process of selecting capabilities.[136] She considers dignity as 'an intuitive notion that is by no means utterly clear'.[137] In fact, Nussbaum holds that there is no solid construction of dignity and that one could not use it to come up with a theory of rights listing specific entitlements.[138] Indeed, although human dignity may be a solid construct, it is not a fixed construction with a single meaning and power.

Nussbaum has presented different justifications of her list of capabilities. In *Frontiers of Justice*, she expresses her most systematic defence of her approach and proposes a justification in the line of Rawls' 'reflective equilibrium'.[139] Rawls' proposal is procedural in nature and contends that a society should be governed by those principles (of justice) on which all individuals could agree under idealized conditions. These individuals engaging in social constructions jointly choose which principles are to be assigned for basic rights and duties as a form of distributive and social justice.[140] Just as each individual should attempt to create a coherent hierarchical whole out of his own set of individual preferences and values, a group of such individuals should strive for such coherence. To that end, they should only adopt those principles that are chosen under a 'veil of ignorance', under which one would not know in which societal position the decision is made or will end up, in order to ensure that the principles are acceptable for everybody.[141]

---

136 ibid 29.

137 id. The idea of capabilities and selecting capabilities also falls in line with Shue's idea of basic rights and their selection. According to Shue, a basic right is a right essential to the enjoyment of other rights. He discerns subsistence and security as 'equally necessary for effective human agency', referring similarly to a certain ability or freedom to act instead of the act or autonomy itself. Selecting basic rights takes place 'upon reflection of what you need to enjoy a right'. See Shue (n 82); Beitz and Goodin (n 30) 4.

138 Nussbaum, *Creating Capabilities* (n 82) 29; Claassen (n 98) 242.

139 Nussbaum, *Frontiers of Justice* (n 110); Nussbaum, *Creating Capabilities* (n 82) 77. The neo-Kantian *a priori* link between autonomy and will states that one acts because one values it – the chosen goal – as good.

140 J Rawls, *A Theory of Justice* (HUP 1971); See also Nussbaum, *Frontiers of Justice* (n 110); R Shafer-Landau (ed), *Ethical Theory* (2nd edn, Wiley-Blackwell 2013) 581.

141 Rawls (n 140).

Along the same chain of thought, Nussbaum proposes a procedural approach via which to select capabilities. In doing so, she refers to the deliberative and reflective individual, contemplating what it means to live a life worthy of dignity. Albeit general, such an intuitive starting point gives definite guidance to the selection of basic entitlements essential to living a life worthy of dignity, according to Nussbaum.[142] Ultimately, Nussbaum maintains that the reflective equilibrium as a justification of selection offers a solid basis for the development of constitutionally anchored political principles in a pluralistic society.[143] Yet, there are several principled objections to the balancing of rights according to the structure of the capability approach, as well as to its justificatory foundation more generally.

Principled objections and problematic foundations

While the theory is strong in conceptualizing an idea of capabilities in line with the view considering dignity as empowerment, there are several problems with balancing capabilities in the first place. First, lifting practical reason and affiliation to the architectonic level seems at odds with the central aim of a non-hierarchical list of basic entitlements to social justice. This is because these two capabilities seem to occupy hierarchically different positions.[144] Second, it is unclear what role Nussbaum attributes to dignity, as well as how she synthesizes the empowerment potential with the constraint potential of her theory. For Nussbaum dignity is fundamentally linked to the freedom to make important choices that concern oneself. But at the same time, she proposes a concept of dignity that limits precisely that freedom that was supposed to be protected by dignity in the first place.[145] How can human dignity limit this exercise without compromising its function as the foundation of the entire idea of the capabilities approach? Third, the primacy of practical reason and affiliation becomes hazier exactly because the scope and content of the capabilities are left to the political domain. In other words, because the theory rests on a deliberative process, selection and weighing of the different capabilities depends on the particular agreement reached amongst individuals.[146] This last point leads to more principled objections to the theory's justification more generally.

This theory is flawed, making it a problematic foundation on which to base the search for a categorically binding moral rule. This impedes its plausibility as a theory of rights, but also its application to the access to medicines and aspects of drug control

142 Nussbaum, *Creating Capabilities* (n 82) 78-79; Nussbaum, *Frontiers of Justice* (n 110) 75-76.
143 Nussbaum, *Creating Capabilities* (n 82) 79; Nussbaum, *Frontiers of Justice* (n 110) 75-76.
144 Nussbaum, *Creating Capabilities* (n 82) 40.
145 Nussbaum, *Frontiers of Justice* (n 110) 172; Claassen (n 98) 243.
146 Ruger, *Health and Social Justice* (n 100) 55.

when seeking to fill a gap in the law.[147] If the theory fails to produce a comparative or otherwise clash-resolving mechanism, the approach would not be able to provide a criterion that would support this prioritized basis. Consequently, an access-led model of drug control would be a political decision, rather than a categorically binding norm. This more general criticism is threefold.

First, Nussbaum views capabilities as identifiable with legal human rights (or rather constitutional civil rights). This is problematic because it blurs the distinction between human rights as moral principles and human rights as legal propositions.[148] Such hazy distinctions also complicate the specification and operationalization of human rights as legal propositions to give meaning to human dignity as a moral demand.[149] Second, humanity or human life cannot play the normative guiding role in selecting central capabilities, as it is assigned in Nussbaum's interpretation of the capability approach.[150] If one takes humanity as a starting point, no human features can be convincingly kept off the list. In other words, Nussbaum's account lacks the ability to distinguish between different human features and demonstrate which human features deserve protection. In addition, Nussbaum fails to convincingly demonstrate that some human features are more important than others and therefore demand different levels of protection and support.[151] Nussbaum aims to construct a universally applicable and convincing theory of justice on the basis of a complex holistic method, inspired by Rawls' reflective equilibrium. Rawls' theory, however, is constructed as a deliberative process rather than an intuitive concept of humanity.[152] Nussbaum's intuitive, virtue-based starting point seems an unconvincing justification of the normative presuppositions underlying the selection of the ten central capabilities.[153]

It should be noted, furthermore, that the concerns discussed are far from exhaustive; more issues could have been addressed. The arguments presented, however, may suffice to conclude that one may have reasons to find Nussbaum's conceptualization and justification of human rights problematic. For the purpose of this book, it is equally important to acknowledge that the approach is difficult to use when it comes to dealing with competing interests, which is evidently the case in the access to medicines and aspects of drug control.[154]

---

147 To recapitulate, Chapter 3 stated that the law in itself is not explicit on the exact interplay of access to medicines and aspects of drug control, but did so only implicitly.

148 Benhabib (n 5) 10; Düwell, 'Human Dignity' (n 6) 32.

149 Benhabib (n 5) 10. Compare with n 89.

150 R Claassen and M Düwell, 'The Foundations of Capability Theory: Comparing Nussbaum and Gewirth' (2013) 16 Ethical Theory and Moral Practice 493, 493, 496-501.

151 ibid 497.

152 ibid 501. See also Rawls (n 140); Shafer-Landau (n 140) 581.

153 Claassen and Düwell (n 150) 498.

154 Ruger, *Health and Social Justice* (n 100) 58.

The theory is difficult to rely on when reconsidering the balancing of access to medicines and aspects of drug control in human rights theory because it is 'deliberately open and underspecified and requires specification before operationalizing it'.[155] Yet, the theory does not simply need specification before its operationalization; it rather requires a categorically binding criterion that trumps all other practical considerations, which, in its current form, it cannot provide.[156] The categorical nature of the argument is important to understand human dignity as a moral demand in its foundational role in the human rights framework. Ruger aims to overcome some of these criticisms by elaborating the health capability and 'fixing' incomplete arguments with complementary arguments derived from social-choice theory. Such a 'patchwork' argument may give more content to the capabilities elaborated on above, but it does not grant the theory a categorically binding force.[157]

4.4.2 The principle of generic consistency

Similar to the idea of capabilities, in giving content to human dignity, is the notion of generic needs and rights of agency, as viewed according to the Principle of Generic Consistency (PGC).[158] In line with the dignity as empowerment interpretation and the capability framing, the PGC focuses heavily on self-determination and self-definition, and sets out a structure of positive and negative rights and obligations focused on creating the enabling conditions of agency. Hence, a State has obligations to create conditions in which agents can act upon freely chosen purposes. As opposed to the capability theory, the PGC starts with a formal analysis of the conceptual presuppositions of agency and autonomous action, from which it subsequently derives substantive content. In fact, the PGC offers a conceptual and operational framework that leads to a hierarchical scheme of positive and negative rights and duties, structured to deal with competing interests.

Yet, apart from this substantive role, the question is whether the PGC can function as a categorical imperative, the necessary acceptance of which was already referred to in the discussion of inalienable rights in the UDHR and other human rights documents (see Section 4.3.2 above). As will be demonstrated, the PGC is capable of reflecting the normative content of the dignity as empowerment interpretation, and occupies a categorically binding position within the human rights framework.[159] However, if the PGC is the categorical imperative, then any rule should be compatible with the

155 id.
156 id.
157 ibid 3.
158 Gewirth, *Reason and Morality* (n 14); Beyleveld, *Dialectical Necessity* (n 82).
159 See also D Beyleveld, 'The Principle of Generic Consistency as the Supreme Principle of Human Rights' (2012) 13 Human Rights Review 1.

PGC and any conflict should be settled in accordance with its structure. This in itself sounds very appealing as a manner in which to settle potential conflicts or tensions in rights protection, as is precisely the purpose of this Part 2.

Generic needs and the degree of needfulness

In brief, the PGC elaborates the idea that agents performatively contradict themselves if they act in discordance with the PGC.[160] The PGC is a principle, but simultaneously provides a formal scheme of reasoning, which gives content to the way in which corresponding rights and duties emerge, relate to one another, and are justified. However, not all agents' needs are necessarily generic. Only those 'needs of agency [that] are prerequisites of an ability to act at all *or* with any *general* changes of success, *regardless of the purposes being pursued*', are.[161] The core factor in evaluating whether a need is generic is therefore the instrumentality of the need vis-à-vis the ability to act in general and for an act to be successful specifically.[162] Those rights that are claims to any aspect of generic needs are generic rights to agency.

So, generic needs or goods are needs inherent to the actual ability to function, or rather to act autonomously on freely chosen purposes.[163] Within generic needs, one can distinguish substantive needs (well-being) and procedural needs (freedom). Gewirth considers freedom as the procedural need reflecting the ability to control and to act according to one's freely chosen purposes. Substantive needs, on the other hand, refer to those goods necessary to do something with this freedom and to control one's agency towards pursuing purposes. Both these dimensions are constantly intertwined.[164]

---

160 ibid 1; Beyleveld, *Dialectical Necessity* (n 82) 1. Gewirth asserts that the dialectical necessity method, which is to be further elaborated on below, implies that a denial of the argument results in self-contradiction of being an agent. Gewirth, *Reason and Morality* (n 14) 23. See also Beyleveld and Brownsword (n 42) 69.

161 Beyleveld and Brownsword (n 42) 70.

162 id.

163 Gewirth, *Reason and Morality* (n 14) 25, 52. Gewirth holds that the normative content of morality should be considered in light of human action and the generic features of such functioning. Moreover, Gewirth dictates that human action lies at the core of human rights. According to Gewirth, no human being can 'evade the context of action'. It follows that the generic needs are those aspects generic or inherent to the ability to act in the first place. See also Gewirth, *Community of Rights* (n 82) 13.

164 Gewirth, *Reason and Morality* (n 14) 32, 44; Beyleveld, *Dialectical Necessity* (n 82) 19. The idea of generic needs is very similar to Beitz's notion of urgent individual interest. Beitz's conceptualization, however, relies on seeking a moral justification of human rights via the practice of human rights. This in itself does not fit with the empowerment concept from which we understand the foundation of human rights to be based in human rights law. To that end, Beitz's interpretation of human rights presupposes a practice of human rights, as well as a political system or order governing this practice. On urgent individual interest, see Beitz (n 9) 109.

Gewirth stresses, moreover, that an agent's right to well-being and freedom has three components: basic goods, non-subtractive goods, and additive goods.[165] Basic goods are those aspects of well-being that are necessary for the actual ability to act. In the case of human beings, such basic goods include 'life and physical integrity [including also] means [such] as food, clothing and shelter'.[166] Non-subtractive and additive goods, in turn, include the aspects of well-being that are relevant for successful action – or at least to the possibility of successful action in general.[167] Interference with a non-subtractive good would mean decreasing or removing an agent's chances to attain specific purposes, without generally diminishing an agent's ability to pursue his or her purposes – i.e. the ability to act as such.[168] Additive goods are those aspects of well-being needed to improve the possibility of successful purposive action.[169] Like the capability theory, the PGC remains neutral to any value judgment about the actual purpose or goal of an action as such. The PGC rather has as its focal point the analysis of the necessary conditions for (successful) agency, regardless of the specific end the agent wants to achieve. However, it obviously does presuppose that the agent determines ends in general, which it considers to be *a priori* connected to the concept of agency as such.[170]

Taking the mere ability of an agent to act as a starting point rather than the specific purpose this action aims to achieve, Gewirth argues that some generic goods (aspects of well-being, as outlined above) are necessary to act at all, or to act successfully, whilst other goods may be important but are not absolutely required.[171] Exactly because various interests may conflict, 'some ordering is necessary'.[172]

The degree of *needfulness to act* is the criterion on the basis of which Gewirth places generic goods, and corresponding rights of well-being and freedom, in a hierarchical order. This degree of needfulness is both a qualitative (rights to maintain

165 Gewirth, *Reason and Morality* (n 14) 52-63; Gewirth, *Community of Rights* (n 82) 13-14.
166 Gewirth, *Reason and Morality* (n 14) 54. See also Beyleveld, *Dialectical Necessity* (n 82) 19; Beyleveld and Brownsword (n 42) 70.
167 Gewirth, *Reason and Morality* (n 14) 54-55; Beyleveld, *Dialectical Necessity* (n 82) 19-20; Beyleveld and Brownsword (n 42) 71.
168 Gewirth, *Reason and Morality* (n 14) 56-57; Beyleveld, *Dialectical Necessity* (n 82) 20.
169 Gewirth, *Reason and Morality* (n 14) 56.
170 ibid 7. Gewirth acknowledges that: [t]he correctness of a morality is not a matter of knowledge or truth at all; rather the moral judgments any person accepts as right or correct can ultimately reflect only his tastes, feelings, conditioning, conventions, decisions, or economic class, and it is only to such noncognitive bases that any moral evaluation can appeal.
171 Moreover, Gewirth contends that the status of these three aspects of well-being is both conceptual and practical, and therefore allows us to analyse human action and interaction from a moral philosophical perspective, whilst still relative and applicable to the context. Gewirth, *Community of Rights* (n 82) 15.
172 Gewirth, *Reason and Morality* (n 14) 3.

the ability to act at all) and a quantitative (rights to the successfulness of acts in general) denominator.[173] Using the degree of needfulness in both its qualitative and its quantitative sense leads to the conclusion that basic rights trump non-subtractive rights, which themselves trump additive rights.[174]

Although the potential gap between agency and human rights has not yet been bridged (see Section 4.5), it is worthwhile to trace a link between Gewirth's degree of needfulness and the priority-setting found in human rights law. The degree of needfulness does not entail an *a priori* priority-setting of rights, granting them different normative and legal status. Rather, Gewirth's hierarchical scheme of needs, as determined by the degree of needfulness, implies the operationalization of the PGC (i.e. generic rights and obligations) that must follow a hierarchical scheme, allowing priority-setting in light of resource constraints, practical realities, and complexities of rights realization and service provision. This feeds well into the urgency of realization found in Chapter 3. Yet, while the PGC maps out an operational framework of how to resolve conflicts, the PGC also requires sufficient empirical insight into what exactly constitutes a generic need and to what extent it is causally diminished by an action in the first instance.[175] Any balancing, according to the structures of the PGC, thus also requires such empirical considerations.

Balancing access to medicines and aspects of drug control via the PGC

As has been described in Chapter 1, there are many controlled substances that have no clear medical designation, but have serious abuse potential. At the same time, there is also a substantial number of controlled substances that carry abuse potential and yet have distinguished, evidence-based medical uses (see Chapter 2). However, it should also be acknowledged that distinguishing a mutually exclusive pharmacological categorization is complex.[176]

Understanding the PGC in its qualitative fashion, access to pain-control medicines, such as morphine and codeine, could be framed as a basic need. Considering a basic need as a generic prerequisite to the actual ability to function, places the denial of pain treatment within the scope of a seriously debilitating factor (see Chapter 2). A key argument in this respect is that it is necessary to differentiate between preventable and unpreventable medical conditions. Usually, a person does not choose to fall ill, to suffer pain or discomfort, or to be unable to access treatment. The fact that so many

173 Beyleveld and Brownsword (n 42) 70.
174 Gewirth, *Reason and Morality* (n 14) 63.
175 Beyleveld and Brownsword (n 42) 71. Gewirth notes that empirical insight is necessary to 'establish the rightness or correctness of a moral principle', see Gewirth, *Reason and Morality* (n 14) 17.
176 S Luper-Foy and C Brown (eds), *Drugs, Morality, and the Law* (Garland Publishing 1994) ix, xi.

people lack access to adequate care, including medicines, indicates that 'individuals have been wronged in some way'.[177] According to Venkatapuram, it is this worry, of being wronged by preventable diseases or of medical conditions constraining one's functioning or life, which is a matter of justice.[178]

However, one should also see the unavailability of controlled medicines generally, and pain-control medicines specifically, as existing on a scale. This is because it is not true to say that a person's basic needs are compromised each time they do not have access to medicines and are thus deprived of adequate health services. If the lack of access to these medicines does not directly keep people from functioning in the first place, we can consider non-subtractive goods and those goods generic to your ability to sustain and continue functioning as the right framing for the availability of medicines. Notably, functioning in this sense should be understood as the ability to act rationally (see below for what it means to act rationally). The empirical arguments developed that state that access to opioid-substitute medicines as part of harm-reduction programmes is, as much as access to pain-control medicines, a matter of health protection and access to medicines provision, apply similarly at the more fundamental moral level.

Yet, the more fundamental issue is how to view the 'other component' of drug control in terms of morality. In other words, the question is not so much whether access to pain-control medicines, controlled essential medicines, or medicine in its widest sense may be a legitimate claim under a theory of basic rights, capabilities, generic rights, or agency rights. The issue is rather what one ought to think of 'the other side' of medicinal use. Ought one to control the non-medical use of controlled substances in a prohibitive, regulatory, or liberal manner, balanced with the access to medicines? The capability approach was found to be inconsistent in this respect. However, on the one hand, it focuses heavily on self-definition and self-choice to support an enabling environment for agents to act. On the other hand, it holds that some freedoms or capabilities should be limited to protect dignity. This is rather confusing because dignity was classified as the ability to act autonomously. Hence, if one wanted to curtail drug control and strictly prohibit the non-medical use of controlled substances regardless individual consent, then such restriction seems hard to defend and justify in terms of the protection of dignity – if dignity is the ability to act on freely chosen purposes in the first place.

In order to understand the normative justification of any approach to drug control, one cannot avoid dealing with the question of whether there could be a right to use drugs –

177 Venkatapuram (n 88) 5.
178 ibid 4-5.

i.e. what the limits to curtailing drug use are. This question is relevant when working from an internal perspective, such as the one presented in this book. Considering human dignity as the ability to act on freely chosen purposes furthermore reflects a coherent interpretation of the foundational claim to dignity found in human rights law (see Section 4.3). What happens if one considers drug use as a freely chosen purpose? The relevant question here becomes whether the PGC supports a right to non-medical use of controlled substances. Stevens answers this question in the affirmative, albeit hesitantly.

Specifically, Stevens holds that 'people may rationally choose to experience the effects of psychoactive substances, even if they have no objective need for them'.[179] At the most, this claim would fall within the category of additive goods. To verify this claim, one needs to understand what it means to act rationally in line with the PGC. Only then can one assess whether drug use could be an additive good in line with the PGC, and confirm or undermine the balancing involved.

A rational justification: dialectical necessity

One may view the PGC as a contemporary interpretation of Kant's maxim to treat each individual, as well as humanity as a whole, as an end in itself and never merely as a means.[180] Starting from the internal perspective of the agent, Gewirth constructs a formal scheme of reasoning from which it follows logically that every prospective purposive agent has generic needs of agency, which he – by virtue of the dialectical necessity of the PGC – ought to defend.[181] Prospective purposive agents are agents whom one may expect to have the capacity to act as such (see below), regardless of whether these agents have explicitly demonstrated this ability yet.

The scheme is dialectical because it deduces binding conclusions from how individuals, as prospective purposive agents, internally reflect on their own agency, rather than deducing conclusions from externally constructed subjective views.[182] It

179 A Stevens, 'Drug Policy, Harm and Human Rights: A Rationalist Approach' (2011) 22 International Journal of Drug Policy 233, 236. As a result of scope-related and textual limitations, the issue of 'enhancing drugs' is not discussed here. See for an ethical reflection on the enhancing ability and drug use, RL Simon, 'Better Performance through Chemistry: The Ethics of Enhancing Ability through Drugs' in S Luper-Foy and C Brown, *Drugs Morality and the Law* (Garland Publishing 1994) 133.

180 See on this I Kant, *Grounding for the Metaphysics of Morals* (tr JW Ellington, 2nd edn, Hackett Publishing 1981). Beyleveld and Brownsword (n 42); Düwell, 'Human Dignity' (n 6).

181 Gewirth, *Reason and Morality* (n 14); A Gewirth, *Human Rights* (The University of Chicago Press 1982) 47-51; Beyleveld, *Dialectical Necessity* (n 82); Beyleveld and Brownsword (n 42); Beyleveld, 'Generic Consistency' (n 159).

182 Gewirth, *Reason and Morality* (n 14); Beyleveld, *Dialectical Necessity* (n 82) 15. Moreover, Gewirth

claims that agents fail to understand what it is to be an agent if they act contrary to the scheme of rights stemming from the PGC. The PGC is necessary in the specific sense in the sense that it is a precondition for agential self-understanding, and it therefore holds normativity for all agents to the extent that they consider themselves capable of acting on freely chosen purposes.[183] Being a will-theory, the rights and obligations emanating from the PGC are categorically binding due to the *a priori* link between the will of an agent and autonomy.[184] The rules derived from the PGC apply to rational agents, including human beings if they are capable of agential self-understanding.[185]

The argument is set up in three stages. The first stage questions what an agent may do by reference to the principle of hypothetical imperatives. The second stage establishes a mutual exchange of generic needs and corresponding rights of agency, being both negative and positive in nature. The third stage ultimately establishes the universal nature of the PGC. More precisely, the argument is constructed as follows:

Gewirth, in stage one, constructs the internal, dialectical reflection of how agents judge their own action.[186] As mentioned, this first stage formulates the principle of hypothetical imperatives or instrumental reason (see below). By definition, a prospective purposive agent (Rachel) claims *I do (or intend to do) X voluntarily to attain my freely chosen purpose Y.*[187] For instance, I open the fridge (X) voluntarily to get a glass of milk (Y). It follows logically that Rachel must value Y, getting a glass of milk, as good. In this scenario, it is sufficient to accept that Rachel values Y as good as otherwise she would not act voluntarily to achieve this purpose.[188] Such voluntary purposeful action expresses the normativity of the principle of instrumental reason.[189] It is irrational for Rachel to voluntarily determine a particular goal if in no sense whatsoever she considers this goal as valuable. Only attaching value – any

---

states that one can justify a supreme moral principle both externally and internally. According to Gewirth, an internal perspective is essential because it is reflective and 'does not merely consist in conforming to some accepted practice; it also carries with it an implicit claim, on part of the person who sets forth the judgment, that he has made it after due consideration and that it is right or correct', see Gewirth, *Reason and Morality* (n 14) 14.

183 Gewirth, *Reason and Morality* (n 14) 32, 43-44; Beyleveld, *Dialectical Necessity* (n 82) 15. The necessity of the argument is reinforced by the fact that denial of any of its stages and implications would be self-contradictory, see Gewirth, *Reason and Morality* (n 14) 23.

184 Beyleveld and Brownsword (n 42) 69.

185 Gewirth, *Reason and Morality* (n 14) 44; Beyleveld and Brownsword (n 42) 126. The prerequisite for the capacity of rational action is controversial when considering rights as human rights. This flaw is rebutted by viewing agents as prospective purposive agents or ostensible agents. This is discussed more extensively later in this section.

186 Beyleveld, *Dialectical Necessity* (n 82) 21-24.

187 ibid 14. 'She' is used generically throughout the scheme.

188 Beyleveld, 'Generic Consistency' (n 159) 4.

189 id.

kind of value – to her freely chosen purpose Y (which could be any purpose) would motivate her to act toward achieving her purpose. Rachel would therefore contradict her own agency if she were not to value purpose Y as good to her whatsoever; she would rather appear to be 'acting' completely randomly. Rachel must therefore first of all accept that she has generic needs of agency, and second of all that having the generic needs of agency is categorically and instrumentally good for her.[190]

In stage two, Gewirth elaborates on the process of internal reflection with the idea that if one understands what it means to be an agent, i.e. to act rationally, then one has to protect and progress those conditions generically relevant to this ability to act rationally.[191] In other words, agents have to defend their generic conditions of agency, both of well-being and of freedom, as set out above.

The logic is that if Rachel values Y, she necessarily has to value the circumstances that make it possible for her to achieve Y as much as Y itself, because without these circumstances she cannot obtain Y in the first place. In other words, if Rachel wants to get a glass of milk, and opening the fridge is both the necessary and sufficient condition to get a glass of milk, it would be irrational for Rachel to hold that she wants to get a glass of milk but is completely neutral with regard to the fridge being opened or not. Neutrality would be irrational because if an agent like Rachel did not value the goal, i.e. getting a glass of milk (Y), she would not open the fridge (X). However, since freedom and well-being are generic conditions to her agency, i.e. things that are *always* presupposed as conditions to *whatever* goal Rachel may set, she must therefore necessarily value her freedom and well-being as good.[192] If these conditions are necessary to Rachel's agency (as stage one demonstrated), Rachel has an obligation to protect them to the extent that she cares about achieving her goal – whichever goal. If she were not to protect them in the case of external infringement, she would not be able to attain her freely chosen purposes. It then again follows logically, that, unless Rachel is willing to accept 'generic damage' to her ability to act, she *ought* to defend her possession of generic conditions, as prerequisites to agency.[193] Because Rachel must value her freedom and well-being as goods, she must accept that she has a claim-right to her freedom and well-being, regardless of whether any other agent has such a claim-right, on the pain of self-contradiction.

Although Rachel must accept that the generic needs of agency are categorically good, the argument at this stage is hypothetical because it places no value judgment on X or Y, but rather demonstrates how one should understand the link between the

190 Gewirth, *Reason and Morality* (n 14) 49.
191 Beyleveld, *Dialectical Necessity* (n 82) 24-42.
192 ibid 14; Gewirth, *Reason and Morality* (n 14) 52-53; Beyleveld, 'Generic Consistency' (n 159) 14.
193 Beyleveld, 'Generic Consistency' (n 159) 4.

will, autonomy, and the ability to act. The argument is still dialectical – i.e. holds normativity from the internal perspective of the individual agent's reasoning – and not yet universal because, so far, Rachel has not interacted with any other agent and the argument presented only reflects her internal reasoning.

In the third and final stage of the argument, the reasoning becomes universally binding and categorical, and includes both positive and negative obligations in relation to all agents: if Rachel is required to make a claim to her generic conditions of agency (stage two) and she is basing this claim on her agency as constructed in stage one, it follows purely logically that every other agent who is capable of making the same claim on the same conditions that Rachel did (stage one and two) has generic rights, and obligations to protect these conditions as well.[194]

If Rachel meets another agent – for instance John – and she attempts to convince John that he must respect her *prima facie* claim-right to freedom and well-being, she cannot rationally explain why she is entitled to these rights on the basis of her being named 'Rachel', having brown eyes, or having a supervisor with an extraordinary loud laugh. Rachel can only claim that John, as any other agent, should respect her rights to freedom and well-being on the basis of her being an agent, on the pain of self-contradiction. This implies that she can no longer hold that only she has these rights, but must – to the extent that she judges John to be a prospective purposive agent – also conclude that John has the same generic rights. John must, to the extent that the requirements of agential self-understanding play any role for John at all, in the same way as Rachel, reach the conclusion that John should be respected in his right to the generic conditions of agency.[195]

From Rachel accepting that she has a claim-right to these conditions it follows naturally that nobody may interfere with Rachel having the generic conditions of agency against her will (negative rights). However, other agents are also categorically bound to assist Rachel in obtaining and defending her generic conditions of agency when she cannot do so on her personal efforts alone (positive rights).[196] This positive right should be understood as a negative framing of non-interference; as a double negative becoming a positive. This is because another agent would contradict his or her own agency if he or she were to hold back from helping Rachel to protect her generic conditions of agency, the other agent (e.g. John) is categorically bound to provide assistance. In fact, Gewirth submits that:

194 Beyleveld, *Dialectical Necessity* (n 82) 42-46.
195 The condition of being a prospective purposive agent is addressed below, when connecting agency rights to human rights.
196 Gewirth, *Community of Rights* (n 82) 42.

> (...) on the basis of the necessity of freedom and well-being for action and successful action in general, no actual or prospective agent can rationally deny that she has a positive right to these necessary goods and that she has a duty to provide for others when they need such help and she is in a position to give it without comparable costs.[197]

While at first sight the PGC may seem rather liberal in nature because of its focus on choice, similarly to the capability approach, it also includes significant social ramifications. The mutual positive duties are a clear example here. By its reference to positive duties, the PGC acknowledges and includes the reality that many agents, including human beings, face structural inequalities.[198] As a result, Gewirth would consider the negative/positive claim-right dichotomy as one which accords negative rights to all agents and positive rights only to governments or social institutions.[199] This subtle nuance, however, requires a reflection on the fact that the theory is neutral on the morality of chosen purposes. The argument is not concerned with whether Rachel's chosen purpose Y, getting a glass of milk, is objectively good. It rather demonstrates that if she opens the fridge (X) to get the milk (Y) then she must value Y as good. Otherwise, she would not voluntarily do Y. Exactly because of the irrelevance of the actual purpose, it would be contrary to stage one and two of the argument to distinguish in the content of the freely selected purposes and the correlative duties at stage three, exactly because the starting point of stage one and stage two is neutral on the normativity of the selected purpose.

As a result, Rachel must accept that she has both negative and positive claim-rights in relation to her generic conditions of agency. Consequently, Rachel must also accept that other prospective purposive agents likewise have claim-rights to generic conditions of agency on the pain of self-contradiction. At this stage, the argument is, although still only dialectically necessary, also categorical and universal in normative appeal because it no longer imposes claims on the agent herself only, but on all prospective purposive agents as well. It is, moreover, at this stage that both Gewirth and Beyleveld prove that the PGC is the normative content of dignity as the categorically binding moral principle, in line with the dignity as empowerment framing, and as such is the basis of the human rights framework.[200]

197 ibid 40.
198 ibid 43.
199 id.
200 Beyleveld and Brownsword argue that the PGC is not only the supreme principle of human rights, but of any action (including all law). It goes beyond the scope of this book to reflect on the broader purpose and implications of the PGC, see Beyleveld and Brownsword (n 42) 77.

Agency and human rights

In both capability theory and the PGC, agency does not equate humanity. An agent can be, but does not have to be, a human being.[201] In turn, while all human rights are agency rights, not all agency rights are human rights.[202] Rights recognized by the PGC, for instance, are not necessarily generic, as they must be justified by reference to a generic need in order to reflect a corresponding generic right.[203] The link between generic rights (as agency rights) and human rights focuses on the rational interaction between agents and non-agents, rather than the 'essence of being human'.[204] This interaction with and focus on rationality raises issues, such as 'Do permanently comatose patients have human rights?' If not – because they do not show any sign of intelligible interaction – how would their interests be protected under human rights law? Similarly, what is the position of children under the PGC and, correspondingly, the human rights framework? As applied to the subject matter: What are the rights of problematic non-medical drug-users if their rationality is challenged in light of dependence disorders? This last question refers to Stevens' argument in favour of a right to non-medical use of controlled substances as long as it does not harm the capacity for rational action.

Maintaining a narrow interpretation, Gewirth holds that it follows from the PGC that everyone unable to act as a rational agent in line with the principle of instrumental reason would have 'quasi-generic' rights of agency – i.e. generic rights proportionate to their ability to act rationally. This means that quasi-generic rights are rights to freedom and well-being proportionate to one's ability to act rationally. Hence, if problematic non-medical use of psychoactive substances affects a person's ability to act rationally, this person holds only partial claim-rights to freedom and well-being.[205] Such a narrow interpretation, however, seems at odds with the central status of the principle of equality in human rights law. As was analysed in Chapter 3, human rights law requires governments and third parties to integrally respect, protect, and fulfil aspects of equality, including non-discrimination. To this end, the rights and interests of vulnerable and marginalized groups should be protected and emphasized in all forms of state planning, policy, and law-making. Vulnerable and marginalized groups especially include patients in a permanent vegetative state, children, and drug-users, whose capacity for rational action is in question, and whose position as rights

201 It is, at least conceptually, possible that artificial intelligence could at some point produce agents.
202 Nussbaum also elaborates on agency and human rights, and has argued that animals also have capabilities which should be protected. Nussbaum, *Creating Capabilities* (n 82) 28-29; Claassen (n 98).
203 Beyleveld, 'Generic Consistency' (n 159) 9.
204 id.
205 Gewirth, *Reason and Morality* (n 14) 120-123; Beyleveld and Brownsword (n 42) 112, 117.

holders is subverted. In fact, such a narrow interpretation seems incompatible with the foundational role of dignity in human rights law (as elaborated in Section 4.3).

In order to deal with this criticism, Beyleveld has adopted a wider notion of agency, which includes these groups. As the PGC operates from an internal perspective (the formal scheme of reasoning is dialectical), one can logically hold that one is never sure as to whether or not 'the other', which could be anything or anyone – your neighbour, pet, plant, or desk – is a prospective purposive agent.

A prospective purposive agent is an agent acting on the basis of the principle of instrumental reason (see stage one of the dialectical necessity method above). By not granting generic rights to 'the other', when you can never categorically demonstrate whether or not they are prospective purposive agents, you run the risk of undermining the PGC on the pain of self-contradiction. To avoid such a contradiction, Beyleveld holds that one has to treat 'the other' as ostensible agent showing agency-expected behaviour. The inability to make any valid truth claim as to whether or not any android is actually an agent or merely acts like one, or acts like an agent but is actually not an agent, is, according to Beyleveld, a 'cognitive deficiency [central] to the very essence of being human'.[206]

Nussbaum submits in this respect that 'we forget that the usual human lifecycle brings with it periods of extreme dependency, in which our functioning is very similar to that enjoyed by the mentally or physically handicapped throughout their lives'.[207] In fact, ignoring this would mean that anyone with a cognitive disorder, for instance, is no longer worthy of human rights protection. It is therefore not a matter of proving whether or not something or someone actually is an agent, but the focus is on granting every apparent (ostensible) agent the generic rights, if you are able to do so, in order to avoid breaching the PGC.[208] This means that one necessarily has positive and negative duties to the generic conditions of all ostensible agents, including in particular to vulnerable and marginalized groups.

Beyleveld and Brownsword label those who show lesser signs of agency – i.e. to be understood as the ability to act rationally in line with the principle of instrumental reason set out in stage one above – as partial agents. On the basis of the precautionary principle, agents must accept duties to partial agents. After all, you cannot know with certainty that partial agents will not display any agency-expected characteristics.

206 Beyleveld, 'Generic Consistency' (n 159) 10.
207 MC Nussbaum, 'Capabilities as Fundamental Entitlements: Sen and Social Justice' (2003) 9 Feminist Economics 33, 52.
208 Beyleveld, 'Generic Consistency' (n 159) 10.

These duties are relative to evidence: androids considered as partial agents possess the likelihood of being an apparent agent.[209]

Ostensible or partial agency and non-medical drug use

Theorizing a potential right to use drugs, we are often confronted with claims that non-medical use is inherently harmful to the capacity for rational action, and that human beings should be protected against inflicting such harm upon themselves. However, Stevens argues that non-medical drug use does not necessarily affect the capacity for rational action.[210] Here it is appropriate to distinguish between problematic and recreational users. While a small minority of drug users may become dependent and can, as such, be classified as problematic users, the vast majority of users have used drugs recreationally without lasting negative effects.[211] Stevens continues to state that recent studies indeed show that dependence disorders have specific effects on the brain and possibly also affect the ability to make rational decisions, although other human action also has this outcome.[212] Singling out drug use as the only behaviour on the list of those which affect the ability to make rational decisions to be strictly prohibited would therefore be unreasonable. The question then becomes whether this ultimately leads to logically accepting that all drug users have the full range of generic rights and duties or not. Here, we can point out that problematic drug use often involves some kind of compulsion, which leads one to question whether the decision to use or abstain is really under the control of the drug user as an agent in line with the PGC.[213]

Yet, viewing drug dependence as a disability resulting from a complex set of brain dysfunctions would place drug users in a similar position as those born with intellectual impairments or, for instance, the comatose patient.[214] By refraining from making value judgments as to the cause of the impairment, in line with the PGC, the ability to act as an agent should be the leading criterion. This, in turn, could vary on

209 Beyleveld and Brownsword (n 42) 113.

210 Stevens (n 179) 235. On autonomy and drug use more generally, see P Scribner, 'Do Drugs Deprive Us of Free Will?' in S Luper-Foy and C Brown (eds), *Drugs, Morality, and the Law* (Garland Publishing 1994); N Leivy, 'Autonomy and Addiction' (2006) 36 Canadian Journal of Philosophy 427. On the ethics of the enhancing abilities of drugs, see eg Simon (n 179); C Scheske and S Schnall, 'The Ethics of "Smart Drugs": Moral Judgments about Healthy People's Use of Cognitive-Enhancing Drugs' (2012) 34 Basic and Applied Social Psychology 508.

211 Stevens (n 179) 235.

212 id; ED London, 'Studying Addiction in the Age of Neuroimaging' (2009) 100 Drug and Alcohol Dependence 182. If it is necessary to medically view drug addiction as a brain disease, this reinforces any claim that views drug users as patients rather than criminals.

213 Stevens (n 179) 236.

214 id.

a case-by-case basis in the context of problematic drug use. Along this same line of reasoning, Beyleveld and Brownsword overall maintain – as opposed to Gewirth – that all agents have generic duties towards all human creatures, regardless of their ability to claim generic rights as such.[215] A right to use drugs as an additive good is, however, in itself also necessarily restricted if it affects the non-subtractive or basic goods of the drug user, or those of others.[216]

4.5 Conceptual criticism

This section deals with some conceptual criticism of various parts of the argument presented above. First, it briefly acknowledges the concerns about dignity as the foundation of human rights and its judicial potential or apparent lack thereof. Second, it addresses issues concerning autonomy in healthcare settings. Finally, it expands on the universality of agency and the paradoxical criticism of the rational approach presented.

4.5.1 Human dignity as the foundation of human rights and its judicial potential

As was previously mentioned, the idea of human rights is certainly not monolithic. The orthodox interpretation of human rights may be found in human dignity. However, many scholars operating from different philosophical traditions argue differently. Waldron, for example, questions whether dignity really is, or even can be, the foundation of human rights.[217] In doing so, Waldron argues that it could be the case that human dignity is the foundation of some, but not all, human rights.[218] The fact that dignity is important does not make it a 'master value' vis-à-vis other features of humanity which might also occupy a foundational role in justifying human rights beyond a set of principles formulated in international law.[219] Moreover, because all human beings possess human rights equally, this 'presumably means that each of them is based on some fact about human nature'.[220] Waldron holds that human dignity is not the only status and/or value that can occupy a foundational role and, moreover,

215 The authors extend the argument to all non-human creatures as well, though this is not relevant for the focus of the present study, see Beyleveld and Brownsword (n 42) 112. In sum, apparent non-agents are granted interest rights, and apparent agents are granted will rights as principally elaborated under the PGC. Beyleveld, 'Generic Consistency' (n 159) 11.

216 See Stevens (n 179).

217 Waldron (n 37) 9. In fact, Waldron questions whether human rights need a foundation like the foundational claim to human dignity.

218 ibid 4-5.

219 id.

220 ibid 5.

that different human rights may be grounded in different aspects of human nature.[221] It is true that human nature is multifaceted, yet the PGC demonstrated that human dignity can be interpreted as encompassing this plurality through its context-blind dialectically necessary justification.

Concerns such as Waldron's address a crucial question in human rights scholarship and moral philosophy, relating to what exactly the substantive meaning of human dignity is. While human dignity certainly became a 'central organizing principle' in the human rights discourse, the various roles ascribed to it seem to complicate, and yet also create, an urge for 'a common core to the idea of dignity'.[222] From a legal perspective, scholars question whether human dignity as a *legal* concept is capable of practically realizing human dignity as a *moral* principle.

McCrudden asserts that apart from its foundational role, human dignity is increasingly referred to as a substantive yardstick in human rights law.[223] Such substantive references complicate opinions regarding the meaning, scope, and role of human dignity in relation to human rights.[224] McCrudden, in relation to human dignity as a legal principle, argues that:

> (…) the use of dignity beyond a basic minimum core, does not provide a universalistic, principled basis for judicial decision-making in the human rights context, in the sense that there is little common understanding of what dignity requires substantively within or across jurisdictions.[225]

The 'judicialization' of human dignity demonstrates that differences exist in the status and normative weight attributed to it. Moreover, practice reveals differences in the individualistic and communitarian conceptions, as well as the rights-supporting or rights-constraining nature of dignity (see Section 4.3.4).[226]

It is, furthermore, important to address the way in which human dignity as a legal concept creates the moral principles underlying human dignity as a central concept in human rights law. However, the fact that across jurisdictions human dignity as a legal concept 'does not provide a universalistic, principled basis for judicial decision-making in the human rights context' should not keep us from analysing what exactly

---

221 id.

222 McCrudden (n 4) 675. On the role of human dignity in law and rights adjudication, see also Dupré (n 33); C Gearty, 'Socio-Economic Rights, Basic Needs, and Human Dignity: A Perspective from Law's Frontline' in C McCrudden (ed), *Understanding Human Dignity* (OUP 2013).

223 McCrudden (n 4) 670.

224 cf n 53-54.

225 McCrudden (n 4) 655.

226 ibid 698.

human dignity as a moral principle is. For, as was mentioned before, the power of an ethical reflection on the human rights framework is found exactly in that it can bridge the difference between the *lex lata* and the *lex ferenda*. Understanding the foundation of human rights law does not mean that one cannot question, challenge, or criticize the human rights machinery, including the juridical interpretation of central principles such as human dignity. If viewed from a moral-philosophical perspective, human dignity informs the human rights framework about what is categorically morally right or wrong (see Section 4.2 above).

4.5.2 Autonomy and agency in healthcare settings

In healthcare settings, autonomy is understood as a central concept alongside dignity and vulnerability. One could challenge the PGC because of its strong emphasis on rational performance. The principal criticism when it comes to applying the PGC to healthcare settings is found in the fact that vulnerability is also a central concept in healthcare, alongside human dignity. Especially in end-of-life situations, one can wonder whether care should rather focus on comforting the patient so that he or she can die with dignity, by focusing on reducing vulnerability instead of focusing on individual autonomy.

While agents are not by definition vulnerable, the agents to whom Gewirth's justification of the PGC applies are. If there were no fear of being harmed, there would be no point in bringing claims to generic conditions of agency – and ultimately in human rights at all. What is the point in protection if you have no violation to fear? This is line of reasoning is similar to the one which claims that one can only have a right if it can be enforced. If there is no correlative duty, what is the power of a right? Yet, it is precisely because one fears violation of one's rights that the aim is for them to be protected. As follows from the principle of instrumental reason, agents proactively value the purposes they freely choose in the sense that their selected purposes motivate their actions to attain these purposes. It is precisely this capacity to make value judgments that leads to agents having generic rights, but also to agents principally valuing their generic conditions of agency as insecure.[227] Hence, all action *a priori* embeds a certain degree of vulnerability.

As has been addressed, in its foundational role human dignity should be understood to be human dignity as empowerment. In line with this reinforced claim to individual autonomy, the PGC understands human dignity to be everything that makes one an agent. As was briefly mentioned, this inevitably includes vulnerability, the '(...) capacity to reason and make choices, life (...), [and what Beyleveld and Brownsword

227 Beyleveld and Brownsword (n 42) 112.

term] mental equilibrium (...) to translate' wishes into actions.[228] The interrelatedness of these features is what could be referred to as 'vulnerable agency'. In addition, Haugen outlines the triangular relation between human dignity, autonomy, and vulnerability in healthcare settings. This is often used to demonstrate the insufficiency of autonomy, or the inability of treatments to empower individuals in order to increase their autonomy.[229] This triangular relationship demonstrates that in healthcare settings adequate care that empowers autonomy, decreases vulnerability and *vice versa.*

4.5.3 Agency, political recognition, and universality

In defining who is the subject of rights, Benhabib raises different conceptual issues. For instance, Benhabib claims it to be evident that any justification of human rights necessarily includes some aspects of agency and some influences of a Rawlsian political context (such as that suggested by Nussbaum). One simply cannot justify human rights without reference to agency.[230] However, on the contrary, Claassen and Düwell note that Rawls based his theory on democratic countries with a constitutional regime, whilst agency accounts of human rights do not make any presuppositions as to the question of constitutional embedding.[231] Constitutional embedding may be contingently important, although not necessary, for people to have rights. Another criticism is that a focus on rational action attests to a Western imperialist interpretation of international law that conflicts with communitarianism, which emphasizes the role of the community as dominant over the individual.[232] Interpreting autonomy as including the ability to reason, however, should be viewed as an objective and broad concept. It does not carry a value judgment as to the purposes chosen by an agent. Rather, it focuses on the potential to act autonomously. In that sense, inaction is as much an autonomous act as action itself. Hence, the protection of human dignity does not reside in the actual act or in its right or wrongness, but rather in a person's ability to choose freely to act or forego action. In this sense, autonomy should be understood as a facilitating capacity. Therefore, even in community-oriented societies, understanding autonomy as a facilitating capacity could well be the universally valid norm through which we can justify the normative foundation of human rights as being grounded in human dignity.

---

228 ibid 115.

229 HM Haugen, 'Inclusive and Relevant Language: The Use of the Concepts of Autonomy, Dignity, and Vulnerability in Different Contexts' (2010) 13 Medicine, Health Care, and Philosophy 203.

230 S Benhabib, 'Reason-Giving and Rights-Bearing: Constructing the Subject of Rights' (2013) 20 Constellations 38, 38.

231 See Claassen and Düwell (n 150) 501.

232 See eg M Werner, 'Individual and Collective Dignity' in M Düwell and others (eds), *The Cambridge Handbook of Human Dignity: Interdisciplinary Perspectives* (CUP 2014).

Precisely because of the global nature and impact of the unavailability of controlled essential medicines, any analysis of a human rights approach to drug control addressing this issue should be context-blind. Such context-blindness is warranted because choosing a frame of analysis that is rooted in any normative or substantive value or viewpoint cannot be applied in a similarly universal way. Applying a human rights approach anchored in a particular substantive viewpoint (for instance a religious interpretation of human rights), presupposes that all people should subscribe to this belief. This is because otherwise the local context fundamentally conflicts with the normative foundation on which the human rights approach analysed rests. By contrast, a context-blind analysis leaves ample space for alterations and substantive interpretations at the practical level, whilst presenting a clear yardstick for moral or immoral action (as the PGC does).

4.5.4 Criticism of a rational approach

Agency accounts of human rights, such as the PGC, have also received criticism.[233] Benhabib, for instance, rules out the possibility of a dialectical justification and instead argues in favour of a justification on the basis of communicative freedom. She holds that the 'capacity to formulate goals of action is not prior to the capacity to be able to justify such goals with reasons to others'.[234] This premise fails to hold as the PGC does not dictate that agents have rights to freedom and well-being because others recognize them. Instead, agents possess such rights because it is dialectically necessary, on the pain of self-contradiction, that an agent must consider them as rights based on their necessity for the general exercise of their agency.

The 'right to have rights' to which Benhabib refers is more of a meta-right, similar to the way in which the PGC is a meta-principle that elaborates a system of meta-rights. These meta-rights are not identifiable with human rights (see Section 4.4.2 above). Benhabib argues that, in contrast with rational action as an aspect of agency, communication and agency are interrelated. She understands that the indispensability of agency abstracts 'from the social embeddedness of agency in (…) shared contexts of speech and action'.[235] However, a situation can exist in which one is the only agent and yet one can still be aware of one's own agency. Reciprocity can be contingently important in justifying agency accounts of human rights, such as that offered by the PGC, but as is demonstrated by the PGC, this is not necessary. Operating on this false premise is what leads Benhabib's argument to wrongly rule out the possibility

233 For an extensive rebuttal of criticism on the Gewirthian approach, see Beyleveld, *Dialectical Necessity* (n 82).
234 Benhabib, 'Another Universalism' (n 5) 15.
235 id.

of the PGC being a categorically binding moral principle that guides the human rights framework.

4.6 Conclusion

This chapter explored the normative justification of the prioritized, access-led approach to drug control, as found in human rights law. As was observed in the introduction, the appeal to absoluteness and priority requires one to think fundamentally differently about the 'principle of balance', as it is currently framed in the field of international drug control. Yet, precisely because the argument found in law is reconstructed, and because the moral principles underlying the human rights framework are not necessarily the same as the legal rights enshrined, the question is whether such approach is normatively defensible.

This chapter presented a normative-ethical defence of the human rights framework. By reflecting on the necessary commitments, which derive from the internal perspective of reasoning of an agent, it found the moral principle on which the human rights framework, and therefore also human dignity as the foundation of inalienable rights, rest. The reference to inalienable rights grounded in dignity, as found in international human rights documents, presupposes that there is a basis for human rights in universal moral principles, and requires us to question whether one can view human dignity as a categorically binding moral norm informing the entire human rights regime. According to this perspective, the role of human dignity is to act as a principle generating rights rather than being a norm or a right in itself. Considering human dignity as a claim *to* autonomy rather than as autonomy itself, allows us to frame human dignity as a categorically binding moral principle underpinning the entire human rights framework. Reflecting on two similar but distinct agency accounts of human rights, which both purport a claim *to* autonomy, leads to the following central points:

Both the capability approach and the PGC conceptualize human rights in a very similar manner. They view human rights as being focused on freedom and well-being, labelled as generic rights, functionings, or capabilities, and deem all agents to hold positive and negative duties to enhance the capabilities or rather the generic conditions of agency. This normative construction of 'human flourishing' as invoking both positive and negative rights is fundamentally different from the way in which economic, social, and cultural rights are framed as political goals instead of as legally enforceable rights. Looking back at Chapter 3, interpreting human dignity as invoking both positive and negative obligations, trumps any idea that the right to health would be conceptually strong but legally weak in reconstructing the 'principle of balance'.

Due to the strong focus on agency, the ability to function, self-definition, and empowerment, it is undisputable that the denial of pain medication and (controlled) medicines more generally, is an affront to dignity. In light of the positive and negative obligations that dignity invokes, governments have obligations to ensure access to pain treatment and access to (controlled) medicines. Yet, the real moral issue in this domain is whether one has a right to use drugs, or whether human dignity, despite being a claim *to* autonomy, can also be the justificatory principle based on which to limit drug use. Moreover, the question of how one should understand any clashes between these two aspects arises, using human dignity as yardstick.

It is at this stage that the PGC demonstrates the power of its dialectical necessity, as opposed to the reflective hypothetical process on which the capability approach is based. The analysis demonstrated that the PGC is capable of purporting dignity as a categorically binding moral principle. Then, the PGC as a rational claim to autonomy is the normative content of dignity as empowerment in its foundational role. Hence, managing an internal perspective demands that we reconsider the 'principle of balance' in line with the degree of needfulness of generic goods and aspects of well-being relevant to the capacity of rational decision-making. The implication of such an approach in relation to the reconsideration of the 'principle of balance' is threefold:

First, regardless of whether there is a right to use drugs, all agents including States, third parties, and other social institutions, hold positive and negative duties regarding the generic rights to well-being and freedom. This includes the access to medicines. Depending on the exact situation, the access to medicines is either a basic or non-subtractive aspect of well-being.

Second, regardless of whether there is a right to use drugs, all agents including States, third parties, and other social institutions, have positive and negative duties to the generic rights of well-being and freedom of drug users. These duties apply regardless of whether or not drug dependence impairs the ability to act in accordance with the principle of instrumental reason, as a result of the precautionary principle.

Third, in light of the juxtaposition of drug-control regulation (i.e. the tension between ensuring access to medicines and control of non-medical drug use and the harms associated to it), if drug use hampers people's access to medicines, then mechanisms ought to be put into place to prioritize the access to medicines as basic or non-subtractive needs over additive aspects of well-being. However, if it is not drug use itself, but rather the regulations put into place to curtail drug use – which are themselves questionable in light of the PGC – that hamper the access to medicines, then these regulations need to be reconsidered. For in accordance with the PGC, the access to medicines must never be limited, not *de jure* or *de facto*, in order to curtail drug use.

The maximum access/minimum diversion approach of the 'principle of balance' is therefore neither wrong nor incompatible with human rights. Rather, both human rights law and theory demonstrate that one cannot equate access to medicines with aspects of non-medical use, and that prioritizing medical access to controlled substances is categorically binding. In fact, the categorically binding dialectical necessity of Gewirth and Beyleveld's moral argument that underpins the access-led approach found in law is morally justified, and all agents, including all social institutions, ought to regulate drug control in such a way that efforts regarding the access to medicines must not be diminished or compromised by drug-control efforts, either *de jure* or *de facto*. This means that the prohibitive and restrictive approach of drug control found in the international drug-control system is highly questionable and is, in places, incompatible with the moral justification presented. The PGC certainly does not entail that all law should be human rights law. Rather, it reasons that if we state that a law is a human rights law, it should be in accordance with the PGC. Moreover, if it concerns a generic condition of agency, it should follow the PGC.

All in all, one can conclude that drug-control regulation can never be managed by a one-size-fits-all approach. This is precisely because the operationalization of the PGC largely depends on the empirical evidence needed to critically assess whether an aspect of freedom or well-being is generic, i.e. instrumental to the ability to function as constructed in the principle of instrumental reason. Yet, finally, the question to take onwards to Part 3 of this book is how States could manage such an access-led approach through the structures provided in the current international drug-control system. One must consider whether, from a practical perspective, the administrative and procedural requirements of the international drug-control system, including specific trade and distribution requirements, hamper States in their ability to ensure access to medicines in accordance with human rights law. This is important to understand what the argument presented in this book may imply.

Part 3

Country Studies

Chapter 5
Bridging Theory and Practice: Introduction to the Country Studies

5.1 Introduction

Various schools of thought claim that international law in general and human rights law in particular are fraught with imperialist and postcolonial incoherencies.[1] Partly building on the traditional discussion on the universality and cultural relativity of human rights, international law is accused of structurally reinforcing the subordinate position of Low and Middle-Income Countries (LMICs).[2] In this respect, Rajagopal considers that the 'human rights discourse and the leading spokespersons for human rights [to] have failed to stop the consolidation of hegemonic international law and [to] have rather been complicit in it.'[3] In light of these concerns, the question is whether new interpretations of existing fields of law, such as the one presented in this book, may also fall victim to similar structural constraints. While this book is neither primarily concerned with the 'colonialist' nature of international law, nor the universality and cultural relativity of human rights per se, these discussions signal the need to continue a more contextual approach.

In this third part of the book, the study takes an 'empirical turn', for as Schaffer and Ginsburg observe, 'international law is the product of specific forces and factors; it accomplishes its ends under particular conditions'.[4] In fact, focusing on local conditions and on implementation is vital because, from a governance perspective,

---

1 See eg U Baxi, 'Too Many or Too Few, Human Rights?' (2001) 1 Human Rights Law Review 1; S Puhaja, 'The Postcoloniality of International Law' (2005) 46 Harvard International Law Journal 459; A Anghie, *Imperialism, Sovereignty, and the Making of International Law* (CUP 2007); S Marks, 'Human Rights and the Bottom Billion' (2009) 1 European Human Rights Law Review 37; S Marks, 'Human Rights and Root Causes' (2011) 74 The Modern Law Review 57; S Pahuja, *Decolonising International Law* (CUP 2011). Notably, any ethical analysis based on the normative foundations of human rights law still allows one to criticize the law in general, including the fields of drug control and human rights.

2 It is submitted here that the concern about the position of LMICs may, depending on the specific context, apply to countries with serious resource constraints in general, including those with high-income levels that face serious limitations in some public sectors (eg the health sector).

3 B Rajagopal, 'Counter-Hegemonic International Law: Rethinking Human Rights and Development as a Third World Strategy' (2006) 27 Third World Quarterly 767, 772.

4 'Empirical turn' is taken from the title of Shaffer and Ginsburg's article on empirical studies and international law, see G Shaffer and T Ginsburg, 'The Empirical Turn in International Legal Scholarship' (2012) 106 American Journal of International Law 1, 1.

'the successful delivery of collective goods and services is not only a question of political preference and public choice, but also a question of the ability of State institutions to function at all'.[5] Part 3, therefore, presents the results of two qualitative country studies conducted in Uganda and Latvia. These studies (Chapters 6 and 7) explore the interplay of the human rights and drug-control frameworks in practice, which may assist in revealing the complexities of and gaps in the international drug-control system with respect to human-rights compliant medicine provision, if any exist at all.

The present chapter provides a brief introduction in terms of design and methodology of this third part, commencing with a description of the research design, which includes the research approach used, the central research question, and the methods of data collection and analysis (Section 5.2). Next, the chapter expands on the rationale behind the country selection (Section 5.3). Finally, it points out various limitations that one must take into account (Section 5.4).

5.2 Research design

5.2.1 Research approach and central question

Chapter 2 demonstrated that medicine provision is generally challenging within the broader healthcare system. In fact, the same chapter introduced the hypothesis that the administrative and procedural requirements originating in Articles 17, 19-20, and 30 of the 1961 Single Convention on Narcotic Drugs possess the potential to complicate a stable and adequate provision of, in particular, controlled essential medicines.[6]

In sum, State Parties to the Single Convention have to manage a special administration to monitor compliance with the provisions contained in the Single Convention.[7] Moreover, they must submit to the International Narcotics Control Board (INCB) annual estimates that at the least include the quantities of substances to be consumed for medical and scientific purposes in the coming year.[8] In addition, State Parties have to furnish the INCB with statistical returns specifying at least the consumption

5 MM Lee, G Walter-Drop and J Wiesel, 'Taking the State (Back) Out? Statehood and the Delivery of Collective Goods' (2014) 27 Governance 635, 635.

6 The author does not claim that the administrative and procedural requirements of the Single Convention necessarily hamper medicine provision. It is rather hypothesized that they could on their own account or in conjunction with other existing complexities prove to have that effect. Single Convention on Narcotic Drugs (adopted 30 March 1961, entered into force 13 December 1964) 520 UNTS 151 (Single Convention) arts 17, 19, 20, and 30. See also Chapter 2.

7 ibid art 17.

8 ibid art 19.

data, import/export data, and production figures.[9] And finally, States also have to implement specific trade and distribution obligations, including those dictating, *inter alia*, that controlled essential medicines should be available on prescription (if deemed necessary written on official forms), ought to be dispensed by authorized staff, and that facilities engaging in the trade or distribution of controlled medicines should be supervised.[10]

Implementation of these procedures to the extent that State Parties ensure adequate access to medicines is crucial because conjointly these obligations reflect a global regulatory structure of import and export licenses. Any State not adhering to these procedures in a sufficient manner is therefore technically sidelined or at least seriously restricted in ensuring its population adequate access to medicines.[11] However, Chapter 2 also explained that medicine provision in accordance with international standards, including human rights, presupposes an impressive series of steps and actions having been taken. The aforementioned administrative and procedural drug-control requirements may, in that regard, only add to the existing complexity of service provision.

The third sub-question of this book is: 'How, if at all, can a normative framework as developed under sub-questions 1-2 be included in the structures of the present international drug-control system?' In order to answer this, it is necessary to gain insight into the local context of medicine provision in light of the administrative and procedural requirements mentioned earlier. Ultimately, the issue is that 'human rights instruments provide a template of domestic governance', whilst the international drug-control system most directly regulates and controls the availability and accessibility of controlled medicines on the pharmaceutical market.[12] Yet, from a legal perspective, one may question what barrier this may constitute, if at all, to the actual medicine provision in compliance with human rights norms. Drawing on the findings of Chapters 3 and 4, the specific central question is:

---

9 ibid art 20.

10 ibid art 30.

11 MEC Gispen, 'Reconciling International Obligations and Local Realities: Provision of Pain Control Medication in Resource-Constrained Countries – Experiences from Uganda' in M Hesselman, A de Wolff and BCA Toebes (eds), *Essential Public Service Provision* (Routledge *forthcoming*).

12 L Reed, WM Reisman and R Dolzer, 'Why Regime Change is (Almost Always) a Bad Idea (Manley O. Hudson Medal Lecture)' (2004) 98 Proceedings of the Annual Meeting (American Society of International Law) 289, 294. See also V Nesiah, 'Resistance in the Age of Empire: Occupied Discourse Pending Investigation' (2006) 27 Third World Quarterly 903, 911. Moreover, the rights-based theories relied on in this book, such as the Principle of Generic Consistency as elaborated on in Chapter 4, are often not designed to deal with issues of implementation.

> How, if at all, can States prioritize, promote and uphold the Availability, Accessibility, Acceptability and Quality (AAAQ standard of healthcare) of medicines in accordance with human rights theory and law, whilst implementing the administrative and procedural requirements of the international drug-control system?

The question has two main aspects, which are each addressed via empirical analysis. First, one needs to generate in-depth understanding of the context in which the administrative and procedural requirements of the international drug-control system come into play. This needs a good grasp of what is called the 'regulatory chain' of pain-control medicines. In parallel with a healthcare-systems analysis, understanding the conditions of service provision in the local context presupposes insight into the structure and process of access to morphine provision in a healthcare system.[13] Structure, process, and outcome-focused healthcare-systems analysis are quite similar to the conceptualization of human rights indicators, which serve as a tool to assess the implementation of human rights norms and State Parties' compliance in this area.[14]

Structural indicators include, for instance, the ratification of legal instruments as well as the 'existence of basic institutional mechanisms necessary for facilitating' implementation and realization of a specific human right.[15] In an attempt to connect the action taken with the corresponding effect in practice, process indicators 'relate State policy instruments to milestones that become outcome indicators'.[16] Finally, outcome indicators are concerned with the result in terms of the realization and actual enjoyment of rights.[17] While the data collected may both be quantitative and qualitative in nature, the results of using human rights indicators are often numerical.[18] Yet, it is important here to not just focus on the quantifiable information of the regulatory requirements, and trade and distribution conditions flowing from drug-control regulations. Instead, the experiences and perceptions of those working with these control procedures, and of those enforcing them, are vital to understanding the local context in which international regulations manifest themselves.

---

13 A Bowling, *Research Methods in Health: Investigating Health and Health Services* (4th edn, Open University Press 2014) 10.

14 See IHRI 'Report of the Inter-Committee Technical Working Group on Harmonized Guidelines on Reporting under the International Human Rights Treaties, Including Guidelines on a Common Core Document and Treaty-Specific Documents' (10 May 2006) UN Doc HRI/MC/2006/3, paras 17-19. See also G de Beco, 'Human Rights Indicators: From Theoretical Debate to Practical Application' (2013) 5 Journal of Human Rights Practice 1.

15 UN Doc HRI/MC/2006/7 (n 14) para 17.

16 ibid para 18.

17 ibid para 19.

18 de Beco (n 14) 4.

In public-health research, qualitative approaches are increasingly common to understand 'experiences and attitudes of patients, the community, or healthcare workers (...) with the goal of informing policy-makers or practitioners'.[19] In fact, 'qualitative methods are intended to convey to policy makers the experiences of individuals, groups, and organizations, who may be affected by policies'.[20] Moreover, the use of qualitative techniques allows one to deepen the understanding of certain phenomena through contextual research. A qualitative approach therefore seems suitable to achieve the objectives in Part 3 of the book.

Second, without establishing any causality, one needs to understand the local realities of service provision in light of the AAAQ standard of healthcare, as relevant, if at all. The qualitative data gathered on the structure, process, and outcome of the administrative and procedural requirements relating to medicine provision is analysed. Furthermore, it is discussed in light of the normative framework of the AAAQ standard of healthcare as developed in General Comment 14 of the Committee on Economic, Social, and Cultural Rights (CESCR). In doing so, the analysis primarily focuses on the Availability and Accessibility requirements, and only if relevant concerns itself with Acceptability standards. Since the administrative and procedural requirements that are studied do not regulate the Quality of medicines, this aspect is not discussed. As part of this second step, the legal commitments made to facilitate the domestic implementation of the right to health are analysed.[21] As a final point of demarcation, in line with the central examples used throughout this book, the country studies also concentrate, in particular, on the access to pain-control medicines and palliative care.[22]

5.2.2 Data collection and analysis

The data collection strategy of the country studies is inspired by the rapid assessment protocol, originally developed by the Insulin Foundation to identify challenges in the provision of insulin for diabetes in resource-constrained countries.[23] The protocol, as

19 MA Duran and T Chantler, *Principles of Social Research* (2nd edn, Open University Press 2014) 44.
20 ibid; R Fitzpatrick and M Boulton, 'Qualitative Methods for Assessing Health Care' (1994) 3 Quality in Health Care 107, 107.
21 On the use of structural human rights indicators, see UN Doc HRI/MC/2006/7 (n 14) para 17.
22 This does not mean that other examples may not be referred to. It merely implies that the studies are designed to focus on pain-control medicines and palliative care. However, for the sake of completeness, comparative arguments and analogous discussions are explored at all stages of the study.
23 See D Beran and M Higuchi, *How to Investigate Access to Care for Chronic Non-Communicable Diseases in Low-and Middle-Income Countries* (International Insulin Foundation 2012).

does this study, operates on the macro (national), meso (regional), and micro (local) level.[24]

The case studies in both countries have been conducted in six sequent phases: (i) initial preparation and desk research; (ii) sampling; (iii) creation of data collection methods; (iv) preparation of fieldwork; (v) data collection itself; and (vi) data analysis.[25] Desk research is carried out by means of a literature analysis. Sampling and the creation of data collection methods, in turn, are carried out on the basis of the desk research.

Data collection tools include in-depth interviews conducted in rural, peri-urban, and urban regions of both countries, as well as participant observations.[26] Respondents were stakeholders in each country's supply/demand chain of morphine. In addition to these core stakeholders, other civil society actors and academics, knowledgeable on the topic, were selected. To increase coherency and facilitate the analysis, respondents were categorized as set out in Table 5.1.[27]

Table 5.1 Overview categories of respondents

Categories of respondents
government officials
civil society representatives
medical store representatives
manufacturing company representatives
head of health facilities
head of pharmacies
legal prescribers (those allowed to prescribe controlled medicines or morphine in particular)
non-prescribing medical staff (e.g. nurses)
dispensers
academics
others

24 ibid 54-57. In contrast to the rapid assessment protocol, the case study component of this research is primarily based on qualitative, instead of quantitative, data.

25 ibid.

26 Duran and Chantler (n 19) 50. In-depth interviews are interviews for which a broad topic, instead of clearly defined questions, is used as a guiding principle.

27 Patients were not included as research participants. Given that they do not occupy any regulatory role, their view as an end user is unlikely to produce the information sought. The decision to omit patients, however, does not detract from the central position these individuals occupy in the book as rights-holders.

Within these categories, references to participants might differ slightly in Chapter 6 and 7, as it was decided, within the categories established, to stick to the most accurate names used in the country-specific context. The categories presented in Chapters 6 and 7 were also used during the data analysis process of each country study. Participants were selected in consultation with a local expert and were further based on informed snowball sampling. An anonymous, country-specific overview of the respondents, their position, and their geographic distribution is provided in Chapter 6 and 7 respectively.

For the interviews, a list of topics was developed and, for each interviewee, amended to suit the position of the actor in question. The list was kept relatively short and general in nature to avoid bias in the discussion as much as possible. The topics include:

i) the position of the respondent in the regulatory chain of controlled medicines (particularly morphine), if applicable;
ii) the respondent's daily routine in their respective position (e.g. as pharmacist, doctor, nurse, wholesaler, or government official) in complying with specific regulations that are applicable to the prescribing, dispensing, ordering, and accounting of controlled medicines relevant to their position. If respondents lack a particular mandate in the regulatory chain of controlled medicines, their general take on these requirements is discussed;
iii) the respondent's view on palliative care policy and the role of human rights in this area;
iv) the respondent's experience, if at all, with any situations in which it was impossible or difficult to sufficiently comply with the applicable procedures;
v) the respondent's view on challenges to service provision in general and specifically in relation to morphine and controlled medicines, if any at all, including success stories.[28]

Short field visits were conducted to collect materials.[29] All interviews were conducted with the informed consent of the participants and recorded with permission.[30] Interviews have been transcribed *verbatim*.[31] The categories of participants, as

28 See eg Gispen (n 11).
29 Data collection took place in July 2014 (Uganda) and in January 2015 (Latvia). In March 2013, a 10-day preliminary field visit was carried out in Uganda to test the feasibility of data collection on site.
30 For the informed consent form used, see Appendixes I and II.
31 *Verbatim* transcription means that interviews were transcribed word-by-word and reflect exactly what the respondent said without amendments. The primary researcher transcribed the interviews conducted in Uganda, while *Uitgetypt*, a fully qualified transcription company, transcribed those held in Latvia. Because of their length, sections that were clearly not relevant to the research in question have been summarized. These instances have been carefully marked throughout the transcription process.

described above, were maintained during the data analysis and the information was analysed by means of a coding system. Throughout the data collection process, any statistical information or objectified data on which participants relied was cross-checked as far as possible by the researcher. During the data analysis, triangulation was used to verify what the participants had submitted (via cross analysis). For instance: if respondent 1 said A, and respondent 2 also said A independently of respondent 1, and this information is further reflected in e.g. policy documents, it is quite likely that the information is valid. If there no such coherence, it is more difficult to base more general conclusions on such findings and, in that case, the data reflects only the perception of the participant.[32]

All the information collected was treated confidentially and results were communicated back to the participants.[33] Subsequent to the data analysis, the findings are discussed as being either general or substance-specific challenges to medicine provision, bearing in mind the AAAQ standard of healthcare developed by the CESCR. Chapter 2 already distinguished between such substance-specific and general challenges. Building on this distinction helps one understand the impact international and domestic drug-control requirements might have on human-rights compliant medicine provision. As mentioned in Chapter 1, the design of both studies was granted ethical approval by the relevant authorities in each country.[34]

5.3 Rationale for country selection

Data from Duthey and Scholten illustrates that a significant part of the global population lacks access to controlled medicines and, in particular, access to pain-control medicines.[35] Precisely due to the ubiquitous nature of such unavailability, any decision relating to country selection is non-exclusive. In an effort to avoid absolutism in this selection procedure, there are various interrelated criteria on the

32 See on the credibility of qualitative research eg JR Cutcliffe, 'Establishing the Credibility of Qualitative Research Findings: The Plot Thickens' (1999) 30 Methodological Issues in Nursing Research 374.

33 All participants will receive an electronic summary of the results. In Uganda, a dissemination event was organized that allowed one to cross-check the information gathered and provided a stage for the distribution of the initial findings to the participants.

34 The design of the study in Uganda was approved by the Medical Ethics Review Committee of the University Medical Centre Utrecht (14-244/C) and by the Uganda National Council for Science and Technology (SS 3477). The former institution also approved the Latvian study (14-532/C).

35 B Duthey and W Scholten, 'Adequacy of Opioid Analgesic Consumption at Country, Global, and Regional Levels in 2010, its Relationship with Development Level, and Changes Compared with 2006' (2014) 47 Journal of Pain and Symptom Management 283. For a discussion of this data and the magnitude of the unavailability of controlled medicines, see also Chapter 2.

basis of which Uganda and Latvia are considered to be suitable case-study countries for the purpose of this book.

First, both countries are so-called 'best practice' countries in the field of palliative care provision or in terms of legislative reform to advance the access to controlled medicines. In Uganda, for instance, access to pain treatment and palliative care has received significant political and civil society attention during the last 20 years. This attention has led to a legislative reform in which specially trained nurses and clinical officers, alongside doctors, are now allowed to prescribe and administer morphine outside hospital settings. The law was reformed to boost accessibility, counter the understaffing of the healthcare system, and respond to the absence of doctors.[36] Uganda's efforts, in this respect, have been acknowledged in, among other areas, academic work.[37] Latvia, on the other hand, has been selected as one of the 12 European countries involved in the *Access to Opioid Medication in Europe* study carried out by a consortium of European universities. Latvia has gone through a substantial policy-reform process to reverse its once restrictive stance, both in the form of laws and policies, on the medical use of controlled substances.[38]

It is important that both countries are classified as 'best practice' countries because, if one wants to study the practical implications of Articles 17, 19-20, and 30 of the Single Convention in the context of human-rights compliant access to medicine provision, some structure has to be in place. Including 'worst practice' countries is considered to frustrate the research and would complicate, instead of support, the approach taken. Exactly due to the inherent need for something to 'go well' in a best-practice scenario, it is believed to be easier to filter out potential gaps, hindrances, or complexities with regard to the service provision. Moreover, the elevated awareness that the topic enjoys is helpful too, meaning that interviews and observations are more likely to render in-depth results if relatively little time is needed to familiarize the research participant with the topic in question.

---

36 JGM Jagwe, 'The Introduction of Palliative Care in Uganda' (2002) 5 Journal of Palliative Medicine 160; A Merriman, *Audacity to Love* (The Irish Hospice Foundation 2010); Ministry of Health, Palliative Care Association of Uganda and Open Society Initiative for East Africa, *The Development of Palliative Care in Uganda* (Ministry of Health 2012).

37 S Ramsey, 'Leading the Way in African Home-Based Palliative Care' (2003) 362 The Lancet 1812; R Harding and IJ Higginson, 'Palliative Care in Sub-Saharan Africa' (2005) 365 The Lancet 1971, 1973; D Lohman, R Schleifer and JJ Amon, 'Access to Pain Treatment as a Human Right' (2010) 8 BMC Medicine 1.

38 L Radbruch and others, *Access to Opioid Medication in Europe: Final Report and Recommendations to the Ministries of Health* (Palliative Medicine Verlag 2014).

Second, both Uganda and Latvia portray inadequate consumption figures despite their reform efforts.[39] In its analysis of this aspect, this book relies on the *Adequacy of Consumption Measure* as used by Duthey and Scholten.[40] If past or current efforts have been significantly successful in improving consumption of pain-control medicines, it is less likely to find structural complexities at the level of local service provision. It is not submitted here that one has to necessarily find such complexities. Rather, the inadequacy of consumption is used as a criterion to propagate at least the possibility of such insight. Yet, perhaps most importantly, the book is concerned with improving access to controlled medicines in regions in which this access is insufficient to date. It would therefore be in contrast with this central ambition to focus on countries with adequate consumption figures.

Third, the healthcare systems of both countries are resource-constrained. In Uganda, this may be the result of its low-income status. Latvia, however, despite being ranked as a high-income country on the Human Development Index (HDI), also suffers serious resource constraints in its healthcare system resulting from the 2008 financial crisis.[41] 'Resource-constrained countries' in the context of this book is therefore to be understood as to include, on the one hand, LMICs that are generally considered resource-poor across many public areas and, on the other, high-income countries of which the healthcare system is subjected to such resource constraints that obstacles in health-service provision occur (possibly similar to those in LMICs).[42] The HDI rank of each country is, in that respect, used to verify the development status of the country.[43] It is important to focus on resource-constrained countries because medicine provision is a resource-intense activity – especially in the case of controlled

39 Duthey and Scholten (n 36) 285, 288.

40 ibid. Duthey and Scholten compare the morbidity-corrected needs of strong opioids such as morphine per capita. Adequacy of consumption is calculated by comparing the actual consumption within a given time span with the pre-calculated need. Such need is calculated by using morbidity-corrected needs of strong opioids, such as morphine per capita, and the actual use of these substances in the top 20 of countries listed on the Human Development Index. For an introduction into this method, see MJ Seya and others, 'A First Comparison between the Consumption of and the Need for Opioid Analgesics at Country, Regional, and Global Levels' (2011) 15 Journal of Pain and Palliative Care Pharmacotherapy 6.

41 C Andersen, 'IMF Survey: Latvia Caught in Vicious Economic Downturn' (28 May 2009) <www.imf.org/external/pubs/ft/survey/so/2009/car052809a.htm> accessed 31 August 2016.

42 These constraints in the conditions of health-service provision in resource-rich countries may lead to results similar to those in resource-constrained countries and in countries with resource-poor healthcare systems, especially if a country has large remote areas. See eg C Coleman and others, 'The International Cancer Expert Corps (ICEC): A Unique Global Mentoring Model for Building Sustainable Expertise in Low- and Lower-Middle Income Countries and Geographically Remote Areas in Resource Rich Countries' (2015) 81 Annals of Global Health 20.

43 See United Nations Development Programme, *Human Development Report 2015: Work for Human Development* (UNDP 2015).

essential medicines. [44] and Latvia[45] have ratified all treaties under study. In this

44 Single Convention (acceded 15 April 1988); Convention on Psychotropic Substances (adopted 21 February 1971, entered into force 16 August 1976, acceded 15 April 1988) 1901 UNTS 175; United Nations Convention Against the Illicit Traffic in Narcotic Drugs and Psychotropic Substances (adopted 20 December 1988, entered into force 11 November 1990, acceded 20 August 1990) 1582 UNTS 95 (1988 Convention Against Illicit Traffic); International Covenant on Economic, Social and Cultural Rights (adopted 16 December 1966, entered into force 3 January 1976, acceded 21 January 1987) 993 UNTS 3 (ICESCR); International Covenant on Civil and Political Rights (adopted 16 December 1966, entered into force 23 March 1976, acceded 21 June 1995) 999 UNTS 171 (ICCPR); Optional Protocol to the International Covenant on Civil and Political Rights (adopted 16 December 1966, entered into force 23 March 1976, acceded 14 November 1995) 999 UNTS 171 (OP-ICCPR); International Convention on the Elimination of All Forms of Racial Discrimination (adopted 7 March 1966, entered into force 4 January 1969, acceded 21 November 1980) 660 UNTS 195 (CERD); Convention on the Elimination of All Forms of Discrimination Against Women (adopted 18 December 1979, entered into force 3 September 1981, ratified 22 July 1985) 1249 UNTS 13 (CEDAW); Convention against Torture and Other Cruel, Inhuman or Degrading Treatment or Punishment (adopted 10 December 1984, entered into force 26 June 1987, acceded 3 November 1986) 1465 UNTS 85 (CAT); Convention on the Rights of the Child (adopted 20 November 1989, entered into force 2 September 1990, ratified 17 August 1990) 1577 UNTS 3 (CRC); Optional Protocol to the Convention on the Rights of the Child on the Involvement of Children in Armed Conflict (adopted 25 May 2000, entered into force 12 February 2002, acceded 6 May 2002) 2173 UNTS 222 (OP1-CRC); Optional Protocol to the Convention on the Rights of the Child on the Sale of Children, Child Prostitution and Child Pornography (adopted 25 May 2000, entered into force 18 January 2002, acceded 30 November 2001) 2171 UNTS 227 (OP2-CRC); Convention on the Rights of Persons with Disabilities (adopted 13 December 2006, entered into force 3 May 2008, ratified 25 September 2008) 2515 UNTS 3 (CRPD); Optional Protocol to the Convention on the Rights of Persons with Disabilities (adopted 13 December 2006, entered into force 3 May 2008, ratified 25 September 2008) UN Doc A/RES/61/106 (OP-CRPD); International Convention on the Protection of the Rights of All Migrant Workers and Members of their Families (adopted 18 December 1990, entered into force 1 July 2003, acceded 14 November 1995) 2220 UNTS 3; International Convention for the Protection of All Persons from Enforced Disappearance (adopted 20 December 2006, entered into force 23 December 2010, signed 6 February 2007) 2716 UNTS 3; African Charter on Human and Peoples' Rights (adopted 27 June 1981, entered into force 21 October 1986, ratified 10 May 1986) 1520 UNTS 217; Protocol to the African Charter on Human and Peoples' Rights on the Rights of Women in Africa (adopted 7 November 2003, entered into force 25 November 2005, ratified 22 July 2010) OAU Doc CAB/LEG/66.6; Protocol to the African Charter on Human and Peoples' Rights on the Establishment of an African Court on Human and Peoples' Rights (adopted 10 June 1998, entered into force 25 January 2004, ratified 16 February 2001) OAU Doc OAU/LEG/EXP/AFCHPR/PROT(III); African Charter on the Rights and Welfare of the Child (adopted 1 July 1990, entered into force 29 November 1999, ratified 17 August 1994) OAU Doc CAB/LEG/24.9/49.

45 Single Convention (acceded 16 July 1993); Convention on Psychotropic Substances (acceded 16 July 1993); 1988 Convention Against Illicit Traffic (acceded 24 February 1994); ICESCR (acceded 14 April 1992); ICCPR (acceded 14 April 1992); OP-ICCPR (acceded 22 June 1994); CERD (acceded 14 April 1992); CEDAW (acceded 14 April 1992); CAT (acceded 14 April 1992); CRC (acceded 14 April 1992); OP1-CRC (ratified 19 December 2005); OP2-CRC (ratified 22 February 2006); CRPD (ratified 1 March 2010); OP-CRPD (ratified 31 August 2010); European Convention for the Protection of Human Rights and Fundamental Freedoms (adopted 4 November 1950, entered into force 3 September 1953, as amended, ratified 27 June 1997) 213 UNTS 222; Charter of Fundamental Rights of the European Union [2000] OJ C364/1 (as amended); European

case, they concern the international drug-control treaties – in particular the Single Convention – as well as the most important (other) international and regional human rights documents. As the study is legal in nature, it would be unintelligible to study the interface between human rights and the practical aspects of international drug-control norms in countries to which the legal instruments analysed do not apply.

Fifth, a local research entry should be available in each country (by recommendation). Such local contact increased the feasibility of conducting the field visits in a sufficient manner.

5.4 Limitations

As is the case with any empirical work, the present analysis comes with its various limitations. Although most documents in Uganda were available in English, some participants needed assistance from colleagues to translate parts of the interview. In Latvia, fewer documents were available in English and some participants also required partial translations (by colleagues). As this barrier appeared unexpectedly, the interviews were conducted in the absence of a professional translator. The interviewees' colleagues can be considered as reliable, and translations do not necessarily make the answers subjective. It is acknowledged, however, that it was impossible to verify whether or not the translators partly added to, changed, or reworded the interviewees' statements.

In addition, the analysis carried out is limited in its regional coverage in the countries in question. Moreover, the limits on the time frame in which both country studies were carried out, prevented participant selection in remote or distant areas. Finally, a dissemination event, at which findings were cross-checked and preliminary outcomes communicated to participants, was only organized in Uganda. It was impossible to organise a similar meeting in Latvia because of time constraints.

More generally, any qualitative study is limited since it reflects an analysis of an observation that is objectified as much as possible, in the most transparent manner.[46]

Convention for the Prevention of Torture and Inhuman or Degrading Treatment or Punishment (adopted 26 November 1987, entered into force 1 February 1989, ratified 10 February 1998) ETS 126; Revised European Social Charter (adopted 3 May 1996, entered into force 1 July 1999, ratified 26 March 2013) ETS 163; Convention for the protection of Human Rights and Dignity of the Human Being with regard to the Application of Biology and Medicine (adopted 4 April 1997, entered into force 1 December 1999, ratified 25 February 2010) ETS 164.

46 Acting as the vehicle for the data collection, the position of the researcher in relation to stereotypes about culture, gender, and social status has been taken into account. On the reflexivity necessary to conduct qualitative fieldwork, see eg L Finlay, '"Outing" the Researcher: The Provenance, Process, and Practice of Reflexivity' (2002) 12 Qualitative Health Research 531.

Furthermore, qualitative case-study research complicates generalizations. Any conclusions based on the analysis, even if presented in a somewhat generalist fashion, should primarily be interpreted in the context of the specific countries under study. Yet, the country studies may serve as pilot studies or vehicles for a more structural analysis into the specific issues found, if any, in a more generalist manner.[47]

47 On the potential and the margins of generalizing case-study findings, see LP Ruddin, 'You Can Generalize Stupid! Social Scientists, Bent Flyvbjerg, and Case Study Methodology' (2006) 12 Qualitative Inquiry 797.

Chapter 6
Country Study I: Uganda

6.1 Introduction

As reflected on in Chapter 5, the objective of the empirical analysis is to explore the interplay of the human rights and drug-control frameworks in practice. This may help to reveal complexities and gaps, if any, in the international drug-control system relating to human rights in accordance with medicine provision.[1] The present chapter reflects on whether or not Uganda is implementing the administrative and procedural requirements of the 1961 Single Convention on Narcotic Drugs in a manner that complies with human rights. More specifically, the chapter attempts to further the understanding of issues, if any, related to the implementation of a special administration, data collection and management, and specific trade and distribution requirements in relation to the Availability, Accessibility, Acceptability and Quality (AAAQ) standard of healthcare.[2]

To this end, this chapter commences by elaborating on the brief comments on the design and methods that were made in Chapter 5. It contains, for instance, an anonymized respondent chart (Section 6.2). Then, it goes on to provide background information on Uganda necessary to contextualize the findings (Section 6.3). Subsequently, revealing the stories found in practice, the chapter discusses experiences in the provision of pain-control medicines in light of drug-control requirements and human rights norms (Section 6.4).

---

1 At no stage in this book is it proclaimed that human rights law is sufficiently capable to bring about its own ambitions in practice. However, because the book operates on the underlying assumptions of human rights law, the primary purpose of the empirical analysis is to understand the ability of States to implement specific requirements of the international drug-control treaties.

2 On the country-specific findings in Uganda, see also MEC Gispen, 'Reconciling International Obligations and Local Realities: Provision of Pain Control Medication in Resource-Constrained Countries – Experiences from Uganda' in M Hesselman, A de Wolff and BCA Toebes (eds), *Essential Public Service Provision* (Routledge *forthcoming*). Parts of the work presented in this publication are included in this chapter (as copyright remains with the author). For details of the obligations listed, see Single Convention on Narcotic Drugs (adopted 30 March 1961, entered into force 13 December 1964) 520 UNTS 151 (Single Convention) arts 17, 19-20, and 30.

6.2 Design and methodology

As mentioned in Chapter 5, which introduced the general methodology underlying the empirical analysis carried out in both countries, the question central to the case study analysis is:

> How, if at all, can States prioritize, promote, and uphold the AAAQ standard of healthcare of medicines in accordance with human rights theory and law, whilst implementing the administrative and procedural requirements of the international drug-control system?

This question presupposes insight into two distinct aspects. First, one needs to generate an in-depth understanding of the context in which the administrative and procedural requirements of the international drug-control system come into play in Uganda. This, in turn, requires insight into Uganda's 'regulatory chain' of pain-control medicines, its institutional and regulatory structure, and the experiences of those working in this system. Second, without establishing any causality, one needs to understand the context of the service provision bearing in mind the AAAQ standard of healthcare when, if at all, relevant.

Relevant laws and policies have been searched for and analysed by means of desk research. Then, the data collection method was expanded. To test its validity, as well as to assess the feasibility of data collection on site, a preliminary visit was carried out. During the field study in Uganda, the African Palliative Care Association (APCA) assisted in finding a research entry. The APCA team helped identify relevant stakeholders, which included the Ministry of Health, Hospice Arica Uganda (HAU) Uganda National Cancer Institute, Mulago National Referral Hospital, the Joint Medical Stores, Makerere University, the Palliative Care Association of Uganda (PCAU), and the Uganda Network on Law Ethics and HIV/AIDS. During this preliminary stage, the focus was on institutions and their position in the 'regulatory chain' of morphine rather than certain individuals or individual experiences of those working in this system.

After this initial research phase, the actual data collection process was prepared. The APCA team provided technical support and guidance in the application process for research clearance (at the Uganda National Council on Science and Technology) and acted as an on-site gatekeeper during the data collection. This was carried out in a period of five weeks in July/August 2014. Data collection methods included participant observation, e.g. by joining one of the HAU medical teams during their home visits, and visits to various health facilities. In addition, 31 in-depth interviews were conducted using the topic guidance mentioned in Chapter 5. Six interviews were conducted as a joint interview with two participants, upon consent of both. Drawing on the categories of actors introduced in the previous chapter, Table 6.1 below supplies a place/date-specific overview of respondents, distinguishing the category of actor to which the respondent belongs, the public/private sector qualification of their position when relevant, the geographical designation, and the location.

Table 6.1 Overview of respondents (Uganda)

Respondent	Health system	Place	Date	Geographic context	Joint interview together with
Academic	n.a.	Kampala	30-7-2014	Urban	n.a.
Civil Society Representative 1	n.a.	Kampala	15-7-2014	Urban	n.a.
Civil Society Representative 2	n.a.	Kampala	24-7-2014	Urban	n.a.
Dispenser 1	Public	Gombe	7-7-2014	Peri-urban	n.a.
Dispenser 2	Public	Masaka	16-7-2014	Rural	n.a.
Dispenser 3	Private	Kampala	18-7-2014	Urban	n.a.
Dispenser 4	Private	Kampala	25-7-2014	Urban	n.a.
Dispenser 5	Private	Mukono	29-7-2014	Rural	Legal Prescriber 8
Dispenser 6	Public	Kampala	30-7-2014	Urban	n.a.
HAU Representative 1 (manufacturer)	Private	Kampala	9-7-2014	Urban	n.a.
HAU Representative 2 (manufacturer)	Private	Kampala	25-7-2014	Urban	n.a.
Health Facility Representative 1	Public	Gombe	7-7-2014	Peri-urban	n.a.
Health Facility Representative 2	Private	Masaka	16-7-2014	Rural	Legal Prescriber 1
JMS Representative (wholesaler)	Private	Kampala	14-7-2014	Urban	n.a.
Legal Prescriber 1	Private	Masaka	16-7-2014	Rural	Health Facility Representative 2
Legal Prescriber 2	Public	Masaka	16-7-2014	Rural	Nurse
Legal Prescriber 3	Public	Kampala	18-7-2014	Urban	n.a.
Legal Prescriber 4	Private	Kampala	18-7-2014	Urban	n.a.
Legal Prescriber 5	Private	Kampala	18-7-2014	Urban	n.a.
Legal Prescriber 6	Public	Kampala	25-7-2014	Urban	n.a.
Legal Prescriber 7	Public	Jinja	29-7-2014	Peri-urban	n.a.

Respondent	Health system	Place	Date	Geographic context	Joint interview together with
Legal Prescriber 8	Public	Mukono	29-7-2014	Rural	Dispenser 5
Ministry of Health Representative 1	n.a.	Kampala	11-7-2014	Urban	n.a.
Ministry of Health Representative 2	n.a.	Kampala	15-7-2014	Urban	n.a.
Ministry of Health Representative 3	n.a.	Kampala	23-7-2014	Urban	n.a.
NDA Representative	n.a.	Kampala	18-7-2014	Urban	n.a.
NMS Representative (wholesaler)	Public	Entebbe	22-7-2014	Urban	n.a.
Nurse	Public	Masaka	16-7-2014	Rural	Legal Prescriber 2
Other 1	Public	Masaka	16-7-2014	Rural	n.a.
Other 2	n.a.	Kampala	31-7-2014	Urban	n.a.
PCAU Representative (civil society)	n.a.	Kampala	10-7-2014	Urban	n.a.

Each interview followed the same procedure. First, the participant was familiarized with the informed consent protocol. After a careful explanation of the purpose of and conditions for participation, the interview started after such consent was given. Recordings were only initiated after participants had consented. Each participant was given the opportunity to raise questions before and after the interview, as well as the time to summarize and reflect on their main message in relation to the topics addressed. Interviews were recorded and, as mentioned in Chapter 5, transcribed *verbatim*. The data collected was analysed relying on the participant categorization similar to that presented above.[3] Coding and triangulation structured the data analysis process. Unless otherwise specified, all information presented on Uganda is based on the 31 interviews conducted.

6.3 Background of Uganda

This section provides some background information and context needed to understand the specific findings on drug control, human rights, and access to medicines provision.

3 *Verbatim* transcription means that interviews were transcribed word-by-word and reflect exactly what the respondent said without amendments. All the interviews that were conducted in Uganda were transcribed by the primary researcher. To limit their length, any parts of the interviews that were not relevant to the research in question have been summarized. These instances have been carefully marked in the respective documents. A distinction is made between quoting respondents and referencing (academic) literature by putting the former in italics.

It briefly describes geographic, demographic, and economic characteristics, as well as the constitutional, legal, and administrative features of the country and its health system.

6.3.1 Geographic, demographic and economic characteristics

Uganda is a landlocked country in Sub-Saharan East Africa. The country has a population of 38.8 million, of which only 16.8 per cent live in urban areas. Uganda's per capita gross national income is $1,613, with a gross domestic product per capita of $1,368. The country's poverty rates show that 37.8 per cent of the population lives on less than $1.25 per day and that 70.3 per cent of the population lives in multidimensional poverty.[4] According to the World Bank, the poverty headcount ratio at national poverty lines is 19.5 per cent.[5]

Life expectancy at birth is 58.8 years. The country's infant mortality rate lies at 43.8 per 1000 live births and the under-five mortality rate is at 66.1 per 1000. Moreover, the adult mortality rates lie at 307 and 380 per 1000 for women and men respectively. HIV affects 7.4 per cent of the population in an age range from 15 to 49.[6]

6.3.2 Legal and administrative context

Uganda has a dualist legal structure. Concretely, this means that all international law instruments ratified by the country have to be transformed into national legislation. Without such transposition, international law has no legal effect in the national legal order. Although Uganda is a State Party to many human rights treaties, as well as other international instruments, the country has a poor record in terms of the transposition of international law into national legislation.

Uganda's administrative machinery divides the country into four regions (North, East, Central, and West) and 111 districts. Districts are further divided into counties, municipalities (parishes), and local villages.[7] Similarly to the decentralized structure

---

4 See United Nations Development Programme, *Human Development Report 2015: Work for Human Development* (UNDP 2015) (Human Development Report 2015).

5 The World Bank, 'Uganda' <http://data.worldbank.org/country/uganda> accessed 31 August 2016. To further the country's economic prosperity and level of development, the government drafted the National Development Plan, which lies at the basis of all the policies and programmes adopted in the country. See The Republic of Uganda, 'National Development Plan (2010/11-2014/15)' (April 2010) <www.undp-alm.org/sites/default/files/downloads/uganda-national_development_plan.pdf> accessed 31 August 2016.

6 See Human Development Report 2015 (n 4).

7 See Ministry of Local Government, 'List of Local Government Districts' <www.uganda-sds.org/local-governments> accessed 31 August 2016. The administrative structure of local government

of local governance, service delivery in Uganda is also decentralized. Yet, although government structures have been decentralized to improve service delivery at local levels, 'effective service delivery has not been realized at these levels'.[8] In fact, it is this lack of effective service delivery, including poor health services, that has led to a multitude of public protests in the country.[9]

In Uganda, most elements of Economic, Social, and Cultural (ESC) rights are not enforceable. Human rights and fundamental freedoms have been laid down in Uganda's Bill of Rights.[10] However, the Bill is strongly focused on civil and political rights and only marginally includes elements of ESC rights, such as property rights, education, work, trade union participation, and a clean and healthy environment.[11] Access to basic medical services, for example, is included in the National Objectives and Directive Principles of State Policy and is not an enforceable right.[12] Despite numerous efforts in public interest litigation to get this motor running, the right to health generally remains non-justiciable in Uganda. To date, the Supreme Court has been reluctant to decide on such matters and holds that it must abstain from entering into political decision-making. In *CEHURD and others v Attorney General*, for instance, the access to maternal care was argued to be a constitutional right. The

is the outcome of a mix of idealism and practical need. Its 20th-century history finds its roots in British colonialism. After years of dictatorship under Obote and Amin (1962-1985), a structure of local governance expressed the (idealist) wish to construct a democratic Nation State from scratch. In 1986, the National Resistance Movement, led by the current president Yoweri Museveni, faced the challenge of delivering services in the aftermath of great political instability. The absence of the provision of basic services throughout Uganda's various regions, combined with the ability of the locally elected councils to deliver such services where the national government failed, incentivized the construction of the administrative machinery based on local governance. Such an idea was, in addition, supported by the notion that a centralized government would be unpopular amongst the population and would, most likely, be objected to by donor countries. However, through the adoption of Chapter 243 of the Laws of Uganda, the Local Governments Act in 1997 recentralized the administrative system to some extent. Its local implementation is supervised by the Ministry of Local Government. See eg TG Manyak and IW Katono, 'Decentralization and Conflict in Uganda: Governance Adrift' (2010) 11 African Studies Quarterly 1, 1, 3, 7.

8 C Mbazira, 'Service Delivery Protests, Struggle for Rights and the Failure of Local Democracy in South African and Uganda: Parallels and Divergences' (2013) South African Journal of Human Rights 252, 274.

9 ibid 259-260. See also OS Caleb, 'Man Undresses in Protest over Poor Health Services' *Daily Monitor* (Kampala, 5 May 2011) <www.monitor.co.ug/News/National/-/688334/1156714/-/c236fjz/-/index. html> accessed 31 August 2016.

10 The Constitution of the Republic of Uganda, 1995, ch 4.

11 JC Mubangizi, 'The Constitutional Protection of Socio-Economic Rights in Selected African Countries: A Comparative Evaluation' (2006) 2 African Journal of Legal Studies 1, 12-13; JC Mubangizi and BK Twinomugisha, 'The Right to Health Care in the Specific Context of Access to HIV/Aids Medicines: What Can South Africa and Uganda Learn from Each Other?' (2010) 10 African Human Rights Law Journal 105, 120.

12 See Ugandan Constitution, National Objectives and Directive Principles of State Policy, obj XX.

Court did not accept this argument, stating that 'the issues as framed by the petitioners fall under the doctrine of a "political question" and therefore the Court is prohibited from hearing such a case on the grounds of [non-justiciability]'.[13] The right to life, however, is included in the Constitution and is therefore used as the starting point of strategic litigation to secure indirect justiciability.[14]

In terms of drug control, a new Narcotics Control Bill was adopted by Parliament in 2014 after having been pending since 2007. The 2015 Narcotic Drugs and Psychotropic Substances (Control) Bill, in that regard, was the first initiative to transpose parts of the international drug-control treaties into national legislation.[15] The increased level of control and the criminal-law provisions adopted in this Bill were heavily scrutinized, both from a human rights and a public health perspective, during public and political debates and among professionals in the field. In the course of these debates, it was even suggested that the new Bill could hamper the access to controlled medication.[16]

6.3.3 Health system

Uganda's health system is organized into national health package services that include cost-effective medical interventions, which should be available to all Ugandans.[17] These health packages include a minimum set of services to which the entire population should have access. In line with the 1995 Constitution and the 1997 Local Government Act, health services are delivered by the District Health Service and are financed through co-payments.[18] In practice, such a payment system requires each patient to pay an out-of-pocket fee.[19] Palliative care services are not considered

13 *Center for Health, Human Rights & Development (CEHURD) and 3 Ors v Attorney General* (Constitutional Petition No 16/2011) [2012] UGCC 4 (5 June 2012).

14 Ugandan Constitution, art 22. On indirect justiciability and strategic litigation in the field of access to medicines more generally, see Chapter 3 of this book.

15 The Narcotic Drugs and Psychotropic Substances (Control) Act of 2015. See also O Nakatudde, 'Parliament Passes Narcotic Drugs and Psychotropic Substances Bill' *Uganda Radio Network* (Kampala, 20 November 2014) <http://ugandaradionetwork.com/story/parliament-passes-narcotic-drugs-and-psycho tropic-substances-bill> accessed 31 August 2016.

16 N Burke-Shyne, 'Four Laws That Are Devastating Public Health in Uganda' (*Open Society Foundations*, 15 December 2014) <www.opensocietyfoundations.org/voices/four-laws-are-devastating-public-he alth-uganda> accessed 31 August 2016; P Kwagala, 'Human Rights and Public Health Implications of the Law on Narcotics and Psychotropic Substance Use in Uganda' (*Parliament Watch*, 25 April 2015) <http://parliamentwatch.ug/human-rights-and-public-health-implications-of-the-law-on-narcotics-andpsychotropic-substance-use-in-uganda/> accessed 31 August 2016.

17 Ministry of Health of Uganda, 'Health Sector Strategic Plan III 2010/11-2014/15' (2010) 49, 78 <www.health.go.ug/docs/HSSP_III_2010.pdf> accessed 31 August 2016.

18 id.

19 id.

a separate pillar in this package system and, as a result, should be delivered in an integrated manner.[20] There is no separate budget for palliative care as distinct from the overall annual budget to ensure free access to morphine.

The health sector is divided into a public and a private sector. The public sector includes 2 national referral hospitals, 11 regional referral hospitals, and 43 general hospitals. In addition, the private sector includes 42 non-profit health facilities and 4 private general practices. Both the public and the private sector also include a district health system of lower-level health centres.[21] Uganda's private healthcare system, furthermore, provides for access to national and international non-governmental organizations, private health practitioners, and traditional and complementary medicine practitioners (either secular or religion-based).[22] The National Medical Stores (NMS) and the Joint Medical Stores (JMS) are responsible for the distribution of all medicinal and health supplies to the public and the private sector respectively. The National Drug Authority (NDA) is the semi-autonomous government institution responsible for the supervision of the pharmaceutical sector –including quality control, inspection, and monitoring and controlling of the import and export of pharmaceuticals.[23]

Health reform and palliative care policy

With the HIV/AIDS crisis of the late 1980s in mind and in order to ease the suffering of untreated patients, since the 1990s Ugandan civil society has pushed for increasingly progressive policy, on the one hand, and legislative reform, on the other. After a statutory amendment was passed in 2004, specially trained nurses and clinical officers were allowed to prescribe morphine for pain and palliative care treatment, both in an in- and out-of-hospital setting.[24] Before the amendment, only doctors were allowed to prescribe such medication in an in-hospital setting.

Notwithstanding these improvements, as is the case in many Sub-Saharan countries, Uganda's health system faces serious challenges in terms of human resources and their deployment. In addition, practice demonstrates that Ugandan patients prefer

---

20 id. Overall, the ambition of the Department of Clinical Services of the Ministry of Health has been to scale up palliative care by 50% between 2010-2015.

21 id.

22 id.

23 The NDA was established through the adoption of Chapter 206 of the Laws of Uganda: the National Drug Policy and Authority Act of 1993. For an overview of its functions, see The National Drug Authority, 'The Functions of the Drug Authority' <http://nda.or.ug/ug/smenu/20/Functions-of-NDA.html> accessed 31 August 2016.

24 The National Drug Authority (Prescription and Supply of Certain Narcotic Analgesic Drugs) Regulations, Statutory Instruments 14/2004, s 4.

home-based treatment, especially in an end-of-life stage.[25] The limited number of doctors available in the country and brain drain, however, makes sustaining an adequate doctor/patient ratio problematic.[26] The absence of treatment, in turn, causes a large financial burden for the State that only further pushes the country into decline. Without access to care, many individuals are unable to sustain themselves. Reform, for this reason, did not only find its incentive in the realm of public health but also in economics.[27] Copying the existing practice of midwives who were allowed to carry controlled medicines used in childbirth into local communities (i.e. outside the hospital), civil society lobbied for a similar arrangement to be applied for trained nurses and clinical officers, to allow them to carry pain-control medicines as well. Although Uganda's progressive reform efforts have considerably increased access to services, access rates still remain limited.[28]

Needs for improved access to essential palliative care

In Uganda, the unavailability and inaccessibility of essential pain-control medicines greatly differs per region and per (type of) healthcare facility; the exact reasons for inadequate access vary across the country. To illustrate this: Harding and colleagues find that the availability of pain-control medication is higher in hospitals than it is in health centres and home-based care facilities.[29] At the same time, however, they noted that stock management systems are hardly in place, resulting in frequent stock-outs.[30]

Like in many Sub-Saharan countries, Uganda is experiencing an increase in non-communicable diseases whilst still suffering from communicable diseases.[31] This

---

25 A Merriman, 'Going the Extra Mile with the Bare Essentials: Home Care in Uganda' (2010) 18 Progress in Palliative Care 18; S Ramsey, 'Leading the Way in African Home-Based Palliative Care' (2003) 362 The Lancet 1812.

26 S Kizito and others, 'Career Intentions of Final Year Medical Students in Uganda after Graduating: The Burden of Brain Drain' (2015) 15 BMC Medical Education (2015) 122. See also Ministry of Health of Uganda (n 17).

27 On Uganda's reform process, see Ministry of Health of Uganda, Palliative Care Association of Uganda and Open Society Initiative for East Africa, *The Development of Palliative Care in Uganda* (Ministry of Health of Uganda 2012). See also A Merriman, 'Uganda: Current Status of Palliative Care' (2002) 24 Journal of Pain and Symptom Management 252.

28 B Duthey and W Scholten, 'Adequacy of Opioid Analgesic Consumption at Country, Global, and Regional Levels in 2010, its Relationship with Development Level, and Changes Compared with 2006' (2014) 47 Journal of Pain and Symptom Management 283, 285; MR Steedman and others, 'Innovation Can Improve and Expand Aspects of End-of-Life Care in Low-and Middle Income Countries' (2014) 33 Health Affairs 1612, 1615.

29 R Harding and others, 'Availability of Essential Drugs for Managing HIV-related Pain and Symptoms within 120 PEPFAR-Funded Health Facilities in East Africa: A Cross-Sectional Survey with Onsite Verification' (2014) 28 Palliative Medicine 293.

30 id.

31 Ministry of Health of Uganda (n 20) 78.

epidemiological shift to non-communicable, chronic diseases, as well as the country's regression in HIV/AIDS prevention,[32] is believed to increase the need for pain treatment and for palliative care. When combined with the trend of understaffing in healthcare facilities, the ever-increasing difficulty in coping with an increasing number of patients becomes particularly noticeable.

The problems that Uganda's health system is facing in terms of human resources and deployment has serious consequences for the health-service provision in general.[33] For instance, in the public and private health sector combined, a 1/1,818 health worker[34] to patient ratio is found.[35] Although most health workers are trained in delivering curative care,[36] such treatment remains limitedly available throughout the country. A lack of curative treatment, furthermore, adds to the need for pain-control and palliative care services. Merriman notes that in 2002 more than 50 per cent of the Ugandan population never saw a health worker in their life. Yet, at the same time, they suffered from diseases for which palliative care and pain control are essential medical treatments.[37] Kiwanuka and colleagues, in this respect, hold that '[t]he poor and vulnerable experience a greater burden of disease but have lower access to health services than the less poor'.[38] This demonstrates that the Ugandan government has a specific responsibility to prioritize and address the situation in the poorest section(s) of the population.

6.4 Results and discussion

This section introduces the findings and the discussion of the results. It elaborates on the relevant actors in the supply/demand chain, the experiences of service providers, and the perceived challenges, if any, in light of specific drug-control requirements. It does so in the context of the aspects relating to the Availability, Accessibility, and Acceptability of healthcare services in accordance with human rights norms. As

32 In recent years, the number of HIV/AIDS contractions has been increasing after having consistently decreased for a period of time. See eg J Kron, 'In Uganda, an AIDS Success Story Comes Undone' *The New York Times* (Kampala, 2 August 2012) <www.nytimes.com/2012/08/03/world/africa/in-uganda-an-aids-success-story-comes-undone.html?r=0> accessed 31 August 2016. On the dual burden of the health system, see Ministry of Health and others (n 27) 5.

33 The shortage of adequately trained health workers is a serious problem throughout Sub-Saharan Africa. See eg S Naicker and others, 'Shortage of Health Workers in Developing Countries – Africa' (2009) 19 Ethnicity & Disease 60.

34 The term 'health worker' covers doctors, nurses, and midwives.

35 Ministry of Health of Uganda (n 20) 20.

36 ibid.

37 Merriman, 'Status of Palliative Care' (n 27) 254.

38 SN Kiwanuka and others, 'Access to and Utilisation of Health Service for the Poor in Uganda: A Systematic Review of Available Evidence' (2008) 102 The Royal Society of Tropical Medicine and Hygiene 1067, 1067.

mentioned in Chapter 5, any quality-related aspects, although interesting and relevant to the broader cause of access to controlled medicines, have been omitted since the Single Convention does not contain quality standards.

6.4.1 Implementation of international human rights and drug-control standards

As described in Section 6.3, Uganda has a poor record of transposing international law – also covering human rights and drug-control – into enforceable domestic legislation. Claims regarding the access to medicines based on human rights find limited legal support. Civil Society Representatives 1 and 2 explained that there is little awareness among the Ugandan population when it comes to claiming public goods and services, such as access to medicines and adequate medical treatment, as an entitlement. In the aftermath of great political instability, Civil Society Representative 2 described, the Ugandan population is simply thankful for any public goods or services provided by the government. The realization would never dawn on them that they should not thank the government for health services, but rather claim them as their right.

While Uganda has a poor record of domestic implementation of international law, the 1993 National Drug Policy & Authority Act holds that Uganda, given its signatory status, is to comply with the obligations ensuing from the international drug-control treaties. As enforced in Section 2 paragraph 1(h) of the Act, '[t]he national drug policy shall be to comply with the international regulations on drugs, including the conventions on narcotic drugs and psychotropic substances under international control' in both the public and private sector.[39]

The Minister of Health can, either on its own account or as advised by the NDA, make changes to the scope of control by means of statutory amendments.[40] This same section states that it is prohibited to supply substances under international control for purposes other than medical, dental, or veterinary purposes.[41] In addition, Sections 38 and 46 respectively limit the manufacture and import/export of internationally controlled substances to these same purposes.[42] Section 46, furthermore, contains a clause stating that no person is allowed to possess internationally controlled substances without a 'lawful excuse'.[43] The Act includes a list of Class A medicines, which includes morphine, to which the regulations apply.[44]

39 The National Drug Policy & Authority Act of 1993, s 2 para 1(h).
40 ibid, ss 13, 20, 26, 39, 43, 47, 64.
41 ibid s 26.
42 ibid ss 38, 46 para 1.
43 ibid s 46 para 1.
44 ibid sch I.

According to the NDA Representative, the Act's regulations relating to import licenses and certificates of suitable premises had been updated (March 2014) to include morphine-specific standards. While it remained unclear what these changes actually mean for the availability and accessibility of pain-control medicines, the respondent held the changes to be significant due to the country's reliance on import/export to manufacture morphine (Uganda does not produce any of the raw materials itself). Overall, however, it was observed that, as also mentioned by the NDA Representative, Uganda might be good at policies but bad at laws.

6.4.2 Relevant policies and regulations to implement specific drug-control requirements

As was observed and explained by the PCAU Representative, three different Class A registration booklets apply to the Class A medicines in Uganda: (i) Class A order books; (ii) Class A record books, and (iii) ward books. Class A order books are to be used to order Class A medicines, including morphine, from either the NMS or JMS. The cover of the Class A order booklet states that filling out the order book is required by the United Nations (UN) and failing to do so prevents the facility from receiving its order. The order book obliges facilities to specify the number of patients, the disease group(s) (i.e. cancer, HIV/AIDS, other), and the amount of medicine needed (i.e. the actual order for new stock). In addition, Class A record books, often referred to as the pharmacy dispense logs, require facilities to register every dose of Class A medication dispensed. When doing so, the date, patient name, patient number, quantity prescribed, and signatures of the dispenser, collector, and person witnessing the dispensing, must be recorded. Finally, ward books are the medical record books used for the internal administration at facilities themselves. These books contain the diagnosis or disease specified per patient. This administration is also used to track the internal distribution of e.g. liquid morphine from the general pharmacy to the ward pharmacy. Being an internal document, the ward book does not have to be submitted to any third party and remains with the facility at all times.

The Ministry of Health of Uganda, in close cooperation with the PCAU, has recently updated the registration booklets to be compliant with the obligation, as dictated by international drug-control treaties, to manage a separate administration. In this process, specific trade and distribution requirements had to be implemented.[45] A special administrative system was adopted to collect all relevant data from the consumer level upwards so as to be able to draft and submit the annual estimates and quarterly statistical returns required.[46]

45 Single Convention, arts 17, 30.
46 ibid arts 19-20.

Representatives of the Ministry and PCAU noted that these revised booklets were being distributed at the time of the data collection. According to Ministry of Health Representative 3, the new booklets reflect the aim to simplify procedures and to overcome fears that had existed among doctors and pharmacists in the past. Moreover, HAU Representative 1 indicated that the previous forms were old, dating back to colonial times, and had been last reviewed in the 1960s. In the recent update of the registration booklets, HAU Representative 1 explained, they were also updated because the NMS only recognizes Class A orders when submitted on specific Class A order forms. Class A orders made on other forms would not be granted. According to the same representative, since many facilities did not have access to these specific forms (or ordering booklets), the accessibility and availability of Class A medicines had been seriously obstructed. In addition, the booklets were improved by using a more easily recognisable format. Previous order forms looked similar to hospital ward books. HAU Representative 1 continued by stating that by creating a 'unique' order form, with specific boxes for the amounts requested and the main disease groups detected in the clinic, the reconciling, monitoring, and managing of data on incoming orders was supposed to become much simpler. The question of whether or not that was indeed the case in practice, is discussed in Section 6.4.4.

In terms of implementing specific trade and distribution requirements, Uganda also works with special Class A prescription forms. As gathered from interviews with legal prescribers, these forms should include at least: the patient's name, the signature of the licensed prescriber, the quantity written in numbers and in letters, as well as the signature of the dispenser, the collector, and the person supervising the distribution. In-hospital pharmacies are often internally provided with a list of authorized prescribers to validate special prescriptions. Copies of these prescriptions must always be kept on file upon dispersal of the medication. Moreover, only accredited facilities may order and stock liquid morphine. The PCAU is mandated by the Ministry of Health to monitor the accreditation process to this end. The requirements for accreditation dictate that facilities must prove that they have at least one legal prescriber under employment – either a physician or qualified nurse/clinical officer – and a secure location to store the liquid morphine (e.g. a double-locked cupboard). The question remains, however, whether accreditation and the related requirements improve or hamper the accessibility and availability of pain-control medicines for the general population (see Section 6.4.4 for a more detailed discussion).

Yet, prior to addressing the implications of said administrative and procedural requirements, the supply/demand chain of morphine is described to contextualize the service delivery. This improves the grasp of the domestic complexities under which international obligations have to be implemented. It also allows one to identify actor-specific responsibilities relating to the compliance with said procedures.

6.4.3 Supply/demand chain of liquid morphine

Based on the interviews with the large variety of actors as described above, the regulatory supply/demand chain of liquid morphine was identified (see Figure 6.1).

Figure 6.1 Uganda's supply/demand chain of liquid morphine

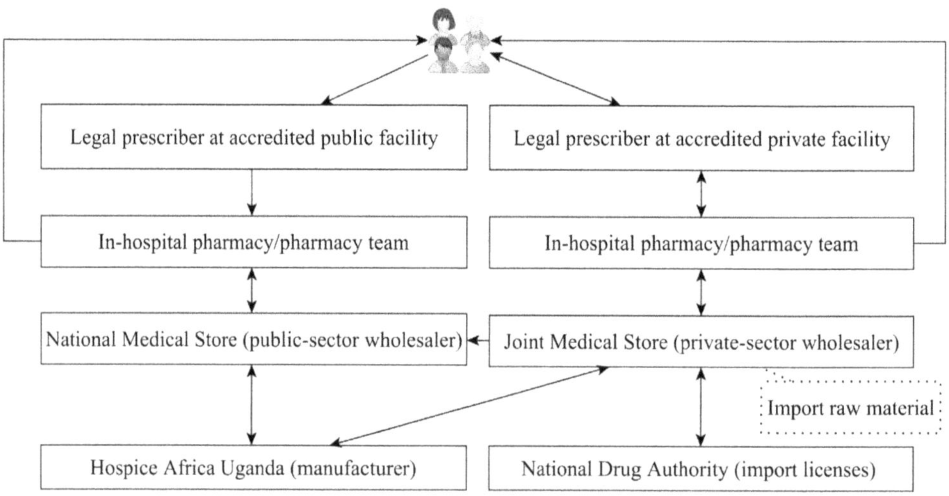

As Figure 6.1 demonstrates, the chain starts with individuals in pain seeking medical assistance.[47] These individuals can opt to either visit a public or a private facility. Upon arrival, the health worker diagnoses whether the patient, for the purpose of this example, either needs pain control or palliative care treatment. If this health worker is a legal prescriber, he or she can take on the case, being allowed to prescribe morphine. In other cases, a non-licensed health worker will have to forward the patient to where he or she can see such a professional.

If a legal prescriber determines that the pain is of such gravity that a strong opioid should be prescribed, then liquid morphine would be the standard treatment in Uganda.[48] To give the patient access to the medication needed, the legal prescriber must use a special prescription format to issue a Class A prescription. With this

47 An out-of-stock situation is described to show how the supply/demand chain operates and to identify actor-specific regulatory responsibilities. Other than being the starting and end point of the chain, the position of individual patients is not included due to the absence of regulatory responsibilities on their part. Despite being the primary rights holder central to this book, their position is not relevant to further the goals and ambitions at which the empirical analysis is aimed.

48 Ministry of Health Representative 3 remarked that liquid morphine was the standard treatment method preferred, as opposed to morphine in tablet form.

special prescription, the patient, a family member, or the attending health worker can obtain the medicine from a licensed pharmacy. The PCAU oversees the licensing of the facilities as instructed by the Ministry, despite the fact that this supervisory role principally falls under the latter's mandate.

If the pharmacy is out of stock, the principle pharmacist or person in charge of the pharmacy has to order morphine by using the Class A order book.[49] Public facilities must order from the NMS – the public-sector wholesaler – and private facilities have to order from the JMS – the private-sector wholesaler.

Should the JMS be out of stock as well, it will have to place an order with the NMS. The NMS receives an annual stipend to ensure that morphine is available free of charge in Uganda, including in the private health sector. In case the NMS is also out of stock, the NMS must place an order with HAU. The HAU is a non-governmental organization and is the only actor in the country licensed by the NDA to manufacture liquid morphine. Due to the public-private partnership that exists between the Ministry of Health, the NMS, and the HAU, the JMS has to place its orders for new stock with the NMS and cannot order directly from HAU itself. Notably, in light of the financial aspect of the availability (i.e. affordability) of health facilities, goods, and services, including medicines, the free obtainability of morphine is a positive element in terms of human rights protection.

Since the HAU is not licensed by the NDA to import raw materials, when needed, it has to place an order with the JMS. The JMS is the only body licensed to import raw materials and, in order to do so, must obtain an import permit from the NDA for each order individually. After having obtained such a permit, the JMS can import and consecutively supply the HAU with the materials needed to manufacture liquid morphine. After which the latter can, in turn, supply the NMS and JMS (and thus both the public and private markets).

Initially, the HAU was to deliver the entire NMS order, including the part designated for the JMS, to the NMS. However, this caused some inefficiency as the NMS is based in Entebbe, whereas the HAU and the JMS are both based in Kampala within a ten-minute distance from one another. Entebbe, on the other hand, is roughly 60 kilometres South-East of Kampala. According to HAU Representative 2, this system was changed and the JMS can now retrieve its part of the order from the HAU directly. The remainder of the order, reflecting the public demand, is consequently supplied to the NMS. A secondary, yet crucial, reason for this adjustment is the short shelf life

49 HAU Representative 1 noted that there is a serious shortage of pharmacies in Uganda. By law, so the representative mentioned, pharmacists can only supervise two pharmacies. Concretely, this means that the principal person in charge does not necessarily have to be a pharmacist.

of liquid morphine. The substance, only containing enough preservatives to last six months, needs to be delivered timely.

Once the NMS and JMS receive or collect their orders, the public and private markets can be supplied. The NMS and JMS Representatives noted that the delivery structures differed in the sense that the NMS utilizes a transport basis, whereas the JMS works on a pick-up basis only. In other words, the NMS delivers on site, whereas private facilities have to pick up their orders from the JMS in Kampala. Expired medication is returned to either the NMS or JMS (and is not included in the overview).

Various administrative and data collection requirements apply throughout the process. The following sections focus on the specific implications resulting from the need to manage a separate administration of the specific trade and distribution requirements (Section 6.4.4), and on the data collection, analysis, and reporting (Section 6.4.5).

6.4.4 Implications of managing a separate administration and specific trade and distribution requirements

The consequences of managing a separate administration, and specific trade and distribution requirements, apply to part of the supply/demand chain as outlined in Figure 6.1. The below Figure 6.2 therefore highlights exactly at which stage in the chain such specific requirements apply (indicated by an envelope).

Figure 6.2 Uganda's separate administration and specific trade and distribution requirements

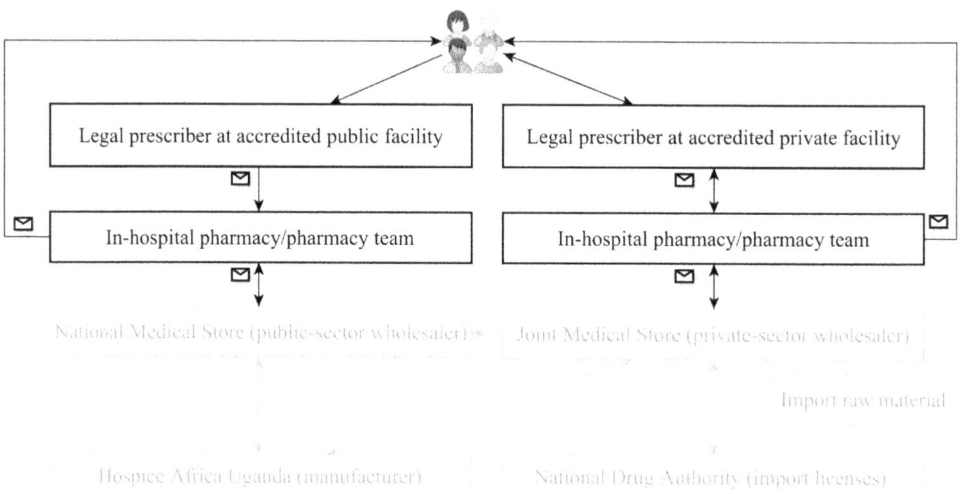

In sum, legal prescribers must use specific prescription forms and health facilities and/or pharmacies have to be accredited in order to request and stock morphine. Dispensers and prescribers are obliged to use the Class A registration booklets – including the registration book, order book, and ward book – to track controlled substances.[50] Such specific requirements presuppose that registration booklets are available, that staff is sufficiently informed on their use, that financial and human resources are available to train qualified staff members, that the additional administration is manageable, and that secured storage needed for accreditation is obtainable. When investigating these (procedural) requirements for the availability and accessibility of liquid morphine, however, several problems were encountered.

Dissemination and information

A first problem is the dissemination of and information on the use of the new registration documentation. Despite being the responsibility of the Ministry of Health, the task is carried out by the NMS and the PCAU. As mentioned earlier, the PCAU has been mandated to oversee the implementation of segments of the special administrative system. To this end, the PCAU Representative indicated that the association does not merely accredit facilities and supervise their efforts in palliative care treatment. Instead, the respondent emphasized *'we do not stop there, we follow up to ensure that they are prescribing it* [i.e. liquid morphine], *it is being utilized, and there are no stock-outs'* (PCAU Representative). While the PCAU provides information on the use of the registration booklets, the dissemination of the new booklets has been a serious concern. As the PCAU Respondent held:

> [*W*]*e get some challenges. For instance, we may go and find they* [i.e. a given health facility] *actually experience stock-outs and what has been causing the stock-outs was the morphine order books, so like the facilities did not know how to order the morphine without the morphine order books* (PCAU Representative).

Yet, while both the PCAU Representative and HAU Representative 1 acknowledged this challenge to be overcome when the Ministry of Health printed the revised order forms, facilities still experience problems on this point. When going around to different facilities in remote, but also urban areas, it became evident that the new registration booklets are neither readily available nor in use. Either the new registration booklets were not available altogether or people had not heard about their existence. In addition, those who were aware of the latest standards had not seen the new booklets yet. Legal Prescriber 6 noted that even though the new regulations had applied for more than a year (at the time of data collection), the hospital where

50 See Section 6.4.1.

the respondent worked had yet to receive the new booklets. Similarly, Dispenser 2 held that *'we do not have a new book (...) they are supposed to be provided by the NMS or palliative care association'* (Dispenser 2). In a similar fashion, Dispenser 1 remarked: *'I have tried to get some more books but I don't know where to get them. We requested [them from the] NMS but we have not received them yet'* (Dispenser 1).

Those who did acquire the new booklets, however, were not always fully informed about its standard of use. The PCAU Representative observed, in this respect, that they monitor compliance with the new regulations. However, while at the national level these documents have been revised in an effort to simplify the procedure involved and are known to apply to all Class A medicines, some local providers understood them as applicable only to liquid morphine (because the booklets were supplied with the liquid morphine order) or a sample of Class A medicines. As one dispenser reported for instance, *'codeine we record on the stock-out card, this one* [i.e. the Class A order book] *is specifically for morphine, eh?'* (Dispenser 1). Codeine, however, like morphine is a Class A substance under the 1993 National Drug Policy & Authority Act.[51]

Overall, visits to various urban, peri-urban, and rural health facilities, both public and private, demonstrated that there might be a significant information gap relating to the purpose and use of the new documentation. While printing and distribution of the updated ordering booklets should have resolved this barrier, it was observed that, at the time of the research, facilities lacked access to these updated booklets altogether or still used old formats, leading to challenges in the access to morphine provision. Although these experiences do not necessarily reveal whether the actual availability or accessibility of care is obstructed, the distribution of and information on these specific forms (and their requirements) is problematic when insufficient. This is especially so when considering the textual warning on the cover of the Class A order booklets, indicating its use to be a requirement of the UN and failure to do so to result in not receiving one's new stock. The latter, in particular, touches on the dissuasive effect and pressure these regulations place on local facilities.

Pressure on local facilities

A second problem relating to the accessibility and availability of morphine is the pressure the special administration in general and the specific trade and distribution requirements place on local facilities. One legal prescriber explained, for instance, *'everything that involves too much paper work tends not to be done well'* (Legal Prescriber 6). Here, the respondent referred to this as being a structural issue, where

51 The National Drug Policy & Authority Act, sch I.

one does not only run out of paper sometimes, but there simply is no embedded system to fill out large quantities of paperwork. Lacking such a system, the respondent continued *'it is not going to work with the best will in the world'* (Legal Prescriber 6).

In terms of the practical feasibility to work with the additional administrative requirements, Ministry of Health Representative 1 held that local realities were not an obstacle in terms of the implementation of and compliance with the registration booklets. According to the respondent, neither the secured storage requirement of the accreditation process, nor the subsequent special administrative tasks, were to be considered a barrier to the provision of health services. In fact, according to Ministry of Health Representative 1, it was not difficult for local facilities to stockpile morphine due to its liquid form and no abuse had been reported.[52] However, representatives of the Ministry of Health did not all share the same view on the ability of local facilities to comply with the special requirements. One of the representatives, for instance, held that:

> [*M*]*any of the facilities despite the formal structures and the required personnel in those structures being set out (...) still have gaps in terms of filling those conditions. What you find on the ground is that the available staff, whoever is responsible for that, really feels a big work load and they may not be able to do that concurrently* (Ministry of Health Representative 3).

Similarly, HAU Representative 2 held that the secure storage (i.e. double lock) requirement could prove problematic. In general, the visits to various health facilities revealed that at some facilities, despite possessing separate storage facilities, locks were broken, only a single lock was used (due to the second being defective), or the cupboard or separate storage facility was too small for the amount of medication to be stored.

In search of experiences of local providers, thus monitoring the opinions on the real implications of the administrative requirements, the opposite of what the Ministry of Health Representative had observed was found in practice. Generally, the system was considered resource intensive. One of the health facility representatives emphasized that *'the records that have the documentation really requires a lot of you, it is quite a lot of accountability'* (Health Facility Representative 2). In this respect, human and financial resources are the most structural and most significant challenge in the implementation of the specific Class A requirements.

As mentioned in Section 6.4.1, the Class A registration booklet among other things, requires a colleague to co-sign each time a Class A medicine is dispensed. Yet, as

52 ibid sch I, A.1.I.

one of the respondents indicated, such cross-checking is often impossible *'because you might find there is only one dispenser. So there is no second person to check'* (Dispenser 6). Similarly, another dispenser stated *'of course sometimes there is no person to check (...) Here before (...) they used to call somebody from another ward to come and check, but sometimes people are busy [and] there is nobody to check the person'* (Dispenser 1). As a result, the same respondent made it clear that even when no second signatory could be located, medicines were distributed and copies of the prescriptions retained. Generally, one observed that the majority of booklets, shown during interviews and field visits, had empty 'checked-by' boxes. Notwithstanding the intention at the national level to simplify the registration of Class A medicines, the reality remained complicated. However, one must highlight that one cannot establish a direct link between the new regulations, on the one hand, and a more complex situation for prescribers and dispenser to ensure access to pain-control medicines, on the other. The reason being that the situation prior to the implementation of the new regulations is unknown to the researcher and, therefore, no comparison can be made. Nevertheless, it is reasoned here that if the revised regulations indeed obfuscate effective compliance due to associated structural constraints, then the goal and the means to attain this goal (i.e. simplified recording) defeat their purpose. This in itself may raise questions with respect to the acceptability criterion of the AAAQ standard of healthcare.

Apart from the actual physical ability to double-check, ambiguity was also found as to the interpretation of this requirement. Dispenser 2 held that such control should be exercised at the ward – exactly because the pharmacist works solo, making checks impossible. The respondent clarified: *'because if I check here, and I am being the only person issuing and checking. Maybe the person who is receiving on behalf of the patient does the check. But this checking was meant at the ward'* (Dispenser 2). Interpreting the booklets in the manner as intended by the drafters at the national level, however, revealed that the secondary check and signature were not supposed to take place at the ward, but at the pharmacy instead. Legal Prescriber 7, furthermore, was confused about the purpose of the 'checked-by' box altogether. When discussing the purpose of this box and the feasibility of filling it out, the respondent replied as follows: *'I was not checking this one* [i.e. referring to the checked-by box] *because (...) I am not sure (...) but I didn't know the reason why (...) I am not saying it is not important but most probably you overlook it'* (Legal Prescriber 7). The specific requirement, moreover, reveals its complexities when one is reminded of the challenges in ensuring adequate staffing. Submitting that the 'checked-by' box is strictly supposed to be filled out, respondent continued by indicating that this is only feasible *'if you find a full blown palliative care unit on its own with enough staff (...) Ideally it should be like that'* (Legal Prescriber 7). This, however, is unlikely in Uganda. In addition, one of the dispensers held the 'checked-by' requirement to only be applicable when administering on the ward *'or if we had more staff members present when you're issuing. We don't have enough members, we are only two (...) that means I would have to call my colleague to come and check'* (Dispenser 2).

Discussing the issue at a more general level, the PCAU Representative acknowledged that indeed human resources are among the most serious concern in the Ugandan health system. According to the respondent, the challenges would:

> *[C]ome back to human resources. You need a lot of time to fill out these things. If you get the opportunity to go in the field you will see what I am talking about. You will find a whole facility, many patients, [and] there are two or three people* [i.e. staff] *(...) Those facilities that have appropriate human resources, or a good number of people, health workers, they will fill in the forms properly. Then you find this person who is struggling, trying to provide the service but in the hardship you will find that the recordings are not really good. You can see they are going a good job, but the hardship* [complicates proper compliance with the administrative requirements] (PCAU Representative).

Similarly, HAU Representative 1 reflected on staffing as being a structural constraint in the health system, which particularly affects the service delivery in the public sector.

Aiming to present a clear picture of the daily reality in which specific drug-control requirements apply, the PCAU Representative continued to emphasize that one cannot blame the health worker on duty for not meeting all the procedural requirements. Often this single individual faces an ever-growing line of patients e.g. waiting for their antiretroviral treatment, has a maternity ward to attend to, and, at the same time, has to clerk patients coming in with pain. In such a scenario, the only check taking place is: *'recorded the name, recorded the drug, give her the instructions, go, OK? (...) I think at times those fields* [may make people] *feel down because the requirement this, the current requirement this (...)'* (PCAU Representative). Even if the nurse cannot comply, he or she will have to ponder whether to distribute the medication or not.

The pressure on local facilities is aggravated in light of the time-intensive nature of palliative care treatment. In this context, one of the legal prescribers held that:

> [t]*here is a tendency to think that actually palliative care* [is] *the same as other treatments but they are very different because you can have a patient and you clerk a patient for three hours, psychological, economic loss, social (...) On average daily we see three* [palliative care] *patients* (Legal Prescriber 7).

Yet, this same respondent also acknowledged that despite this, *'I meet this challenges, I meet this rigor resources, the patients are getting analgesics (...) It is maybe haphazard but at least they get it'* (Legal Prescriber 7).

Indeed, it seems that the issues ensuing from a lack of staff or overburdening thereof, an increasing number of patients, and the time-intensive nature of palliative care, are all further complicated by the special administrative requirements. Legal Prescriber 1 noted for instance that the accounting and registration following the reception of a palliative care patient made the assessment in general even more time intensive. Nevertheless, both Legal Prescriber 1 and Health Representative 2 emphasized that even with the extra time the administration takes, they do not fail to give patients adequate treatment in their practice (as a result of these procedures). Legal Prescriber 4 reinforced this assertion, stressing that at times a special palliative care unit is called into the hospital to clerk a palliative care patient thoroughly due to the high time allocation needed. Nonetheless, the respondent also mentioned that the situation never became so strenuous that the ability of their staff to deliver services in the limited time was undermined. Pharmacists, for example, were never unable to comply with the dispensing regulations.

In contrast to the challenges experienced, other respondents submitted that the specific administrative requirements neither increased the current workload nor contributed to complexities of service provision. Health Facility Representative 1, for instance, held that the special procedures were fully implemented into the daily routine. While the procedures may be formally implemented, Dispenser 1, employed at the same facility, acknowledged that challenges existed in the practical implementation of said procedures. Moreover, Dispenser 3 noted that the facility at which the respondent worked had increased the level of control for Class A medicines and, in fact, expanded the administrative requirements. It remained unclear in the interview and during the observations whether this had any effect on the feasibility to work in these enhanced procedures.

Nonetheless, even though some respondents held that the requirements did not obstruct their work, similar experiences were found in the context of the structural challenges to Uganda's health system. In this respect, their experiences, whether devoid of challenges or not, would resemble those considering that the additional regulatory requirements exerted pressure on their daily work and the health system more generally. For this reason, the question is whether challenges to comply with the administrative and procedural requirements are the problem. Or whether challenges to comply with specific drug-control requirements are part of a larger complexity of the service provision in Uganda. Even if the latter holds true, the broader complexities in service provision may indeed be aggravated by the requirements stemming from specific drug-control regulations.

Late detection, limited awareness, and the geographic accessibility/inaccessibility of health clinics all lead to an increase of the need for palliative care, especially when combined with the elevation in the presence of non-communicable diseases. A legal prescriber observed *'by all means* [there is] *a great increase of the need for palliative care'* (Legal Prescriber 4). Legal Prescriber 5 submitted that Uganda is not ready to deal with the increase of cancers, diabetes, and cardiovascular diseases. The health system is overstretched, according to the respondent, and despite there being a system to address cancers, the rudiments of treatment plans for other non-communicable diseases is lacking. While, according to Legal Prescriber 5, pain is not the most common side effect of those other non-communicable diseases, their treatment still requires at least some form of pain control and therefore pain-control medication. The absence of a systematic approach to the treatment of non-communicable diseases (other than cancer) is a structural challenge that, in turn, is complicated when one is reminded of the specific administrative requirements that are applicable to Class A medication.[53]

Moreover, the necessity to have authorized staff prescribe morphine could prove problematic considering the general deficiency in human resources. In order to acquire the status of legal prescriber, clinical officers and nurses can take a special training at HAU. This training, however, is expensive. The limited availability of financial support, in addition, requires facilities to cover the tuition fee (for the training) from their own resources should they want one of their staff members to become a qualified prescriber. Notably, Ministry of Health Representative 1 stressed that scholarships were available, while the APCA team mentioned that these used to be available when this type of training first started. Actors like the HAU and the APCA also offer some financial assistance. Nevertheless, more generally, the output of the training course is too low to adequately scale up services in the country. In these circumstances, it seems that know-how and experience trump actual qualification. One dispenser illustrated in this regard that *'one clinical officers who was trained, partly trained, but not fully trained – he hasn't qualified* [to become a legal prescriber], *he does not have a diploma in palliative care to be allowed to prescribe morphine (...) He prescribes because he has the knowledge'* (Dispenser 1). Finally, it must be noted that not just staff-related pressure could exist; a lack of other resources may also complicate the implementation of specific record-keeping requirements. One of the legal prescribers

53 The same respondent submits, however, that in comparison to other countries, Uganda's health system is coping relatively well.

explained, for instance, that the patient charts were used to prescribe: *'we just have our charts for the patients, you prescribe in the patient chart'* (Legal Prescriber 8).

Even though service providers explained that the complexities they experience do not hamper them in their ability to ensure access to pain-control medicines, the above clearly demonstrates that the additional requirements, and ensuing challenges in light of the structural difficulties that exist in the Ugandan health system, do not foster the accessibility to and availability of treatment. Yet, if the special administration complicates the service provision at a variety of facilities (in all geographical regions, i.e. urban, peri-urban, rural), then one may wonder what professionals do in situations when they feel unable to comply with the regulations applicable to prescribing or dispensing Class A medicines.

Customized registration procedures and negative compliance incentive

A third problem encountered is that of the adoption of customized procedures to implement and comply with the specific Class A registration requirements. Despite the fact that service providers describe their daily practice to already be burdensome, many facilities opt for such procedural customization. Legal Prescriber 1 and Health Facility Representative 2 noted that in their clinic, the reporting was not done straight after having seen a patient. To increase the manageability of their job, an internal system was developed, which allowed for all accounting and registration to be done on the day after their home visits. They acknowledged, however, that gaps in the registration occur from time to time due to the attending staff being unable to fill out a form after consultation with a patient.

Similarly, HAU Representative 2 explained that the HAU maintains a monthly (internal) accumulative reporting procedure, in which the full amount of morphine dispensed in that month is listed and cross-referenced with the stock levels. Moreover, Dispenser 6 noted that isolated errors occur in the system, which, according to the respondent, is natural since it relies on manual, instead of computerized, input. Examples include the dispensing of erroneous quantities to the patient (from a medical point of view).

However, as was mentioned earlier, the Class A order booklet points out that if facilities fail to adhere to the administrative requirements, they cannot be supplied with new stock. Adequately completing these documents is, after all, emphasized to be a requirement set by the UN. The PCAU Representative, discussing the message this statement brings across to local service providers, said *'actually* [these regulations are] *very scary to the health workers. And what usually happens, if they have written the name, they may end up adding it up. You follow what I mean?* [They] *make it up'* (PCAU Representative). It seems that when local service providers struggle to comply with regulations in the manner intended at the national – and perhaps also international – level, regulations produce a negative compliance incentive, i.e. accepting to meet the applicable regulations in a manner contrary to the actual regulation.

Nevertheless, similarly to the previous subsection, one cannot state that a negative compliance incentive directly hampers the access to medicines. Rather, it is submitted here that this at least renders the enforcement of these rules and their purpose questionable.

Inconsistent enforcement

Bearing in mind the role of the NMS, being one of the primary bodies in the assessment of the Class A orders submitted by health facilities, and its power to either honour or refuse such orders, the NMS Representative disclosed that there had indeed been instances of non-compliance after which facilities were not supplied with new stock. Most of these cases were the result of improperly signed forms having been submitted or the incorrect form having been used, i.e. other than the official format included in the Class A order book. When linked to the problems relating to the dissemination of the revised registration booklets, in particular to public facilities, any facility not yet having access to the new forms therefore faces serious obstacles in its efforts to refill its stock. Contrastingly, the registration requirements were simplified and the new booklets were distributed, among other reasons, to prevent facilities from facing unnecessary stock-outs.[54]

Interestingly, when discussing the manner in which the order forms were handled by the NMS, it was observed that two example orders were reviewed differently. Both, however, were approved. In an attempt to identify what would exactly be the 'deal breaker' for the organization, the NMS Representative explained that while the most commonly encountered mistake was that of unduly signed forms and the use of incorrect formats, the quantity needed is the most decisive factor when verifying orders. Yet, confusingly, when probed on this matter, it appeared that even when a form is filled out in full, a missing signature (of a person authorized to sign such forms) is considered a threshold on the basis of which orders are denied. For the NMS, in other words, the most important markers for acceptance of an order are that the order is submitted on the official form, requests a reasonable amount of medication, and is accompanied by an authorized signature.

54 See Section 6.4.1.

In sum, order forms are reviewed differently in the private and the public sector (and potentially also within these sectors), which leads to inconsistent enforcement. The ambiguity found in this respect signals the need for the provision of additional training for local facilities on the relevance and the practical implications of the specific Class A requirements. In fact, the knowledge and information gaps that exist between the international level, the national level, and the local reality of service provision, leads one to question the value of the administrative requirements implemented. First of all, it seems largely irrelevant how local facilities fill out the required information. Second, there is no consistent enforcement of these procedures despite ongoing monitoring.

Accreditation and splintered mandates

Splintered mandates and accreditation issues are a final problem encountered in relation to the administrative necessities, and the specific trade and distributional restrictions. The discussion concerning the absence of financial resources to pay for training can already be considered an example of this. Legal Prescriber 6 noted, in addition, that morphine is classified as being precious and made out to be far too special (in comparison to other medicines). According to the respondent, instead of making rules more flexible, previous reform efforts in Uganda had actually added another layer of regulation, increasing its complexity. In spite of the HAU's training programme, which authorizes nurses and clinical officers to act as prescribers, individuals are not allowed to order liquid morphine upon successful completion of their training. Only accredited facilities can order morphine and, moreover, accreditation can only be obtained upon inspection by the PCAU. Concretely, Legal Prescriber 6 continued, you might be able to place an order for morphine, but not in its liquid state. This, evidently, is counterproductive as the accreditation of health facilities was created to protect nurses and clinical officers.

While it is sufficient to inspect facilities, the respondent continued, it is inconsistent that a doctor, who by virtue of their training is allowed to prescribe morphine and does not require any additional training to do so, can only order morphine if employed at an accredited facility. Some private clinics and private hospitals cannot stock liquid morphine for that same reason, unless a PCAU inspection has taken place. The PCAU, however, is a palliative care institution and morphine use is not limited to palliative care purposes. As Legal Prescriber 6 explained, these private hospitals, despite performing major surgeries, cannot stock liquid morphine as long as accreditation is absent. Regardless of the relative ease with which these facilities could pass an inspection, the respondent wondered whether advanced private clinics really need to be inspected. The geographical distribution of health facilities could, in terms of accreditation, act as a barrier. Such geographic accessibility/inaccessibility, after all, is a concern in Uganda and may be particularly problematic in relation to access to pain-control medicines. Accreditation requirements therefore divide accessibility into a two-pronged question: first, does the patient live within a reasonable distance of the health facility and, if so, is this facility accredited to provide the pain-control treatment (i.e. liquid morphine) he or she needs.

Moreover, the supply/demand chain is generally considered lengthy, easily disturbed and includes splintered mandates, which affect the service provision. While at the national level the supply/demand chain is generally considered sufficient, service providers operating in the system complain about the challenges they face. Of particular concern is the short shelf life of liquid morphine (six months). Should obstacles hamper the supply/demand chain, the newly arriving liquid morphine could be set to expire. In such instances, the availability of and accessibility to pain-control medicine is undoubtedly threatened. Moreover, it has been reported that the buses distributing morphine to public facilities leave at set times irrespectively of all orders having been dropped off or not. As these buses only venture out to rural areas at fixed moments, results can be devastating for those facilities that have run out of stock or are about to run out. Such inefficiencies, experience shows, become more frequent the longer the bureaucratic loop is.

While a direct and causal relationship cannot be established between any of the specific requirements implemented in Uganda and an obstruction in the availability of, accessibility to, or even acceptability of pain-control treatment, one must acknowledge that these requirements at least fail to promote the use of said medication in practice. In fact, they seem to aggravate the structural challenges in Uganda's health system and affect, in one way or another, the ability of local health workers to perform their job in accordance with the relevant regulations. This last issue is mentioned specifically as respondents had held that implementation of any of the regulations had not directly resulted in a patient not receiving care. It became evident, however, that the care provided did not always follow the strict regulatory requirements applicable.

6.4.5 Implications of data collection, analysis, and reporting procedures

Theory of data management

In addition to applying to the specific administrative, trade, and distributional requirements, the consequences of the types of data collection, analysis, and reporting are also germane to a section of the supply/demand chain (outlined earlier in Figure 6.1, Section 6.4.2). Figure 6.3 indicates the structure of data collection, analysis, and reporting, based on the initial observations made during the preliminary field visit.

Here too, similarly to the previous section, the envelopes indicate the stage of the process where specific administrative requirements are relevant.

Figure 6.3 Uganda's data collection, analysis, and reporting procedures in theory

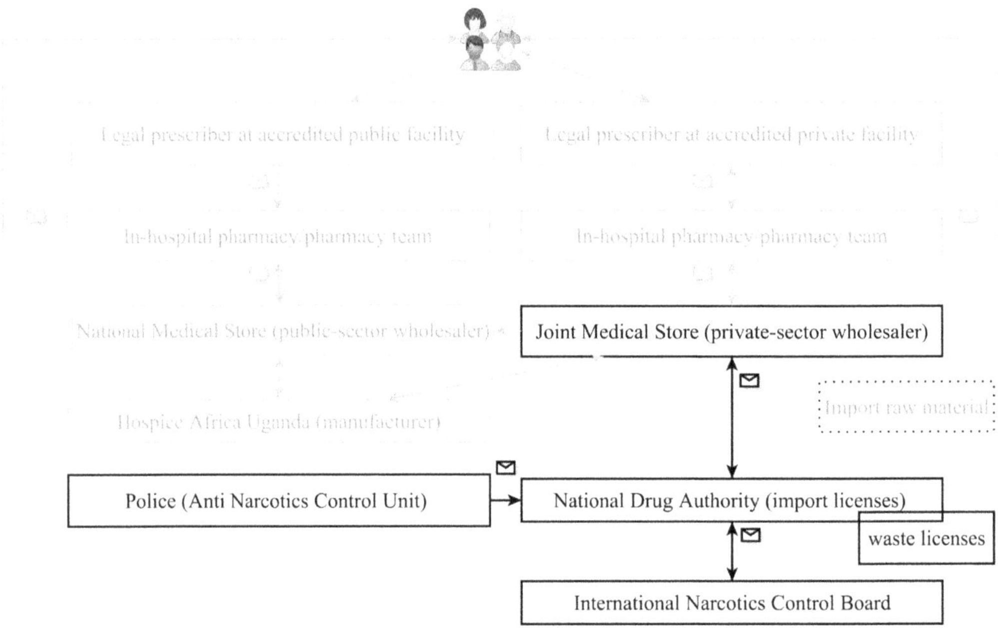

Legal prescribers at both public and private facilities register all single doses prescribed and administered in the Class A registration booklets. The health facilities, in turn, submit these documents to the NMS (public) and JMS (private) respectively. The JMS, then, provides the documentation it collects to the NMS so that the latter is able to compile an overview to be presented to the Ministry of Health. The Ministry, subsequently, provides this information to the NDA. According to Ministry of Health Representative 1, the NDA then drafts the estimates and statistical returns reported to the INCB. Estimates included in the report are based on consumption figures. Figure 6.3 demonstrates at which stage of the supply/demand chain the collected information is used, and also indicates when information is *not* used: in the transparent parts.

Consumption-based methods and reporting

Ideally, data collection, via the special administration requirements, and reporting to the INCB, would be based on the regulatory supply/demand chain depicted in Section 6.4.2. If the technical guidance, as provided by the WHO and INCB, on how to draft estimates and on which quarterly statistical returns methods to use were accepted, a combination of consumption-based and morbidity-based data would be relied on in this system. As was mentioned in Chapter 2, the WHO and INCB recommend the use of combined methods to ensure that the absolute need is reflected in such estimates (rather than only the registered demand). Without entering into complex statistical and methodological discussions, one may note that this bottom-up approach, which includes individual consumption data into the documents to be submitted to the INCB, was also recommended during regional training sessions. The researcher observed this during a workshop in Entebbe (July 2014) that had been jointly organized by the Pain and Policy Study Group and the APCA.

Nonetheless, it appeared that the process involved and outcome of the compilation of documents to be submitted to the INCB remained versatile and, at times, unclear. Ministry of Health Representative 1 stated that before the NDA received its reporting mandate (see Figure 6.3), the Ministry of Health and the NMS were responsible for the communication with the INCB. Upon the establishment of the NDA, tasks were shifted. In the current structure, the Ministry is not involved in the reporting process. Nevertheless, the Ministry of Health is still the body receiving all the forms distributed by the INCB. Yet, as one of the representatives aptly phrased, it *'is no longer* [involved] *in the direct line of communication'* (Ministry of Health Representative 2). Despite the absence of direct communication with the INCB, Ministry of Health Representative 1 emphasized that the Ministry remains chiefly responsible for the monitoring of compliance with the procedural obligations and is charged with the compilation of reports on this subject, to be delivered to the NDA.

Ministry of Health Representative 2 further explained that the NMS is tasked with totalling all orders and consolidating all information gathered by means of the special administration. This data is, subsequently, compiled into a report for the NDA, which then provides it to the INCB. The same respondent described, moreover, that the JMS submits a similar 'accounting overview' to the NDA on the basis of which the latter assembles the report. Such a report also includes all import data of raw material for which the JMS needs an import license from the NDA. The mutual cooperation required is illustrated in Figure 6.3. However, when digging more deeply into the subject matter, it remains unclear as to who analyses what or submits exactly what information to whom.

The NDA is the body designated to correspond with the INCB. The NDA Representative explained, on this point, that a separate unit within the NDA prepares the information submitted to the INCB. Ideally, the information provided would originate from a quantification of consumption, as compiled by the Ministry of Health, and confiscations by the Anti-Narcotics Control Unit of the police. Yet, the NDA bases its estimates on the import/waste ratio. This implies that import data, i.e.

the number of import licenses issued to the JMS, is compared with the bulk stock of morphine manufactured for medical purposes. The NDA operates on the assumption that *'whatever comes in is consumption* [because] *if it is not consumed there are returns of destruction'* (NDA Representative). Destruction data originates from the JMS and NMS respectively, despite the fact that the NDA should have such data in its possession, being the body designated to supervise the destruction process.

The NDA Representative described that, in practice, distribution centres collect expired morphine and move to destroy it. The NDA does not receive any specific documentation on this and is merely provided with a collection of data (from the JMS and NMS). In relation to the data collection and compilation of information, the NMS Representative confirmed that it receives quarterly data from the JMS. All data is, furthermore, kept on file in case the NDA or the police (Anti-Narcotics Control Unit) would require access to such information. The NMS neither analyses nor audits (backward or forward) the supply/demand chain, as according to the NMS Representative, it is not their role to do so. The respondent held, on this topic, *'even if we would have to do any auditing (...) I do not think we are* [obliged to]*'* (NMS Representative). While it is unclear who exactly carries such responsibility, the respondent said that those responsible for auditing would investigate consumption per facility and check whether or not a facility has properly accounted for this.

In contrast, the JMS Representative asserted that the JMS does not provide information other than reports on import data, including permits and received quantities of raw material. In search of the origin of the NDA's consumption data, the respondent was asked whether facilities provide the JMS with any specificities on their consumption. The JMS Representative held that it does not perform any facility-level monitoring as this falls within the purview of the NDA. Instead, the JMS looks at the ordering trend of a facility, which means that an order simply must 'make sense' in comparison to previous orders. Yet, if estimates are solely based on consumption data, which is fully order-based, one has to understand how local facilities make their orders, and which formats or methods are used. This leads to the first problem.

Ordering and forecasting

Dispenser 5 explained that orders are calculated on the basis of what has been used. Similarly, one of the dispensers noted that they *'(...) base* [orders] *on consumption of the previous months to project how much will be needed for the future'* (Dispenser 6). This same respondent clarified that the ordering procedures neither forecast nor employ morbidity-based quantification techniques. In general, consumption figures are used to reflect a responsive as opposed to a pro-active methodology.

The JMS Representative, on the other hand, acknowledged that forecasted ordering of local facilities was a serious challenge. The respondent described it to be difficult to accurately predict the number of health clinic visitors and estimate who, of those patients, is in need of pain control, especially because pain control (morphine) is not just a component of palliative care, but is also required for a range of other medical treatments. The complexity lies in the indiscernibility of patterns in the manner in, and particularly the location at, which patients present themselves to health workers. Geographic inaccessibility of clinics is a serious issue in this respect. People have to travel far to reach the appropriate health clinic. If one, moreover, cannot reach individuals who reside in remote areas, then one cannot be informed about disease patterns, its prevalence in a particular region, or forecasted medicinal demand. Consequently, the practice is rather *ad hoc*. This same respondent described *'whatever you have you treat those who are there, then when it is finished, those who come do not get'* (JMS Representative). Likewise, the lack of adequate epidemiological data is a problem.

In general, Ministry of Health Representative 2 described that there are no structural issues in the health system causing non-compliance, i.e. situations in which Uganda is unable to submit annual estimates or quarterly statistical returns. Uganda tenders estimates, quarterly returns, and if needed supplementary estimates to correct the demand. Yet, in view of the above, the danger in solely relying on consumption data – regardless of whether or not Uganda is able to come up with other figures – is in the assumption that the registered need reflects the absolute need in a country. Although they are formally compliant with reporting obligations, the techniques relied on could well structurally rule out the needs of a large part of the population, who are not able to express their needs to a health worker. The JMS Representative held, in this respect, that 'only those that arrive will be captured but they are just a small fraction of those who would actually need, so that is an issue' (JMS Representative). This is a structural challenge at the core of Uganda's health system and, more generally, hinders geographic accessibility in accordance with human rights norms. One must note, however, that it is not submitted that the ordering techniques complicate geographic accessibility, but rather that the inaccessibility of health facilities makes consumption-based ordering and forecasting questionable.

Quantification, data analysis, and capacity building

Nonetheless, the current consumption-based approach is considered sufficient. As there is only one manufacturer and just one party licensed to order raw material, the NDA Representative considered the methods currently in use adequate. Should any other information be needed, the NDA can request it. Still, however, the respondent observed that *'a quantification exercise would be ideal'* (NDA Representative).

Preferably, the NMS and the Ministry of Health, who seem jointly responsible for quantifying the country's consumption data, would provide such information. To date, no link has been established between the recorded consumer data and the annual estimate, the NDA official indicated. In fact, the quantification exercise referred to by the NDA Representative refers to an overview of the consumption data collected through the separate Class A administration analysed by the Ministry of Health. In contrast with the intentions of the Ministry of Health,[55] interviews with various stakeholders in the regulatory supply/demand chain made it clear that the information obtained through the separate Class A registration is not supplied to the NDA. Neither is it used to draft estimates or compile quarterly statistical returns, with the exception of the JMS import license returns and JMS/NMS destruction returns. In terms of scaling up and increasing supply, Ministry of Health Representative 2 noted that a proportionate increase of morphine for clinical purposes also increased the volume of raw materials. According to the respondent, such a scale-up was reported to the INCB.

The exact approach in terms of capacity-building so as to scale up quantification also remains unclear. The NMS, as explained earlier, does not provide a capacity-building programme and relies on the Ministry of Health. However, one of the representatives of the Ministry of Health noted that '[the] *PCAU has been doing that on our behalf'* (Ministry of Health Representative 3). Nevertheless, Ministry of Health Representative 2 stated that the Ministry does get involved when necessary. According to this respondent, there is a national group of trainers that provide various workshops, including on pain control (i.e. its do's and don'ts) and the potential dangers of opioid analgesics. It remains ambiguous whether this capacity-building focuses on pain treatment and palliative care in particular or if it is broader.

The JMS Representative explained that the JMS does run a specific capacity-building programme primarily focused on non-morphine opioids. The exclusion of morphine, the respondent made clear, was due to the HAU's involvement in the technical training on routines and forecasting for morphine use. For all other Class A medicines, the JMS provides assistance concerning the requirements, retention periods, logistical support for ordering, and how to scale up (step 1-3) analgesics to identify equivalent dosing (e.g. between codeine and morphine). One of the educational tools used is a newsletter in which a specific issue or theme is highlighted in each edition.

55 As was elaborated in Section 6.4.2, the intention of the government of Uganda to implement the special administration for Class A medication was to give effect to the country's obligations under the international drug-control treaties. It was also meant to synergise data collection tools and methods so as to harmonize the system, making it easier to collect the relevant data.

Practice of data management

Based on the above, without deeming it absolutely accurate due to the diversity of respondents' comments on the topic, Figure 6.4 depicts the data management chain in practice (as opposed to its theoretical implementation).

Figure 6.4 Uganda's data collection and analysis, reporting, and enforcement in practice

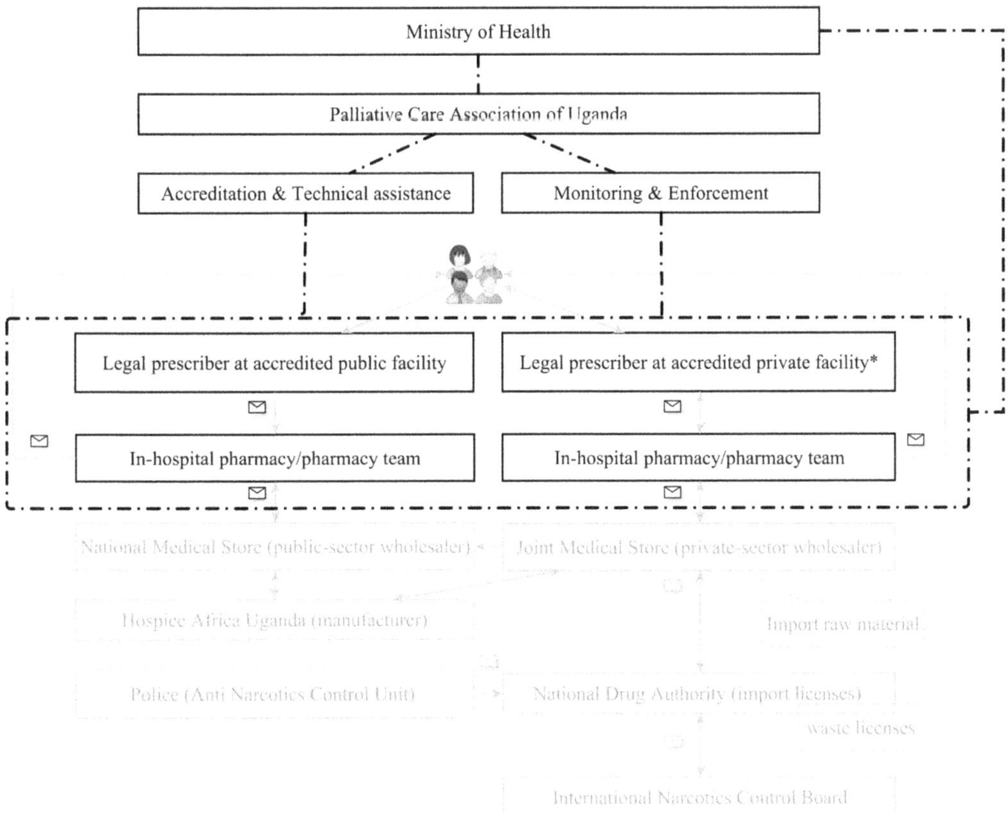

As one may notice, Figure 6.4 is an amended version of Figure 6.1 and, as illustrated, is clearly different from the ideal situation and initially reported structure mapped by Figure 6.3.

In short, the INCB sends the form to the Ministry of Health, which forwards them to the NDA. The NDA drafts the estimates and reports statistical returns, solely based on the import/waste ratio. Import data is collected on the basis of the licenses issued to the JMS and on the correspondence with the JMS on the subject. For waste data, the NDA relies on its own databases.

Public and private facilities keep track of and report on medicines by means of Class A record books, order books, and ward books. Ward and record books stay at the facility. Order forms are submitted to the NMS or JMS. These two organisations review documents to either approve or deny orders. However, they do not analyse them. Even though the Ministry of Health mentioned that the PCAU is, together with the Ministry, involved in the analytical quantification, it remains vague on which data such an analysis, if at all performed, is based and to whom this data is submitted, if at all. This is unknown because the NDA Representative mentioned that the NDA would ideally be able to rely on quantification data provided by the Ministry of Health and NMS jointly. The precise role of the NMS in this respect, however, remains uncertain as well. It is for this reason that the quantification exercise has not been included in this overview. This absence, nevertheless, is not to be regarded as indicative of its practical likelihood. The monitoring role of PCAU in general, on the other hand, does not necessarily seem to include data analysis.

Questioning the purpose of administration

Attempting to understand the implications of administrative requirements and data management leads to questions regarding the purpose of the administration. This was already briefly addressed in the context of the enforcement of the Class A registration booklets. It also manifests itself in relation to the data management chain.

While recorded data does not seem to be transferred beyond the wholesale level, at which it is not analysed, the information does not seem to undergo any analysis at all. This means that the data registered in the Class A order book is not directly used to arrive at estimates and calculate statistical returns by use of quantification, despite the fact that the NDA had indicated that it wished to do so. Indirectly, one could argue, this affects the availability of and accessibility to controlled medicines, including pain-control medication. Managing an administration that is simply filed and remains unused in the fulfilment of its overall purpose, does nothing more than create undue pressure on local facilities, hampering them in the provision of services in the process. Moreover, when data on use reflects only the registered (instead of an absolute) need, this causes a structural gap in demand figures. Such a discrepancy indirectly complicates the availability of and accessibility to medicines for many vulnerable and marginalized sections of society who cannot access or struggle in accessing a health facility accredited to provide pain-control treatment. This in itself would also threaten the principle of non-discrimination. In an effort to respect the principle of non-discrimination in an integrally effective manner, States have to prioritize the needs of vulnerable and marginalized groups including the elderly, women, children, HIV/AIDS patients, persons living with disabilities, people of the LGBT community, indigenous people, and people living in remote areas. The same problem is observed in the fact that morphine consumption, and the number of legal prescribers and accredited facilities are used as key indicators in the analysis of the coverage and adequacy of morphine consumption.

6.4.6 Some key challenges to the provision of controlled medicines

Apart from strictly relating to or being revealed in the context of the Class A administrative requirements and aspects of data management, there are some key challenges to the provision of controlled medicines. First, the lack of financial resources in the health system itself, the general socio-economic context in which service provision takes place, and the individual financial capacity of patients are problematic. As was also briefly touched on in the context of the specific administrative requirements, some facilities simply lack the means to buy the equipment or other goods necessary to provide services. According to Civil Society Representative 2, Uganda's co-paid health system had increased out-of-pocket payments – a development many people struggle with. In addition, poverty and food access is a serious concern. As both Legal Prescriber 2 and a Nurse described, some patients *'will show some kind of pain, because of just mere hunger'* (Nurse). While the public hospital at which these respondents work used to provide breakfast and dinner, budget cuts have led to the supply of only one meal a day being feasible. The socio-economic status of patients may, moreover, even prevent patients from receiving care despite its availability and accessibility. Dispenser 5 and Legal Prescriber 8 explained they had to stop a patient's treatment because the patient could not afford any food and experienced discomfort when consuming morphine without an appropriate nutritional intake, meaning that the usual side effects were aggravated due to the lack of nutrition.

Second, corruption poses a serious challenge to Uganda's health system. Corruption includes embezzlement of medication and intentional inflation to heighten out-of-pocket payments. Civil Society Representative 2 explained that health centres submit their order of medicines to either the NMS or the JMS, but the consignment is delayed. In such instances, what happens is that medicines are intentionally delivered late to create scarcity, which due to an increase in demand inflates prices. Alternatively, medicines that are not supposed to be sold, but are to be available free of charge in public hospitals, are found to be sold in private pharmacies. In those cases, health workers in public hospitals declare a particular medicine to be out-of-stock, whilst taking the medicines to private clinics to make more money. According to the respondent, while it is uncertain whether or not morphine is embezzled or inflated, one can never be too sure. If it happens with other medicines, it could well happen with morphine or other Class A medicines too.

Civil Society Representative 1 described another example of corruption. Every year, by July, all medicines are out of stock. The respondent explained that in an attempt to obscure the stock-out, however, the NMS in these situations holds that medication is available but, since it is not claimed, nobody is in need of it. To prevent this from happening, a dual push/pull system could prove fruitful. Civil Society Representative 1 continued by explaining that the NMS, in such a system, would list the essential medicines that ought to be available in all health centres so that the most common illnesses can be treated. It would push facilities, in other words, to request stock. Patients, on the other hand, can 'pull' from them the medication they require. This would mean that people could receive what they ask for and not just be provided with what is deemed an absolute necessity. These are two examples of corruption within an array of problems that Uganda faces in its health system.

Third, Uganda is experiencing the difficulties caused by a reorganization to move from an acute care oriented health system – focused on infectious diseases – to a chronic care oriented system – focused on non-communicable diseases.[56] Yet, despite numerous successful campaigns, widespread awareness and information distribution remains problematic for Uganda's health system. As was also discussed in previous sections, Uganda's health system is demand driven and responsive by nature. According to Ministry of Health Representative 2, the demand created is not only simply determined by patients visiting a health facility, but also by the judgment of the health worker. In other words, a structural challenge to the health system itself is the low level of advocacy and mobilization of those who need treatment. In addition, the importance of the effective implementation of adequate training must be highlighted. This, after all, is required so as to ensure that the clinical officer or nurse on duty can identify pain and is able to direct the patient to appropriate treatment. Whereas one problem is that the patient might not go to the clinic, another problem is that health workers might struggle to diagnose an illness as until now their practice has predominantly focused on infectious rather than non-communicable diseases. Ministry of Health Representative 1 noted that the Ministry had started providing education and information on non-communicable diseases to educate and train both health workers and patients.

Fourth, effective pain treatment requires the availability of adjuvants (e.g. to treat common side effects of morphine). Managing side effects is a crucial component in effective pain control yet, at the same time, presents a challenge due to the inherent complexities associated with medicine provision. Legal Prescriber 4 emphasized that adjuvant medicines are adequately available unless there is a national stock-out.

56 Notably, this matter has been placed the political agenda as, at the time of research, the National Development Plan was under revision.

Therefore one cannot deem adjuvants to be generally unavailable; rather one must note that when unavailable, the availability and accessibility of morphine may be complicated.

Fifth, while hardly any abuse is actually detected, fear of abuse or of the development of dependence still seems to exist among senior doctors, hindering effective pain control. For instance, The PCAU Representative noted that:

> [*t*]*here is a knowledge gap amongst health workers (...) especially amongst the ones who have qualified sometime back. I would say old doctors and consultants; there is also still a challenge there because (...) they have a fear for morphine (...) The young ones* [have been] *taught in the medical school* [or] *in the nursing school. They are very fast at acknowledging this patient* [is in] *pain* [and needs morphine] *but they are frustrated sometimes by the consultants who will block the usage of it* (PCAU Representative).

Legal Prescriber 3 held that the lack of knowledge among senior doctors even discouraged patients from using pain-control medication. According to the respondent, the scepticism of senior doctors has somehow spilled over to the public, which has increased the fear among patients. Moreover, as Legal Prescriber 1 and Health Facility Representative 2 said, the perception dominating the community, having seen patients on morphine dying, is one in which morphine consumption equates death.

Fear was also detected amongst some pharmacists. From time to time, a pharmacist would consider the prescribed dosages too high and intervals between which patients have to take medicines too short. Cases have been reported in which, as a result, pharmacists amended prescriptions, with a serious impact on patients' palliative care treatment. It is not an understatement to say that communication is poor between pharmacists and doctors on this subject. It occurs that despite having been prescribed morphine for several weeks, the pharmacist alters the treatment to span only a couple of days. This evidently hampers access to adequate treatment. This is the reason that pharmacy schools now also include distinctive palliative care training.

Opinions are diverse, however, when it comes to fear of abuse. While some acknowledged such fear to still exist in practice, Ministry of Health Representative 1 reported the variance in the perceptions of senior and junior prescribers to be fading out. Similarly, the JMS Representative held that *'in Uganda, at least now, people have recognized when somebody needs it you get it. There is no fear that dependency occur, if the patient actually has severe pain'* (JMS Representative). Moreover, Health Facility Representative 1 continued by clarifying that *'we started with the fear but that fear is gone now, we now prescribe this drug with that confidence of following the guidelines and we have them benefit'* (Health Facility Representative 1).

Strikingly, in contrast, Legal Prescriber 4 noted that there used to be a practice of 'overprescribing'. Explaining the practice, the respondent illustrated that, in the case of cancer, as soon as a patient was diagnosed, morphine treatment would be started. Often (but not always), however, cancer is diagnosed at a stage where it results in moderate to severe pain. Such side effects should be treated appropriately. Upon identification of the problem, the prescription practice was adjusted to fall within the ambit of adequate behaviour. Now, liquid morphine is only prescribed and administered in cases where it is necessary and does not automatically accompany the mere diagnosis of cancer.

The fear and abuse described above seems distinct from the fear of non-compliance discussed in Section 6.4.4. Yet, as widely discussed in other publications, the fear of abuse may still complicate the adequate provision of pain and palliative care treatment.[57]

6.4.7 Potential reform

Whilst the NMS Representative perceived an increase in the use of morphine on the basis of the orders, consumption levels remain far from satisfactory. In order to scale up accessibility to and availability of pain-control medicines, such as liquid morphine, reform initiatives have been discussed in Uganda. Leading up to these proposals, Ministry of Health Representative 3 linked various aspects of this empirical analysis carefully together:

> *I think the issue of coming up with the proper estimates for purposes of whatever may not be precise. Because of those challenges* [i.e. challenges discussed in previous sections] *as we send the returns to INCB we may not be very accurate. So when countries place the supplementary orders, I think it is based on those kind of challenges which were not seen during that process of compiling of what basically the quota should be (...) So that would, I think, lead to that the controls are so stringent. For example if countries have like something in our case, we have observed or we have proved that there is no formulation that we are using or should we again continue to, you know. There should be some leeway depending on what kind of formulation we are using. Because for many of the health workers are really involved in this that has been a challenge of filling down each and every record. At the end of the day, or over 10 years when we have implemented this nobody has ever craved for this oral morphine. So could there be a de-classification of that particular formulation other than maybe the other formulations like the oral tables or the injectable* (Ministry of Health Representative 3).

57 See eg HL Fields, 'The Doctor's Dilemma: Opiate Analgesics and Chronic Pain' (2011) 69 Neuron 591.

It is exactly these years of experience without serious abuse issues or diversion that contributed to the government's investigation into the declassification of some formulas with the aim to improve accessibility and decrease the regulatory burden. However, as Ministry of Health Representative 1 described, much more evidence is needed to support the claim that the morphine solutions used in the country are neither abused nor diverted. The respondent explained that the Ministry of Health had initiated discussions on declassifying morphine solutions and making it an over-the-counter medicine. The representative immediately placed this assertion into perspective and noted that such a declassification would come too early according to the NDA.

Still, however, Ministry of Health Representative 3 believed that declassification of certain formulas could indeed suit the particular context of service provision in resource-constrained countries better. The representative stated that *'given the fact that the human resources capacities in many of these facilities and the number of patients and whatever, so, it becomes a big challenge in many African countries. Really you know complying with all those detailed, you know, requirements'* (Ministry of Health Representative 3). Not just the Ministry of Health, but also service providers would be happy with such a move. For example, Legal Prescriber 6 noted:

> *I would be totally happy with that, personally, I have just said to you I am in favour of really getting it to be a normal medication that people can use. I would probably be comfortable with that for the lowest concentration because then you actually are never going to get in trouble. We produce a couple of pretty high concentrations and I would not like that to be readily available, also because people are most used to the first one (...) I am a huge fan of low concentration of morphine because we use it here as a step 2* [i.e. analgesics on the WHO pain ladder] *because the alternative step 2s like codeine (...) and tramadol are either not available at all or very expensive with more side effects (...) I do not think it would happen – but I would personally be very happy to say that you know really extending the availability and access to the lower dose regimes, and even having some guideline that says if you feel your patient needs more than 50 milligrams per or (...) that's a referral. Or you have a flowchart. We're not quite there yet* (Legal Prescriber 6).

Moreover, the special administrative system is essentially manual. The general medicine-ordering system, on the other hand, is computerized and believed to be more efficient and user-friendly. Some service providers believe that merging morphine ordering into the general ordering system would improve morphine use and be beneficial to its availability.

Despite there being no lack in ambition it remains difficult to push for change. Perhaps Uganda's frontrunner position in the field of palliative care reform is making it difficult to challenge or question one's own approach. Nonetheless, any future reform will have to find its roots in evidence, not just in practice.

6.4.8 Particular issues around other (controlled) medicines

Step 1 pain-control medicines such as paracetamol

In order to understand whether or not issues surrounding the availability of morphine for pain control could truly be attributed to the medicine's controlled nature, problems related to other controlled medicines in general and uncontrolled *pain-control* medicines were explored. Paracetamol, a step-1 medicine for pain-control treatment, is widely available. Paracetamol is an over-the-counter medicine and therefore accessible without prescription. There is no permit, special license, or retention period applicable. The JMS Representative mentioned that the coverage of paracetamol is substantially higher than the coverage of liquid morphine. Similarly, Health Representative 1 indicated that despite morphine often not being available in smaller health facilities, these facilities do have paracetamol and ibuprofen in stock.

Anti-epileptics

According to Health Facility Representative 1, the availability of anti-epileptic medicines had recently received attention. The respondent continued by clarifying that anti-epileptics are included on the list of medicines ordered and that, at least in the last 7-10 years, these have been readily available most of the time, the reason being that the NMS had better organized itself over time. The representative emphasized that, in contrast to morphine, no double prescription requirement applies to anti-epileptic medicines, despite the fact that these medicines, as much as morphine, are considered a controlled essential medicine and therefore falls under the same regulatory scheme of the international drug-control system. It was observed, in addition, that it had never occurred to the respondents to use a similar advocacy strategy or line of argumentation to secure the widespread provision of morphine.

Opioid substitute treatment

At present, methadone – a frequently used medicine in opioid substitute treatment – is not registered by the NDA, meaning that the medicine has yet to be granted market authorization and, as such, cannot be manufactured, imported, dispensed, prescribed, or used in the country. Ministry of Health Representative 1 said, however, that registration is *'something which we will have to think about'* (Ministry of Health Representative 1). According to the respondent, harm-reduction measures are increasing in the country because of a growth in drug use. However, no link has been realised between rehabilitation services and palliative care services thus far.

In sum, the findings relating to morphine seem rather specific. In other words, whereas in law and theory a similar argument may be presented in relation to any controlled essential medicines, practice in Uganda demonstrates that one has to consider the availability of specific controlled medicines in their own context. In the case of liquid morphine, even though this might also apply to other controlled medicines, such a context refers to the new Class A registration booklets.

6.5 Conclusion

Seeking an answer to the question of whether Uganda, as an example, is able to provide access to pain-control medication in accordance with human rights law within the remit of their obligations under the international drug-control treaties, the following can be concluded. First, in Uganda, law is of not much help to advance the access to medicines. The country has not transposed any of the human rights treaties it is a party to into national legislation, and the right to health is generally not enforceable or justiciable in Uganda's legal system. In its recently adopted new Narcotics Bill, it has limitedly started to transpose the international drug-control treaties. In fact, the Bill only includes parts of the 1988 UN Convention Against the Illicit Traffic in Narcotic Drugs[58] but not the Single Convention. This Bill, however, has received much criticism because it is held to violate human rights law and also to potentially decrease the access to controlled medicines in the country. Regardless of the more practical findings on service provision, any human rights claim regarding the access to pain-control medicines is unlikely to be successful in court. The country's legal system, moreover, does not offer any real legal backing for health matters in the first place. In essence, as the NDA Representative also contended, Uganda may be good at policies but bad at laws. In this respect, there is little awareness amongst the Ugandan population when it comes to claiming public goods and services, such as medicines and adequate medical treatment, as an entitlement.

Second, in the context of Uganda, one can conclude that the implementation of Articles 17, 19-20, and 30 of the Single Convention causes problems, in general but especially when viewed in the context of the AAAQ standard of healthcare. The Class A registration booklets are found to place an additional burden on already overburdened health workers. Reporting is 'wobbly around the edges', registered consumption contains errors, whilst enforcement is inconsistent, and there is a lack

58 United Nations Convention Against the Illicit Traffic in Narcotic Drugs and Psychotropic Substances (adopted 20 December 1988, entered into force 11 November 1990) 1582 UNTS 95.

of information on the implementation of said procedures. The requirements carry a certain dissuasive effect and some health workers develop a negative compliance incentive. Even if facilities do not directly link their experience to the specific Class A requirements, a similar result is observed. The administrative measures are resource-intensive and therefore challenging in a resource-constrained context. Without establishing any causality, this would suggest at least that the way in which these regulations play out in practice could obstruct the availability and accessibility of medicines, and health services more generally. Yet indeed, as Lee, Walter-Drop, and Wiesel stressed, 'the successful delivery of collective goods and services is not only a question of political preference and public choice, but also a question of the ability of State institutions to function at all'.[59]

Moreover, one can question the purpose of the separate administration, including specific trade and distribution requirements, if in practice it hardly works to arrive at adequate estimates and quarterly statistical returns. It is difficult for Uganda to have adequate insight into the absolute need for pain treatment due to a lack of epidemiological data and an absence of forecasted ordering. The supply/demand chain of liquid morphine is a responsive system based on consumption data, despite a significant discrepancy between the registered demand and the absolute need. Such a gap in consumption data is caused by structural challenges that include the geographic accessibility of health clinics, a lack of finances, and understaffing. This is only complicated further by the accreditation requirement. In light of the structural constraints Uganda faces, the needs of vulnerable and marginalized groups are most likely to fall outside the ambit of any orders or estimates established, which compromises the principle of non-discrimination.

Therefore, one could conclude that solely relying on consumption methods seems problematic from a human rights perspective in the context of Uganda. One could attribute blame to Uganda for applying such methodology, or for ineffectively or insufficiently fulfilling its obligations under the international drug-control and human rights frameworks. Doing so, however, would be ill-founded. Contrastingly, the Ugandan case study rightfully reflects a 'best practice' situation, which may be in a structurally disadvantaged position to effectively discharge its dual obligations due to the resource-intensive nature of international and domestic drug-control requirements in particular. In this sense, the chapter emphasises the need to start viewing the human rights and drug-control systems as complementary and reinforcing, instead of mutually exclusive frameworks of law: viewing them as mutually exclusive clearly

59 MM Lee, G Walter-Drop and J Wiesel, 'Taking the State (Back) Out? Statehood and the Delivery of Collective Goods' (2014) 27 Governance 635, 635.

hampers effective service provision more generally. In this respect, one should see the Ugandan example as a timely warning.

The INCB calls upon States to address their country-specific challenges. However, it does so without providing sufficient background and context as to the flexibilities that exist within the international drug-control system itself to adopt country-specific measures. The regulations in their current form may not be culturally acceptable because of their resource-intensive nature. Yet, any progressive reform discussed in Uganda should be supported by actors, such as the INCB, with specific information clarifying which interventions are deemed acceptable to foster access to controlled essential medicines on site. It is not submitted here that without drug-control measures service provision in Uganda would be flawless. Instead, it is concluded that at least the administrative and procedural obligations, as well as the national implementation and interpretation of these obligations, potentially conflict with the country's ability to provide services in accordance with the AAAQ standard of healthcare.

In sum, whereas it is complicated for Uganda to ensure the access to medicines in accordance with human rights norms in general, the implications of the Single Convention in particular only make this more complex. In many countries, the private health system is often better organized than the public health system. The fact that private health facilities also struggle with the implications of the specific domestic and international drug-control requirements ought to be considered as indicative of a wider problem, something that only aggravates the above. If it is already complex to implement aspects of the AAAQ standard of healthcare within the remits of specific drug-control requirements, it may also be difficult to prioritize access over control efforts. This is demonstrated by the adoption of the new Narcotics Bill and its possible negative effect on the access to medicine. The new Bill increases drug-enforcement measures and is therefore believed to include a potentially negative impact on the progress made in the field of access to controlled-medicine provision.

Chapter 7
Country Study II: Latvia

7.1 Introduction

This chapter investigates whether Latvia is able to implement the administrative and procedural requirements of the 1961 Single Convention on Narcotic Drugs in a human rights compliant manner. Similarly to Chapter 6, it deals more specifically with understanding the issues, if any exist, in implementing a special administration, data collection and management, and specific trade and distribution requirements in relation to the Availability, Accessibility, Acceptability, and Quality (AAAQ) standard of healthcare.[1] As indicated in Chapter 5, the objective of the empirical analysis is to explore the interplay of the human rights and drug-control frameworks in practice. In doing so, this chapter aims to reveal the complexities and gaps that may be found in the international drug-control system in terms of human rights compliant medicine provision.[2] As was also highlighted in Chapter 5, Latvia is a high-income country with a seriously constrained health system. As a result, the population is faced with the repercussions of inadequate access to opioid analgesics, including morphine for pain treatment.

This chapter first elaborates briefly on the research design and methodology introduced in Chapter 5 and presents an anonymized chart that outlines all the respondents that participated in the study (Section 7.2). Next, the chapter provides background information on Latvia so as to ensure that the reader is able to contextualize the findings (Section 7.3). Focusing on the real-life experience of those working with the specific drug-control requirements, this chapter finally discusses the experiences of and context in which the provision of pain-control medicine takes place in Latvia (Section 7.4).

1 For an elaboration of the obligations listed, see Single Convention on Narcotic Drugs (adopted 30 March 1961, entered into force 13 December 1964) 520 UNTS 151 (Single Convention) arts 17, 19-20, and 30.

2 As mentioned before, at no stage in this book is it proclaimed that human rights law, on its own, is sufficient to bring about its own ambitions in practice. However, because the analysis is based on the assumptions on which human rights law rests, the primary purpose of the empirical analysis is to understand the ability of States to implement specific requirements of the international drug-control treaties.

7.2 Design and methodology

As for the country study conducted in Uganda, the question central to the empirical analysis is:

> How, if at all, can States prioritize, promote, and uphold the AAAQ standard of healthcare of medicines in accordance with human rights theory and law, whilst implementing the administrative and procedural requirements of the international drug-control system?

Answering such a question presupposes twofold insight. First, one needs to generate an in-depth understanding of the context in which the administrative and procedural requirements of the international drug-control system come into play in Latvia. This requires one to understand Latvia's 'regulatory chain' of pain-control medicines, its institutional and regulatory structure, and the experiences of those working within the system. Second, without establishing any causality, one needs to comprehend the context of service provision bearing in mind the AAAQ standard of healthcare when, if at all, relevant.

Through desk research, the relevant laws and policies were identified and analysed. Then, the data collection methods, as summarized in Chapter 5, were described. A representative from the World Health Organization (WHO) Europe Office recommended Ilze Aisilniece as the primary contact during the research stay. Vilnis Sosars, in turn, came recommended by members of the Access to Opioid Medication in Europe (ATOME) project. The ATOME team, having researched aspects of drug-control regulation within the country, was well-informed about whom to speak to in Latvia.

Drawing on the categorization, as introduced in Chapter 5, relevant stakeholders were identified in consultation with the aforementioned contact persons. To select respondents, on-site snowball sampling was used. Data collection was carried out during a period of three weeks (in January 2015). The data collection methods included participant observations and 17 in-depth interviews. Interviews were conducted using a topic guide (see also Chapter 5). Eight interviews were held as joint interviews upon consent of both participants. Out of these eight interviews, one participant translated the interview for the other participant. In addition, in another interview a participant who had previously been interviewed acted as the translator for the interviewee. Table 7.1 provides an exhaustive overview of the respondents. Identical to the table in Chapter 6, details listed include: the time, place, and date at which the interview took place; the category of actor to which respondent belongs; the public/private sector qualification of their position when relevant; and the geographic context in which the respondent works.

Table 7.1 Overview of respondents (Latvia)

Respondent	Health system	Place	Date	Geographic context	Joint interview together with
Civil Society Representative	n.a.	Riga	26-1-2015	Urban	n.a.
Ministry of Health Representative 1	n.a.	Riga	12-1-2015	Urban	Ministry of Health Representative 2
Ministry of Health Representative 2	n.a.	Riga	12-1-2015	Urban	Ministry of Health Representative 1
Narcologist 1	Public	Riga	13-1-2015	Urban	Narcologist 2
Narcologist 2	Public	Riga	13-1-2015	Urban	Narcologist 1
NHS Representative (government)	n.a.	Riga	21-1-2015	Urban	n.a.
Pharmacist 1	Public	Riga	20-1-2015	Urban	Translated by Narcologist 2
Pharmacist 2	Private	Riga	22-1-2015	Urban	Pharmacist 3
Pharmacist 3	Private	Riga	22-1-2015	Urban	Translated by Pharmacist 2
Pharmacist 4	Private	Riga	29-1-2015	Urban	Pharmacist 5
Pharmacist 5	Private	Riga	29-1-2015	Urban	Pharmacist 4
Pharmacist 6	Private	Riga	30-1-2015	Urban	n.a.
Physician 1	Public	Riga	14-1-2015	Urban	n.a.
Physician 2	Private	Riga	29-1-2015	Urban	n.a.
Physician 3	Private	Riga	29-1-2015	Rural	n.a.
SAM Representative (government)	n.a.	Riga	26-1-2015	Urban	n.a.
WHO Representative	n.a.	Riga	16-1-2015	Urban	n.a.

The Latvian Centre for Human Rights (LCHR) allowed the use of their office as a base of operations. Although the LCHR does not specialize in health rights, such an in-house arrangement was tremendously helpful when organizing meetings with various stakeholders. The LCHR team, furthermore, provided careful feedback on and assistance in how to approach participants.

The interview procedure followed in Latvia was similar to the one used in Uganda. First, each participant was familiarized with the informed consent protocol and the purpose and conditions of the interview were carefully explained.[3] The actual interview commenced upon consent of the participant and interviews were only recorded with permission of the interviewee. Each participant was given the opportunity to raise questions before and after the interview, as well as the time to summarize and reflect on their main message in relation to the topics addressed. All interviews were transcribed *verbatim*.[4] The data collected was analysed relying on the participant categorization as presented in Table 7.1. Coding and triangulation structured the data analysis process. Unless otherwise specified, all information presented on Latvia is based on the 17 interviews that were carried out.

7.3 Background of Latvia

7.3.1 Geographic, demographic and economic characteristics

Latvia is one of the Baltic States in North East Europe. Formerly a part of the Union of Soviet Socialist Republics (USSR), Latvia has been an independent republic since 1991 and, in 2004, became a member of the European Union. The country has an estimated population of 2 million, 67.7 per cent of which lives in urban areas and 19 per cent of which is 65 years old or older.[5]

The World Bank considers Latvia a high-income country with a Gross National Income of $14,900 per capita.[6] In 2014, life expectancy at birth was 74.2.[7] The WHO estimates the country to reserve 5.9 per cent of its Gross Domestic Product for health expenditure.[8] The country's poverty headcount ratio at national poverty lines lies at 22.5 per cent of the population.

7.3.2 Legal and administrative context

Latvia is a civil-law country that is largely monistic. Concretely, this means that all international law that has been ratified is enforceable in the domestic legal order. As

3 See Appendix II for the informed consent protocol used in Latvia.
4 *Verbatim* means that interviews were transcribed word-by-word and reflect exactly what the respondent said without amendments. Transcription was outsourced to *Uitgetypt* and, upon return, carefully reviewed for errors.
5 The World Bank, 'Latvia' <http://data.worldbank.org/country/latvia?display=map> accessed 31 August 2016; CIA World Factbook, 'Latvia' <www.ciaworldfactbook.us/europe/latvia.html> accessed 31 August 2016; WHO, 'Noncommunicable Diseases (NCD) Country Profiles – Latvia' <www.who.int/nmh/countries/lva_en.pdf> accessed 31 August 2016.
6 See World Bank (n 5).
7 United Nations Development Programme, *Human Development Report 2015: Work for Human Development* (UNDP 2015).
8 id; see also World Bank (n 5).

opposed to dualist legal systems, a monistic system does not require the adoption of national legislation to transpose international obligations into domestic law.[9] Administratively, Latvia is divided into 26 counties and 7 municipalities.[10] Similarly to Uganda, service delivery is partly decentralized.

International treaties that have been ratified take precedence over national legislation.[11] The Law on the Constitutional Court, furthermore, goes on to dismiss any distinction between instruments that have been ratified and those that have been signed.[12] The presence of a signature of a government official, in other words, is sufficient to declare an international treaty superior to any domestic legal Act, except the Constitution.[13] As Van Elsuwege points out, the case law of the Constitutional Court confirms the doctrine of monism and therefore the hierarchy of legal norms.[14]

Fundamental rights are enshrined in Chapter VIII of the Constitution, of which Article 111 contains the right to health and medical assistance.[15] This right to health is enforceable and justiciable, as is evidenced by a range of cases dealing with matters that are related to health and the access to medicines.[16]

7.3.3 Health system

Decentralization is, as briefly hinted at before, also visible in the health system. In Latvia, it is common for smaller hospitals and regional centres to be municipality-owned. University hospitals and 'single speciality hospitals', on the other hand, are state-owned. In contrast to the public facilities, most pharmacies are privately run.[17]

Recently, Mitenbergs and colleagues found that '[t]he Latvian health care system is based on [a] general tax-financed statutory health care provision, with a purchaser-

---

9 P van Elsuwege, *From Soviet Republics to EU Member States: A Legal and Political Assessment of the Baltic States' Accession to the EU* (Martinus Nijhoff Publishers 2008) 157, 161-165.

10 CIA World Factbook (n 5).

11 Law on International Treaties of the Republic of Latvia of 1994, s 13. Van Elsuwege (n 9) 162, 163.

12 Constitutional Court Law of 1997, s 16(2). Van Elsuwege (n 9) 162, 163.

13 id.

14 Van Elsuwege (n 9) 162, 163.

15 Article 111 states that '[t]he State shall protect human health and guarantee a basic level of medical assistance for everyone.' See the Constitution of the Republic of Latvia, 1922 (as amended).

16 T Birmontiene, 'Health Legislation in Eastern European Countries: the Baltic States' (2004) 11 European Journal of Health Law 77, 80. See also *Roberts Mutulis v the Republic of Latvia* (Case No 2008-48-01) [2009] LVCC 6 (29 September 2009); *Vitālijs Orlovs and 19 Ors v the Republic of Latvia* (Case No 2012-14-03) [2013] LVCC 6 (9 April 2013).

17 U Mitenbergs and others, 'Latvia: Health System Review' (2012) 14 Health Systems in Transition 1, 18.

provider split and a mix of public and private providers'.[18] This means that Latvia's health system is based on a statutory system of co-financing. The budget of the National Health Service (NHS), the branch of the Ministry of Health responsible for health financing, is raised via a system of income-blind general taxation. Both private and public service providers are given the option to contract with the NHS. Unfortunately, in the aftermath of the 2008 financial crisis, Latvia had to introduce one of the highest out-of-pocket payments in Europe to sustain its health system.

General practitioners (GP), Mitenbergs and colleagues argue, are the system's gatekeepers to any type of 'secondary ambulatory and hospital care'.[19] In theory, patients are free to choose any care provider upon receipt of a referral from their GP. However, their health expenses are only covered – albeit via the system of co-financing – when the service provider has concluded a contract with the NHS. In practice, the pool of providers from which to select is therefore much smaller and particularly small in the countryside.[20] In addition, there has been a decline in the hospital-bed/population ratio (to 3.4/1000 for acute care) and in in-patient hospitals in general (to 67).[21]

To improve access to care, despite the decline in hospital beds available, since 2009 day care has played an important role in Latvia's health system. Although home care has been included to improve access to treatment, however, financial constraints continue to limit individuals' real access to health services.[22] Moreover, human resources are seriously constrained also, with the country operating on a 2.91/1000 physician-to-population ratio.[23]

Relevant health policy in Latvia

The Latvian Centre of Oncology at Riga East Hospital was the first to open a specialized palliative care unit providing 25 beds. Divided over four regional hospitals there are an additional 55 palliative care beds available in the country.[24] The unit's multidisciplinary team consists of at least 'oncologists, nurses, nurse assistants, psychologists, social workers, chaplains, and voluntary care providers'.[25] If necessary, in addition to this team, other specialists can be involved. Mortality rates suggest that

18 ibid xviii.
19 ibid xx.
20 id.
21 ibid 87-88, 90.
22 ibid xix.
23 ibid 96-97.
24 ibid 132.
25 id.

palliative care patients either suffer from cancers or HIV/AIDS – although the latter is much less common.[26] Apart from several guidelines, there are no general palliative care standards for GPs. Home care providers – e.g. nurses, physician's assistants, or social workers – usually do not receive specific palliative care training in their respective standard curricula.[27]

There is, however, a national Palliative Care Association of Latvia. Support for palliative care initiatives, as well as recognition for it, originates from, among others, the Latvian Physician's Society, the Ministry of Health, and the National Institute of the Society of Health. Financial support, in turn, has also been provided by the European Social Fund Programme and has been obtained through collaboration with the WHO, the European Association for Palliative Care, and other international organizations with a palliative-care agenda.[28]

In light of the increasing prevalence of non-communicable diseases, as also seen in Uganda, the need for palliative-care services is an ever-increasing one. This seems aggravated by the fact that the number of people dying from cancer in Latvia is decreasing.[29] Moreover, as will also be discussed below, people living in remote areas often struggle, both in terms of geographic access and in overcoming financial constraints, to access treatment in time. Yet, if an individual presents himself or herself at a late or fairly late stage in their disease, palliative care and, in particular, pain control is likely to be needed.[30] In addition to palliative care, much attention is focussed on drug-control policy and on the minimization of social harm caused by illicit drug use. Harm-reduction services are, moreover, considered effective healthcare services for drug users and are available throughout the country.[31]

7.4 Results and discussion

This section introduces the findings and the discussion of the results. It elaborates, among other aspects, on the implementation of specific international obligations, the background and context of controlled medicine use in Latvia, the supply/demand chain of controlled medicines (including morphine), the experiences of service providers, and the perceived challenges, if any, in working with specific drug-control

26 ibid 12.
27 Mitenbergs and others (n 17) 133.
28 L Radbruch and others, *Access to Opioid Medication in Europe: Final Report and Recommendations to the Ministries of Health* (Palliative Medicine Verlag 2014) 7.
29 WHO, 'Country Profiles – Latvia' (n 5).
30 Mitenbergs and others (n 17) 164-167.
31 See EMCDDA, 'National Drug Strategy' <www.emcdda.europa.eu/publications/country-overviews/lv> accessed 31 August 2016.

requirements. As was done in Chapter 6, the section analyses these findings in the context of the Availability, Accessibility, and Acceptability of healthcare services in accordance with human rights norms. Quality-related aspects, again as similar to the previous chapter, are not discussed despite being relevant to access to controlled medicines in its broadest form. Because they are absent in the Single Convention, however, such requirements are not discussed here.

7.4.1 Implementation of international human rights and drug-control standards

Although Latvia has ratified the most relevant international drug-control and human rights treaties, Section 7.3.2 clarified that international law takes precedence over domestic law even if an instrument has been signed but not ratified. Even though this makes the various international obligations analysed in previous chapters directly applicable in Latvia, it is important to note that a variety of national legislative acts include relevant provisions on the implementation of international drug-control treaties.[32]

In terms of human rights protection, it was generally observed that human rights protection in Latvia focuses on civil and political rights in particular. Bearing the country's Soviet history in mind, it comes as no surprise that language-related and citizen rights dominate both the public and the political discourse. Still, the right to health is an enforceable and justiciable right. In this respect, the WHO Representative noted that Latvia does not systematically review its domestic regulation in view of international law. However, Ministry of Health Representatives 1 and 2 also held that all Latvian laws comply with the relevant human rights norms.

7.4.2 Relevant policies and regulations to implement specific drug-control requirements

As the ATOME project revealed, the accessibility and availability of opioid medication for pain treatment – including morphine – is regulated by an overwhelming list of regulations.[33] Part of these regulations relate directly to the implementation of the aforementioned international drug-control requirements.

---

32 Law on Procedures for the Legal Trade of the Narcotic and Psychotropic Substances and Medicinal Products of 1996 (as amended); Pharmaceutical Law of 1997 (as amended); Law on Precursors of 1996 (as amended); Criminal Law of 1998 (as amended); Latvian Administrative Violations Code of 2007.

33 L Radbruch and others, *Report and Recommendations to the Ministries of Health Annex* (Palliative Medicine Verlag 2014).

In relation to the special administration, and the specific trade and distribution requirements, only physicians employed at medical treatment institutions are authorized to issue special prescriptions – i.e. prescriptions that include controlled medicines although still only up to a set maximum.[34] To issue such prescriptions, special forms must be used and the prescription should be registered in a registration journal. When doing so, an entry should, moreover, be included on the patient's chart or on their outpatient card. All special prescriptions should, in other words, be written out and, furthermore, should include a stamp of the medical institution/practitioner issuing it.[35]

Likewise, a strict accountability register should be kept on file for at least ten years and must be updated monthly.[36] Concretely, this means that each month it should be checked whether the stock that is said to remain on paper and the actual stock match. The outcome of this check is recorded in the register. To ensure that the accountability register is up to date, all special prescriptions issued during a day must be recorded at the end of said day.[37] In terms of authorization, only those medical treatment and/or social care institutions that have a special licence, issued by the Ministry of Health, are allowed to purchase controlled medicines from wholesalers or pharmacies.[38] Evidently, the institution in question is only permitted to do so for as long as the licence remains valid. Specific storage requirements dictate that controlled medicines are to be stored in a safe or metal locker, placed in a dedicated room, which is equipped with an alarm (sound or light) that during the absence of personnel is linked to the alarm system.[39]

Pharmacists also have to keep records on their purchases for a minimum of ten years and, similar to medical treatment centres, must keep an accountability register.[40] In the pharmacies, the pharmacist or their assistant shall include the name of the medicine, its dosage, the quantity, the date, and a signature or personal stamp.[41] In addition, special prescription forms with light red margins have to be used. It is prohibited to dispense controlled medicines on other forms.[42] Suspicious or forged prescriptions have to be kept separate and must be reported to the National Health

34 ibid 132, 134.
35 ibid 137-141.
36 ibid 140.
37 ibid 137-141.
38 ibid 142.
39 ibid 153.
40 ibid 148.
41 ibid 147-148.
42 ibid 137, 149-150.

Inspectorate (NHI) by the pharmacy's manager or whoever else holds the managerial responsibilities.[43]

Different dispensing privileges apply, including license requirements, and the NHI will examine the trade and distribution procedures in general-type pharmacies, medical treatment institutions without a closed-type pharmacy, and social care institutions that trade in or dispense controlled medicines.[44] In addition, in medical treatment centres only pharmacists who have been granted permission by the head of the institution are allowed to dispense opioid medication.[45] Finally, licence holders have an obligation to ensure that all data relating to the manufacturing and handling of controlled medicines is kept on file for a period of ten years and presented upon request of the NHI. The extracts, in turn, can be delivered in print or electronically and must both be dated and duly signed.[46]

To prevent non-compliance and prevent the requirements from being insufficiently adhered to, the following applies. As was mentioned earlier, an accountability register must be updated at the end of each day. Records of incorrect prescriptions, in other words, are kept on file. On the pharmacy level, the individual who has managerial responsibility must inform the NHI of any suspicious cases or cases where there are doubts about the validity of a prescription of controlled medicines.[47] The manager of the health institution in question must submit information on incorrect prescriptions, regarding the medical practitioner who issued the prescription, to the NHI.[48] In doing so, the NHI is able to keep track of any practitioners who make mistakes.

The state police have to be notified when a shortage or surplus in special prescriptions is detected, even if caused by natural disaster.[49] In this case, the manager of the institution where the error was found establishes a commission to investigate the matter and specify at least the type of incident, series of prescription forms (via their serial number), and the quantity involved.[50] Such a commission is to include at least the manager or authorized official responsible for the institution in question and a representative from both the State Sanitary Inspection and the NHI.[51]

43 ibid 150.
44 ibid 143-145, 147-152.
45 ibid 148.
46 ibid 148-149.
47 ibid 150-151.
48 ibid 159.
49 id.
50 ibid 160.
51 ibid 159-160.

In terms of data collection and reporting, pharmacies have to provide a variety of information to the State Agency of Medicines (SAM) when medicines have been dispensed or medical devices have been ordered by means of special prescription forms. Such information includes: the prescription series and number; the type of e-form, if applicable; the date on which the prescription was issued; the full name and personal identification number of the patient; the name of the medical treatment institution; the code of the diagnosis; the compensation percentage to be applied for insurance purposes; the name of the insurance company; the name of the medicinal products ordered; the code and quantity of the products; and the dispensing date.[52]

A pharmacy must, at least once a month, process all data concerning special prescriptions issued to the NHS.[53] Treatment facilities and social care institutions shall provide the SAM with quarterly updates on the consumption of listed controlled medicines at their establishment. The SAM, in turn, uses this information for the analysis and monitoring of narcotic and psychotropic medicinal products.[54] All in all, however, the aforementioned requirements only provide a glimpse into the long list of regulatory and administrative requirements applicable to the use of controlled medicines identified during the ATOME project.

7.4.3 Background and context of the domestic interpretation of drug-control requirements

It became clear during the interviews that Latvia's domestic drug-control system has largely been shaped by its Soviet era. In spite of their stringent nature, Ministry of Health Representative 2 indicated that regulations had previously been stricter. Elaborating on the interpretation of the specific regulations applicable, the respondent enunciated: *'take into account that we were previously in the USSR many years ago. There were very strict and strong regulations concerning narcotics'* (Ministry of Health Representative 2). Physician 1 confirmed that indeed regulations were 'very extremely strict', submitting that every ampoule (i.e. vial) of controlled medicines had to be checked individually so as to confirm its whereabouts or usage. Physician 3, also representing a professional organization, confirmed that the level of control in Latvia finds its roots in Soviet times but also highlighted that reform is on its way. The respondent held that *'[the] control system we have very strong [comes from] Soviet times. Unfortunately. But step-by-step, maybe it's getting better'* (Physician 3). Pharmacists 2 and 3 held Latvia to be conservative due to the country's Soviet history – it had been under Soviet rule for 50 years after all. Nevertheless, similar to

52 ibid 175.
53 ibid 151.
54 ibid 141.

the observation of Physician 3, these respondents observed that such conservative opinion was changing.

Whether reform is truly on the horizon or whether the aforementioned conservativeness is in fact changing, will be further elaborated on in the subsequent sections. Here, the local realities of service provision will be discussed in relation to Latvia's obligations under international law. First, however, it is worth noting that in light of the domestic interpretation of these rules, Ministry of Health Representatives 1 and 2 expressed their concern that 'outsiders' might deem the Latvian regulatory system too harsh, but, according to them, drug control must be strong. The respondents explained that practitioners are afraid that individuals other than the patient might consume the substances prescribed.

Such fear among practitioners, and the ensuing reluctance to prescribe controlled medicines, however, is paradoxical as it is also suggested to have its roots in the Soviet era. Briefly commenting on whether or not these procedures are considered as functional, purpose-fit, or by all any feasible tools to attain a certain regulatory goal, the WHO Representative said:

> *(...) again coming from our history from Soviet times when it was really prohibited and it was really very strong controlled (...) This still continues, and we see a lot of procedures, a lot of requirements, a lot of, in my mind, not always needed procedures and requirements, which really keeps doctors, you know, distant, reluctant. They do not want. Better not to start* (WHO Representative).

Not only the interviews, but also the meetings and interaction with a variety of actors in governmental and non-governmental settings, strongly suggested that the Latvian health system's strict regulation might be perpetuating a structural fear to prescribe. Generally, a culture of control and enforcement seems to reign in which individuals at different levels are afraid, refuse, or are just reluctant to take responsibility. In fact, Civil Society Representative 1 compared the health system to the army, suggesting that they both operate under a cloak of discipline and in the same hierarchical manner. When relating the former to the availability of controlled substances for medical use, the same respondent submitted that the need to control scheduled substances seems to outweigh the importance of their accessibility and availability. The respondent also perceived the consequences of control to be lessening, however. Civil Society Representative 1 held: *'maybe it* [i.e. the strict level of control] *has some kind of Soviet roots because it was harsh as well during Soviet times where everything was controlled. But it's still in place'* (Civil Society Representative 1). Yet, not all service providers agree on this. Similarly to the observations of Ministry of Health Representatives 1 and 2, Pharmacist 3 believed the current level of control to be fine and, in fact, endorsed its stringency.

Before investigating these local realities in more detail and elaborating on the respondents' views regarding the potential challenges faced, one must map an actor-specific outline of the supply/demand chain of morphine in Latvia. This overview will serve as a point of departure for the discussion of the implications of the administrative and procedural obligations contained in the Single Convention and will provide the contextualization needed to interpret this analysis.

7.4.4 Supply/demand chain of morphine

Participant observation and interviews with all different actors as identified allowed one to establish the regulatory supply/demand chain of morphine (see Figure 7.1).[55]

Figure 7.1 Latvia's supply/demand chain of morphine

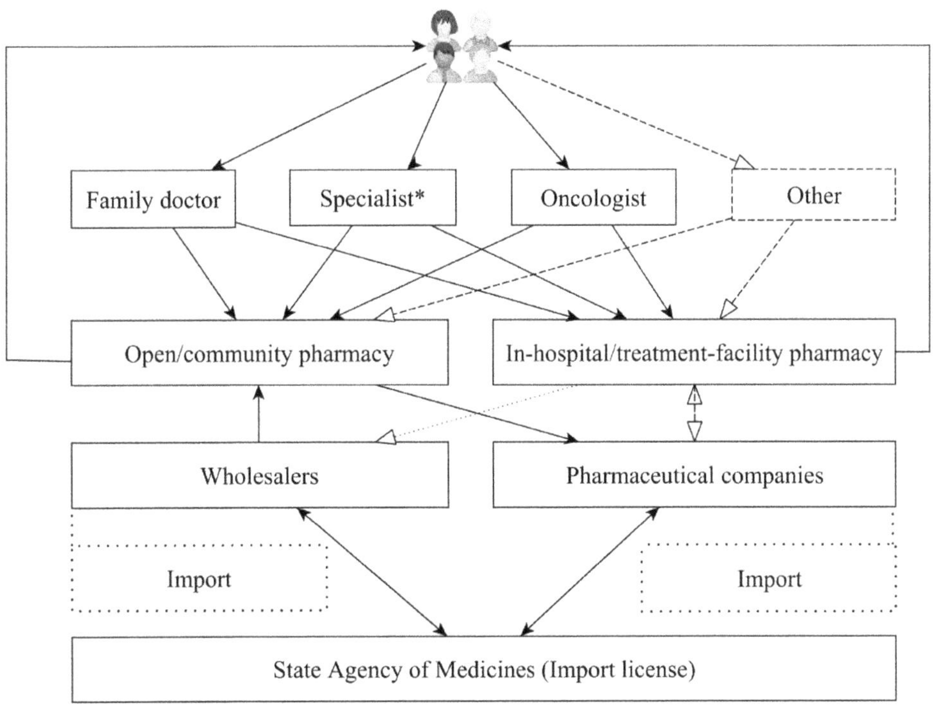

55 The asterisk behind 'specialist' indicates that medicines prescribed by an in-hospital specialist for an in-hospital patient is always reimbursed. Prescriptions by in-hospital specialists prescribing morphine for out-hospital patients, however, are not reimbursed if needed for other purposes than the diagnosis, as defined by the NHS.

A patient who, for example, has received a diagnosis for oncology-related or neuropathic pain can obtain full (100 per cent) reimbursement for their opioid medication, if prescribed by a licensed family doctor, an in-hospital specialist, or oncologist.[56] When one seeks medical assistance from another doctor, not classified as one of those mentioned above, or receives another diagnosis, the patient can obtain opioid medication but the NHS will not reimburse it. The category 'other' in Figure 7.1 demonstrates the supply/demand of such non-reimbursed morphine for pain treatment.

Patients can pick up their special prescriptions, including those for controlled medication, at licensed in-hospital pharmacies or at open pharmacies. This means that not all pharmacies are licensed to stock and purchase controlled medicines. If the licensed facility does not have the required medicine on stock – or if it is unavailable altogether – it can place an order with a wholesaler or pharmaceutical company. Pharmacies carry out a cost/effectiveness analysis via questionnaires to determine which pharmaceutical company or wholesaler is most suitable to acquire the product from. These suppliers, also wholesalers or pharmaceutical companies, must possess a special licence issued by the SAM to operate. In the event of stock-out, open pharmacies can turn to wholesalers, if necessary. Suppliers, moreover, can apply for an import permit with the SAM after which they can import controlled medicines and fulfil their role in the supply chain, as discussed above.

7.4.5 Implications of managing a separate administration and specific trade and distribution requirements

The consequences of managing a separate administration and specific trade and distribution requirements affect one part of the supply/demand chain outlined in Figure 7.1. As indicated by the envelopes, Figure 7.2 visualizes the stage in the supply/demand chain at which specific requirements apply.[57]

---

56 Similarly to the supply/demand chain of Uganda (see Chapter 6, Section 6.4.3), an out-of-stock situation is taken as the example to reveal all, if any, actor-specific regulatory responsibilities that exist. Moreover, like for Uganda, individual patients have neither been included in the overview nor been studied due to their lack of regulatory authority – despite being the primary rights holders central to this book.

57 Similar to Figure 7.1, the asterisk behind 'specialist' indicates that medicines prescribed by an in-hospital specialist for an in-hospital patient is always reimbursed. Prescriptions by in-hospital specialists prescribing morphine for out-hospital patients, however, are not reimbursed if needed for other purposes than the diagnosis, as defined by the NHS.

Figure 7.2 Latvia's separate administration and specific trade and distribution requirements

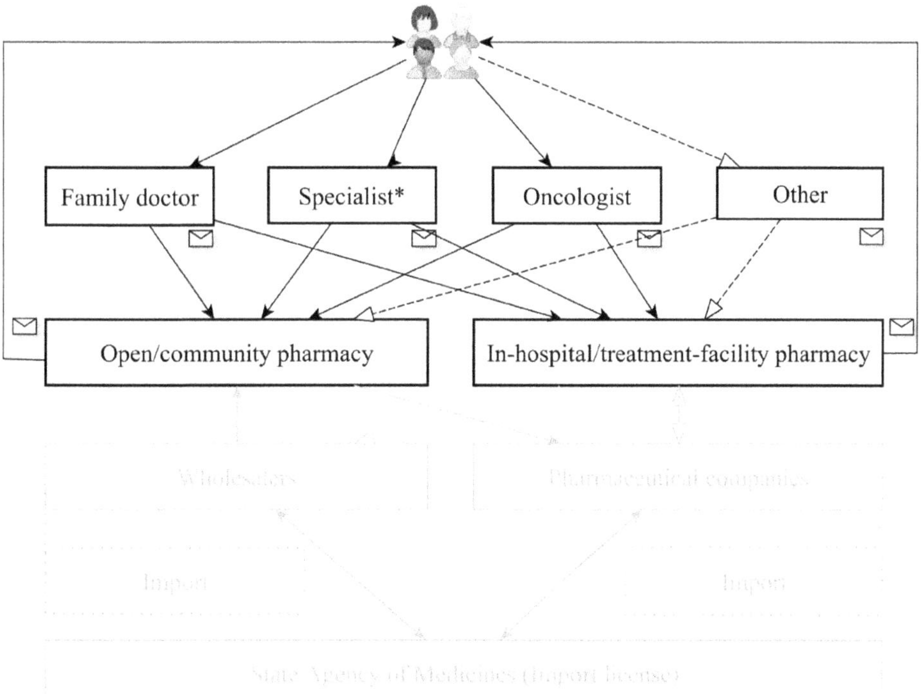

In short, prescribers must use special prescription forms. For such forms to be filled out correctly, they need to be handwritten and to include both a stamp of the health facility at which the prescriber is employed and a stamp that contains the individual prescriber's professional information. Each special prescription should be registered in the registration journal and a reference should be included on the patient's chart. Pharmacists have to manage an accountability register that is updated daily to list the new special prescription forms handled and issued. This special administration is to be kept on file for a period of ten years. Overall, licence requirements apply to pharmacists and regulate their ability to order controlled medicines from wholesalers or pharmaceutical companies (issued by the SAM). As mentioned in Section 7.4.4, medicines are only reimbursed by the NHS if prescribed for oncological or neuropathic pain, in in-hospital settings, and by a licensed family doctor, oncologist, or hospital specialist. Various problems have been observed concerning the implementation of a range of regulations and policies applicable.

Geographic accessibility and NHS contracts

The first problem relates to geographic accessibility and contracts with the NHS. The NHS Representative explained that only a limited number of doctors and pharmacists have reimbursement contracts with the NHS. A patient, the NHS Representative continued, can only receive reimbursement for their pain-control medication e.g. for oncology care in an outpatient setting, when obtaining the prescription from and submitting it to a doctor and pharmacist who have such a contract. The NHS Representative described that the NHS' contracting policy is based on a quota of practitioners per defined regions. When seeing a prescriber who does not have the aforementioned contract, the patient must therefore pay out-of-pocket. Bearing the economic crisis of 2008 and its aftermath in mind, heightened out-of-pocket payments are likely to affect at least the affordability aspect of accessible care. Moreover, while perhaps not necessarily a problem in Riga, the limited distribution of NHS reimbursement contracts in remote areas might further lead to complications with respect to geographic accessibility.

According to the NHS Representative, pharmacists, especially those located in the countryside, have a considerable interest in obtaining an NHS contract due to the accompanying income stability. Whereas the NHS Representative was rather positive about the current policy in place, Pharmacist 1 noted that there are only a few pharmacies in Riga licensed to dispense controlled medicines. At the same time, the respondent held this to not present a problem since patients know at which pharmacies controlled medicines can be purchased and no stock-outs have been experienced in Riga itself. The story is different for rural areas. Civil Society Representative 1 revealed that in these areas there is a general lack of pharmacies and, in particular, a shortage of those authorized to stock controlled medicines. In practice, this lack means that patients have to reach out to local centres to collect their medicines, making medication unavailable exactly where they are needed most.

Bureaucracy and customized procedures

The second problem is the large quantity of paperwork at odds with the daily realities of service provision and the continuous struggle the Latvian health system experiences in terms of human resources. The large number of regulations leads to the adoption of a wide range of internal procedures, which may differ per institution, that aim to facilitate compliance with the system's regulatory requirements.

Civil Society Representative 1 provided an example of the dispensing of controlled medicines by an in-hospital pharmacy. As illustrated before, a licensed pharmacy has to maintain an accountability register. Such a register is, in essence, an internal reviewing procedure to ensure that appropriate accounting of dispensed controlled medicines takes place. If an in-hospital pharmacy dispenses controlled medicines to a patient on one of the hospital's wards, the head nurse on duty must register the action in a designated journal – it remained unclear, however, which journal the respondent referred to exactly, since numerous journals ought to be kept at various stages of the supply/demand chain. When controlled medicines are disposed of, in addition, each ampoule has to be accounted for individually. The head of the ward, in turn, reviews the journal each week. Then, an internally established committee goes around the hospital to crosscheck the actual number of controlled medicines with those recorded in said journal.

National regulations do not mandate such frequent crosschecking. Yet, according to Civil Society Representative 1, the applicable national regulations do dictate a monthly review of the onward accounting and checks of the absolute amounts in stock. There, in other words, might be some discretion as to how a hospital implements the various requirements (since the above only reflects an example). Discussing the functionality of the process, Civil Society Representative 1 proclaimed that *'it is just a big bureaucracy actually. It takes so much time. I'm with the committee that goes around the hospital each month. It takes two days actually and that's two days in a month we have to do this (...) I see a great burden here'* (Civil Society Representative 1). There seems to be no direct purpose other than administration for the sake of administration and Civil Society Representative 1 questioned whether the data collected is of much value in itself. Exactly because it was considered a waste of time, the hospital committee referred to above had agreed amongst itself that quarterly, instead of monthly, checks would suffice. In doing so, the hospital does not strictly observe national regulations.

On a similar note, pharmacists adopt customized internal procedures to comply with the obligation to update the strict accountability register daily. Despite the fact that the accountability register in theory is to be updated at the end of each day, Pharmacists 2 and 3 noted that all their accounting is done at the end of the month. Updating the register tends to involve a lot of extra paperwork. Pharmacist 6 indicated, for instance, that *'usually, you should do it every day, but we usually do it on Saturday'* (Pharmacist 6). In this respect, Civil Society Representative 1 observed *'the procedures* [for] *scheduled drugs are quite, I would say, burdensome. They are creating a big burden and a big bureaucracy around them'* (Civil Society Representative 1).

What becomes clear from the above is that controlling the dispensing of medicines to avoid diversion of controlled medicines through illicit channels seems to be prioritized over the access to controlled substances in Latvia's medical system. The requirement to account for every ampoule of a controlled medicine exemplifies how strenuous the burden on the staff can be, and even unrealistic. Civil Society Representative 1 used atropine, utilized frequently in surgical wards, as a concrete example. The respondent held that when raising such issues with the Ministry of Health, the latter claims to be unable to change anything and refers one to the police instead. Confirming the bureaucracy involved in the recording procedure, Physician 2 reiterated that:

> *(...) actually, this accounting system and this registration of prescription forms is really stupid. You know how much work it is to register all those prescription forms? It is stupid and we have been arguing about this for many years. But we still have, the Soviet bureaucracy is not leaving us, even after 25 years* (Physician 2).

However, not all service providers experience the stringent regulatory requirements in a negative manner. Pharmacist 5 regarded the applicable regulations not to be strict but to be normal. According to this respondent, it is not difficult to comply with any regulatory requirements. The prevalence of narcotics abuse, furthermore, makes compliance even less problematic. This respondent, thus, seemed to link the purpose of the recording requirements with the overall goal and ambition of drug control and did not question whether the specific requirements were purpose-fit. Along the same line of reasoning, Physician 5 held that the special booklets in fact made it much easier to forecast how much morphine, for instance, would be needed for the next three days. Moreover, this respondent described that it really only takes seconds to write down all the required data, as you can prepare the information on the basis of the case histories.

Although service providers remain divided on whether or not the bureaucracy involved hampers the access to medicines and adequate treatment in practice, one cannot conclude *a priori* that these rules complicate the accessibility and availability of controlled medicines. However, as described in subsequent subsections, one can state that if the bureaucratic process indeed frustrates the daily work of service providers, it at least does not foster the provision of medicines (as is the case in Uganda).

Fear of non-compliance and a negative compliance incentive

Linked to the special registration and accounting requirements is the fear that if perceived burdensome, the irritation could foster reluctance among prescribers and dispensers alike to prescribe or dispense controlled medication at all. A secondary problem, in this respect, is the fear of non-compliance and the creation of a negative compliance incentive, i.e. accepting to meet the applicable regulations in a manner contrary to the regulation. These issues may, like the bureaucracy relating to the administrative requirements, hamper instead of promote the access to medicines.

The Latvian NHI is the designated body responsible for the enforcement of the special administrative procedures (see Figure 7.3).

Figure 7.3 Latvia's monitoring and enforcement mandates

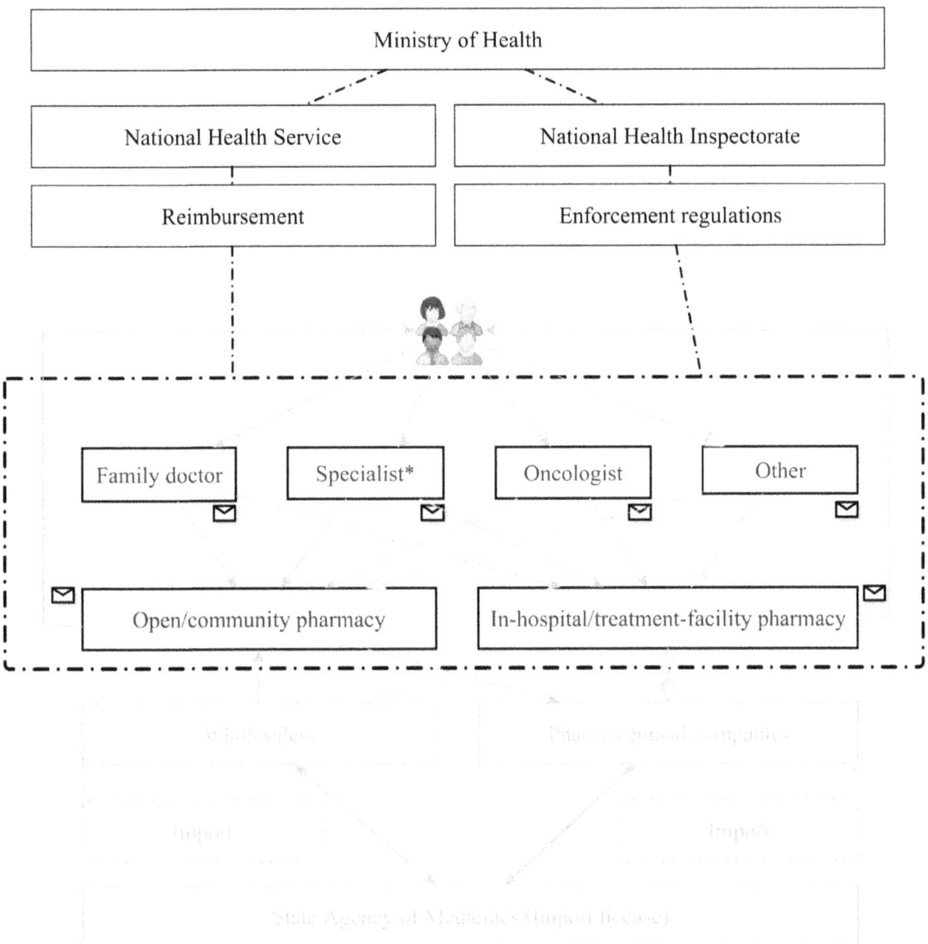

Attributing the lack of trust in institutions to the days of Soviet rule, the WHO Representative confirmed that the NHI is indeed enforcing compliance with the administrative procedures and continued to add that *'(...) if there is something wrong, and you always can find something wrong, then there are penalties and they will be introduced'* (WHO Representative).

Generally service providers fear non-compliance and some develop a negative compliance incentive. Physician 3 indicated, for instance, that controlled medicines are sometimes not prescribed due to the accompanying administrative burden. According to this respondent, the underlying cause is not the know-how of these physicians, but rather them feeling unsafe in the system. This respondent revealed that *'[t]here is always fear, doctors don't feel free to raise an issue with the health inspectorate'* (Physician 3). The respondent continued to explain that many sanctions apply, which mainly constitute fines or administrative protocols. In light of these enforcement mechanisms, however, Physician 3 emphasized: *'I repeat once more, because these controls don't link with the content of our work with bureaucratic mistakes. I know that we are very busy and we have really human mistakes (...) It is normal. I am not God'* (Physician 3).

Likewise, the NHS Representative declared in this respect that *'there were some pharmacies who don't like these recipes (...) because they have special requirements for it'* (NHS Representative). Similarly, the SAM Representative clarified that not many wholesalers are interested in dispensing controlled medicines exactly because of the strict nature of the applicable regulations. Civil Society Representative 1, moreover, remarked in this respect:

> *(...) for a very big part, yes. That's a factor. I mean even for physicians it's an additional burden if they want to prescribe scheduled medicines (...) It's really burdensome. I guess they are quire reluctant (...) But we put just restrictions on restrictions to make it look quite harder to deliver* (Civil Society Representative 1).

Physician 2 submitted that in particular in-hospital specialists do not want to be bothered with the hassle of paperwork and, therefore, either refer a patient to a GP or ask the GP to write a special prescription on their behalf. In the event of the latter, the problem then is, according to the respondent, that a doctor cannot prescribe medication without tending to the patient first.

While, as indicated earlier, other respondents do not perceive the administrative requirements to be burdensome because the Latvian health system is generally strictly controlled, Physician 2 pointed out that the special administrative requirements embed a certain fear of governmental oversight and for the consequences of non-compliance. Yet, in contrast, even though the prescription of controlled medicines is subject to strong bureaucracy, Civil Society Representative 1 held that this neither always creates a reluctance to prescribe nor does it hamper the access to medicines. Still, in relation to the potentially embedded fear, the respondent admitted that:

> *(...) of course there are physicians who just use this system* [i.e. the administrative requirements] *as a basis for not prescribing. That's what they say or tell the patients.*

It's not so easy or it's so complicated. Then we'll try to stay out of it. I guess it could specifically apply for general practitioners because hospital physicians and specialists actually they feel much safer (...) [i.e. in-hospital physicians] *have more people to cover them* (Civil Society Representative 1).

Indeed, Physician 3 declared that GPs do not feel safe to prescribe controlled medication due to the intensive control system enforced by the government. This respondent expressed that *'they* [i.e. family doctors] *don't feel safe to prescribe because we have big control system from government if we prescribe these medicines. We have very very controlled systems not horizontal level but vertical'* (Physician 3). In this respect, the respondent observed that if GPs were to refrain from prescribing controlled medicines, then the access to these medicines would be complicated in practice.

Discussing the matter at the national level shows a different perspective, however. For instance, Ministry of Health Representatives 1 and 2 stated that although one could claim that in theory the administrative requirements present a burden, practice shows an entirely different picture. In their view, strict control is beneficial to service providers as it raises awareness and forces them to take a precautionary approach when dealing with controlled-medicine prescriptions. The respondents emphasised their argument by remarking that the Ministry of Health had not received any complaints about the special administrative requirements – or its burdensome nature. On the contrary, the officials emphasized that the visual effect of the coloured special prescription forms assists physicians in their work. Whereas the Ministry of Health Representatives referred to the colour coding of the special prescription booklet as an aid, Pharmacists 4 and 5 referred to the same labels as warnings instead.

In terms of the regulatory requirements posing an additional barrier to the delivery of palliative care, which on its own is already considered to be time-intensive treatment, Ministry of Health Representative 2 said: *'the question is whether we also see complaints from doctors, from pharmacists. But there were no complaints'* (Ministry of Health Representative 2). However, the WHO Representative held that constraints are both a theoretical possibility under the current regulatory framework and a practical reality. Complaints on this issue simply have not reached the Ministry of Health. There, perhaps worryingly, is a lack of trust in this respect, which became particularly evident through a comment by Physician 3 that read: *'I have no trust to speak about this field with the Ministry* [of Health] *because we are at the opposite sides'* (Physician 3).

Recognizing this same fear of control and enforcement, Pharmacist 6 explained that the NHI should conduct its checks every two years – especially because the pharmacy at which the respondent was employed also produces prescription medicines. The respondent revealed, furthermore, that there was much tension amongst the staff, as it had been two years since the last NHI visit and a follow-up was expected at any time. At the time of research, the pharmacy in question had not detected any errors in their accounting system. Admittedly, the reason could be their expectation to be audited soon by the NHI. In fact, the respondent clarified that the staff was rather tense and particularly careful in their dispensing behaviour. All prescriptions were double-checked to see if the correct information had been included and to prevent false prescriptions from being honoured. Their tense behaviour, according to the respondent, in this particular case was caused by the fear of losing their licence.

Civil Society Representative 1 elaborated on this fear, highlighting that the hospital's internal quality assurance committee, according to the regulations, is obliged to report any accounting mistakes to the police. In other words, committee members are mandated to report colleagues who make such mistakes to the police. The same respondent continued to reveal that such harsh requirements lead to serious concern and distress amongst committee members. Such concern, the respondent indicated, was caused by the magnitude of regulations that are applicable and must be adhered to.

When drawing a clearer picture of the intensity of control enforcement and the accompanying fears, Ministry of Health Representative 1 referred once more to the Soviet period in which one could be imprisoned if even a single ampoule was lost. According to the respondent, it is precisely due to this past that service providers choose not to complain about the present level of enforcement.

Even though fear seems to be widespread in the practical application of specific drug-control requirements, not many mistakes are detected at the national level. Moreover, Ministry of Health Representatives 1 and 2 held little diversion to be reported in the country. In other words, they submitted that misuse is infrequent and substances dispensed on the legal market do not end up in illegal channels. Pharmacist 1 also observed that mistakes were hardly ever detected. More pragmatically, Pharmacist 2 and 3 noted that a patient always gets their medication, even if in a rush there is no time to fill out all the paperwork. In such a case, the pharmacy at which the respondents' work would ensure that, at the end of the day, all regulations were complied with. Moreover, Pharmacists 4 and 5 confessed that at times the prescribing doctor had to be contacted to verify mistakes in the prescription.

Yet, given the highly restrictive nature of the regulatory system and the fear relating to its enforcement, a negative compliance incentive seems to have developed in the system, meaning that the law is circumvented in order to comply with it. For instance,

Pharmacist 6 disclosed that at the pharmacy where the respondent works, staff tries to fix any mistakes internally first. The respondent set out that:

> *(...) after we find that we made a mistake,* [we] *go to the doctor and ask them to prescribe a prescription for us. If* [we have] *given out too many or something like that. But we don't have many mistakes in that... Usually we somehow make a deal 'please cover our assess' (...) Usually willing to help us (...) I have never done it because I am too young to get any of those* [connections]. *The older colleague, she does every two, three months to get her eye prescription, she has heart disease problem. She has better communication with her doctor. So, she usually asks* (Pharmacist 6).

Although it does not happen often, the respondent essentially described a violation of the law that has the aim to facilitate compliance with said law. Similarly, Civil Society Representative 1 said that one could always play the system. According to this respondent, many wards keep a small extra stock of controlled medicines just in case an ampoule breaks. This stock is kept off the record and has the aim to simplify the procedure when mistakes do occur.

The question remains, however, what this all means in terms of the availability and accessibility of medicines. While a reluctance to do paperwork may indeed complicate a patient's access to medicines, it cannot be claimed with the same ease that the fear of non-compliance and a negative compliance incentive have the same outcome. Not having the intention to establish causal relationship in this part of the book, the above rather emphasises a similar question raised in Chapter 6: What is the purpose of the regulation, and is the regulation implemented fit to reach its own goal? This indirectly relates to the accessibility and availability of medicines because if these regulations are indeed ineffective, their inability to ensure that their own purposes are achieved hampers the availability of controlled substances, including morphine for pain treatment.

Storage facilities

A final problem is related to storage facilities. Controlled medicines must be stored in a safe or metal locker, and an alarm system is mandatory. Civil Society Representative 1 signalled, however, that some pharmacies purposefully choose not to apply for a special licence for the distribution of controlled substances because of their inability to comply with such a secure storage requirement. Physician 2, in addition, indicated that by law it is mandatory to keep special prescription booklets in a safe also. This, according to the respondent, is reminiscent of so-called 'Soviet bureaucracy'. Clearly upset with the rigorous regulatory framework, the respondent held: *'it is enough, because I cannot buy a safe. If someone wants me to keep it in safe, I say please provide me with a safe and I'll keep in the safe, because it is stupid'* (Physician 2).

Financial limitations, in other words, can pose a serious problem in one's attempt to comply with the storage requirements.

Nevertheless, according to Physician 2, the alternative, i.e. not keeping prescription booklets in a safe, would mean violating the rules if the same logic were applied. This respondent, however, dismissed this, referring to the purpose of the regulation. According to the respondent, even if one were to keep the prescription booklets outside a safe, the practitioner could still be complying with the purpose of the law. Physician 2 held, for example, that *'I worked with lawyers and I have the system that ensures that no one can steal prescription forms. And that's the main thing'* (Physician 2).

Pharmacist 6, furthermore, pointed out that the pharmacy for which the respondent worked resembled a collection of boxes due to the amount of paperwork that has to be stored for a long period of time. According to this respondent, both normal prescriptions and special prescriptions have to be kept for one year and three years respectively, whereas accounting journals must be kept in secured storage for five to ten years, depending on the journal. Ultimately, the underlying question relates to the purpose of an obligation, so as to assess which tools best serve its realization. This having been said, Civil Society Representative 1 suggested, as was also stated by other respondents, that inefficient, inconsistent, or even over-enforcement of controlled-medicine regulations does not prevent people from getting their medication. This last point, however, is questioned in light of the observation that the control procedures create a fear of non-compliance and a reluctance to prescribe among service providers, which evidently do affect the access to medicines in practice.

7.4.6 Implications of data collection, analysis, and reporting procedures

Similarly to the special administrative requirements, and specific trade and distribution regulations, data collection, analysis, and reporting obligations are reflected in the morphine supply/demand chain. Figure 7.4 demonstrates at which stage of the chain the collected information is used. Consequently, the figure also demonstrates when information is not used. The envelopes indicate the exact stage in the process at which specific administrative requirements apply, as relevant to the study.

Figure 7.4 Latvia's data collection, analysis, and reporting procedures

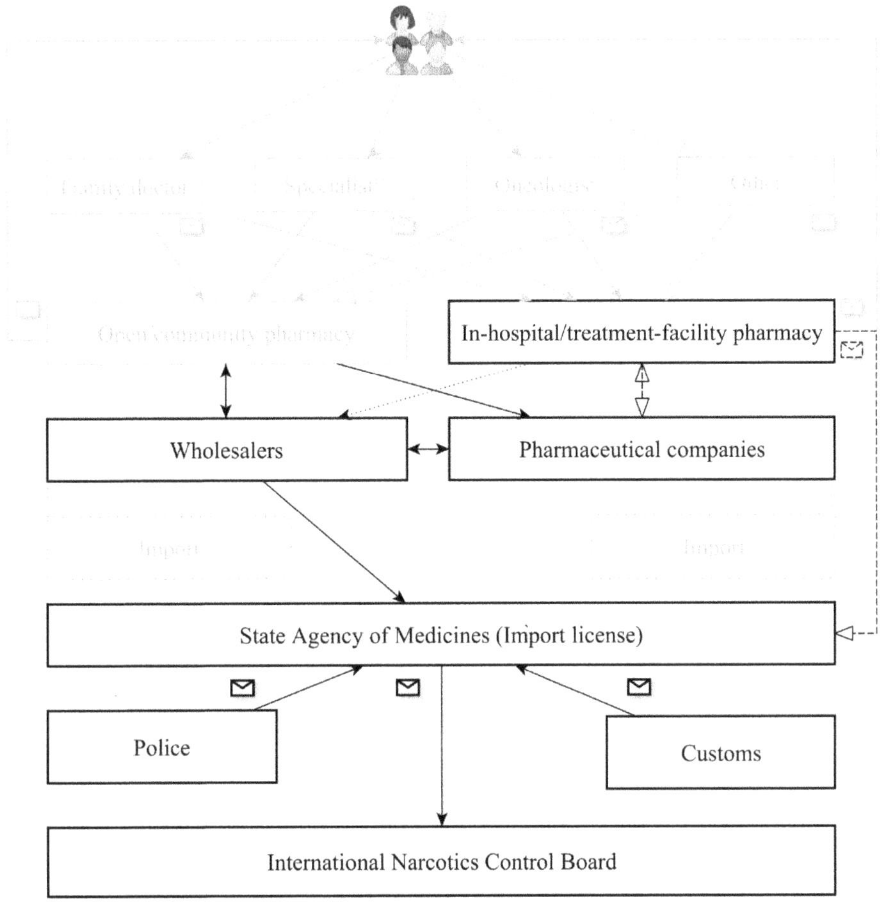

As also summarized in Chapter 6, the WHO and the International Narcotics Control Board (INCB) recommend States to base their estimates on a combination of consumption and morbidity-based data. After a discussion of the estimation techniques used, the SAM Representative revealed that Latvia bases its estimates on a combination of data about import/export licences and the illegal consumption of medicines (obtained from customs and police). On this basis, the SAM develops consumption statistics that are compiled in a report submitted to the INCB. With respect to the method used to compile the data, the representative explained: *'we calculate estimates from previous years and then calculate how many we need this quantity, how many quantity we need (...) Every year we calculate the last three years consumption, and multiply'* (SAM Representative).

The SAM collects data from wholesalers who record their information through a special portal. The purpose hereof is *'only* [to compare] *(...) how much wholesalers said that they sell to* [a] *pharmacy* [with, on the part of the] *(...) pharmacy how much they used'* (SAM Representative). In addition, the SAM also gathers data from hospitals on their opioid-medicine consumption. As the SAM Representative explained, however, this last set of data, collected in the form of a Microsoft Excel spreadsheet, is not used to produce estimates. Staff shortages prevent a full analysis of the hospital data collected from taking place. According to the respondent, although the SAM cannot analyse the additional data collected, the representative confirmed that it continues to collect this information because the law requires it to do so. The respondent, furthermore, went on to state *'I think that it is* [a] *need for* [the] *future, because we will* [move towards an] *electronic* [system] *(...) And then these data collects in all system. And then this data will be used'* (SAM Representative).[58] Hence with this extra information, the SAM aims to gain better insight into the in-hospital consumption patterns. If supplementary estimates are needed to increase coverage, the SAM Representative submitted this to be a mere formality since, despite being different every year, such supplementary estimates are included in the annual overviews.

It may be difficult to obtain data in many countries where the opioid consumption data seemingly reflects a gap between the country's estimated absolute need and its registered consumption. Civil Society Representative 1 indicated this to be paradoxical, because the majority of relevant epidemiological data, which could accommodate forecasted ordering, is collected through the reimbursement system of the NHS. This data, however, is not used beyond the financial aspect. The data in question includes the geographical dispersion of the controlled-medicine demand and patient diagnoses, which could be relevant to bridge the supposed gap between the absolute need and the registered consumption in Latvia. To put it bluntly, according to the respondent, the NHS data collected is not used to forecast demand out of fear of the control system.

According to the SAM Representative, the country has never experienced problems with its calculations and estimates. In fact, the respondent believed that:

> *(...) that our system is very good. We see all demands and estimates, consumption we see all together, and I think our system is good from this point of view. We received all information about it, and we see all situations in our country (...) but we see only high level* (SAM Representative).

---

58 The SAM Representative also explained that there is no need to collect additional data on all out-hospital settings. The pharmacy data, the representative highlighted, is already included in the data the wholesalers submit during the special entry.

Concretely, the SAM does not have insight into the consumption figures at facility level. Regardless, the SAM Representative deemed the current system adequate because all information on e.g. imports, exports, consumption data, and information on wholesalers and licences issued is shared and compiled into reports. In fact, the respondent proclaimed that in the event of any mistakes or incoherencies in the data collected, any issue could be resolved. In contrast, Civil Society Representative 1 emphasized that not only does the data remain untouched in the NHS system, the data that is analysed is merely analysed superficially. However, this respondent also acknowledged that an internal discussion had been initiated at the Ministry of Health on how to use the collected data in a more advanced manner. Yet, actual progress has not been made yet, as improvement of data analysis is not considered a priority by the Ministry.

Pharmacist 1 indicated that complexities present itself in relation to the accuracy of forecasting at open pharmacies. Forecasting concerns whether or not orders reflect as much as possible the absolute need of the country. These needs, moreover, must take special note of vulnerable and marginalized groups whose interests should be protected with priority under human rights law. According to the respondent, open pharmacies – i.e. non-hospital pharmacies – lack insight into the number of patients purchasing controlled medicines at their facility. This lack, in turn, prevents open pharmacies from managing their stock in an efficient manner. This respondent claims that this is mainly due to the rigid legislative framework applicable to controlled medicines. In contrast, Pharmacists 4 and 5 denied said deficiency and claimed that there is always stock, regardless of the demand levels the pharmacy is confronted with.

Yet, similarly to the concerns raised in the context of Uganda, it seems problematic to solely rely on consumption data when a significant segment of the population might struggle to visit a licensed health facility or doctor due to the geographic inaccessibility of such facilities. Although this structural constraint in itself might challenge service provision, it might also compromise the principle of non-discrimination, as exactly the needs of those e.g. living in remote areas should be secured with priority. In cases where relevant epidemiological data that can be used to produce a forecast is simply unavailable, such as in Uganda, arriving at adequate estimates is structurally challenging and the unfeasibility of adequately complying with the estimation requirement is part of a larger structural problem.

Along this same line of reasoning, one does not blame a country for inadequately discharging its obligations under international law, but rather challenges international law because a country is unable to effectively discharge its obligations. Despite this logic, the case of Latvia is rather the contrary because country-specific epidemiological data is collected but not used nor prioritized.

It is clear that in countries struggling to provide access to health facilities, focusing on consumption data is difficult. However, the simple decision of Latvia not to use otherwise available data which one could use to forecast the need of those unable to reach health facilities may in itself be a breach of the principle of non-discrimination. In order to further substantiate and interpret this point, some key challenges to the service provision in Latvia are discussed below.

7.4.7 Some key challenges to the provision of controlled medicines

As was also seen in Uganda, even if some respondents hold the administrative requirements to be incorporated into their daily tasks not to be an extra burden, other general and specific challenges, both structural and temporary, may well result in these administrative and procedural obligations hindering effective service provision.

Fear of abuse

The first challenge specifically related to controlled medicines, although structural in Latvia, is the fear of abuse. As the WHO Representative succinctly distinguished, any fear in relation to controlled medicines should be broken down into fear of dependence, on the one hand, and fear of enforcement of the applicable regulations, on the other. In relation to the dependency-related and abuse-related fear, as was addressed in Section 7.4.3, Ministry of Health Representatives 1 and 2 both indicated that outsiders might consider the Latvian regulations too strict. The representatives implied that the regulations must be strict because practitioners are worried that individuals other than the patients might consume the controlled medicines too. In spite of the impact that the control procedures have on the access to controlled medicines, Physician 2 clarified that those working in the system are used to the level of control. Bearing in mind, moreover, the prevalence of addiction in countries such as the United States of America, the respondent referred to the care that physicians must take to prevent people from becoming addicted to controlled substances.

The SAM Representative, furthermore, addressed the fear of dependence as a potential challenge to service provision. According to this respondent, there is an increase in demand and this could well lead to an increase in consumption. The problem, the respondent pointed out, is that doctors do not prescribe the medicine. While this is mainly attributed to the reluctance to work with the control procedures enforced, such non-prescribing behaviour is also partly due to an ingrained fear to facilitate or instigate dependence.

Additionally, Pharmacist 6 identified a key challenge to be the fear that still exists among GPs to prescribe controlled medicines. In contrast, however, Physician 2 noted in relation to doctors' prescription behaviour that the high dosages of opioid medication registered in the country is the key issue. This respondent declared that if lower dosages or formulas were allowed in the country, it would become easier or more comfortable for doctors to prescribe, in turn combating the fear of abuse.

Perceptions of pain and controlled-medicine use

Another substance-specific, yet seemingly structural challenge Latvia's health system is confronted with, is the perception of pain and the use of controlled medicines. Civil Society Representative 1 held that there are still many myths about the use of controlled medicines. According to this respondent, the dominant perception in society is that *'when you're real, you have to have pain'* (Civil Society Representative 1). This means that pain is 'part of the deal' and people can live without medication. In fact, the respondent stated that *'not all physicians realize that every pain should be relieved'* (Civil Society Representative 1). Instead, the representative explained, there have been instances in which patients who did receive treatment and consumed controlled medicines were made to feel bad about it.

Similarly to the dominant perception amongst Ugandan patients, Physician 2 observed that many patients regard the use of morphine as meaning that one is in the final stage of life, making the provision of adequate treatment increasingly complex. In this respect, the use of controlled medicines, including morphine, remains greatly stigmatized. Physician 1 traced this perception of pain back to Soviet times as well. This respondent held that during that time, hardly any pain control was available so patients would, for example, have to wait until the next day to receive additional assistance if the treatment they had received proved inadequate to alleviate the pain experienced.

False and stolen prescriptions

A third structural yet substance-specific challenge is that of false or stolen prescriptions, which require pharmacists to be particularly cautious when dispensing controlled medicines. As mentioned, some respondents asserted that the administrative requirements do not necessarily lead to *de facto* denial of access to controlled medicines. They emphasise the importance of strict control in light of the country's considerable black market for non-medical use of prescription medicines. Physician 1 noted, for instance, that all elements of special prescription forms are equally important and vital to identify which prescriptions are copied or stolen.

Pharmacists 2 and 3 explained, for example, to be extra cautious and that, when anything inconsistent or suspicious is discerned on a prescription, the doctor is contacted. Unfortunately, false or stolen prescriptions constitute a larger problem than general mistakes. The respondents explained that they are occasionally informed by the NHS about a pack of stolen special prescription forms circulating on the black market. As all special prescriptions are numbered, the NHS provides them with the range of numbers stolen to ensure that none of these prescriptions are used. However, copies are sometimes so realistic that it is difficult to distinguish between false and real prescriptions. Not only are pharmacists informed about stolen forms, they also flag suspicious prescriptions themselves. Pharmacists 2 and 3 provided the example of a doctor who kept issuing the same controlled medicines to the same patient, leading them to question whether the prescription was stolen. To check their suspicions, they called the doctor who answered that the prescription was correct and to not contact him again. This incident suggests that doctors also have the ability to corrupt the system, should they wish to do so; Pharmacist 2 said *'if everything is cool, I'm cool too'* (Pharmacist 2).

While in this case the actual availability and accessibility of medicines seems to be unhampered, it was observed that false prescriptions could lead to fear or cause pharmacists to feel unsafe at work. This, in turn, could also result in them being wary of dispensing controlled medicines. As Pharmacist 6 indicated *'almost every day we get these fake receipt (...) Since they come in the evening and usually you're alone in the evening, we don't have a guard or nothing; just do not pull a fuss. Just send them away. We have to say that we were out of it'* (Pharmacist 6). In terms of detection, Pharmacists 4 and 5 described that if customers cannot provide detailed information, such as personal identification or names when asked, this gives them a warning to be more cautious. However, once detected, Pharmacist 6 said it involves too much bureaucracy to report the detection of false prescriptions to the NHI.

In general, Civil Society Representative 1 stated that pharmacists fear drug users coming in with false prescriptions, which makes them feel unsafe and in danger. This respondent explained that there are areas in Riga known for drug users using false prescriptions visiting pharmacies. While acknowledging that there is a valid basis for the fear of such false prescriptions, this respondent suggested that it is also a bit exaggerated. According to the respondent, in day-to-day practice this fear is a distant reality for many and only valid for some. Nevertheless, false prescriptions might fuel concern and reluctance to dispense controlled medicines, including morphine. If this is the case, this could indirectly hamper the access to adequate care, including morphine for pain treatment. Moreover, the issue of fear of false prescriptions goes hand-in-hand with the lack of human resources in Latvia's health system.

Human resources

Throughout all interviews, it became clear that one of the key challenges in Latvia's health system is the lack of human resources. It is a general challenge that could also affect the provision of controlled medicines. Respondents identified two issues, namely: (i) the lack of staff; and (ii) the brain drain to other European countries resulting from the decreasing salaries in Latvia. In this respect, Physician 1 held that the country's uneven doctor-to-patient ratio results in an excessive workload, as their practice contains a disproportionate number of patients.

Respondents indicated that it is not so much doctors' willingness or fear regarding the prescription of opioid medication that limits controlled-medicine provision, but the workload instead. As was true for the observations in Uganda, it may very well be that the burdensome nature of the regulatory requirements related to prescribing and dispensing controlled medicines are aggravated in light of the workload that service providers face due to understaffing.

Financial resources

Latvia, furthermore, faces structural constraints in health-system financing, which constitutes a general yet structural challenge, aggravating the complexities related to the provision of controlled medicines, including morphine. Ministry of Health Representatives 1 and 2 submitted that the annual health budget is too low and out-of-pocket payments are too high. The NHS Representative explained that Latvia's health-financing system is based on a limited list of diagnoses or diseases for which certain medicines are reimbursed. The list is not comprehensive, meaning that not all treatments are refunded. In light of the licence requirement discussed above, the availability and accessibility of controlled medicines might be impeded. The NHS Representative explained this issue in relation to morphine:

> *(...) in case of oncology, the rate of reimbursement is hundred per cent (...) But of course we understand that these two groups of diagnosis are not covered all needs for painkillers (...) Unfortunately (...) pain killers for rheumatology is not covered by our system (...) It is because of restriction in budget mostly. Because our budget is very small for the reimbursement system* (NHS Representative).

The respondent indicated that the list was established ten years ago (at the time of data collection). While pain treatment for oncology was part of the list from the beginning, neuropathic pain was later included as an indication for which medicines ought to be reimbursed. This suggests that access to reimbursed pain-control medication may have increased.

Also at facility level, Physician 2 presented the lack of national finances allocated to healthcare to be the main barrier to affordable treatment:

> *(...) the problem with reimbursement, again, we don't have enough funds for this reimbursement system. Therefore, it is controlled through the budget of family doctors. But all, any doctor has his budget for the reimbursement of medicines. And if you exceed, then you may have to pay back (...) yes it is a strict system. That is because we don't have money now* (Physician 2).

Nevertheless, Latvian doctors may also circumvent the system. Civil Society Representative 1 explained that although the reimbursement system is based on diagnosis, staff is skilled at finding ways around the system to get what they need. For example, if a patient is diagnosed with disease X that should be treated with medicine Y, which is not reimbursed for disease X but is reimbursed for disease Z, this respondent stated that physicians usually add the code of the diagnosis for which that particular medicine is reimbursed. According to the respondent, *'I guess, physicians who care for their patients just find their way around the system'* (Civil Society Representative 1).

Likewise, Physician 2 stated that there is no difficulty in Latvia to obtain pain treatment. This respondent noted, however, that the actual accessibility is highly dependent on the willingness of, in particular, GPs to provide this type of treatment and to organize all support, such as home-based or hospice care. Especially in relation to this last point, the respondent observed that this could present a major problem because of the out-of-pocket payments required for home care. The respondent also explained that costs, as well as the reliability of the home-care system, differ per municipality. This is further addressed below when discussing geographic accessibility/inaccessibility of health facilities as a key challenge.

Returning to the aspect of finances, out-of-pocket payments remain an issue as well. Patients whose care is 100 per cent reimbursed by the NHS are still required to pay an administrative fee. According to the WHO Representative, while the amount of such administrative fees seems surmountable, additional fees could contribute to *de facto* unequal access to health facilities, goods, and services. According to this respondent, Latvia's tax-paid system does not differentiate between incomes, resulting in everyone receiving the same basic package of health services. The respondent explained *'a visit to the general practitioner is very cheap. Like it will be 5 Euro, a visit. But of course it is only a visit of doctor, which always involves lab tests and a lot of other things people have to pay. So this is the reason they* [i.e. patients] *really do not attend'* (WHO Representative). Physician 3 also noted that out-of-pocket payments are generally burdensome for patients living in rural areas, as the socio-economic conditions of those patients are usually quite poor.

Moreover, as is true for costs associated with storage facilities, financial challenges can prove problematic in relation to the requirement for pharmacists to work with a computerized system. Lacking the finances to afford a computer means you cannot comply with this regulation. Pharmacist 6 explained that pharmacies in rural areas in particular do not have computers or have a very bad or slow Internet connection. This respondent explained that although physicians do receive government support for it, many physicians in remote areas neither have a computer nor Internet access. Physician 3 added that there is little to no government assistance to help physicians work online. This might be problematic in light of the e-health system that Latvia aims to introduce. If many facilities struggle financially to ensure sufficient computer and Internet access, an e-health system could complicate access to care rather than foster it. This may not directly affect the access to controlled medicines, as this is a manual system, but would affect the health system in general, thus unavoidably affecting the access to controlled medicine to some extent.

Geographic accessibility/inaccessibility of health clinics

A final key challenge to the provision of controlled medicines is the geographic accessibility/inaccessibility of health facilities, goods, and services. This is a general structural challenge, which may decrease the access to controlled medicines in light of the applicable licensing. Access to health facilities is increasingly difficult in remote areas during wintertime, as roads are literally blocked with snow and parts of the country are cut off. Moreover, a significant challenge in ensuring access to treatment in rural areas is found in the reimbursement system that limits the number of home visits a doctor can make. Physician 2 explained that because of this quota system *'it is very difficult to provide it if you are like 30 kilometres from his doctor and the roads aren't so good. In the city we can ensure that there is a nurse going every day'* (Physician 2). Actual service delivery therefore seems highly dependent on service providers' willingness to work around the system. According to Physician 2, it is extremely impractical to make actual service delivery rely essentially on the preparedness of doctors to put in extra effort to work around the system.

Regarding the actual availability of and access to pain treatment and palliative care in Latvia's rural areas, Physician 2 stated that there are small regional hospitals where palliative care patients could stay. However, the prevalence of such facilities is much higher in urban areas compared to the country's rural areas. The respondent explained that accessibility to home care therefore very much depends on the social and medical services provided per municipality and indicated that accessibility is increasingly complex in rural areas.

According to the WHO Representative, the lengthy waiting lists are another structural challenge for Latvia's countryside. A possible explanation for these waiting lists is the general scarcity of available services. Pharmacist 6 identified that it is generally unattractive for both doctors and pharmacists to work in rural areas due to the areas' living standards. Physician 3 submitted that the government does not make it appealing to work in rural areas, as there is insufficient infrastructure in place and a lower standard of education. Yet, the accessibility/inaccessibility of health facilities, goods, and services in remote areas are not limited to the doctor's or nurse's inability to attend to the patient at home. As mentioned earlier, the socio-economic status of many rural dwellers and their physical distance from health facilities makes it difficult to get the medical treatment one requires – especially in view of the high out-of-pocket payments.

Other

Three other key concerns were observed. One of these concerns is that the general public, or layperson, is relatively uninformed. Civil Society Representative 1 attributed this to the fact that it is unclear to people where to obtain information. Moreover, a certain level of corruption seems to exist in the health system. Fuelled by the black market, in some cases doctors attempt to profit individually by prescribing controlled medicines and selling them to drug users, for example. Lastly, and perhaps most importantly, not all medicines are authorized for distribution on the Latvian market. The country is small and therefore has a relatively small market. Because of the absence of authorization, it happens that medicines are unavailable. This would particularly affect the most vulnerable individuals, and those in rural areas. While such unavailability has yet to be evidenced in relation to controlled medicines, their availability and accessibility could, in theory, be complicated by this.

7.4.8 Potential reform

As was briefly mentioned in the context of finances, the Ministry of Health is planning to carry out an e-health/e-prescription pilot. Ministry of Health Representative 1 and 2 noted that with the implementation of e-prescriptions, it will be determined to what extent changes will (need to) be made to the present system. The implementation of this reform initiative also serves as a moment of reflection, according to these respondents. However, service providers complain about the government's progress. For instance, Pharmacist 6 pointed out that the start of the pilot has been delayed several times due to technical problems. The same respondent suggested that the administrative requirements could be more manageable in a digital system, rather than manually having to complete a stack of paperwork. As the respondent explained, normal prescriptions, i.e. containing non-controlled medicines, are accounted for electronically whereas that of controlled medicines has to be done on paper. The desire to integrate controlled medicine accounting and ordering into the 'normal medicine system' was also observed in Uganda.

In general, there is much interest in this e-health programme amongst physicians and pharmacists. Civil Society Representative 1, in this respect, said: *'our system is very bureaucratic, very bureaucratic (...) We don't want to do it manually. We want the e-system'* (Civil Society Representative 1). While many welcome the initiative, Pharmacists 2 and 3 also expressed some concern in regard to data protection. On a different note, Pharmacist 6 suggested that digitalizing the storage requirements would also facilitate compliance with the applicable regulations. However, it is unclear whether the e-health/e-prescription pilot also includes digitalizing the requirement to keep copies of dispensed prescriptions, for instance.

When discussing the potential of the e-health system in relation to compiling estimates, the SAM Representative indicated that the wholesaler information used at the moment is sufficient. In other words, the potential of collecting currently unavailable information would – in this respondent's opinion – not help draft more complete or adequate estimates. However, when further discussing this issue, the respondent held that it would be better if the SAM received information both from wholesalers and from pharmacies and hospitals. The reason for this remains unclear, making the respondent's last statement seem slightly contradictory.

7.4.9 Particular issues regarding other controlled medication

Apart from pain-control medicines, an advanced regulatory system for opioid-substitute medication was observed, even though Narcologist 1 submitted that Latvia only counts 300 patients on such treatment.[59] The ATOME country report for Latvia demonstrated that the regulations described below apply specifically to opioid-substitute medicines.

The decision about one's suitability for and participation in opioid-substitute treatment, including methadone and buprenorphine, is limited to narcologists who have entered into a contractual relationship with the NHS (although even then a set maximum of allowed prescriptions applies).[60] Narcologists treating out-hospital patients with buprenorphine are required to supervise the patient at all times.[61]

59 The fieldwork is primarily focused on pain-control medication as an example for the wider group of controlled medicines. The findings on opioid-substitute treatment summarize all comparative elements as found during the fieldwork but are by no means presented as comprehensive.

60 Radbruch and others (n 33) 133.

61 ibid 136.

Narcological treatment institutions keep and register the controlled medicines issued in the institution itself, and maintain a strict accountability register.[62] Dispensing of designated controlled medicines is limited, e.g. buprenorphine may only be dispensed upon presentation of a special prescription, a personal identification card, and a patient's programme card for the therapy in question; GHB, fentanyl injection solution, and diethyl ether are prohibited from being dispensed in a pharmacy.[63]

Supply/demand chain opioid-substitute medicines

A narcologist is a physician specifically licensed to work in addiction therapy. As Figure 7.5 illustrates, the supply/demand chain of opioid-substitute treatment differs from the supply/demand chain of pain-control medicines described in previous sections.

Figure 7.5 Latvia's supply/demand chain of opioid-substitute medicines

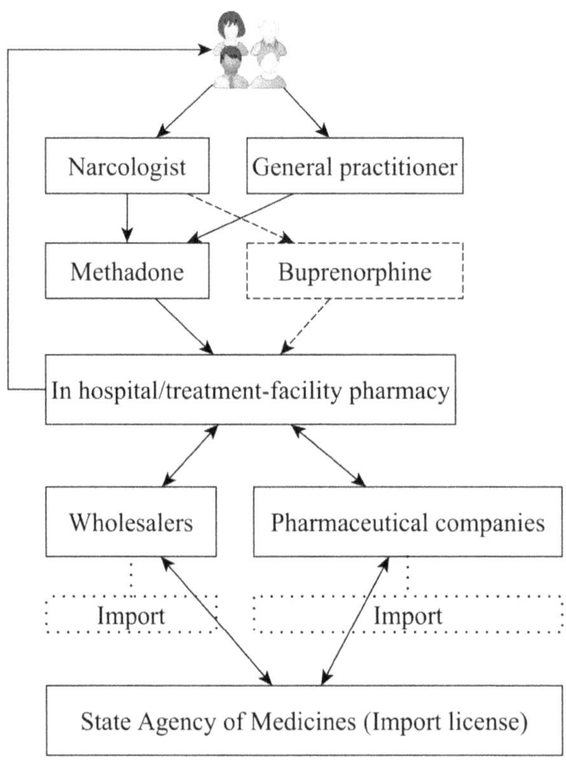

62 ibid 152.
63 ibid 146.

While allowed in general practice, it was observed that methadone is predominantly dispensed in treatment facilities per daily dose and is not available on prescription. Buprenorphine, on the other hand, is available on prescription but is only prescribed and distributed in special health facilities. In terms of the supply/demand chain, methadone is prescribed by either a narcologist or a GP, while buprenorphine can only be prescribed by a narcologist. Methadone is fully covered by a special scheme of the NHS (the medicine falls outside the scope of the general reimbursement list). Buprenorphine, on the other hand, is not reimbursed.

The SAM Representative explained that there is only one wholesaler licensed to import buprenorphine. This respondent indicated that the SAM was investigating whether all buprenorphine imported into the country in 2014 was really used for medical purposes only (as the country had seen a 30 per cent increase). According to this respondent, this vast increase in buprenorphine imports was subject to additional control due to the risk of buprenorphine being sold onto the black market.

Implications of administrative requirements and data collection and analysis

In relation to the special administrative requirements, Narcologists 1 and 2 considered it a problem that neither methadone nor buprenorphine are mainstreamed, but are kept in a separate administrative system instead. In fact, these respondents held that the strict regulations obstruct the access to opioid-substitute treatment, as one cannot ensure the access to the treatment without completing all mandatory forms. Yet, according to Narcologists 1 and 2, it is difficult to have sufficient stock exactly because these requirements are mandatory. In other words, the lengthy and intensive bureaucracy involved hampers the supply/demand chain. Moreover, Narcologists 1 and 2 highlighted the fact that buprenorphine is neither included in the positive list of reimbursement medicines nor in a separate programme such as the NHS' special scheme for methadone. The respondents noted this lack of government involvement as a significant challenge to the availability of buprenorphine.

The buprenorphine market is a monopoly with a single pharmaceutical company acting as the supplier. This makes it an expensive medicine. As a direct result of buprenorphine's small market, the respondents held that institutions are not interested in scaling up treatment or in ensuring its availability in a more mainstreamed manner, which, in turn, has led to stock-outs and serious challenges in the access to treatment. In fact, when discussing government involvement to push for greater availability of this medicine, Narcologists 1 and 2 submitted that the government states that there is nothing they can do precisely because the medicine is not reimbursed.

Narcologists 1 and 2, furthermore, stated that forecasting is difficult because the pharmaceutical company delivering buprenorphine does not want to take the facility-based analytics into account. According to these respondents, the supplier importing buprenorphine bases its stock management on responsive, instead of proactive, data. The internal data of the company, therefore, only includes the demand of patients who are at that particular moment receiving treatment and therefore excludes the demand of patients who still have to start treatment. According to the narcologists, calculating stock without taking into account the proactive figures, including prospective patients entering treatment, may lead to a stock-out crisis similar to what happened at the end of 2014. Narcologist 2 explained:

> *(...) in the end of the last year* [2014] *we didn't have in our country buprenorphine. Our patients stayed without this mediation. It's because those regulations are very strong and the stock couldn't be full with those medications because they* [i.e. the wholesaler] *don't know, for example, how many patients could enter in the end of the year. Ten or five or twenty? They couldn't make like a big reservation. Like that for this medication, they couldn't* (Narcologist 2).

Pharmacist 1 added, moreover, that even when discussing a major stock-out, the company was not interested in the facility's proactive data since the company itself had not foreseen the increase in demand. This example supports the importance of needs-based information and, additionally, demonstrates that facility-level data collection of opioid-substitute medication remains unused.

Likewise, certain practical elements of the specific administration seem to hamper actual access. This complexity is aggravated by the requirements one needs to meet to enter treatment. Narcologists 1 and 2 explained that doctors have to follow a five-step procedure to begin treatment, including finding financial support for the treatment. Respondents observed that there are not always sufficient funds to allow all eligible patients to enter the programme. This is particularly problematic for buprenorphine because the medicine is not listed on the positive list of reimbursed medicines. Furthermore, the extensive assessment criteria could be perceived as an additional burden when viewed in relation to the general lack of staff and the inadequate budget for addiction psychiatry. In addition, it takes time to define the best dose per patient.

The in-hospital pharmacy that Narcologists 1 and 2 work at relies on an advanced internal ordering system using local software that registers daily demands of controlled medicines. The statistical information collected is not provided to the wholesaler because, as was addressed above, the wholesaler does not request such information. However, regulation requires pharmacies to keep track in the strict accountability register. The internal system the respondent refers to is simply a system adopted at their health institution. Each hospital or treatment centre uses its own procedures.

Nevertheless, Pharmacist 1 proposed that it would be ideal if the system used at their institution could be improved and implemented at a national level, so as to ensure that the Ministry of Health and the NHI receive all relevant data on forecasted consumer use.

Key structural challenges

The key challenges to the access to opioid-substitute treatment include the lack of government support, geographic accessibility, licensed institutions, and insufficient human and financial resources. It was observed that, although also available in ten other districts in the country, methadone is best accessible in Riga. However, access to treatment is still challenging, especially in rural and remote areas. Access is further complicated due to the high out-of-pocket payments, particularly in relation to buprenorphine. Not only is buprenorphine not reimbursed, but patients must also pay for each doctor's visit. Moreover, as there is a prescription limit of two weeks for buprenorphine, patients must essentially pay for both the medicine and doctors' appointments every two weeks. According to Narcologists 1 and 2, the general low or instable socio-economic conditions in which most patients live, combined with the out-of-pocket payments, further complicate the access to treatment.

Potential reform

The WHO Representative submitted that scaling up methadone treatment is difficult due to its sensitive nature amongst politicians. Narcologists 1 and 2 observed that while it has been possible for GPs to prescribe methadone for opioid dependence in their practice since 2012, there has not been a single GP who prescribed opioid-substitute medicines since the regulations have been relaxed. This is largely due to reimbursement issues. However, according to the respondents, as long as GPs are not prescribing methadone, the government will not consider opioid-substitute treatment as a serious (public) health concern. Moreover, respondents submit that there should be an increase in facilities that can distribute methadone to boost geographic coverage and accessibility.[64]

7.5 Conclusion

In formulating an answer to the question of whether Latvia, as a second example, is able to provide access to pain-control medicines in a manner consistent with

64 According to the European Monitoring Centre for Drugs and Drug Addiction, methadone maintenance treatment is available at nine treatment facilities, and buprenorphine treatment at eight. See EMCDDA, 'Drug Treatment Overview for Latvia' <www.emcdda.europa.eu/data/treatment-overviews/Latvia> accessed 31 August 2016.

the human rights obligations contained in international drug-control treaties, the following can be concluded.

First, in Latvia, international law is directly applicable in the domestic legal order. The international obligations under study are therefore of direct relevance and do not have to be transposed into domestic legislation. Although human rights protection in the country seems much more focused on civil and political rights, the right to health is an enforceable and justiciable right in Latvia.

Second, in the context of Latvia, one can conclude that, even if different from Uganda, the implementation of Articles 17, 19-20, and 30 Single Convention also leads to a variety of problems; both generally and specifically in relation to the AAAQ standard of healthcare.

Overall, Latvia has adopted an abundance of regulations to control the manufacturing of, trade in, and use of controlled substances. Latvia's health system should, however, be considered in the context of the country's Soviet past. In particular, its vast hierarchical structure generally makes it difficult for the system's workers to take responsibility. On the one hand, an outsider would probably regard the applicable regulations as strict or even too strict and would question their purpose in the context of medicine provision. On the other hand, an insider would likely be pleased with the already more flexible approach that has been introduced since the Soviet era. However, this does not imply that service providers are satisfied with the status quo of regulations. In contrast, it became clear that the bureaucracy surrounding controlled medicines is an unwanted remnant from Soviet times. Notably, this does not necessarily mean that those frustrated by the current level and scope of control reject the purpose of control itself.

When compared to respondents in Uganda, respondents in Latvia were even more vocal and questioned the purpose of certain regulatory requirements in relation to the practice of complying with that specific rule. For instance, the storage requirement, including the mandatory alarm system, was challenged from the perspective that the purpose of the rule is to secure the prescription forms. Yet if a facility has a general alarm system and the prescriptions are under lock and key at the facility, then one could hold there is no need for an additional metal safe or dedicated alarm.

In addition, while the regulations are more flexible now than before, they are still so stringent and extensive that they can have a dissuasive effect on service providers; even if not necessarily perceived as such by all service providers themselves. Reluctance to perform additional paperwork ensuing from the prescription of a controlled medicine or being afraid of non-compliance with specific regulatory requirements affects the availability and accessibility of medicines. Moreover, similarly to Uganda – although perhaps motivated by different reasons – the specific regulatory requirements fuel a certain negative compliance incentive following which staff circumvent the strict implications of a regulation in order to comply with them on paper.

As was also observed in Uganda, even if service providers are disturbed by the additional requirements, but their abilities to provide services are not affected by additional regulatory procedures, several fundamental constraints cause these providers to state that their work is hampered by the regulatory burden. These constraints include human resources, financial constraints, a fear of abuse, geographic accessibility, and licensing of prescribers and dispensers. These are also amongst the core issues impeding access to controlled medicines, including pain-control medicines. Hampering the access to medicines in this context should not necessarily be interpreted as directly decreasing the current level and scope of access. Rather, hampering the access implies that at least a certain regulatory requirement does not advance the availability and accessibility of, in this case, pain-control medicines.

For instance, the Latvian health system suffers from understaffing and those working in the system generally face a work overload. Any additional requirement embedded in a system of over-enforcement and strict control is likely to dissuade prescribers and dispensers from prescribing controlled medicines. Moreover, geographic accessibility/inaccessibility to health facilities, goods, and services affects those living in remote areas specifically. This is especially so in the context of the licensing agreements with the NHS, which might compromise the principle of non-discrimination as States – including Latvia – are bound to prioritizing the needs of vulnerable and marginalized segments of society in particular, such as those living in remote areas. In fact, the challenges faced in opioid-substitute treatment and the perceived lack of government involvement in improving the access to these services may also clash with the principle of non-discrimination – especially so when viewing drug users as vulnerable and marginalized groups of society.

Whereas in Uganda the level of control and specific requirements were questioned for their cultural appropriateness in relation to the AAAQ standard of healthcare, such a conclusion seems inappropriate for Latvia. In light of its Soviet past, the stringent control seems to suit its culture. However, this does not mean that further liberalization is not needed. In fact, the opposite seems true as participants welcome additional reform initiatives to overcome a regulatory system that is considered by some as having been put in place just to make service delivery harder.

The purpose of regulatory requirements is particularly questioned if examined in the context of data collection and analysis procedures. As in Uganda, the administrative requirements do not contribute to arriving at adequate and accurate estimates. In fact, in both Latvia and Uganda estimation techniques are based on consumption data, meaning many patients' needs are not forecasted due to their inability to obtain access to health facilities, goods, and services caused by financial and geographic reasons. One could therefore conclude that, in the context of Latvia, solely relying on consumption methods seems problematic from a human rights perspective.

It should be noted, however, that the context of the access to controlled medicines and the need for regulations significantly differs between Uganda and Latvia. Latvia suffers from a black market in false prescriptions, which limits the access to medicines provision in general. Such abuse was not identified in Uganda. While this context of abuse fuels the need for regulations, the question that needs to be explored is what the extent of these regulations should be. With due respect for the differences between Uganda and Latvia, the Latvian example also demonstrates the need to start viewing the human rights and drug-control systems as complementary rather than mutually exclusive frameworks of law.

The Latvian example also reveals that the leeway that States possess to adopt stricter rules than those laid down in the international drug-control treaties should be revisited, in regard to the implementation of the resulting administrative and procedural obligations. It illustrates that more guidance is necessary at the international level to overcome a structural information gap. Finally, like Uganda (although for different reasons), Latvia also finds itself in a suboptimal position to effectively discharge its obligations under international law due to its seriously resource-constrained health system. The different socio-economic contexts of both countries and their distinct history and culture of substance use, prove that more research is needed on the implementation of resource-intensive international drug-control procedures in countries facing significant resource constraints.

Part 4

Conclusions and Recommendations

Chapter 8
Conclusions and Recommendations

8.1 Recalling the questions and ambitions of this book

Concerned with the access to controlled essential medicines under the interplay of human rights and drug-control norms, this study explored a human rights approach to the international drug-control system. Analysing the availability and accessibility of these medicines in theory and practice, the book used morphine as essential pain-control medicine as leading example. In its analysis, both a general focus on controlled essential medicines, as well as a more applied focus on pain-control medicines, was employed.

As described in Chapter 1, Remedios was lucky to receive palliative care and pain-control treatment at Mexico's National Cancer Institute.[1] Unlike Remedios, millions of patients around the world continue to suffer in dire conditions, as pain-control medicines like morphine and codeine remain largely unavailable or inaccessible. In fact, despite their multifaceted need, Duthey and Scholten concluded that 66 per cent of the global population are unable to access, for whatever reason, opioid analgesics.[2] Even though the authors found the global unavailability of opioid analgesics to affect all levels of development, the deficit is worst in Low- and Middle-Income Countries and, in particular, in the Sub-Saharan region. The suffering caused by the unavailability and inaccessibility of pain-control treatment raises serious concerns in light of human rights protection. States, after all, have the obligation to respect, protect, and fulfil the right to health and the prohibition of torture and cruel, inhuman, and degrading treatment (CIDT).[3]

While there are many general and substance-specific factors challenging the access to medicines, the provision of controlled essential medicines is particularly influenced

1 Human Rights Watch, *Care When There is no Cure* (HRW 2014).

2 Moreover, consumption is very low in 10%, low in 3%, moderate in 4%, and adequate in a mere 7.5% of the global population. See B Duthey and W Scholten, 'Adequacy of Opioid Analgesic Consumption at Country, Global, and Regional Levels in 2010, its Relationship with Development Level, and Changes Compared with 2006' (2014) 47 Journal of Pain and Symptom Management 283.

3 International Covenant on Economic, Social and Cultural Rights (adopted 16 December 1966, entered into force 3 January 1976) 993 UNTS 3 (ICESCR) art 12; Convention against Torture and Other Cruel, Inhuman or Degrading Treatment or Punishment (adopted 10 December 1984, entered into force 26 June 1987) 1465 UNTS 85, arts 1, 16.

by the international drug-control treaties. Taking into account the multifaceted complexity of health-service provision, and the general and specific conditions in which to provide for pain-control medicines, this book examined the international drug-control treaties as a potential barrier.[4] Despite States' obligation to ensure access to medicines in adherence to the regulatory monitoring requirements enshrined in the international drug-control system, the normative foundation, interpretation, application and implementation of said system may raise questions regarding States' obligations under human rights law.

The dual nature of controlled substances makes it imperative to regulate their production, manufacturing, import/export, distribution, and use. The question being, however, how far regulation should and can go, both in terms of scope and level, to ensure the availability of controlled essential medicines. This issue was found particularly acute for two distinct reasons.

First, the international drug-control framework operates a delicate equilibrium. States have to curb all production, manufacturing, import/export, distribution, and use of controlled substances. Medical and scientific purposes are the only legitimate exception to this otherwise strict rule.[5] This 'principle of balance', as the foundation of drug control is often referred to, requires States to maximize availability for medical and scientific purposes whilst minimizing harm caused by non-medical drug use.[6] However, States have complementary obligations under the human rights framework. In fact, human rights norms construct a framework of balancing to settle competing interests and rights clashes. Analysing any human rights approach to drug control presupposes understanding whether the 'principle of balance', as framed and understood in the international drug-control system, is compliant with human rights norms.

Second, the administrative, procedural, and trade and distribution-related requirements of the international drug-control system jointly compose the primary regulatory system to which States have to adhere in order to ensure access to controlled essential medicines. For the purpose of controlling diversion and to manage the licit supply/demand chain of controlled medicines, the technical requirements oblige States to manage a separate administration, compose estimates and statistical returns, and adopt specific trade and distribution regulations.[7] As health-service provision is generally

4 See Chapter 2.
5 Single Convention on Narcotic Drugs (adopted 30 March 1961, entered into force 13 December 1964) 520 UNTS 151 (Single Convention) art 4.
6 WHO, *Ensuring Balance in National Policies on Controlled Substances: Guidance for Availability and Accessibility of Controlled Medicines* (WHO 2011).
7 Single Convention, arts 17, 19-20, 30.

complex in resource-constrained regions, or in countries with large remote areas and/or significant resource constraints in their health system, these particular drug-control requirements may complicate, instead of foster, controlled medicine provision.[8]

Indeed, it has been increasingly acknowledged that the monitoring mechanisms of the international drug-control system might be the core of the deficit in pain-control medicine in particular and, more generally, of the inaccessibility of controlled essential medicines. One may therefore wonder whether States can realistically implement a human rights foundation for drug control within the ambit of the current regulatory framework embodied in the international drug-control treaties – regardless of what the substantive normative implications of a human rights foundation for drug control would be. This book placed this second issue in the context of governance and a State's ability to effectively provide for public services, including health services.

Taking these two aspects into account, the central research question was:

> Which structural, mandate-related, or behavioural changes, if any, does a human rights approach imply in the field of drug control focused on the access to controlled medicines provision in resource-constrained countries in particular?

Answering this question presupposed elaborating three sub-questions:

1) How would human rights norms frame the regulation of controlled substances, given their dual individual and public-health implications?

Having some understanding of the manner in which human rights norms frame the regulation of controlled substances, the second question aimed to explore the conditions of human-rights compliant service provision:

2) What are the conditions based on human rights norms, if any, in line with which States have to ensure the provision of controlled medicines?

Finally, upon gaining in-depth understanding of the foundation and criteria of a human rights approach to drug control, the third question was:

3) How, if at all, can a normative framework as developed under sub-questions 1-2 be included in the structures of the present international drug-control system?

8 See eg AL Taylor, 'Addressing the Global Tragedy of Needless Pain: Rethinking the United Nations Single Convention on Narcotic Drugs' (2007) 35 Journal of Law, Medicines and Ethics 556; KI Pettus, 'Rhetoric and the Road to Hell: The International Narcotics Control Regime and Access to Essential Medicines' (2012) 1 Bulletin Health Policy and Law 1.

Bearing the aforementioned duality in mind, the book aimed to explore what it means, both in theory and in practice, to discuss, advocate, and enforce a human rights approach to drug control. To this end, the book aimed to improve and contribute to the interpretation of these two frameworks of law as mutually reinforcing, instead of exclusive, fields of public international law. This was particularly deemed necessary – and innovative – because the current body of human rights and drug control mainly analyses the effects of drug-control efforts in light of human rights law, but neglects to question its basis when it comes to human rights norms or any issues concerning their interpretation and implementation.

From an academic perspective, this book fills a gap in the current body of knowledge on the interplay of human rights and international drug control. By doing so, it contributes to a more comprehensive understanding of the access to medicines in general, and the research on the access to medicines and human rights in particular. Even though law is the central discipline based on which the analysis takes place, the study required input from disciplines such as ethics, and life and social sciences. As such, the book relies on a multidisciplinary selection of methods. While legal at its core, this book transcends the more conventional legal analysis often used in academic writing, by including an ethical reflection and qualitative case study approach.

In doing so, this book highlights the current political debates on human rights and drug control and provides information for current reform initiatives in this area. For this purpose, it produces a set of normative human rights requirements and thresholds, which can be used to explore current drug-control reform initiatives. Finally, it is hoped that the normative and analytic framework produced in this book, if used in its guiding capacity, may directly affect the approaches of national and international policy-makers and legislators: to stimulate human rights compliant law and policy changes in the field of controlled medicine regulation, and improve the medication's availability on a global scale.

8.2 Human rights and drug control: normative and empirical findings

This section reflects on the main findings expressed throughout this book. Seeking an answer to sub-questions 1 and 2, this section first reflects on what a human rights foundation for drug control entails (Section 8.2.1). Addressing sub-question 3, this section subsequently focuses on the key lessons learnt from the implementation of and practical constraints observed in the service provision in Uganda and Latvia (Section 8.2.2).

8.2.1 Human rights foundation of drug control

Mutually reinforcing fields of public international law

As explained in Chapter 2, human rights are integrally relevant to the interpretation of the international drug-control treaties. Their relevance applies irrespectively of the horizontal or hierarchical position one grants the human rights system in the field of public international law. This book argues in favour of a constitutionalist interpretation of international law in which human rights are granted normative priority over other branches of public international law.[9] In light of the ongoing debate regarding the fragmentation of international law, this study demonstrates that a constitutionalist approach survives the criticism of its opponents. Human rights have to be integrated into the interpretation and implementation of the international drug-control regime on the basis of the general rules of treaty interpretation as well.[10] Therefore, one can consider the human rights approach to drug control not to be based on arbitrary political decision-making, but reflective of a legitimate interpretation of international law on all accounts.

The principle of balance in human rights law

As briefly recapitulated in Section 8.1, the international drug-control system operates a delicate equilibrium, which is often referred to as the 'principle of balance'. Human rights law, however, frames any perceived conflict between the medical and non-medical use of controlled substances in a different manner. As set out in Chapter 3, notwithstanding the theoretical equality of all rights, human rights law itself provides a legal structure by which to implement and enforce human rights in an effective and prioritized manner. This means that human rights law recognizes priority-setting and balancing to the extent that such priority-setting or balancing can find a basis in and be justified by human rights law. Consequently, any balancing which would ignore or disrespect important human rights requirements would be unacceptable.

Placing the aforementioned balanced foundation of drug control in the context of human rights law results in what this book referred to as an 'access-led' approach to drug control. Exactly because human rights law may attribute the various aspects of drug control a different normative value, a balanced approach may in fact be a

---

9 See ILC, 'Report of the Study Group of the International Law Commission on the Fragmentation of International Law: Difficulties Arising from the Diversification and Expansion of International Law' (13 April 2006) UN Doc A/CN.4/L.682, para 85 (ILC Report); J Vidmar, 'Norm Conflicts and Hierarchy in International Law: Towards a Vertical International Legal System?' in E de Wet and J Vidmar (eds), *Hierarchy in International Law* (OUP 2012) 20.

10 See Chapter 2.

prioritized one. Mainly on the basis of the right to health, the prohibition of torture, and CIDT, the access to medicines, including controlled essential and pain-control medicines, is not *a priori* a more dominant aspect of drug control or human rights protection. Rather, the obligation to secure access to medicines, including controlled essential medicines, is attributed more importance when considered in relation to the obligation to control the non-medical use of controlled substances and, in particular, to offer protection against their hazardous use.[11]

At least in light of the normative framework of the right to health, the legal status of the access to medication and the control of non-medical use may be the same. Yet, in terms of implementation and enforcement of the right to health, access to medicines is part of its core and therefore subject to priority realization. In contrast, efforts to control the hazardous use of substances are considered to be part of the general aspects of the right to health and therefore subject to progressive realization. While certainly less explicit, the prohibition against torture and CIDT supports such a modest hierarchy.

In an attempt to distinguish the extent to which States are obliged to secure human rights protection, and thus to enquire which normative requirements can be distilled, this book demonstrates that the access to controlled essential medicines is subject to the Availability, Accessibility, Acceptability, and Quality (AAAQ) standard of healthcare. The AAAQ standard is formulated as an interpretation of Article 12 ICESCR and implies that all healthcare facilities, goods, and services should be available, accessible, acceptable, and of sufficient quality.[12]

Viewing drug control primarily as a concern of the right to health, any aspect of drug control should be realized in accordance with the AAAQ standard of healthcare. Yet, this begs the question of whether Uganda and Latvia, as country-specific examples, are sufficiently equipped to implement and realize access to medicines in accordance with the AAAQ standard via the structures provided in the international drug-control system itself. The specific structures referred to particularly include the administrative and procedural obligations, and trade and distribution requirements of the Single Convention on Narcotics Drugs (Single Convention).[13] However, before delving into the practical aspects of service provision and its implementation, this book reflects on the normative justification of the approach presented.

---

11 See Chapter 3, Sections 3.4-3.5.

12 See ICESCR; CESCR, 'General Comment No 14: The Right to the Highest Attainable Standard of Health (Art. 12)' adopted at the Twenty-Second Session (11 August 2000) UN Doc E/C.12/2000/4, para 12.

13 Single Convention, arts 17, 19-20, 30.

A normative justification

The appeal of absoluteness and priority, as found in human rights law, requires a fundamental shift in the understanding of the 'principle of balance' in international drug control. However, one should explore the normative justification of an 'access-led' approach as found in law exactly because the moral principles at the heart of the human rights framework are not necessarily identical to the legal rights enshrined in it.

Operating on the assumptions of the human rights framework implies viewing human dignity as its central overriding principle and the foundation of inalienable rights. Such an interpretation, moreover, attributes to human dignity the role of a principle generating rights rather than recognizing it as being a norm or right in itself. Viewing human dignity as a claim *to* autonomy rather than autonomy itself, allows one to frame human dignity as a categorically binding moral principle at the core of the entire human rights framework. Yet, if human dignity is the ability to act autonomously, then human rights are claims to freedom, goods, and services that require protection and to which access is a prerequisite in order to live an autonomous life.

This study based the normative arguments presented on capability theories and specifically explored the capability theory of Martha Nussbaum and the Principle of Generic Consistency (PGC) of Alan Gewirth as further conceptualized and justified by Deryck Beyleveld.[14] The theories relied on conceptualizing human rights as claims aiming to enhance and enable conditions of freedom and well-being. These claims are both positive and negative in nature implying both the realization of facilities, goods, and services as well as respect for one's liberty.[15] Exactly because these theories embrace a strong focus on agency and functioning, it is undisputable that the denial of pain medication and, more generally, controlled essential medicines may compromise human dignity. While it is clear that States have moral obligations to ensure the adequate availability and accessibility of controlled essential medicines, the real moral issue lies in whether or not people have a right to use drugs for non-medical purposes.

It has been demonstrated that the capabilities approach of Nussbaum remains unclear, and at times unconvincing, with respect to the selection of capabilities and in discerning how one could justifiably settle conflicts between various competing

14 A Gewirth, *Reason and Morality* (The University of Chicago Press 1978); D Beyleveld, *The Dialectical Necessity of Morality* (The University of Chicago Press 1991); MC Nussbaum, *Frontiers of Justice* (HUP 2006); MC Nussbaum, *Creating Capabilities* (HUP 2011).

15 See Chapter 4, Section 4.4 in which the normative content of human dignity is analysed in light of both theories.

interests.[16] As a result, the capabilities approach may be sufficiently in scope for the access to medicines and aspects of drug control individually, but remain unclear (as developed to date) insofar that it can provide guidance in the balancing between these two interests. The PGC, on the other hand, provides a powerful argument that not only justifies human rights as empowerment entitlements but also supports the 'access-led' approach found in law. The PGC is a rational claim to autonomy and establishes a need for generic goods and aspects of well-being relevant to the capacity of rational decision-making. The capacity of rational action is captured in the principle of hypothetical imperatives, reflecting a dialectically necessary interpretation of rational action.[17]

The power of the PGC's justification lies in the fact that an agent would contradict their own agency if rejecting the premise that having access to certain goods and services or respect of freedom are necessarily good for the attainment of a certain freely chosen purpose, regardless of what such a freely chosen purpose may be. The generic claim-rights resulting from these freely chosen purposes are limited to the extent that they may not harm others (both individual and society) in exercising generic rights. Instead, the degree of needfulness of generic needs of agency produces a hierarchical structure along which to balance competing interests and claims.[18]

One therefore has to reconsider the 'principle of balance' in line with the degree of needfulness the principle determines. Doing so demonstrates that regardless of whether people have a *right* to use drugs, all agents, including state and non-state parties have positive and negative duties to ensure the access to medicines, including controlled essential medicines. Moreover, in spite of the defensibility of a right to use drugs, these agents hold positive and negative duties in relation to the generic rights of drug users. The precautionary principle, in this respect, requires one to treat others as agents and attribute to them generic rights unless it has been unequivocally demonstrated that the 'agents' are incapable of rational action. Duties toward drug users, in other words, apply regardless of whether or not drug dependence impairs the ability to act in accordance with the principle of instrumental reason.

Finally, in an attempt to settle a perceived conflict between the access to medicines and drug-control efforts, the PGC states that if non-medical drug use hampers individuals' access to medicines, then regulations ought to be put into place to prioritize such

16 See eg R Claassen and M Düwell, 'The Foundations of Capability Theory: Comparing Nussbaum and Gewirth' (2013) 16 Ethical Theory and Moral Practice 493; R Claassen, 'Human Dignity in the Capability Approach' in M Düwell and others (eds), *The Cambridge Handbook of Human Dignity: Interdisciplinary Perspectives* (CUP 2014).

17 Gewirth (n 14); Beyleveld (n 14).

18 Beyleveld (n 14) 21-46.

medical use. Depending on the exact situation, access to medicines may classify as a basic or non-subtractive need, while a right to use drugs can be classified as additive need, if at all. The degree of needfulness determines that basic needs trump non-subtractive needs and additive needs and non-subtractive needs, in turn, trump additive needs.[19] Moreover, if not drug use itself but rather the regulations to curb drug use, which are in itself questionable in light of the PGC, obstruct or impede access to medicines, then one needs to reconsider these regulations in accordance with the PGC. In this respect, the PGC supports the 'access-led' approach found in law and inspires discussion on the manner in which a human rights approach to drug control can be achieved. It does so, furthermore, taking into account aspects of cultural, traditional, and religious use. Hence, in line with the PGC, efforts to control the non-medical use of substances may not negatively impact efforts to ensure the access to medicines.

While a principle like the PGC provides a categorically binding moral criterion according to which to balance competing interests, such balancing is not necessarily the same as that found in law. The PGC, moreover, does not deal with issues concerning the operationalization of the 'access-led' approach contained in this book. Hence, looking at what the law says, the right to health may by law be limited to the extent that any of these limitations contribute to progressive realization of the rights laid down in the ICESCR. While it is beyond the scope of this study to reflect on the empirical implications of various drug-control approaches, it suffices to acknowledge that progressively achieving the rights laid down in the ICESCR implies that none of these measures may limit the enjoyment of such rights disproportionately.

To conclude, while *de jure* balancing in the international drug-control and human rights frameworks may be fairly similar in terms of the nature of the norms involved, the picture changes drastically when viewing drug-control matters with the implementation and enforcement of human rights law in mind, due to the priority-setting prescribed by human rights norms.

8.2.2 Implementation and practical constraints of service provision in Uganda and Latvia

Addressing the third sub-question, this book explored issues of implementation of the 'access-led' approach through case studies in Uganda and Latvia. These country studies explored whether the States in question were realistically able to uphold the

19 As set out in Chapter 4, basic needs include those aspects of well-being necessary for the actual ability to act. Non-subtractive needs are those aspects of well-being relevant to the possibility of successful action. Additive needs, in turn, are those aspects that would improve the possibility of successful action. See also Gewirth (n 14) 54-57.

AAAQ standard of healthcare within the ambit of the administrative, procedural, and trade and distribution requirements contained in the international drug-control system. The empirical analysis was specifically focused on the implementation of Articles 17, 19-20, and 30 of the Single Convention.[20]

While considerably different in context, background, and regulatory system, both countries face substantial difficulties in their implementation of the aforementioned requirements in a human-rights compliant manner. In their distinct ways, both countries have adopted domestic regulations to implement and comply with the drug-control requirements analysed. Bearing in mind the general/substance-specific distinction in factors hindering medicine provision, some factors were found to specifically relate to the international drug-control treaties, whilst other factors were more general in nature and indirectly complicated the implementation of said procedures. Although the book did not scrutinize the countries in a comparative manner, their similarities and differences are jointly summarized and culminate in lessons learnt.[21]

Challenges of medicine provision specifically related to drug-control requirements

With respect to the administrative and the specific trade and distribution requirements, service providers in both countries demonstrated a fear of non-compliance and even a negative compliance incentive. Supplementary administrative tasks were generally deemed obstructive even if the service providers did not consider the procedures to be burdensome – the reason being the structural lack of human and financial resources.

More generally, a multilevel information gap was identified in the implementation of a range of administrative, estimate-related, reporting, and trade and distribution requirements enshrined in the Single Convention. This gap implies, for instance, that actors at the international level, such as the International Narcotics Control Board (INCB), are insufficiently aware of the impact the international obligations and their domestic counterparts at the local level have. While by law, the international drug-control system may be interpreted as sensitive to country-specific resource-constrained situations, practice shows the control of illicit dispersion of controlled substances to be favoured over ensuring their medical availability.

At the national level, the Ugandan and Latvian examples demonstrate that the various Ministries involved continue to have insufficient insight into the potential flexibilities found in the international drug-control treaties and about the purpose of the international procedures applicable. In Uganda, moreover, the fear of non-compliance,

20 On the research design and methodology, see Chapter 5; Chapter 6, Section 6.2; and Chapter 7, Section 7.2.
21 See for a more in-depth discussion Chapters 6 and 7.

based on misinformation, has led to the adoption of rules stricter than necessary, which are also not fit for the purpose they aim to achieve. This is problematic because at the local level the purpose of both the domestic and international procedures is often misunderstood. This, in addition, fuels a fear of non-compliance that, in turn, can result in a 'negative compliance incentive', i.e. accepting to meet the applicable regulations in a manner contrary to the regulation as such. Furthermore, service providers at the local level face, either directly or indirectly related to drug-control procedures, an increased workload. Regardless, in both countries, the data collected at facility level is not used to compose estimates or quarterly statistical return reports.

General challenges complicating the implementation of and compliance with specific drug-control requirements

In both countries, although for each in their own way, a lack of human resources, financial constraints, and geographic (in)accessibility of health facilities are among the core general complexities that complicate their ability to implement the specific administrative, procedural, and trade and distribution requirements in accordance with human rights.

As has already been briefly suggested in the previous paragraphs, both countries adopted resource-intensive domestic procedures. Compliance with these procedures is proving increasingly complex given the suboptimal and resource-constrained conditions in which both countries have to provide health facilities, goods, and services. Moreover, both countries lack insight into country-specific epidemiological data. This lack, in turn, complicates the drawing up of accurate estimates. This last aspect is due to a plurality of reasons, of which geographic accessibility/inaccessibility of health clinics is a fundamental one. The inability of people to see a health worker within a reasonable distance of their homes complicates the composition of accurate estimates in general. It also proves problematic in light of human rights protection, as the needs of vulnerable and marginalized segments of society are likely to be excluded from the estimates.

Bearing these specific challenges, and challenges at the local level, in mind, one can question whether the regulatory requirements of the international drug-control system fit their purpose and whether they are handled by international actors in a desirable manner. The INCB calls upon States to address their country-specific challenges. However, it does so without providing sufficient background and context as to the flexibilities that exist in the international drug-control system to adopt country-specific measures. One does not submit that without drug-control measures the access to pain-control medicines in Uganda or Latvia would be flawless. However, it is concluded that the administrative and procedural obligations and their national implementation and interpretation may potentially conflict with the country's ability to provide for services in accordance with the AAAQ standard of healthcare.[22]

8.3 Towards a human rights approach of drug control to improve the access to controlled medicines

Having reflected on this book's central normative and empirical messages, this section looks ahead and reflects on the changes, if any, that should be adopted regarding the present scope and level of drug control. In doing so, this section describes the book's central message, includes a set of recommendations (Section 8.3.1), and identifies areas that could benefit from further investigation (Section 8.3.2).

8.3.1 Central message and key recommendations

Having elaborated on the normative and empirical implications of analysing a human rights approach to drug control to improve the access to controlled essential medicines, the question remains as to which structural, mandate-related, or behavioural changes such an approach would require.

Structural changes

In the context of this study, structural changes include any legal technical or institutional amendment necessary to further develop a human rights approach to drug control (as analysed in this book). The study's normative section (Part 2) demonstrated that a human rights approach to drug control implies an 'access-led' approach to drug-control regulation. In other words, the access to medicines, including controlled essential medicines, must not be disproportionately compromised or obstructed by efforts to curb drug use and control their dispersion. Any obstruction is strictly invalid if denial of the access to controlled medicines were to result in a violation of the prohibition of torture and CIDT. The strict prohibition clause as adopted in Article 4 of the Single Convention may neither *de jure* nor *de facto* impede or obstruct efforts to secure the access to medicines. Moreover, any international or domestic drug-control law or policy either in theory or in practice obstructing the access to medicines is void.

One may question, however, whether the text of the strict prohibition clause as contained in Article 4 Single Convention allows one to prioritize the access to medicines in a human-rights compliant manner. A legal codification of the way in which the access

22 The impact of these procedures on AAAQ-conform medicine provision is purposefully referred to as potential, even in the conclusions, because no quantitative data has been structurally gathered nor was the empirical analysis set up to distinguish causal relationships.

to medicines is prioritized in terms of the enforcement and implementation of human rights would look similar to a general clause in which the access to medicines is the starting point and the protection against non-medical use the exception. By no means is this argument a blunt call for liberalization, it is rather the conclusion of a legal-technical argument which may result in liberalization if the latter is the only route through which one can move towards an 'access-led' approach. This makes the maximum access/minimum diversion approach of the 'principle of balance' neither wrong nor incompatible with human rights. Rather, both human rights law and theory demonstrate that one cannot equate access to medicines to aspects of non-medical use and that it is categorically binding to prioritize the medical access to controlled substances.

Consequently, it is recommended that the international community, including all State Parties to the international drug-control treaties as well as the entire UN community, contribute to and work towards modifying the international drug-control system to the extent that it no longer obstructs the access to medicines. However, although the 'access-led' approach this book advocates may legal-technically be suitable within the framing of the foundation of drug-control regulation, it also requires structural change from a more legal-substantive perspective.

This is especially so because the country studies conducted in Uganda and Latvia – although set up in pilot fashion – demonstrated that resource-constrained countries experience problems in arriving at adequate estimates and/or to run smooth administrative procedures, including specific trade and distribution requirements. Seeing that composing accurate estimates (i.e. estimates that cover the real need of a country's population and not just the registered need of those able to visit a health facility) is complex and that structural problems, such as a lack of staff, an absence of funds, and geographic accessibility/inaccessibility of health clinics, complicate estimating the real demand in a country, one can question whether the international drug-control system places these countries in a structurally disadvantaged position when it comes to achieving compliance. Moreover, leeway should be provided in managing a separate administration and implementing specific trade and distribution requirements.

It is therefore recommended that the international drug-control bodies, including the INCB, the United Nations Office on Drugs and Crime (UNODC), and the Commission on Narcotic Drugs (CND) produce General Comments to provide normative guidance on the scope, content, and purpose of the administrative and procedural obligations. When doing so, the aforementioned bodies ought to take a complementary, instead of mutually exclusive, approach to human rights law and the general and specific obligations stemming from drug-control treaties. It is recommended that the drug-control bodies work closely with the Committee on Economic, Social and Cultural Rights (CESCR), the UN Special Rapporteurs on health and torture, and the Committee against Torture in this regard to ensure that the related General Comments reflect a comprehensive and synergetic approach.

In fact, the international community ought should reconsider the monitoring mechanisms in their entirety due to the disadvantaged position in which they seem to place countries providing health services in suboptimal conditions. This study found that the international drug-control system takes what one could call a substance-specific approach since the listing of substances in different schedules of preparations corresponds to different levels of control. However, when considering the regulatory mechanisms, one could argue that the drug-control treaties largely take a one-size-fits-all approach. This in the sense that all States Parties not sufficiently accommodating the particular resource-constrained conditions of certain countries actually enforce resource-intensive standards and procedures. Against this backdrop, it is therefore highly recommended that the international community, including both human rights and drug-control monitoring bodies and State Parties, explores regulatory mechanisms which take into account the structural constraints of service provision that is present in a majority of the State Parties (in which the access to controlled medicines, including pain-control medicines, remains below par). This means that one should abolish overly restrictive or unsuitable specific trade and distribution requirements at the international and domestic level in order to improve the accessibility of controlled medicines. To this end, the freedom of States to adopt stricter rules than those laid down in the international drug-control treaties should be curbed in order to ensure that the access to medicines can never be obstructed, in law and in practice. When making such considerations, however, one should necessarily also take into account a substance's abuse potential.

Revisiting international drug-control laws from the perspective of the local realities presented is also particularly acute in light of debates on the universality of human rights and the central role diversity plays in its realization. Exactly because of its universal nature, human rights law is quite open-ended; there is no hierarchy relating to the world's different cultures, customs, and perceptions. In order for human rights to be truly universal beyond their moral foundation or explication in law, one therefore has to relate to their practical reality and allow for a certain degree of variation in strategies for its realization. Brems speaks in this regard of 'inclusive universality'.[23] Moreover, Merry acknowledges that the implementation of human rights standards,

23 E Brems, 'Reconciling Universality and Diversity in International Human Rights: A Theoretical and Methodological Framework and Its Application in the Context of Islam' (2004) 3 Human Rights Review 5.

either by law, training, or other processes is naturally 'both global and local at the same time'.[24]

The current debates on universal human rights standards should inform debates on the universality of drug-control standards. In general, the international community should be alarmed by the normative and technical challenges found in the current scope and level of international drug control and start reform initiatives to adapt the internal structure of the regime itself in order to halt its perpetuation of structural disadvantages.

If States or the present international political arena are unwilling or unable to foster progressive structural reform to improve the access to controlled essential medicines, States could take Bolivia as an example and withdraw from the international drug-control treaties, aiming to re-accede with a specific reservation.[25] States could also take a bottom-up approach by creating customary international law. Any State starting an 'access-led' practice, such as partly demonstrated by the country studies, contributes to the creation of *opinio juris*. *Opinio juris* and state practice are, as one is aware, the prerequisites for customary international law.[26] It may be unlikely, however, for an 'access-led' practice to turn into customary international law in the foreseeable future.

---

24 SE Merry, 'Legal Transplants and Cultural Translation: Making Human Rights in the Vernacular' in M Goodale (ed), *Human Rights: An Anthropological Reader* (Blackwell 2009) 266. The necessary link between culture and universalism is also widely discussed by other authors including F Lenzerini, *The Culturalization of Human Rights Law* (OUP 2014); J Donnelly, *International Human Rights* (3rd edn, Westview Press 2013). As was also mentioned in Chapter 3, this is what partly distinguishes this book from the newly emerged 'Receptor Approach', which predominantly advocates using social institutions other than laws to implement international (human rights) standards. See on the receptor approach, T Zwart, 'Using Local Culture to Further the Implementation of International Human Rights: The Receptor Approach' (2012) 34 Human Rights Quarterly 546; Y Donders and V Vleugel, 'The Receptor Approach: A New Human Rights Kid on the Block or Old Wine in New Bags?' (2014) 36 Human Rights Quarterly 654.

25 'Bolivia Withdraws from the UN Single Convention on Narcotic Drugs' (Washington Office on Latin America, 30 June 2011) <www.wola.org/2011/06/bolivia-withdraws-from-the-un-single-convention-on-narcotic-drugs/> accessed 31 August 2016; International Drug Policy Consortium, 'Bolivia's Legal Reconciliation with the UN Single Convention on Narcotic Drugs' (July 2011) <www.undrugcontrol.info/images/stories/documents/IDPC-advocacy-bolivia-july2011.pdf> accessed 31 August 2016; UNODC, 'Bolivia to Re-accede to UN Drug Convention, While Making an Exception on Coca Leaf Chewing' <www.unodc.org/unodc/en/frontpage/2013/January/bolivia-to-re-accede-to-un-drug-convention-while-making-exception-on-coca-leaf-chewing.html> accessed 31 August 2016.

26 See eg C Chinkin, 'Sources' in D Moeckli, S Shah and S Sivakumaran (eds), *International Human Rights Law* (2nd edn, OUP 2014) 81-82.

At country level, States should review their drug-control legislation in light of human rights law, and prioritize and focus legislation on providing the access to medicines in a manner sensitive to the country's conditions of service provision. Moreover, instead of adopting rules that are stricter than those laid down in the international drug-control treaties, States should explore making drug-control laws more flexible. This includes exploring reform initiatives and entering into constructive dialogues with the international community and the respective treaty monitoring bodies.

Not just the degree of needfulness as contained in the PGC, but specifically also the proportionality test discussed in Chapter 3, should inform such reform initiatives. Relying on proportionality as a benchmark and framework on which to base legitimate drug-control standards is particularly helpful as it substantiates issues about whether or not current and future drug-control efforts are fit for their purpose. A proportionality test in law includes weighing a pressing social need (i.e. the interest of society) against the individual's interest of rights enjoyment.[27] Such a proportionality test, in which the standards legality, necessity, and subsidiarity are key criteria, determines whether a given rule is sufficient to attain its goal, as well as whether interference with a right is justified to attain that goal.[28] If used in this guiding capacity, both the PGC and the proportionality test as developed in law reveal the framework using which States and the international community can explore and revise drug-control regulations in order to tailor drug-control efforts so as to support instead of hamper the access to medicines.

Any structural changes this book proposes – at both the international and the national levels – are designed to work towards ensuring that regulations become purpose-fit instead of remaining ill-informed (by a lack of constructive guidance and being insensitive to the local context in which they are to be implemented).

Mandate-related changes

Mandate-related changes include any suggested revision of the mandates of the various human rights and drug-control actors addressed in the analysis of this book. While the international drug-control system includes the main regulatory system of controlled substances, the human rights framework is in the forefront in terms of providing for a legitimate basis for drug control.

Apart from recommended structural changes, the book also identifies mandate-related changes. The AAAQ standard of healthcare, as developed in the human rights

27 See Chapter 3, Section 3.3.3.
28 JH Gerards, *EVRM – Algemene Beginselen* (SDU Uitgevers 2011) 97.

system, is crucial for drug control. As the book clearly revealed, it is necessary and important to view the international drug-control and human rights system as mutually reinforcing instead of exclusive. One must note, however, that this does not mean that the international drug-control bodies have to get involved in human rights monitoring to the extent the human rights bodies do. Neither does it imply that the human rights bodies must be mandated to regulate drug-control matters.

Nevertheless, a human rights approach to drug control does imply that the INCB, when assessing estimates and acting as the gatekeeper of the supply/demand chain of controlled medicines, should include the AAAQ standard of healthcare in carrying out its mandate. Similarly, the UNODC and CND should take notice of the AAAQ standard of healthcare as important human rights monitoring tool and integrate this in their work if they have not done so yet. The international drug-control system, in other words, should actively and effectively support and improve the access to medicines in regions where it is most needed. In doing so, the international drug-control bodies, even more so than they have been doing, can learn from the constructive dialogue of state reporting on the substantive implementation of specific human rights provisions. Especially the INCB should take the 'progressive realization approach' into account. If adopting a practice similar to state reporting under human rights law in order to enter into a constructive dialogue with State Parties, progressive implementation should be monitored.

It is not submitted here, however, that the actors involved fail to monitor implementation at this stage. Instead, it is contended that the present efforts should be synergized and that efforts to ensure the access to medicines should be understood with the technical constraints of the current international drug-control regime in mind. The reference to the international drug-control treaties in General Comment 15 of the Committee on the Rights of the Child, for example, is a welcome development.[29]

In addition, human rights bodies should be aware of the technical and substantive implications that the international drug-control regime has for the access to medicines and should reflect on this when monitoring the AAAQ standard of healthcare and human rights protection more generally.

Behavioural changes

Finally, in addition to the structural and mandate-related changes listed above, this study has also produced recommendations related to behavioural changes.

29 CRC Committee, 'General Comment No 15: The Right of the Child to the Enjoyment of the Highest Attainable Standard of Health (Art. 24)' adopted at the Sixty-Second Session (17 April 2013) UN Doc CRC/G/GC/15, para 66. See also Chapter 3.

Behavioural changes refer to aspects related to the interpretation and attitude of the individuals occupying a position in any of the drug-control and human rights bodies. For instance, the unfounded fear of and myths surrounding the use of controlled medicines, and in particular the use of pain-control medication such as morphine and codeine, should be discouraged and corrected. Although any law, regulation, and policy adopted to regulate the dual nature of controlled substances should be evidence-based, the mindset of legislators, regulators, service providers, educators, patients, and all other actors involved should be informed by medical evidence, not by a fear of abuse.

It is not contended that one should think lightly of drug-control matters and the potential public hazard that non-medical substance use can produce, but such negative consequences should never overshadow their medical potential and hinder their availability and accessibility in practice. While applauding the bulk of constructive initiatives taken to this end, more extensive education, training, information, capacity and community-building is required to inform actors on adequate treatment standards, including those relating to the use of controlled essential medicines.

Moreover, those working in the international drug-control system should develop a certain 'human rights mindset'. They should not only talk about human rights protection but also act according to their mandates and use human rights as a 'yardstick' in their decision-making.

The question is, however, whether the international drug-control and human rights bodies possess or have access to the necessary know-how to realize this necessary double awareness. While the collaboration of the WHO and INCB is an example of knowledge exchange, joining forces has so far been technical as opposed to normative in nature. Human rights education and training has been widely discussed by academics as a tool to integrate and implement human rights norms.[30] These debates should be used as an inspiration and may guide the creation of the awareness that the international drug-control treaties require of the human rights system, norms, and requirements, and *vice versa*.

---

30 See eg, F Tibbitts and WR Fernekes, 'Human Rights Education' in S Totten and JE Pedersen (eds), *Teaching and Studying Social Issues: Major Programs and Approaches* (Information Age Publishing 2011) 88. Tibbitts and Fernekes refer to the UN standpoint that human rights education should not just be taught in schools but rather should be available to all segments of society. See also UNGA 'Report of the Secretary-General on the United Nations Decade for Human Rights Education (1995-2004) and Public Information Activities in the Field of Human Rights' (20 October 1997) UN Doc A/52/469/Add.1.

8.3.2 Areas of further investigation and broader implications

Although much has been addressed in this book, other urgent human rights and drug control related topics have fallen outside the scope of the book. Drawing on the ambitions, analysis, and reflections of this book, two such topics should be mentioned specifically for attention in future work.

First, additional research is needed into the balancing of the protection against hazardous use of controlled substances against cultural, religious, and traditional substances use. This is necessary to reconsider and frame a human rights foundation of drug control in a holistic manner. As stated in Chapter 1, the analysis presented, although focused on the access to controlled essential medicines, is relevant to the potential tensions between other drivers of substance use and the strict prohibition clause. The thresholds and criteria that human rights norms provide to legitimately strike a balance in competing interests are equally relevant and applicable to cultural, religious, and traditional forms of substance use. One, therefore, does not have to scrutinize human rights norms and the structures they provide from scratch. Rather, one should build on the systematic legal and ethical analysis provided in this book. In doing so, however, one should also fill in the framework provided with relevant empirical and background information on these other areas of substance use. To this end, further analysis should be equally legal, ethical, and empirical in nature.

Such new research would extend this book's central message and contribute to a complete picture of human rights and drug control in all its facets and from a grassroots level. The purpose of this book, after all, was to go beyond a mere analysis of the effects of drug-control regulations on human rights protection. Rather, it aimed to illustrate the relevance of human rights to drug-control regulation from an internal perspective, in line with Pettus' suggestion to review the internal structures of the international drug-control regime instead of the external application of the global drug enforcement efforts.[31]

Second, more research into the practical implications that the technical and administrative drug-control requirements have for the local service provision is also much needed. It is always tricky to use words such as 'effective', 'significant', 'disadvantaged', or 'structural', for how can one substantiate such claims, especially if no quantitative data has been used and the purpose of this book was not to reflect on causal relationships per se. In this regard, it is noted once more, that the country studies fulfil an exploratory role, highlighting avenues for future research.[32] However,

31 KI Pettus, 'Rhetoric and the Road to Hell: The International Narcotics Control Regime and Access to Essential Medicines' (2012) 1 Bulletin Health Policy and Law 1. See also Chapter 1.

32 See Chapters 6 and 7.

one must also note that using a case-study approach complicates the generalization of its outcome. This does not mean no generalization is possible at all, but that the approach taken and the insightful findings urge additional research into local health-service provision, specific drug-control requirements, and human-rights compliant access to medicines.

While the present book provides the normative foundations, academic and political debates on human rights, drug control, and access to medicines would benefit from additional health systems research into the structures of governance concerning local service provision.[33] Supplementing the qualitative work presented in this book with quantitative data would provide an important contribution to the determination of the avenues of reform that the current monitoring and regulatory bodies ought to explore.

In addition, as ample references throughout the study have shown, the conclusions should be understood while bearing in mind that at no stage is it submitted here that human rights standards are sufficiently capable of realizing their own normative purpose in practice. In fact, as also stressed in Chapter 3, the selection of core obligations of the CESCR, for instance, has been criticised. Critics have asserted in this regard that the list of core obligations of the right to health presupposes sufficient and well-advanced health systems.[34] Paradoxically, one could even question whether regulations in accordance with the AAAQ standard of healthcare would be capable of turning around the public health deficit of controlled medicine provision. For this reason, in addition to supplementary research into the practical applications of drug-control requirements, it is much-needed to map and analyse the practical implications and feasibility of specific human rights standards, adopted and formulated to improve the local realization of human rights.[35] For example, the potential of the AAAQ standard of healthcare has been extensively scrutinized in relation to the right to water.[36] It should also be acknowledged, however, that this comment does not subtract from the conclusions presented. The research at the heart of this book operated on the assumptions of human rights law and was therefore not necessarily set up to question the human rights system per se. However, future research into the ability of

33 See eg D Beran, 'The Impact of Health Systems on Diabetes Care in Low and Lower Middle Income Countries' (2015) 15 Current Diabetes Reports <doi:10.1007/s11892-015-0591-8> accessed 31 August 2016.

34 See Chapter 3.

35 On the necessity of looking into local realities to understand rights realization, see also B de Gaay Fortman, *Political Economy of Human Rights* (Routledge 2011).

36 MH Jensen, M Villumsen and TD Petersen, *The AAAQ Framework and the Right to Water: International Indicators for Availability, Accessibility, Acceptability and Quality* (Danish Institute for Human Rights 2014); M Villumsen and MH Jensen, *The AAAQ Manual and the Right to Water: Contextualising Indicators for Availability, Accessibility, Acceptability and Quality* (Danish Institute for Human Rights 2014).

human rights standards to realize their own normative ambitions should benefit from the collaboration amongst human rights bodies. In relation to health and the access to medicines in particular, such research should benefit from a collaboration with international drug-control bodies as well.

In light of these future research areas, this book contains some broader implications that deserve special attention. First, the in-depth empirical analysis presented has broader implications for research on the realization of economic, social, and cultural rights in countries with suboptimal conditions of service provision. Using a similar approach, more research is needed to reveal technical and practical complexities of service provision, e.g. in the fields of education and employment. Second, this book supports the idea that a one-size-fits-all approach in medicine regulation is insufficient. Additional medicine-specific research should be carried out in the field of pharmaceutical regulations to create a comprehensive overview of the applicability and impact of various competing or reinforcing regulatory structures regarding medicine development, market authorization, and consumer/patient use.

8.4 Final thoughts

This book has touched on one of the most latent, yet devastating human rights and public health crisis the world is facing today. The dire situation in which millions of people suffer on a daily basis due to a lack of access to adequate pain control and palliative care treatment inspired and informed the approach taken. Although the study relied on pain control as the central example, the findings similarly apply and should be viewed as relevant to the access to controlled essential medicines more generally.

The lack of an injection of the system of human rights norms and its moral foundation into international drug-control debates, politics, and academic thinking in a constructive and concise manner, fuelled the ambitions of this book. While any academic work inspires new questions, and innovative and necessary areas of research are identified, it is important to recognize the contribution this book has made. It is evident that one may not, cannot, and should not rule out or minimize the importance of human rights for drug-control regulation at any time. Any law, regulation, or policy regulating the dual nature of controlled substances should find its basis in human rights norms. In relation to the access to controlled essential medicines, this implies that balancing in the field of drug control is a prioritized one and the access to medicines must never be obstructed by interventions designed to curb drug use. To this end, the specific resource-intensive monitoring requirements should be reconsidered in light of human rights standards.

The visible and invisible impact that the domestic regulations, adopted by both Uganda and Latvia to comply with international requirements, have on the local service provision is devastating and defeats their purpose. The international community and individual States should be alarmed by the practical realities found in these countries and domestic interventions should be considered. Progressive reform in laws, regulations, and policy, aiming to protect the dignity of all patients experiencing inadequate care due to regulatory complexities and structural challenges that aggravate their situation, is more than just a simple call as advocated here. Instead, it reflects the way forward: a moral and legal obligation imposed upon the entire international community to prioritize lives and safety.[37]

37 KA Annan, 'Lift the Ban! Kofi Annan on Why It's Time to Legalize Drugs' *Der Spiegel* (22 February 2016) <www.spiegel.de/international/world/kofi-annan-on-why-drug-bans-are-ineffective-a-107840 2.html> accessed 31 August 2016.

APPENDIXES

APPENDIX I: INTERVIEW PROTOCOL UGANDA

Universiteit Utrecht

SIM

Utrecht University
Netherlands Institute of Human Rights (SIM)
P.O. Box 80125
3508 TC Utrecht
The Netherlands

Research Participant Information and Consent Form

1. **Title of the Study:** 'Advancing Access to Opioid Analgesics'

2. **Principle Investigator:** M.E.C. (Marie Elske) Gispen, LLM, Ph.D. Researcher at the Netherlands Institute of Human Rights (SIM), Utrecht University. Ph. +31(0)6 43 43 99 18; E-mail: m.e.c.gispen@uu.nl

3. **Context and Justification**
   You are asked to participate in a research, which sets out to analyse a human-rights based model of drug-control to advance access to opioid analgesics such as morphine in resource poor countries. This research is carried out under the supervision of Professor J.E. (Jenny) Goldschmidt (Director of the Netherlands Institute of Human Rights, Utrecht University) and Professor M. (Marcus) Düwell (Director of the Ethics Institute, Utrecht University), by Ms. M.E.C. (Marie Elske) Gispen, LLM. Before you decide, you can talk to anyone you would feel comfortable with about the research. This consent form may contain words you do not understand. Please ask me to stop as we go through all the information and I will take the time to explain anything you do not clearly understand. If you have questions later, you can ask me at any time.

   The purpose of the study is to get insight in Uganda's reform process and present regulatory system of controlled substances applying to morphine, and to map the link between the regulatory demands of the procedural obligations anchored in international drug control treaties and morphine availability. In doing so, the study will also compare access to morphine with an uncontrolled medicine necessary for pain treatment. We believe that you can help us better understand the regulatory chain of morphine in Uganda by telling your experience as one of the actors in the system.

4. **Research participation and procedures**
   Your participation will comprise of one, one-on-one interview lasting for approximately one hour, with the possibility of a follow-up interview for clarification purposes if mutually agreed upon between the PI and the participant. You are being invited to take part in this research because the African Palliative Care Association (APCA) has recommended you as relevant actor in the regulatory chain of morphine.

   If you decide to participate you will be asked questions about your role in the regulatory chain of morphine, the pros and cons of the present system and the way it affects delivering adequate standards of palliative care and pain treatment in particular. In particular we would like to ask you a few questions about the registration of consumer data, estimate techniques and reporting procedures and Uganda's treaty reporting procedure to the International Narcotics Control Board as the monitoring body of the International Drug Control Treaties. From a legal/regulatory perspective, we would like to hear about the differences, if any, between the accessibility of oral morphine and as compared to paracetamol, which is an uncontrolled medicine, used to treat pain, so we grant a better understanding of the legal control of controlled medicines. To make sure we have the correct information, the interview will be tape-recorded and only if you agree we will take some pictures. The tapes will be destroyed after the research project finished – no later than January 2016.

5. **Voluntary Participation**
   Your participation in this research is entirely voluntary. It is your choice whether or not to participate. The choice you will make will not have any effect on your current and future job position, it also has no effect on your work evaluation.

6. **Risks**
   We don't envision any risks involved in this study. We are asking you to share with us sometimes very personal or confidential information, and you may feel uncomfortable talking about some of the topics. You are entirely free to refuse to answer any (or all) question(s), which you do not want to answer. You do not have to give any reason for not responding.

7. **Benefits and Reimbursements**
   There is no direct benefit to you, but your participation is likely to help us to increase better access to controlled medication in resource poor countries. You will not be provided any incentive to take part in the research. Also, we will not give any reimbursement of travel costs or loss of time.

8. **Confidentiality and Dissemination of Results**
   The research being done in the community might draw attention to you if you participate and other people in the community may ask you questions about it. We will not be sharing any information about you to anyone outside the research team. All information collected will be kept private and the study is strictly confidential. Your name and identity will also not be disclosed at any time. The data, however, may be published in academic publications without disclosing your identify or giving your name. We will share the knowledge we get from this research with all participants by providing a summary of the results first before we make it widely available to the public.

9. **Right to Refuse or Withdraw**
   Your participation in this research is entirely voluntary. It is your choice whether or not to participate. The choice you will make will not have any effect on your current and future job position, it also has no effect on your work evaluation. You may decide to refuse to participate without any loss of benefits, which you are otherwise entitled to. At the end of the interview you will be given the opportunity to review your remarks and modify if necessary to clear any misunderstandings.

10. **Contact**
    If you have any questions you can ask me now or later. If you wish to ask questions later, you may contact the following people: Principal Investigator (see contact details under section 2), or the principal contact person in Uganda: Ms. Eve Namisango, via: eve.namisango@africanpalliativecare.org/African Palliative Care Association P.O. Box 72518 Plot 95, Dr. Gibbons Road, Makindye Kampala, Uganda, Ph. +256 312 264 978.

AUTHORISATION FORM

Statement by the participant

I have been invited to participate in research about access to controlled medicine in resource poor countries. I have read the foregoing information, or it has been read to me. I have had the opportunity to ask questions about it and any questions I have been asked have been answered to my satisfaction. I have read and understand this consent form, and I volunteer to participate in this research study. I acknowledge that I will receive a copy of this form. I voluntarily choose to participate, but I understand that my consent does not take away any legal rights in the case of negligence or other legal fault of anyone who is involved in this study. I was also explained that nothing in this consent form is intended to replace any applicable Federal, state, or local laws. I consent voluntarily to be a participant in this study

Name of participant	Date	Signature of participant
	—/—/— (day/month/year)	

If illiterate

I have witnessed the accurate reading of the consent form to the potential participant, and the individual has had the opportunity to ask questions. I confirm that the individual has given consent freely.

Print name of witness	Date	Signature of witness
	—/—/— (day/month/year)	

Thumb print of participant

Statement by the researcher
I have accurately read out the information sheet to the potential participant, and to the best of my ability made sure that the participant understands that we will have an interview in which we will ask a few questions about the availability of controlled medicine in resource poor countries. I confirm that the participant was given an opportunity to ask questions about the study, and all the questions asked by the participant have been answered correctly and to the best of my ability. I confirm that the individual has not been coerced into giving consent, and the consent has been given freely and voluntarily.

A copy of this ICF has been provided to the participant.

Name of researcher	Date	Signature of researcher
	—/—/— (day/month/year)	

Appendix II: Interview Protocol Latvia

Universiteit Utrecht

SIM

Utrecht University
Netherlands Institute of Human Rights (SIM)
P.O. Box 80125
3508 TC Utrecht
The Netherlands

Research Participant Information and Consent Form

1. **Title of the Study:** 'Advancing Access to Opioid Analgesics'

2. **Principle Investigator:** M.E.C. (Marie Elske) Gispen, LLM, Ph.D. Researcher at the Netherlands Institute of Human Rights (SIM), Utrecht University. Ph. +31(0)6 43 43 99 18; E-mail: m.e.c.gispen@uu.nl

3. **Context and Justification**
   You are asked to participate in a research, which sets out to analyse a human-rights based model of drug-control to advance access to opioid analgesics such as morphine. This research is carried out under the supervision of Professor J.E. (Jenny) Goldschmidt (Director of the Netherlands Institute of Human Rights, Utrecht University) and Professor M. (Marcus) Düwell (Director of the Ethics Institute, Utrecht University), by Ms. M.E.C. (Marie Elske) Gispen, LLM. Before you decide, you can talk to anyone you would feel comfortable with about the research. This consent form may contain elements you do not fully understand. Please ask me to stop as we go through all the information and I will take the time to explain anything you do not clearly understand. Also, should you have any questions later, you can ask me at any time.

   The purpose of the study is to get insight in Latvia's present regulatory system of controlled substances applying to morphine, and to map the link between the regulatory demands of the procedural obligations anchored in international drug control treaties and morphine availability in the country. If relevant, this study also purposes to gain insight in any reform processes. In doing so, the study will also compare access to morphine with an uncontrolled medicine necessary for pain treatment. We believe that you can help us better understand the regulatory chain of morphine in Latvia by telling your experience as one of the actors in the system.

4. **Research participation and procedures**
   Your participation will comprise of one, one-on-one interview lasting for approximately one hour, with the possibility of a follow-up interview for clarification purposes if mutually agreed upon between the PI and the participant. You are being invited to take part in this research because the you have been recommended as relevant actor in the regulatory chain of morphine.

   If you decide to participate you will be asked questions about your role in the regulatory chain of morphine, the pros and cons of the present system and the way it affects delivering adequate standards of palliative care and pain treatment in particular. In particular we would like to ask you a few questions about the registration of consumer data, estimate techniques and reporting procedures and Latvia's treaty reporting procedure to the International Narcotics Control Board as the monitoring body of the International Drug Control Treaties. From a legal/regulatory perspective, we would like to hear about the differences, if any, between the accessibility of oral morphine and as compared to paracetamol, which is an uncontrolled medicine, used to treat pain, so we grant a better understanding of the legal control of controlled medicines. To make sure we have the correct information, the interview will be tape-recorded and only if you agree we will take some pictures. The tapes will be destroyed after the research project finished – no later than January 2016.

5. **Voluntary Participation and Right to Refuse or Withdraw**
   Your participation in this research is entirely voluntary. It is your choice whether or not to participate. The choice you will make will not have any effect on your current and future job position, it also has no effect on your work evaluation. You may decide to refuse to participate without any loss of benefits, which you are otherwise entitled to. At the end of the interview, you will be asked whether there are any issues you would like to clarify or whether you would like to provide any additional information you feel is missing from the interview.

6. **Risks**
   We don't envision any risks involved in this study. We are asking you to share with us sometimes information which you may feel uncomfortable talking about. You are entirely free to refuse to answer any (or all) question(s), which you do not want to answer. You do not have to give any reason for not responding.

7. **Benefits and Reimbursements**
   There is no direct benefit to you, but your participation is likely to help us to increase better access to controlled medication in resource constraint countries in particular. You will not be provided any incentive to take part in the research. Also, we will not give any reimbursement of travel costs or loss of time.

8. **Confidentiality and Dissemination of Results**
Potentially, the research being done might draw attention to you if you participate and other people may ask you questions about it. We will not be sharing any information about you to anyone outside the research team. All information collected will be kept private and the study is strictly confidential. Your name and identity will also not be disclosed at any time. The data, however, may be published in academic publications without disclosing your identify or giving your name but with reference to organisations or the different regulatory actors. We will share the knowledge we get from this research with all participants by providing a summary of the results.

9. **Contact**
If you have any questions you can ask me now or later. If you wish to ask questions at a later stage, please get in touch via: Achter Sint Pieter 200, 3512 EM Utrecht, The Netherlands; Ph. (work landline) +316 30 253 8407; or Ph. (mobile) +31(0)6 43 43 99 18; E-mail: m.e.c.gispen@uu.nl.

AUTHORISATION FORM

Statement by the participant

I have been invited to participate in research about access to controlled medicine in Latvia. I have read the foregoing information, or it has been read to me. I have had the opportunity to ask questions about it and any questions I have been asked have been answered to my satisfaction. I have read and understand this consent form, and I volunteer to participate in this research study. I acknowledge that I will receive a copy of this form. I voluntarily choose to participate, but I understand that my consent does not take away any legal rights in the case of negligence or other legal fault of anyone who is involved in this study. I was also explained that nothing in this consent form is intended to replace any applicable Federal, state, or local laws. I consent voluntarily to be a participant in this study

Name of participant Date Signature of participant

— /— /— (day/month/year)

If illiterate

I have witnessed the accurate reading of the consent form to the potential participant, and the individual has had the opportunity to ask questions. I confirm that the individual has given consent freely.

Print name of witness Date Signature of witness

— /— /— (day/month/year)

Thumb print of participant

Statement by the researcher
I have accurately read out the information sheet to the potential participant, and to the best of my ability made sure that the participant understands that we will have an interview in which we will ask a few questions about the availability of controlled medicine in Latvia. I confirm that the participant was given an opportunity to ask questions about the study, and all the questions asked by the participant have been answered correctly and to the best of my ability. I confirm that the individual has not been coerced into giving consent, and the consent has been given freely and voluntarily.

A copy of this ICF has been provided to the participant.

Name of researcher Date Signature of researcher

— /— /— (day/month/year)

Samenvatting

Probleemstelling en methode

Miljoenen mensen lijden wereldwijd aan de gevolgen van onbehandelde chronische en acute pijn, onder andere door de slechte beschikbaarheid van geneesmiddelen als morfine en codeïne. Dit is met name een probleem in landen met beperkte hulpbronnen, en specifiek in Afrikaanse landen ten zuiden van de Sahara, bij ziektebeelden als kanker en hiv/aids.

Onbehandelde pijn kan leiden tot een verhoogd risico op onder andere depressieve klachten maar zorgt er ook voor dat patiënten vaak niet, of niet goed meer, in hun eigen levensonderhoud kunnen voorzien en/of hun zorgtaken voor familie kunnen uitvoeren. Het verschil tussen onbehandelde en behandelde pijn is daarbij een verschil van dag en nacht. Deze sluimerende mondiale volksgezondheidscrisis heeft niet alleen grote invloed op het maatschappelijk welzijn vanuit sociaaleconomisch perspectief, maar roept ook dringende vragen op vanuit het beschermen van de rechten van de mens.

Het internationale mensenrechtensysteem stelt overheidsverplichtingen in op basis waarvan adequate gezondheidszorg beschikbaar moet zijn en individuen tegen onmenselijke en mensonterende behandeling beschermd moeten worden. Speciale gezanten van de Verenigde Naties ondersteunen het idee dat tekortschietende pijnbestrijding (al dan niet als onderdeel van palliatieve zorg) niet slechts een schending van kortgezegd het recht op gezondheid is, maar ook een schending kan zijn van het folterverbod waar de vrijwaring van onmenselijke en mensonterende behandeling onder valt. Een veel gehoord argument hierin is dat morfine en codeïne als adequate pijnbestrijdingsmedicatie afdoende beschikbaar en toegankelijk moeten zijn, onder andere omdat zij genoemd staan op de Lijst van Essentiële Medicijnen zoals opgesteld door de *World Health Organisation* (WHO). Op basis van het recht op gezondheid zijn overheden verplicht genoemde medicijnen beschikbaar te stellen conform de *AAAQ standard of health care*. Deze *AAAQ*-standaard betekent dat gezondheidsinstellingen, goederen en diensten, in voldoende mate beschikbaar, toegankelijk, geschikt en van kwaliteit aanwezig moeten zijn in een land (AAAQ staat voor *availability, accessibility, acceptability,* en *quality*).

Echter, het is niet het mensenrechtensysteem maar het internationale drugscontrolerecht dat de beschikbaarheid, toegankelijkheid en het gebruik van geneesmiddelen als morfine en codeïne specifiek reguleert. Dit komt omdat morfine en codeïne zogeheten gecontroleerde essentiële medicijnen zijn: geneesmiddelen die dus enerzijds op de WHO-lijst staan en waarvan tegelijkertijd het actieve bestanddeel onder de reikwijdte van het internationale drugscontrolerecht valt omdat dit bestanddeel een verslavende werking kan hebben.

Zowel morfine als heroïne wordt gemaakt van een actief bestanddeel van opium. Doorgaans kan men stellen dat morfine een wetenschappelijk bewezen medische werking heeft, terwijl heroïne zeer verslavend is als het recreatief wordt gebruikt. Het is moeilijk om een harde lijn te trekken tussen medisch en niet-medisch (en verslavend) gebruik omdat als morfine recreatief wordt gebruikt dit ook tot afhankelijkheidsproblemen kan leiden. Tegelijkertijd zijn er studies die bevestigen dat heroïne een medische relevantie heeft. Sterker nog, heroïne is ooit ontdekt als medicijn om morfineverslaving tegen te gaan. De verslavende werking van heroïne bleek echter aanzienlijk groter dan van morfine. Het gaat hier niet om de strikte scheidslijn tussen deze twee middelen maar meer algemeen om de onderliggende problematiek: het tweeledige karakter van gecontroleerde essentiële medicijnen.

Dit tweeledige karakter maakt dat het belangrijk is de productie, import/export, handel en het gebruik van deze middelen te reguleren. De vraag is echter wat de aard en reikwijdte van dergelijke regelgeving zou moeten zijn. Dit boek formuleert een wetenschappelijk antwoord op deze politiek gevoelige vraag door te onderzoeken welke structurele, mandaat en interpretatie gerelateerde veranderingen nodig zijn om te spreken van een mensenrechtenbenadering van drugscontrole. Het richt zich daarbij specifiek op het belang te voorzien in de toegang tot gecontroleerde medicatie in landen met beperkte hulpbronnen.

Het boek omvat een normatief kader (hoofdstuk 3-4) en toepassing van twee landenstudies (hoofdstuk 5-7). Het presenteert een juridische analyse die de meer conventionele juridische methodiek overstijgt, en bevat ook een ethische analyse en empirische studies in Oeganda en Letland. De juridische analyse gaat uit van de hiërarchie van rechtsbronnen zoals deze is opgenomen in Artikel 38 van het Statuut van het Internationaal Gerechtshof. Het uitgangspunt van de ethische analyse en daarmee ook verantwoording van theoriekeuze is een 'intern perspectief'. Daarmee wordt in de context van dit boek de conventionele interpretatie van het internationale mensenrechtensysteem bedoeld; het doel van het boek is niet het mensenrechtensysteem als zodanig te bekritiseren, maar in plaats daarvan de morele waarden waarop het systeem is gebaseerd uit te lichten en toe te passen op het centrale thema van het boek. De landenstudies zijn kwalitatief van aard. Zie voor een uitgebreide toelichting op de methode hoofdstuk 1 en 5. De context, achtergrond en inkadering van de probleemstelling wordt besproken in hoofdstuk 2.

Normatief kader

Het internationale drugscontrolesysteem bestaat nu meer dan honderd jaar. In die periode is het pas heel recent dat mensenrechten een in toenemende mate belangrijke rol krijgen in hervormingsdiscussies. De manier waarop mensenrechten tot nu toe worden betrokken in deze discussies is niet optimaal. Veelal worden slechts de effecten van internationale en nationale drugscontrolemaatregelen bekritiseerd vanuit een mensenrechtelijk perspectief. Een dergelijke aanpak heeft een belangrijke alarmerende functie maar stelt het uitgangspunt van het internationale drugscontrolesysteem niet ter discussie. Dit boekt plaatst het uitgangspunt van het internationale drugscontrolesysteem wel in licht van mensenrechtennormen om zo een legitieme basis van wet- en regelgeving op het gebied van drugscontrole te formuleren (hoofdstuk 3-4).

Het uitgangspunt van het internationale drugscontrolesysteem wordt vaak geformuleerd als het *principle of balance*. Uitgaande van een algeheel en strikt verbod, met als enige legitieme uitzondering productie, import/export, distributie en gebruik voor medische en wetenschappelijke doeleinden, moeten staten medisch (en wetenschappelijk) gebruik maximaliseren terwijl zij de negatieve consequenties van drugsgebruik moeten minimaliseren. Het internationale drugscontrolesysteem geeft verder niet of nauwelijks normatieve richting over hoe, of conform welke standaarden, staten dit moeten doen (zie hoofdstuk 2). Er zijn wel een aantal administratieve en procedurele verplichtingen van toepassing op het realiseren van toegang tot medicatie; deze worden later besproken.

Op zichzelf is het uitgangspunt aannemelijk. Echter, wanneer men probeert de onderliggende spanning tussen het tegengaan van misbruik en het realiseren van medisch gebruik binnen de reikwijdte van mensenrechtennormen te plaatsen, moet men de systematiek van het mensenrechtensysteem respecteren. Hoofdstuk 3 zet uiteen dat het mensenrechtensysteem veel specifieker dan het internationale drugscontrolesysteem een kader omvat van legitieme belangenafwegingen. Het komt vaak voor dat verschillende belangen of rechten in de samenleving of op individueel niveau met elkaar in conflict zijn. In zulke gevallen moet het recht een antwoord bieden op de vraag welk belang (algemeen of individueel) voorrang geniet. Een dergelijke afweging kan worden gemaakt op basis van de aard van een recht, de al dan niet van toepassing zijnde beperkingsclausule en daarin opgenomen proportionaliteitseisen, en de gradatie in het verwezenlijken van rechten. De eerste twee aspecten hebben betrekking op een afweging tussen verschillende individuele rechten en/of het belang van de samenleving. De gradatie van verwezenlijking heeft betrekking op een urgentie-afweging tussen verschillende aspecten van een recht.

Uitgaande van genoemde normen en kwalificaties uit het mensenrechtensysteem, blijkt uit hoofdstuk 3 dat het internationale mensenrechtensysteem zich noch direct noch in verdragen, begeleidende documenten of jurisprudentie uitspreekt over hoe een belangenafweging tussen het tegengaan van misbruik en het medisch beschikbaar stellen van gecontroleerde stoffen eruit moet zien. Impliciet doet dit het wel en daarbij is de uitkomst van de belangenafweging dat de toegang tot medicatie net iets meer gewicht in de schaal legt dan het belang om misbruik en de negatieve consequenties van drugsgebruik tegen te gaan. Dit betekent geenszins dat het laatstgenoemde niet belangrijk zou zijn of in mindere mate binnen de reikwijdte van het internationale mensenrechtensysteem valt. Dit bekent slechts dat met name in de implementatie van het recht op gezondheid een staat direct toegang tot essentiële medicatie moet garanderen en slechts geleidelijk (d.w.z. gefaseerd naar maximale kunnen) preventiemaatregelen moet treffen.

Hoofdstuk 4 behandelt de vraag of een dergelijke op medische toegang georiënteerde benadering van wet- en regelgeving op het gebied van drugscontrole legitiem en verdedigbaar is op basis van de morele waarden waarop het internationale mensenrechtensysteem rust. Dit is belangrijk, zeker omdat het recht zich niet expliciet uitspreekt over de onderhavige belangenafweging en des te meer ook omdat de morele waarden waarop het recht is gebaseerd niet noodzakelijk een-op-een hetzelfde zijn, of hoeven te zijn, als de rechten zoals deze uit het geldende recht spreken.

Uit verschillende internationale verklaringen en documenten blijkt dat mensenrechten worden gelegitimeerd in de inherente menselijke waardigheid. Artikel 1 van de Universele Verklaring voor de Rechten van de Mens stelt bijvoorbeeld dat ‘alle mensen vrij en gelijk in waardigheid en rechten [worden] geboren’. Menselijke waardigheid staat daarmee niet gelijk aan de rechten die het mensenrechtensysteem inroept. In plaats daarvan is het een categorische norm waaruit verschillende rechten (kunnen) voortkomen en worden gelegitimeerd.

Er wordt vaak gezegd dat het begrip ‘menselijke waardigheid’ te vaag is, slecht te duiden, en juridisch zwak door de tal van uitleggen die aan het begrip worden gegeven. In de conventionele uitleg van het mensenrechtensysteem wordt menselijke waardigheid of inherente waardigheid vaak begrepen als een aanspraak op autonomie (in plaats van autonomie als zodanig). Dat wil zeggen, de materiële invulling van menselijke waardigheid als categorisch bindende norm moet worden uitgelegd als de mogelijkheid om autonoom te handelen. Dat is dus iets anders dan autonomie als zodanig. Op basis daarvan kan men mensenrechten als volgt begrijpen: als menselijke waardigheid de mogelijkheid om autonoom te handelen betekent (ongeacht wat dit autonome handelen precies betekent), dan zijn mensenrechten aanspraken op vrijheden, goederen en diensten die zowel beschermd als verwezenlijkt moeten worden en waarvan de toegang daartoe een voorwaarde is om überhaupt een autonoom leven te leiden (nogmaals, ongeacht wat dit autonome leven of handelen betekent). Dit is een *empowerment*-gedachte: het gaat hier om het respecteren, beschermen en verwezenlijken van basisbehoeften om een zelfstandig leven te leiden.

Uitgaande van deze redenering zijn er een aantal theorieën uit de normatieve ethiek, politieke filosofie, en/of rechtstheorie die belangrijk zijn in de vraag hoe deze aanspraken moeten worden geconcipieerd en gerechtvaardigd. Op basis daarvan kan worden bekeken of de uitkomst van de belangenafweging zoals afgeleid van het bestaande recht ook standhoudt als deze in het licht van de aan het recht onderliggende morele waarden wordt geplaatst.

Het boek past de *capability*-theorie (*Capabilities Approach*) van Martha Nussbaum, en de theorie van generieke consistentie (*Principle of Generic Consistency*) van Alan Gewirth en Deryck Beyleveld toe. Beide theorieën werken op vrij vergelijkbare wijze basisbehoeften uit als criteria voor de mogelijkheid tot succesvol handelen, deelname aan de samenleving, en in bredere zin het bereiken van eigen geformuleerde doelen. Zowel de toegang tot geneesmiddelen als het tegengaan van misbruik daarvan valt binnen de reikwijdte van deze theorieën.

De rationele benadering van Gewirth en Beyleveld is echter overtuigender wanneer verschillende belangen tegen elkaar moeten worden afgewogen (wat in dit boek het geval is). De theorie van het *Principle of Generic Consitency* gaat uit van generieke behoeften om vrijheid en welzijn te garanderen. Deze generieke behoeften worden gerangschikt aan de hand van de noodzakelijkheid van het beschermen en verwezenlijken van die aspecten welke belangrijk zijn om autonoom te kunnen handelen. Deze *degree of needfulness* biedt een duidelijk houvast in het beslechten van conflicterende behoeften. De mate waarin de mogelijkheid om autonoom, en in het geval van Gewirth en Beyleveld rationeel, te handelen is dus bepalend voor de rechtvaardiging van een inperking van een recht. De manier waarop deze handelingsbekwaamheid wordt begrepen, is belangrijk voor de rechtvaardiging van de uitkomst van een belangenafweging. Want steeds blijft de vraag: waarom is het ene belang wellicht belangrijker dan het andere, of misschien zijn beide belangen qua aard wel van vergelijkbaar belang maar zijn er toch gewichtige redenen om het ene belang voorrang te laten genieten boven het andere. Dat is een vraag die bij ieder conflict opspeelt en die, zoals hoofdstuk 3 liet zien, in het recht via juridische beginselen en criteria wordt geregeld.

Gewirth en Beyleveld reconstrueren rationeel handelen aan de hand van het *principle of instrumental reason*. Dit is een redenering waarbij wordt uitgegaan van een intern (*dialectical*) perspectief. De gedachte is dat een *agent* slechts handeling X uitvoert om Y te bereiken als dezelfde *agent* Y zelfstandig als goed beschouwd. Om het iets concreter te maken: Rachel zal de koelkast openen (X) als zij een glas melk wil drinken (Y). Op basis van deze eerste premisse leidt het argument in twee vervolgstappen uiteindelijk tot wederzijdse erkenning van positieve en negatieve rechten en plichten.

Het belang van toegang tot geneesmiddelen, in het bijzonder pijnbestrijdingsmedicatie, is een generieke behoefte. De vraag is echter in hoeverre recreatief drugsgebruik binnen de reikwijdte van de theorie valt. Zoals hoofdstuk 4 laat zien, verdedigt de toepassing van deze generieke consistentie dat een balans binnen drugscontroleproblematiek moet worden begrepen als een uitgangspunt waarbij geneesmiddelengebruik nooit bij wet of praktijk mag worden beperkt door maatregelen die als oogmerk hebben de volksgezondheid en openbare orde tegen drugsmisbruik te beschermen. Nogmaals, ook vanuit ethisch perspectief betekent dit geenszins dat het niet belangrijk zou zijn om drugsmisbruik tegen te gaan en/of dat dit geen verplichting (vanuit het recht of moraal) zou zijn voor staten. Drugscontrolemaatregelen mogen geneesmiddelengebruik simpelweg noch juridisch noch praktisch in de weg staan. Daarbij komt dat een ethische analyse van het recht juist de mogelijkheid biedt om het recht te bekritiseren.

Landenstudies

Na het formuleren van een op mensenrechten gestoelde basis van drugscontrolemaatregelen slaat het boek een brug naar de praktijk. De vraag is namelijk of het mogelijk is om een normatieve basis zoals geformuleerd te implementeren in de huidige structuren van het internationale drugscontrolerecht (hoofdstuk 5-7).

Het belang van die vraag komt voort uit twee aspecten. Allereerst wordt het internationaal recht als zodanig bekritiseerd vanuit een postkoloniaal perspectief; het universele karakter van het recht is niet daadwerkelijk universeel maar in plaats daarvan een westerse interpretatie die wordt opgelegd als universeel. Nu gaat dit boek niet over deze kritisch juridische discussies. Een dergelijk kritiek laat slechts de noodzaak zien van het slaan van een brug omdat het boek een nieuwe interpretatie van het (internationaal) recht betoogt. Het is daarnaast zeker ook belangrijk de praktijk in ogenschouw te nemen aangezien het boek zich met name richt op landen met beperkte hulpbronnen (veelal niet-westers).

Ten tweede is er een reden die veel dichter bij de centrale problematiek van het boek ligt. De Artikelen 17, 19-20, 30 Enkelvoudig Verdrag (*Single Convention on Narcotic*

Drugs) verplichten staten om een aparte administratie bij te houden, jaarlijkse schattingen en kwartaalcijfers op te maken en deze ter controle in te dienen bij de *International Narcotics Control Board* (INCB) die toezicht houdt op de naleving van de internationale drugscontroleverdragen. Daarnaast zijn verdragspartijen ook gehouden verschillende handel- en distributiegerelateerde maatregelen op te nemen in hun nationale wet- en regelgeving. Hoewel een deel van deze verplichtingen is gericht op het beschermen van de 'legale drugsmarkt' en het aldus verwezenlijken van medisch gebruik van gecontroleerde stoffen, veronderstellen de vereisten praktisch gezien een gevestigde bureaucratie en een goedlopende distributieketen. Condities die juist in landen met beperkte hulpbronnen, waar de meeste patiënten wonen die voor pijnbestrijdingsbehandelingen in aanmerking komen, niet of in slechte mate aanwezig zijn. Daar zijn tal van redenen voor, maar dit onderzoek heeft niet als doel om die redenen aan het licht te brengen. Echter, tegen de achtergrond van bestuurlijke structuren en gezondheidssystematiek is het wel zeer belangrijk te onderzoeken of een *AAAQ*-standaard zoals geformuleerd binnen het mensenrechtensysteem überhaupt succesvol kan worden geïmplementeerd in samenhang met de implementatie van genoemde technische maatregelen die uit het drugscontrolesysteem voortvloeien.

Om meer zicht te krijgen op de lokale realiteit waarin genoemde verplichtingen moeten worden geïnterpreteerd, is het eerst belangrijk per land vraag en aanbod en de distributieketen van morfine voor pijnbestrijding in kaart te brengen. Dit maakt inzichtelijk welke actoren op nationaal, regionaal en lokaal niveau in een land voor welke administratieve of technische handelingen, voortvloeiend uit de implementatie van genoemde artikelen, verantwoordelijk zijn en aan wie deze actoren daarover verantwoording moeten afleggen. Tegen de achtergrond van dergelijke overzichten (zie hoofdstuk 6 en 7, in het bijzonder figuur 6.1 en 7.1) zijn er een aantal belemmeringen in het voorzien in toegang tot pijnbestrijdingsmedicatie die nauw gerelateerd zijn aan drugscontrolemaatregelen. Daarnaast zijn er ook een aantal belemmeringen die meer algemeen van aard zijn, maar die toch ook in meer indirecte zin de implementatie van drugscontrolemaatregelen op een manier waarop de *AAAQ standard of healthcare* wordt gerespecteerd kunnen bemoeilijken.

Uit beide landenstudies bleek een reeks specifieke belemmeringen, zoals de angst die heerst bij artsen, verpleegkundigen en apothekers in Oeganda en Letland dat ze niet aan specifieke administratieve en handel- en distributiegerelateerde verplichtingen voldoen. Deze angst lijkt in sommige gevallen zelfs te leiden tot een soort negatieve *compliance*-incentive: de drijfveer om aan een verplichting te voldoen is de angst om er niet aan te voldoen waardoor ook gesjoemeld wordt in de marge. Aanvullende administratieve regels, zoals het dubbel ondertekenen van de uitgifte van morfine in Oeganda, werden doorgaans in beide landen als onnodig belemmerend ervaren. Daarnaast bleek in beide landen een gebrek in de informatievoorziening op internationaal, nationaal en lokaal niveau. Voorbeelden zijn dat actoren op het nationale niveau onvoldoende zicht hebben op de dagelijkse realiteit van lokale *service providers*, maar ook dat internationale actoren zoals de *INCB* onvoldoende zicht hebben op de impact van internationale regels op nationaal en lokaal niveau in een land.

Een meer structurele factor die evenzeer de adequate voorziening van gecontroleerde geneesmiddelen kan belemmeren, is in grote mate het gebrek aan hulpbronnen. In beide landen zijn met name financiële en personeelstekorten een belangrijke reden waarom het lastig is om aan aanvullende regelgeving te voldoen. Zoals hierboven beschreven is het in Oeganda belangrijk dat iedere uitgifte van morfine door een collega wordt gesuperviseerd en dat deze medeondertekent. Echter, Oeganda wordt met name in de gezondheidssector geplaagd door een chronisch en structureel personeelstekort. Iedere regel die dus extra mankracht vereist is *a priori* lastig te implementeren. Een ander voorbeeld uit Letland is een gebrek aan financiële middelen, wat een barrière vormt om de verplichting om een apart alarmsysteem te installeren voor de ruimte waarin medische logboeken worden bewaard na te leven.

Een ander structureel probleem is de geografische spreiding van gezondheidsinstellingen in beide landen. De in te dienen schattingen van onder andere de hoeveelheid te gebruiken morfine in komend kalenderjaar worden vaak opgemaakt op basis van consumptiecijfers in plaats van een gecombineerde methode van consumptie- en ziektebeelddata. Wanneer het structureel moeilijk is voor patiënten om überhaupt bij een gezondheidsinstelling te komen die een licentie heeft om gecontroleerde middelen te hanteren, dan is het heel waarschijnlijk dat de schattingen die worden ingediend niet op de daadwerkelijke maar op de geregistreerde behoefte aan een middel zijn gebaseerd en dus *a priori* niet adequaat zijn vanuit een mensenrechtenperspectief. Juist omdat een mensenrechtenbenadering ook betekent dat kwetsbare groepen in de samenleving speciale aandacht vereisen. Hieronder vallen expliciet ook groepen die in rurale gebieden wonen.

Genoemde voorbeelden zijn slechts een greep uit de bevindingen van het onderzoek maar laten zien dat er gegronde reden is om de vraag te stellen of de technische procedures zoals deze voortvloeien uit het internationale drugscontrolesysteem landen met beperkte hulpbronnen niet structureel in een achtergestelde positie stellen om in afdoende mate de *AAAQ standard of healthcare* te hanteren. In geen van de voorbeelden kan worden gezegd dat de ondervonden belemmeringen er voor hebben gezorgd dat patiënten geen toegang tot geneesmiddelen hadden. De uitkomst is eerder dat de technische drugscontrolemaatregelen veelal voorbijgaan aan de lokale realiteit waarin zij moeten worden geïmplementeerd. De vraag is dus of de controlemaatregelen uit de internationale drugscontroleverdragen wel voldoende doeltreffend, proportioneel, en subsidiair zijn. Hoewel men niet zomaar kan generaliseren op basis van twee landenstudies, ondersteunen beide deelonderzoeken in ieder geval een negatief antwoord op deze vraag.

Conclusies en aanbevelingen

De conclusies van het boek zijn kort gezegd dat een mensenrechtenbenadering een genuanceerde op medische toegang georiënteerde benadering is, die niet of problematisch kan worden toegepast binnen de huidige structuren van het recht. Grondige herziening is dus noodzakelijk. Het boek formuleert uiteindelijk een overzicht van structurele, mandaatgerelateerde en interpretatie- en/of gedraggerelateerde conclusies en aanbevelingen op (zie hoofdstuk 8).

In het kort: structurele veranderingen zijn juridisch technische veranderingen en institutionele amendementen die op basis van het onderzoek noodzakelijk worden geacht om de opgestelde mensenrechtenbenadering door te voeren. De tekst van het strikte verbod uit Artikel 4 Enkelvoudig Verdrag moet worden herzien. Het uitgangspunt van drugscontrole zou de toegang tot medicatie moeten zijn en dit zou ook moeten blijken uit de meest fundamentele algemene bepaling uit het internationale drugscontrolerecht. De internationale gemeenschap is gehouden samen toe te werken naar een aanpassing van het internationale drugscontrolerecht zodat dit de toegang tot medicatie niet langer belemmert. Deze verantwoordelijkheid spreekt met name ook uit de conclusies van de landenstudies. Het wordt daarbij aanbevolen dat internationale drugscontroleorganen zoals de *INCB*, *United Nations Office on Drugs and Crime* en *Commission on Narcotic Drugs general comments* (zeer gezaghebbende achtergronddocumenten die met name in het mensenrechtensysteem worden opgesteld door verdragsorganen) aannemen waarin de aard en reikwijdte van verschillende (technische) drugscontroleverplichtingen anders wordt toegelicht en uitgediept. Het is daarbij van belang dat de internationale drugscontroleorganen nauw samenwerken met mensenrechtenlichamen zoals het comité van het Internationaal Verdrag inzake economische, sociale en culturele rechten (IVESCR).

Met het oog op deze kritische noot moet men zich ook afvragen of de technische procedures wellicht structureel niet passend zijn en moeten worden herzien. Dit boek betoogt dat de internationale gemeenschap integraal aandacht moet besteden aan de specifieke condities waarin landen met beperkte hulpbronnen internationale verplichtingen dienen te verwezenlijken. In ieder geval op basis van de landenstudies blijkt duidelijk dat genoemde procedures grondig moeten worden herzien. Een dergelijke herziening is uitermate relevant en noodzakelijk in het kader van discussies rondom de universaliteit van mensenrechten. Diversiteit speelt in toenemende mate een belangrijke rol in de implementatie van rechten; herziening van specifieke drugscontrolemaatregelen moet in het licht van die discussie worden bezien. Op nationaal niveau is van enorm belang dat staten hun nationale wetgeving herzien wegens het normatief kader dat dit boekt schetst.

Mandaatgerelateerde veranderingen hebben, zoals het woord al aangeeft, betrekking op het mandaat van de verschillende mensenrechten- en drugscontrolelichamen. Een van de belangrijkste mandaatgerelateerde veranderingen die dit boekt voorstelt, is het belang van het overnemen van de *AAAQ standard of healthcare* door de internationale drugscontroleorganen, en het overnemen van de *constructive dialogue* uit het landenrapportageproces van het mensenrechtenkader. Daarbij is het van belang dat het juridisch concept 'geleidelijke verwezenlijking' wordt overgenomen in de beoordelingen en toepassing van actoren zoals de INCB.

Tot slot hebben gedragsgerelateerde veranderingen te maken met de interpretatie en attitude van de personen die bepalende functies vervullen in belangrijke drugscontrole- en op mensenrechten gestoelde organen. Het is met name in de drugscontrolesector van groot belang dat de veelal ongefundeerde angst voor misbruik van gecontroleerde geneesmiddelen wordt tegengegaan. Daarbij is het belangrijk dat de veelal niet-juridische specialisten in drugscontroleorganen een 'mensenrechtenblik' krijgen. Daarmee wordt bedoeld dat zij zich terdege bewust zijn van het mensenrechtensysteem en enig inzicht hebben in de manier waarop mensenrechten van belang zijn en moeten worden toegepast in de internationale drugscontroleproblematiek.

Uitgaande van deze drie aspecten laat het boek duidelijk zien dat verandering gewenst en noodzakelijk is om de schrijnende positie waarin miljoenen mensen onnodig lijden terug te dringen. De *war on drugs* heeft gefaald, niet alleen in het tegengaan van misbruik van gecontroleerde stoffen maar dus ook duidelijk ten aanzien van het beschikbaar stellen van gecontroleerde medicatie. De les die hieruit te leren valt is dat de huidige maatregelen, in welke vorm dan ook, niet voldoen. In ieder aanpak van drugscontroleproblematiek is het meest essentiële belang dat de patiënt (of die nu een kankerpatiënt is of een problematisch drugsgebruiker) centraal staat en diens rechten worden gerespecteerd, beschermd en verwezenlijkt.

Selected Bibliography

Ahern J, Stuber J and Galea S, 'Stigma, Discrimination and the Health of Illicit Drug Users' (2007) 88 Drug and Alcohol Dependence 188.
Alston P and Goodman R, *International Human Rights* (OUP 2013).
Ando N, 'National Implementation and Interpretation' in D Shelton (ed), *The Oxford Handbook of International Human Rights Law* (OUP 2013).
Arendt H, *The Origins of Totalitarianism* (Harcourt 1951).
Arras JD, Fenton E and Kukla R (eds), *The Routledge Companion to Bioethics* (Routledge 2015).

Ballantyne JC, Kalso E and Stannard C, 'WHO Analgesic Ladder: A Good Concept Gone Astray' (2016) 352 The British Medical Journal 1 <http://dx.doi.org/10.1136/bmj.i20>.
Bantekas I and Oette L, *International Human Rights: Law and Practice* (CUP 2013).
Barbour R, *Introducing Qualitative Research* (SAGE Publications 2008).
Barreto JM (ed), *Human Rights from a Third World Perspective: Critique, History and International Law* (CUP 2013).
Barrett D and Nowak M, 'The United Nations and Drug Policy: Towards a Human Rights-Based Approach' in A Constantinides and N Zaikos (eds), *The Diversity of International Law: Essays in Honour of Professor Kalliopi K Koufa* (Martinus Nijhoff Publishers 2009).
Barrett D and others, 'Recalibrating the Regime: The Need for a Human Rights-Based Approach to International Drug Policy' (The Beckley Foundation 2008) <www.hrw.org/sites/default/files/related _material/beckley0308exec.pdf>.
Barrett D, *The Impacts of Drugs Policies on Children and Young People* (Open Society Foundations 2015).
Baxi U, 'Too Many or Too Few, Human Rights?' (2001) 1 Human Rights Law Review 1.
Beauchamp TL and Childress JF, *Principles of Biomedical Ethics* (7th edn, OUP 2013).
Beitz CR and Goodin RE (eds), *Global Basic Rights* (2009 OUP).
— —, *The Idea of Human Rights* (OUP 2009).
Benhabib S, 'Another Universalism: On the Unity and Diversity of Human Rights' (2007) 81 Proceedings and Addresses of the American Philosophical Association 7.
— —, 'Reason-Giving and Rights-Bearing: Constructing the Subject of Rights' (2013) 20 Constellations 38.
Bennett D and Carr D, 'Opiophobia as a Barrier to the Treatment of Pain' (2002) Journal of Pain & Palliative Care Pharmacotherapy 105.

Beran D and Higuchi M, *How to Investigate Access to Care for Chronic Non-Communicable Diseases in Low- and Middle-Income Countries* (International Insulin Foundation 2012).
Beran D, 'The Impact of Health Systems on Diabetes Care in Low and Lower Middle Income Countries' (2015) 15 Current Diabetes Reports < doi:10.1007/s11892-015-0591-8>.
Berterame S and others, 'Use of and Barriers to Access to Opioid Analgesics: A Worldwide, Regional, and National Study' (2016) 387 The Lancet 1644.
Bewley-Taylor D and Jelsma M, 'Regime Change: Re-Visiting the 1961 Single Convention on Narcotic Drugs' (2011) 23 International Journal of Drug Policy 72.
Bewley-Taylor D, *International Drug Control: Consensus Fractured* (CUP 2012).
Beyleveld D and Brownsword R, *Human Dignity in Bioethics and Biolaw* (OUP 2001).
Beyleveld D, *The Dialectical Necessity of Morality* (The University of Chicago Press 1991).
— —, 'The Principle of Generic Consistency as the Supreme Principle of Human Rights' (2012) 13 Human Rights Review 1.
— —, 'Human Dignity and Human Rights in Alan Gewirth's Moral Philosophy' in M Düwell and others (eds), *The Cambridge Handbook of Human Dignity: Interdisciplinary Perspectives* (CUP 2014).
Bideli M and others, 'Access to Medicines from a Health Systems Perspective' (2013) 28 Health Policy and Planning 692.
Bilchitz D, 'Socio-Economic Rights, Economic Crisis, and Legal Doctrine' (2014) 12 International Journal of Constitutional Law 710.
Birmontiene T, 'Health Legislation in Eastern European Countries: the Baltic States' (2004) 11 European Journal of Health Law 77.
Boister N, 'Waltzing on the Vienna Consensus on Drug Control? Tensions in the International System for Control of Drugs' (2016) Leiden Journal of International Law 389.
Bomhoff J, *Balancing Constitutional Rights: The Origins and Meanings of Postwar Legal Discourse* (CUP 2013).
Bowling A, *Research Methods in Health: Investigating Health and Health Services* (4th edn, Open University Press 2014).
Brems E, 'Reconciling Universality and Diversity in International Human Rights: A Theoretical and Methodological Framework and Its Application in the Context of Islam' (2004) 3 Human Rights Review 5.
Brennan F, Carr DB and Cousins M, 'Pain Management: A Fundamental Human Right' (2007) 105 Anesthesia & Analgesia 205.
Brownsword R, 'Human Dignity from a Legal Perspective' in M Düwell and others (eds), *The Cambridge Handbook of Human Dignity: Interdisciplinary Perspectives* (CUP 2014).

Cameron A, 'Understanding Access to Medicines in Low- and Middle-Income Countries through the Use of Price and Availability Indicators' (DPhil thesis, Utrecht University 2013).

Campagna N, 'Human Dignity and Prostitution' in M Düwell and others (eds), *The Cambridge Handbook of Human Dignity: Interdisciplinary Perspectives* (CUP 2014).
Cassese A, *The Human Dimension of International Law* (OUP 2008).
Chinkin C, 'Sources' in D Moeckli, S Shah and S Sivakumaran (eds), *International Human Rights Law* (2nd edn, OUP 2014).
Claassen R and Düwell M, 'The Foundations of Capability Theory: Comparing Nussbaum and Gewirth' (2013) 16 Ethical Theory and Moral Practice 493.
Claassen R, 'Human Dignity in the Capability Approach' in M Düwell and others (eds), *The Cambridge Handbook of Human Dignity: Interdisciplinary Perspectives* (CUP 2014).
Cleary J and others, 'Formulary Availability and Regulatory Barriers to Accessibility of Opioids for Cancer Pain in Africa: A Report from the Global Opioid Policy Initiative (GOPI)' (2013) 24 Annals of Oncology xi14.
Cleary J and others, 'Formulary Availability and Regulatory Barriers to Accessibility of Opioids for Cancer Pain in Asia: A Report from the Global Opioid Policy Initiative (GOPI)' (2013) 24 Annals of Oncology xi24.
Cleary J and others, 'Formulary Availability and Regulatory Barriers to Accessibility of Opioids for Cancer Pain in Latin America and the Caribbean: A Report from the Global Opioid Policy Initiative (GOPI)' (2013) Annals of Oncology xi41.
Cleary J and others, 'Formulary Availability and Regulatory Barriers to Accessibility of Opioids for Cancer Pain in the Middle East: A Report from the Global Opioid Policy Initiative (GOPI)' (2013) 24 Annals of Oncology xi51.
Cleary J, 'Essential Medicines in Palliative Care' (2014) 28 Palliative Medicine 291.
Cleary J, A Husain and M Maurer, 'Increasing Worldwide Access to Medical Opioids' (2016) 387 The Lancet 1597.
Coleman C and others, 'The International Cancer Expert Corps (ICEC): A Unique Global Mentoring Model for Building Sustainable Expertise in Low- and Lower-Middle Income Countries and Geographically Remote Areas in Resource-Rich Countries' (2015) 81 Annals of Global Health 20.
Coomans F, 'Reviewing Implementation of Social and Economic Rights: An Assessment of the "Reasonableness" Test as Developed by the South African Constitutional Court' (2005) 65 Heidelberg Journal of International Law 167.
Crenshaw K, 'Mapping the Margins: Intersectionality, Identify Politics, and Violence against Women of Color' (1991) 43 Stanford Law Review 1241.
Curry-Summer I and others, *Research Skills* (Ars Aequi Libri 2010).
Cutcliffe JR, 'Establishing the Credibility of Qualitative Research Findings: The Plot Thickens' (1999) 30 Methodological Issues in Nursing Research 374.

De Beco G, 'Human Rights Indicators: From Theoretical Debate to Practical Application' (2013) 5 Journal of Human Rights Practice 1.
De Gaay Fortman B, *Political Economy of Human Rights* (Routledge 2011).

De Schutter O, 'The Status of Human Rights in International Law' in C Krause and M Scheinin (eds), *International Protection of Human Rights: A Textbook* (Institute for Human Rights Åbo Akademi University 2009).

De Wet E, 'Jus Cogens and Obligations Erga Omnes' in D Shelton (ed), *The Oxford Handbook of International Human Rights Law* (OUP 2013).

— —, 'The International Constitutional Order' (2006) 55 International and Comparative Law Quarterly 51.

Dembour MB, 'What Are Human Rights? Four Schools of Thought' (2010) 32 Human Rights Quarterly 1.

Den Hartogh G, 'Is Human Dignity the Ground of Human Rights?' in M Düwell and others (eds), *The Cambridge Handbook of Human Dignity: Interdisciplinary Perspectives* (CUP 2014).

Dobson M and others, *Surgical Care at the District Hospital* (WHO 2003).

Donders Y and Vleugel V, 'The Receptor Approach: A New Human Rights Kid on the Block or Old Wine in New Bags?' (2014) 36 Human Rights Quarterly 654.

Donnelly J, *International Human Rights* (3rd edn, Westview Press 2013).

Dupré C, 'Constructing the Meaning of Human Dignity' in C McCrudden (ed), *Understanding Human Dignity* (OUP 2013).

Duran MA and Chantler T, *Principles of Social Research* (2nd edn, Open University Press 2014).

Dussault G, Correia T and Pontes C, 'Impact of the Economic Crisis on Human Resources for Health Policies in Southern EU Countries' (2015) 25 European Journal of Public Health 32.

Duthey B and Scholten W, 'Adequacy of Opioid Analgesic Consumption at Country, Global, and Regional Levels in 2010, its Relationship with Development Level, and Changes Compared with 2006' (2014) 47 Journal of Pain and Symptom Management 283.

Düwell M and others (eds), *The Cambridge Handbook of Human Dignity: Interdisciplinary Perspectives* (CUP 2014).

Düwell M, *Bioethics* (Routledge 2013).

— —, 'Human Dignity: Concepts, Discussions, Philosophical Perspectives' in M Düwell and others (eds), *The Cambridge Handbook of Human Dignity: Interdisciplinary Perspectives* (CUP 2014).

Eide A and others, *The Universal Declaration of Human Right: A Commentary* (SUP 1992).

Elliot R and others, 'Harm Reduction, HIV/AIDS, and the Human Rights Challenge to Global Drug Control Policy' (2005) 8 Health and Human Rights 104.

Ezard N, 'Public Health, Human Rights and the Harm Reduction Paradigm: From Risk Reduction to Vulnerability Reduction' (2001) 12 International Journal of Drug Policy 207.

Fields HL, 'The Doctor's Dilemma: Opiate Analgesics and Chronic Pain' (2011) 69 Neuron 591.

Finlay L, '"Outing" the Researcher: The Provenance, Process, and Practice of Reflexivity' (2002) 12 Qualitative Health Research 531.
Finnis J, *Natural Law and Natural Rights* (2nd edn, OUP 2011).
Fitzmaurice M and Elias O, *Contemporary Issues in the Law of Treaties* (Eleven International Publishing 2005).
Fitzpatrick R and Boulton M, 'Qualitative Methods for Assessing Health Care' (1994) 3 Quality in Health Care 107.
Foley KM and others 'Pain Control for People with Cancer and AIDS' in DT Jamison and others (eds), *Disease Control Priorities in Developing Countries* (2nd edn, OUP 2006) 981.
Fortin KMA, *The Accountability of Armed Groups under Human Rights Law* (DPhil thesis, Utrecht University 2015).
Forzley M, Walker DM and Gispen MEC, 'Essential Laws for Medicines Access: A Pilot Study on National Legislation' (WHO 2014) <http://apps.who.int/medicinedocs/documents/s21443en/s21443en.pdf>.
Freeman M, 'Universalism of Human Rights and Cultural Relativism' in S Sheeran and N Rodley (eds), *Routledge Handbook of International Human Rights Law* (Routledge 2013).
Fuo O and Du Plessis A, 'In the Face of Judicial Deference: Taking the "Minimum Core" of Socio-Economic Rights to the Local Government Sphere' (2015) 19 Law, Democracy & Development 1.

Gearty C, 'Socio-Economic Rights, Basic Needs, and Human Dignity: A Perspective from Law's Frontline' in C McCrudden (ed), *Understanding Human Dignity* (OUP 2013).
Gerards JH, *EVRM - Algemene Beginselen* (SDU Uitgevers 2011).
Gewirth A, *Reason and Morality* (The University of Chicago Press 1978).
— —, *Human Rights* (The University of Chicago Press 1982).
— —, *The Community of Rights* (The University of Chicago Press 1996).
Ghai Y, 'Understanding Human Rights in Asia' in C Krause and M Scheinin (eds), *International Protection of Human Rights: A Textbook* (Institute for Human Rights Åbo Akademi University 2009) 547.
Ghodse H (ed), *International Drug Control into the 21st Century* (Ashgate 2008).
Gispen MEC, *Poor Access to Pain Treatment* (International Federation of Health and Human Rights Organization 2011).
— —, 'A Human Rights View on Access to Controlled Substances for Medical Purposes under the International Drug Control Framework' (2013) 719 European Journal of Pharmacology 16.
— —, 'Reconciling International Obligations and Local Realities: Provision of Pain Control Medication in Resource-Constrained Countries – Experiences from Uganda' in M Hesselman, A de Wolff and BCA Toebes (eds), *Essential Public Service Provision* (Routledge *forthcoming*).

Gispen-de Wied CC and Leufkens HGM, 'From Molecule to Market Access: Drug Regulatory Science as an Upcoming Discipline' (2013) 719 European Journal of Pharmacology 9.
Goldschmidt JE and Gispen MEC, '*Aanvullend Rapport Ratficatie... En dan?*' (SIM 2012).
Gorove K, 'Shifting Norms in International Health Law' (2004) 98 American Society of International Law Proceedings 18-20.
Gostin L, *Global Health Law* (HUP 2014).

Hägglöf I and Holmgren Å, 'Regulatory Affairs' in HP Rang (ed), *Drug Discovery and Development: Technology in Transition* (Elsevier 2006).
Hallam C, Bewley-Taylor D and Jelsma M, 'Scheduling in the International Drug Control System' (2014) TNI Series on Legislative Reform of Drug Policies No 25 <www.tni.org/files/down load/dlr25_0.pdf>.
Hannum H, 'The Status of the Universal Declaration of Human Rights in National and International Law' (1995-1996) 25 Georgia Journal of International and Comparative Law 287.
Harding R and Higginson IJ, 'Palliative Care in Sub-Saharan Africa' (2005) 365 The Lancet 1971.
Harding R and others, 'Availability of Essential Drugs for Managing HIV-related Pain and Symptoms within 120 PEPFAR-Funded Health Facilities in East Africa: A Cross-Sectional Survey with Onsite Verification' (2014) 28 Palliative Medicine 293.
Harding R and others, 'Provision of Pain- and Symptom-Relieving Drugs for HIV/AIDS in Sub-Saharan Africa' (2010) 40 Journal of Pain and Symptom Management 405.
Hart HLA, 'Are There Any Natural Rights?' (1955) 64 The Philosophical Review 175.
Hastie B and others, 'An Examination of Global and Regional Opioid Consumption Trends 1980-2011' (2014) 28 Journal of Pain & Palliative Care Pharmacotherapy 259.
Haugen HM, 'Inclusive and Relevant Language: The Use of the Concepts of Autonomy, Dignity, and Vulnerability in Different Contexts' (2010) 13 Medicine, Health Care, and Philosophy 203.
Hayward T, 'On Prepositional Duties' (2013) 123 Ethics 264.
Hoffmann FF, 'Human Rights, the Self and the Other' in A Orford (ed), *International Law and Its Others* (CUP 2006).
Hogerzeil HV and others, 'Is Access to Essential Medicines as Part of the Fulfilment of the Right to Health Enforceable through the Courts?' (2006) 368 The Lancet 305.
Hogerzeil HV and others, 'Promotion of Access to Essential Medicines for Non-Communicable Diseases: Practical Implications of the UN Political Declaration' (2013) 381 The Lancet 680.
Huber M and others, 'How Should We Define Health?' (2011) The British Medical Journal 343.
Hunt N, 'Public Health or Human Rights: What Comes First?' (2004) 15 International Journal of Drug Policy 231.

Jagwe JGM, 'The Introduction of Palliative Care in Uganda' (2002) 5 Journal of Palliative Medicine 160.
Jensen MH, Villumsen M and Petersen TD, *The AAAQ Framework and the Right to Water: International Indicators for Availability, Accessibility, Acceptability and Quality* (Danish Institute for Human Rights 2014).
Jensen SLB, *The Making of International Human Rights: The 1960s, Decolonization, and the Reconstruction of Global Values* (CUP 2016).
Joseph S and Fletcher A, 'Scope of Application' in D Moeckli, S Shah and S Sivakumaran (eds), *International Human Rights Law* (2nd edn, OUP 2014).

Kant I, *Grounding for the Metaphysics of Morals* (tr JW Ellington, 2nd edn, Hackett Publishing 1981).
Kaplan W and Mathers C, 'Global Health Trends: Global Burden of Disease and Pharmaceutical Needs' in L Bero and others (revs), *World Medicines Situation Report 2011* (3rd edn, WHO 2011).
Kennedy D, 'One, Two, Three, Many Legal Orders: Legal Pluralism and the Cosmopolitan Dream' (2006/2007) NYU Review of Law and Social Change 641.
Kiwanuka SN and others, 'Access to and Utilisation of Health Service for the Poor in Uganda: A Systematic Review of Available Evidence' (2008) 102 The Royal Society of Tropical Medicine and Hygiene 1067.
Kizito S and others, 'Career Intentions of Final Year Medical Students in Uganda after Graduating: The Burden of Brain Drain' (2015) 15 BMC Medical Education (2015).
Klein Goldewijk B and De Gaay Fortman B, *Where Needs Meet Rights* (WCC Publications 1999).
Koch IE, 'Dichotomies, Trichotomies, or Waves of Duties?' (2005) 5 Human Rights Law Review 81.
Koskenniemi M and Leino P, 'Fragmentation of International Law? Postmodern Anxieties' (2002) 15 Leiden Journal of International Law 553.
Koskenniemi M, 'Human Rights Mainstreaming as a Strategy for Institutional Power' (2010) 1 Humanity 47.
Krashin D, Merrill J and Trescot A, 'Opioids in the Management of HIV-Related Pain' (2012) 15 Pain Physician 157.
Krommendijk J, *The Domestic Impact and Effectiveness of the Process of State Reporting under UN Human Rights Treaties in the Netherlands, New Zealand and Finland* (Intersentia 2014).

Labate BC and Canvar C (eds), *Prohibition, Religious Freedom and Human Rights: Regulating Traditional Drug Use* (Springer 2014).
Laing R and others, '25 Years of the WHO Essential Medicines Lists: Progress and Challenges' (2003) 361 The Lancet 1723.
Lande A, 'The Single Convention on Narcotic Drugs, 1961' (1962) 16 International Organization 776.

Lauren PG, 'The Foundations of Justice and Human Rights in Early Legal Texts and Thought' in D Shelton (ed), *The Oxford Handbook of International Human Rights Law* (OUP 2013).
Lee MM, Walter-Drop G and Wiesel J, 'Taking the State (Back) Out? Statehood and the Delivery of Collective Goods' (2014) 27 Governance 635.
Leijten AEM, *Core Rights and the Protection of Socio-Economic Interests by the European Court of Human Rights* (DPhil thesis, Leiden University 2015).
Leivy N, 'Autonomy and Addiction' (2006) 36 Canadian Journal of Philosophy 427.
Lenzerini F, *The Culturalization of Human Rights Law* (OUP 2014).
Lines RM, 'The 'Fifth Stage' of Drug Control: International Law, Dynamic Interpretation and Human Rights' (DPhil thesis, Middlesex University 2014).
— —, *Human Rights and Drug Control in International Law* (CUP *forthcoming*).
Lohman D and Burke-Shyne N, 'The Impact of International Drug Policy on Access to Controlled Medicines' (Open Society Foundations 2015).
Lohman D, 'Pain Care as a Human Right' (2014) 14 Pain Practice 199.
Lohman D, Schleifer R and Amon JJ, 'Access to Pain Treatment as a Human Right' (2010) 8 BMC Medicine 1.
London ED, 'Studying Addiction in the Age of Neuroimaging' (2009) 100 Drug and Alcohol Dependence 182.
López-Gómez M and others, 'Cancer in Developing Countries: The Next Most Preventable Pandemic. The Global Problem of Cancer' (2013) 88 Critical Reviews in Oncology/ Hematology 117.
Lu L, Fang Y and Wang X, 'Drug Abuse in China: Past, Present and Future' (2008) 28 Cellular and Molecular Neurobiology 479.
Luper-Foy S and Brown C (eds), *Drugs, Morality, and the Law* (Garland Publishing 1994).

Macklin R, 'Dignity is a Useless Concept' (2003) 327 The British Medical Journal 1419.
Manyak TG and Katono IW, 'Decentralization and Conflict in Uganda: Governance Adrift' (2010) 11 African Studies Quarterly 1.
Marks S, 'Human Rights and the Bottom Billion' (2009) 1 European Human Rights Law Review 37.
— —, 'Human Rights and Root Causes' (2011) 74 The Modern Law Review 57.
Marks SP, 'Access to Essential Medicines as a Component of the Right to Health' in A Clapham and M Robinson (eds), *Realizing the Right to Health*, vol 3 (Rüffers & Rub 2009).
Mason Meier B and Fox AM, 'Development as Health: Employing the Collective Right to Development to Achieve the Goals of the Individual Right to Health' (2008) 30 Human Rights Quarterly 259.
Mbazira C, 'Service Delivery Protests, Struggle for Rights and the Failure of Local Democracy in South African and Uganda: Parallels and Divergences' (2013) South African Journal of Human Rights 252.

McCrudden C, 'Mainstreaming Human Rights' University of Michigan (2004) Public Law & Legal Theory Research Paper Series No 47 <http://papers.ssrn.com/sol3/papers.cfm?abstract_id=568642>.

——, 'Human Dignity and Judicial Interpretation of Human Rights' (2008) 19 European Journal of International Law 655.

—— (ed), *Understanding Human Dignity* (OUP 2013).

McLachlan C, 'The Principle of Systemic Integration and Article 31(3)(c) of the Vienna Convention' (2005) 54 International and Comparative Law Quarterly 279.

——, 'Investment Treaties and General International Law' (2008) 57 International and Comparative Law Quarterly 361.

McNair A, *The Law of Treaties* (OUP 1961).

Merriman A, 'Uganda: Current Status of Palliative Care' (2002) 24 Journal of Pain and Symptom Management 252.

——, *Audacity to Love* (The Irish Hospice Foundation 2010).

——, 'Going the Extra Mile with the Bare Essentials: Home Care in Uganda' (2010) 18 Progress in Palliative Care 18.

Merry SE, 'Legal Transplants and Cultural Translation: Making Human Rights in the Vernacular' in M Goodale (ed), *Human Rights: An Anthropological Reader* (Blackwell 2009).

Mitenbergs U and others, 'Latvia: Health System Review' (2012) 14 Health Systems in Transition 1.

Mock C and others, *Guidelines for Essential Trauma Care* (WHO 2004).

Moore GE, 'The Subject Matter of Ethics' in R Shafer-Landau (ed), *Ethical Theory* (2nd edn, Wiley-Blackwell 2013).

Motta Ferraz OL, 'Brazil: Health Inequalities, Rights, and Courts: The Social Impact of the Judicialization of Health' in AE Yamin and S Gloppen (eds), *Litigating Health Rights: Can Courts Bring More Justice to Health?* (HUP 2011).

Moyn S, 'The Secret History of Constitutional Dignity' in C McCrudden (ed), *Understanding Human Dignity* (OUP 2013).

Mubangizi JC and Twinomugisha BK, 'The Right to Health Care in the Specific Context of Access to HIV/Aids Medicines: What Can South Africa and Uganda Learn from Each Other?' (2010) 10 African Human Rights Law Journal 105.

Mubangizi JC, 'The Constitutional Protection of Socio-Economic Rights in Selected African Countries: A Comparative Evaluation' (2006) 2 African Journal of Legal Studies 1.

Naicker S and others, 'Shortage of Health Workers in Developing Countries – Africa' (2009) 19 Ethnicity & Disease 60.

Nesiah V, 'Resistance in the Age of Empire: Occupied Discourse Pending Investigation' (2006) 27 Third World Quarterly 903.

Nowak M and McArthur E, *The United Nations Convention against Torture: A Commentary* (OUP 2008).

Nowak M, 'Torture and Enforced Disappearance' in C Krause and M Scheinin (eds), *International Protection of Human Rights: A Textbook* (Institute for Human Rights Åbo Akademi University 2009) 151.

Nussbaum MC, 'Capabilities as Fundamental Entitlements: Sen and Social Justice' (2003) 9 Feminist Economics 33.

——, *Frontiers of Justice* (HUP 2006).

——, *Creating Capabilities: The Human Development Approach* (HUP 2011).

Obrist B and others, 'Access to Health Care in Contexts of Livelihood Insecurity: A Framework for Analysis and Action' (2007) PLOS Medicine 1584.

O'Neill O, 'The Dark Side of Human Rights' (2005) 81 International Affairs 427.

Orakhelashvili A, 'Article 30 Convention of 1969' in O Corten and P Kleinne (eds), *The Vienna Conventions on the Law of Treaties: A Commentary* (vol 1, OUP 2011).

Pahuja S, *Decolonising International Law* (CUP 2011).

Pattinson SD, *Medical law and Ethics* (3rd edn, Sweet & Maxwell 2011).

Paul SM and others, 'How to Improve R&D Productivity: The Pharmaceutical Industry's Grand Challenge' (2010) 9 Nature Review Drug Discovery 203.

Perehudoff SK, Laing RO and Hogerzeil HV, 'Access to Essential Medicines in National Constitutions' (2010) 88 Bulletin of the World Health Organization 800.

Perehudoff SK, Toebes BCA and Hogerzeil HV, 'Access to Essential Medicines in National Constitutions: Progress Since 2008' (2016) 18 Health and Human Rights 1.

Pettus KI, 'Rhetoric and the Road to Hell: The International Narcotics Control Regime and Access to Essential Medicines' (2012) 1 Bulletin Health Policy and Law 1.

Pogge TW, *World Poverty and Human Rights* (2nd edn, Polity Press 2008).

Porat I, 'The Dual Model of Balancing: A Model for the Proper Scope of Balancing in Constitutional Law' 27 (2005-2006) Cardozo Law Review 1393.

Potts H, *Accountability and the Right to the Highest Attainable Standard of Health* (Human Rights Centre 2008).

Puhaja S, 'The Postcoloniality of International Law' (2005) 46 Harvard International Law Journal 459; A Anghie, *Imperialism, Sovereignty, and the Making of International Law* (CUP 2007).

Pullman D, 'Human Dignity and the Ethics and Aesthetics of Pain and Suffering' (2002) 23 Theoretical Medicine 75.

Radbruch L and others, 'The Lisbon Challenge: Acknowledging Palliative Care as a Human Right' (2013) 16 Journal of Palliative Medicine 301.

Radbruch L and others, *Access to Opioid Medication in Europe: Final Report and Recommendations to the Ministries of Health* (Palliative Medicine Verlag 2014).

Radbruch L and others, *Report and Recommendations to the Ministries of Health Annex* (Palliative Medicine Verlag 2014).

Rajagopal B, 'Counter-Hegemonic International Law: Rethinking Human Rights and Development as a Third World Strategy' (2006) 27 Third World Quarterly 767.

Ramcharan BG, 'The Law-Making Process: From Declaration to Treaty to Custom to Prevention' in D Shelton (ed), *The Oxford Handbook of International Human Rights Law* (OUP 2013).
Ramsey S, 'Leading the Way in African Home-Based Palliative Care' (2003) 362 The Lancet 1812.
Rang HP (ed), *Drug Discovery and Development: Technology in Transition* (Elsevier 2006).
— —, 'The Development of the Pharmaceutical Industry' in HP Rang (ed), *Drug Discovery and Development: Technology in Transition* (Elsevier 2006).
Rawls J, *A Theory of Justice* (HUP 1971).
Reed L, Reisman WM and Dolzer R, 'Why Regime Change is (Almost Always) a Bad Idea (Manley O. Hudson Medal Lecture)' (2004) 98 Proceedings of the Annual Meeting (American Society of International Law) 289.
Reuter P and Trautmann F (eds), *A Report on Global Illicit Drug Markets 1998-2007* (European Communities 2009).
Rhodin A, 'The Rise of Opiophobia: Is History a Barrier to Prescribing?' (2006) 30 Journal of Pain & Palliative Care Pharmacotherapy 31.
Riedel E, 'Economic, Social, and Cultural Rights' in C Krause and M Scheinin (eds), *International Protection of Human Rights: A Textbook* (Institute for Human Rights Åbo Akademi University 2009).
— —, 'The Human Right to Health: Conceptual Foundations' in A Clapham and M Robinson (eds), *Realizing the Right to Health* (Rüffers & Rub 2009).
Rishmawi M, 'The Revised Arab Charter on Human Rights' in C Krause and M Scheinin (eds), *International Protection of Human Rights: A Textbook* (Institute for Human Rights Åbo Akademi University 2009).
Rolles S and others, *The Alternative World Drug Report* (2nd edn, Transform Drug Policy Foundation 2016).
Rosen M, 'Dignity: The Case Against' in C McCrudden (ed), *Understanding Human Dignity* (OUP 2013).
Ruddin LP, 'You Can Generalize Stupid! Social Scientists, Bent Flyvbjerg, and Case Study Methodology' (2006) 12 Qualitative Inquiry 797.
Ruger JP, 'Health Capability: Conceptualization and Operationalization' (2010) 100 American Journal of Public Health 41.
— —, *Health and Social Justice* (OUP 2010).

Samnøy A, 'The Origins of the Universal Declaration of Human Rights' in G Alfredsson and A Eide (eds), *The Universal Declaration of Human Rights: A Common Standard of Achievement* (Martinus Nijhoff Publishers 1999).
Sánchez-Moreno MM, 'The Human Rights Case for Drug Reform: How Drug Criminalization Destroys Lives, Feeds Abuses, and Subverts the Rule of Law' in Human Rights Watch (ed), *World Report* (HRW 2014).
Saul B, Kinley D and Mobray J (eds), *The International Covenant on Economic, Social, and Cultural Rights: Commentary, Cases, and Materials* (OUP 2014).

Scheinin M, 'Characteristics of Human Rights Norms' in C Krause and M Scheinin (eds), *International Protection of Human Rights: A Textbook* (Institute for Human Rights Åbo Akademi University 2009).

— —, 'Impact on the Law of Treaties' in M Kamminga and M Scheinin (eds), *The Impact of Human Rights Law on General International Law* (OUP 2009).

Scheske C and Schnall S, 'The Ethics of "Smart Drugs": Moral Judgments about Healthy People's Use of Cognitive-Enhancing Drugs' (2012) 34 Basic and Applied Social Psychology 508.

Schleifer R, Sagredo J and Avafia T, 'Addressing the Development Dimensions of Drug Policy' (UNDP 2015).

Scribner P, 'Do Drugs Deprive Us of Free Will?' in S Luper-Foy and C Brown (eds), *Drugs, Morality, and the Law* (Garland Publishing 1994).

Sellin J, *Access to Medicines* (Intersentia 2014).

Sen A, 'Capability and Well-Being' in MC Nussbaum and A Sen (eds), *The Quality of Life* (OUP 1993).

— —, 'Human Rights and Capabilities' (2005) 6 Journal of Human Development 151.

Sepúlveda M and others, *Human Rights Reference Handbook* (4th edn, Icelandic Human Rights Centre 2009) 5; J Donnelly, *International Human Rights* (3rd edn, Westview Press 2013).

Seya MJ and others, 'A First Comparison Between the Consumption of and the Need for Opioid Analgesics at Country, Regional, and Global Levels' (2011) 15 Journal of Pain and Palliative Care Pharmacotherapy 6.

Shafer-Landau R (ed), *Ethical Theory* (2nd edn, Wiley-Blackwell 2013).

Shaffer G and Ginsburg T, 'The Empirical Turn in International Legal Scholarship' (2012) 106 American Journal of International Law 1.

Shaw M, *International Law* (6th edn, CUP 2008).

Shue H, *Basic Rights: Subsistence, Affluence, and U.S. Foreign Policy* (2nd edn, Princeton University Press 1996).

Simon RL, 'Better Performance through Chemistry: The Ethics of Enhancing Ability through Drugs' in S Luper-Foy and C Brown, *Drugs Morality and the Law* (Garland Publishing 1994).

Skogly SI, 'The Human Rights Obligations of the World Bank and IMF' in W van Genugten, P Hunt and S Mathews (eds), *World Bank, IMF and Human Rights* (Wolf Legal Publishers 2003).

Ssenyonjo M, *Economic, Social and Cultural Rights in International Law* (Hart Publishing 2009).

Steedman MR and others, 'Innovation Can Improve and Expand Aspects of End-Of-Life Care in Low-and Middle Income Countries' (2014) 33 Health Affairs 1612.

Stephens P, 'Access to Medicines: Common Problems, Common Solutions?' (DPhil thesis, Utrecht University 2016).

Stevens A, 'Drug Policy, Harm and Human Rights: A Rationalist Approach' (2011) 22 International Journal of Drug Policy 233.

Stitsen JMA and others (eds), *Farmalogie* (2nd edn, Elsevier 2001).

Takahashi S, 'Drug Control, Human Rights, and the Right to the Highest Attainable Standard of Health: By No Means Straightforward Issues' (2009) Human Rights Quarterly 748.

Tasioulas J, 'Human Dignity and the Foundations of Human Rights' in C McCrudden (ed), *Understanding Human Dignity* (OUP 2013).

Taylor AL, 'Addressing the Global Tragedy of Needless Pain: Rethinking the United Nations Single Convention on Narcotic Drugs' (2007) 35 Journal of Law, Medicines and Ethics 556.

Thomas L, Lohman D and Amon JJ, 'Access to Pain Treatment and Palliative Care: A Human Rights Analysis' (2010) 24 Temple International & Comparative Law Journal 365.

Tibbitts F and Fernekes WR, 'Human Rights Education' in S Totten and JE Pedersen (eds), *Teaching and Studying Social Issues: Major Programs and Approaches* (Information Age Publishing 2011) 88.

Tobin J, *The Right to Health in International Law* (OUP 2012).

Toebes BCA, *The Right to Health as a Human Right in International Law* (Intersentia 1999).

——, 'Human Rights, Health Sector Abuse and Corruption' (2011) HRHW Working Paper No 64 <www.du.edu/korbel/hrhw/workingpapers/2011/64-toebes-2011.pdf>.

——, 'Schets van het Internationaal Gezondheidsrecht' Tijdschrift voor Gezondheidsrecht (*forthcoming*).

Tomuschat C, *Human Rights: Between Idealism and Realism* (2nd edn, OUP 2008).

Uebelacker L and others, 'Chronic Pain in HIV-Infected Patients: Relationship to Depression, Substance Use, and Mental Health and Pain Treatment' (2015) 16 Pain Medicine 1870.

Van Boven T, 'Categories of Rights' in D Moeckli, S Shah and S Sivakumaran (eds), *International Human Rights Law* (2nd edn, OUP 2014).

Van den Ham R, Bero L and Laing R, 'Selection of Essential Medicines' in L Bero and others (revs), *World Medicines Situation Report 2011* (3rd edn, WHO 2011).

Van Elsuwege P, *From Soviet Republics to EU Member States: A Legal and Political Assessment of the Baltic States' Accession to the EU* (Martinus Nijhoff Publishers 2008).

Van Kempen PHPHMC and Fedorova MI, *Internationaal Recht en Cannabis* (Kluwer 2014).

——, *Internationaal Recht en Cannabis II: Regulering van Cannabisteelt en -Handel voor Recreatief Gebruik: Positieve Mensenrechtenverplichtingen versus VN-Drugsverdragen* (Wolters Kluwer 2016).

Vargas-Schaffer G, 'Is the WHO Analgesic Ladder Still Valid?' (2010) 56 Canadian Family Physician 514.

Venkatapuram S, *Health Justice* (Polity Press 2011).

Vidmar J, 'Norm Conflicts and Hierarchy in International Law: Towards a Vertical International Legal System?' in E de Wet and J Vidmar (eds), *Hierarchy in International Law* (OUP 2012).
Villumsen M and Jensen MH, *The AAAQ Manual and the Right to Water: Contextualising Indicators for Availability, Accessibility, Acceptability and Quality* (Danish Institute for Human Rights 2014).
Vranken M and others, 'Legal Barriers in Accessing Opioid Medicines: Results of the ATOME Quick Scan of National Legislation of Eastern European Countries' (2014) 48 Journal of Pain and Symptom Management 1135.

Wacks R, *Understanding Jurisprudence: An Introduction to Legal Theory* (OUP 2005).
Waddell IG, 'International Narcotics Control' (1970) 64 American Journal of International Law 310.
Waldron J, 'Is Dignity the Foundation of Human Rights' (2013) NYU Public Law & Legal Theory Research Paper 12/73 <http://papers.ssrn.com/sol3/papers.cfm?abstract_id=2196074>.
Walsh C, 'Psychedelics and Cognitive Liberty: Reimaging Drug Policy through the Prism of Human Rights' (2016) 29 International Journal of Drug Policy 80.
Weimar L, 'The Nature of Claim-Rights' (2013) 123 Ethics 202.
Weissbrodt D, 'Roles and Responsibilities of Non-State Actors' in D Shelton (ed), *The Oxford Handbook of International Human Rights Law* (OUP 2013).
Werner M, 'Individual and Collective Dignity' in M Düwell and others (eds), *The Cambridge Handbook of Human Dignity: Interdisciplinary Perspectives* (CUP 2014).
Westerman PC, 'Natural Rights versus Human Dignity: Two Conflicting Traditions' in M Düwell and others (eds), *The Cambridge Handbook of Human Dignity: Interdisciplinary Perspectives* (CUP 2014).
Wiech K and Tracey I, 'The Influence of Negative Emotions on Pain: Behavioural Effects and Neural Mechanisms' (2009) 47 NeuroImage 987.
Wilson DP and others, 'The Cost-Effectiveness of Harm Reduction' (2015) 26 International Journal of Drug Policy s5.
Wolfe D and others, 'Human Rights and Access to Hepatitis C Treatment for People who Inject Drugs' (2015) 26 International Journal of Drug Policy 1072.
Wright H, 'International Opium Commission' (1909) 3 American Journal of International Law 828.

Yamin AE and Gloppen S (eds), *Litigating Health Rights: Can Courts Bring More Justice to Health?* (HUP 2011).
Yin RK, *Case Study Research: Design and Methods* (4th edn, SAGE Publications 2009).
Young KG, 'The Minimum Core of Economic and Social Rights: A Concept in Search of Content' (2008) 33 The Yale Journal of International Law 113.
Zinzombe SP, *The Right to Health, Pharmaceutical Corporations and Intellectual Property: Access to Medicines* (Intersentia 2015).

Zwart T, 'Using Local Culture to Further the Implementation of International Human Rights: The Receptor Approach' (2012) 34 Human Rights Quarterly 546.

Index by Paragraph

Curriculum Vitae

Marie Elske Gispen currently works as postdoctoral researcher on children's rights and tobacco control at the Global Health Law Groningen Research Centre of Groningen University and is a senior research associate at the International Centre on Human Rights and Drug Policy of Essex University. She carried out her PhD research on human rights and drug control at Utrecht University's Netherlands Institute of Human Rights (SIM) and Ethics Institute. As part of her PhD research Marie Elske has been a visiting scholar at Durham University, and a visiting fellow at the African Palliative Care Association in Uganda and the Latvian Centre of Human Rights. Alongside her research Marie Elske is a member of the honours programme (2015/2016) of the Royal Netherlands Academy of Arts and Sciences. She frequently presents at international and national conferences and regularly teaches on human rights. Previously, Marie Elske has interned for the Essential Medicines and Pharmaceutical Products Department of the World Health Organization in Geneva and worked as a junior researcher with SIM on a government commissioned project on the UN Convention on the Rights of Persons with Disabilities. She is also the past editor-in-chief of the Utrecht Journal of International and European Law. Marie Elske obtained her bachelor degree (LL.B.) in international law and European law in 2009 and her master degree (LL.M.) in legal theory in 2011 from Utrecht University.

School of Human Rights Research Series

The School of Human Rights Research is a joint effort by human rights researchers in the Netherlands. Its central research theme is the nature and meaning of international standards in the field of human rights, their application and promotion in the national legal order, their interplay with national standards and the international supervision of such application. The School of Human Rights Research Series only includes English titles that contribute to a better understanding of the different aspects of human rights.

For previous volumes in the series, please visit http://shr.intersentia.com.

Published titles within the Series:

71. Karel De Meester, *The Investigation Phase in International Criminal Procedure: In Search of Common Rules.*
    ISBN 978-1-78068-305-8
72. Nelleke Koffeman, *Morally sensitive issues and cross-border movement in the EU. The cases of reproductive matters and legal recognition of same-sex relationships.*
    ISBN 978-1-78068-349-2
73. Roland Moerland, *The Killing of Death. Denying the Genocide against the Tutsi.*
    ISBN 978-1-78068-351-5
74. Andrea Broderick, *The Long and Winding Road to Disability Equality and Inclusion. The United Nations Convention on the Rights of Persons with Disabilities.*
    ISBN 978-1-78068-358-4
75. Christina Peristeridou, *The principle of legality in European criminal law.*
    ISBN 978-1-78068-357-7
76. Emilie Ellen Kuijt, *Humanitarian Assistance and State Sovereignty in International Law. Towards a Comprehensive Framework.*
    ISBN 978-1-78068-366-9
77. Lize R. Glas, *The Theory, Potential and Practice of Procedural Dialogue in the European Convention on Human Rights System.*
    ISBN 978-1-78068-375-1
78. Paulien de Morree, *Rights and Wrongs under the ECHR. The prohibition of abuse of rights in Article 17 of the European Convention on Human Rights.*
    ISBN 978-1-78068-418-5
79. M.P. Beijer, *Limits of Fundamental Rights Protection by the EU. The Scope for a Development of Positive Obligations.*
    ISBN 978-1-78068-455-0

www.ingramcontent.com/pod-product-compliance
Ingram Content Group UK Ltd.
Pitfield, Milton Keynes, MK11 3LW, UK
UKHW051920100926
8556IPUK00021B/1273

9 781780 684543